COLLECTED WHEEL PUBLICATIONS

VOLUME 4

NUMBERS 47 – 60

I0249482

BPE

BPS Pariyatti Editions

BPS Pariyatti Editions
An imprint of Pariyatti Publishing
www.pariyatti.org

© Buddhist Publication Society, 2008

All rights reserved. No part of this book may be used or reproduced in any manner whatsoever without the written permission of BPS Pariyatti Editions, except in the case of brief quotations embodied in critical articles and reviews.

Although this is an American edition, we have left any British spelling of words unchanged.

First BPS Pariyatti Edition, 2019
ISBN: 978-1-68172-136-1 (Print)
ISBN: 978-1-68172-137-8 (PDF)
ISBN: 978-1-68172-138-5 (ePub)
ISBN: 978-1-68172-139-2 (Mobi)
LCCN: 2018940050

Contents

WH 47 Buddhism and the God-Idea
Nyanaponika Thera 1

WH 48 & 49 The Discourse on the Snake Simile
Nyanaponika Thera 27

WH 50 Knowledge and Conduct
Prof. O. H. de A. Wijesekera, Dr. K. N. Jayatilleke
Prof. E. A. Burtt 63

WH 51 Taming the Mind
Nyanaponika Thera 107

WH 52 & 53 Pathways of Buddhist Thought
Ñāṇamoli Thera 135

WH 54 The Mirror of the Dhamma
Nārada Thera, Bhikkhu Kassapa 173

WH 55 The Five Precepts
Dr. Paul Dahlke, Bhikkhu Sīlācāra,
L.R. Oates, G. Constant Lounsbery 215

WH 56 Ordination in Theravada Buddhism
J. F. Dickson, F. L. Woodward 237

WH 57 & 58 A Discourse to Knowers of Veda
Prof. T. W. Rhys Davids 263

WH 59 Stories of Old 309

WH 60 The Satipaṭṭhāna Sutta and Its Application to Modern Life
V. F. Gunaratna 335

Key to Abbreviations

A	Aṅguttara Nikāya	Paṭis	Paṭisambhidamagga
Ap	Apadāna	Peṭ	Peṭakopadesa
Bv	Buddhavaṃsa	S	Saṃyutta Nikāya
Cp	Cariyāpiṭaka	Sn	Suttanipāta
D	Dīgha Nikāya	Th	Theragātha
Dhp	Dhammapada	Thī	Therigātha
Dhs	Dhammasaṅgaṇī	Ud	Udāna
It	Itivuttaka	Vibh	Vibhaṅga
Ja	Jātaka verses and commentary	Vin	Vinaya-piṭaka
Khp	Khuddakapāṭha	Vism	Visuddhimagga
M	Majjhima Nikāya	Vism-mhṭ	Visuddhimagga Sub-commentary
Mil	Milindapañha	Vv	Vimānavatthu
Nett	Nettipakaraṇa	Nidd	Niddesa

The above is the abbreviation scheme of the Pali Text Society (PTS) as given in the *Dictionary of Pali* by Margaret Cone.

The commentaries, *aṭṭhakathā*, are abbreviated by using a hyphen and an "a" ("-a") following the abbreviation of the text, e.g., *Dīgha Nikāya Aṭṭhakathā* = D-a. Likewise the sub-commentaries are abbreviated by a "ṭ" ("-ṭ") following the abbreviation of the text.

The sutta reference abbreviation system for the four Nikāyas, as is used in Bhikkhu Bodhi's translations is:

AN	Aṅguttara Nikāya	DN	Dīgha Nikāya
MN	Majjhima Nikāya	Sn	Saṃyutta Nikāya
J	Jātaka story	Mv	Mahāvagga (Vinaya Piṭaka)
Cv	Cullavagga (Vinaya Piṭaka)	SVibh	Suttavibhaṅga (Vinaya Piṭaka)

Buddhism and the God-Idea

Selected Texts

Edited and introduced by

Nyanaponika Thera

WHEEL PUBLICATION NO. 47

Copyright © Kandy: Buddhist Publication Society
(1962, 1970, 1981)

Buddhism and the God-Idea

Quite contradictory views have been expressed in Western literature on the attitude of Buddhism toward the concept of God and gods. From a study of the discourses of the Buddha preserved in the Pali Canon, it will be seen that the idea of a *personal deity*, a creator god conceived to be eternal and omnipotent, is incompatible with the Buddha's teachings. On the other hand, conceptions of an *impersonal godhead* of any description, such as world-soul, etc., are excluded by the Buddha's teaching on *anattā*, non-self or unsubstantiality.

In Buddhist literature, the belief in a creator god (*issara-nimmāna-vāda*) is frequently mentioned and rejected, along with other causes wrongly adduced to explain the origin of the world, as, for instance, world-soul, time, nature, etc. God-belief, however, is not placed in the same category as those morally destructive wrong views which deny the kammic results of action, assume a fortuitous origin of man and nature, or teach absolute determinism. These views are said to be altogether pernicious, having definite bad results due to their effect on ethical conduct.

Theism, however, is regarded as a kind of kamma-teaching in so far as it upholds the moral efficacy of actions. Hence a theist who leads a moral life may, like anyone else doing so, expect a favourable rebirth. He may possibly even be reborn in a heavenly world that resembles his own conception of it, though it will not be of eternal duration as he may have expected. If, however, fanaticism induces him to persecute those who do not share his beliefs, this will have grave consequences for his future destiny. For fanatical attitudes, intolerance, and violence against others, create unwholesome kamma leading to moral degeneration and an unhappy rebirth.

Although belief in God does not exclude a favourable rebirth, it is a variety of eternalism, a false affirmation of permanence rooted in the craving for existence, and as such an obstacle to final deliverance.

Among the fetters (*saṃyojana*) that bind to existence, theism is particularly subject to those of personality-belief, attachment to rites and rituals, and desire for fine-material existence or for a "heaven of the sense sphere," as the case may be.

As an attempt at explaining the universe, its origin, and man's situation in his world, the God-idea was found entirely unconvincing by the Buddhist thinkers of old. Through the centuries, Buddhist philosophers have formulated detailed arguments refuting the doctrine of a creator god. It should be of interest to compare these with the ways in which Western philosophers have refuted the theological proofs of the existence of God.

But for an earnest believer, the God-idea is more than a mere device for explaining external facts like the origin of the world. For him it is an object of faith that can bestow a strong feeling of certainty, not only as to God's existence "somewhere out there," but as to God's consoling presence and closeness to himself. This feeling of certainty requires close scrutiny. Such scrutiny will reveal that in most cases the God-idea is only the devotee's projection of his ideal—generally a noble one—and of his fervent wish and deeply felt need to believe. These projections are largely conditioned by external influences, such as childhood impressions, education, tradition and social environment. Charged with a strong emotional emphasis, brought to life by man's powerful capacity for image-formation, visualization and the creation of myth, they then come to be identified with the images and concepts of whatever religion the devotee follows. In the case of many of the most sincere believers, a searching analysis would show that their "God-experience" has no more specific content than this.

Yet the range and significance of God-belief and God-experience are not fully exhausted by the preceding remarks. The lives and writings of the mystics of all great religions bear witness to religious experiences of great intensity, in which considerable changes are effected in the quality of consciousness. Profound absorption in prayer or meditation can bring about a deepening and widening, a brightening and intensifying, of consciousness, accompanied by a transporting feeling of rapture and bliss. The contrast between these states and normal conscious awareness is so great that the mystic believes his experiences to be manifestations of the divine; and given the contrast, this assumption is quite understandable. Mystical experiences are also characterized by a marked reduction or temporary exclusion of the multiplicity of sense-perceptions and restless thoughts. This relative unification of mind is then interpreted as a union or communion with the One God. All these deeply moving impressions, and the first spontaneous interpretations of them, the mystic subsequently identifies with his particular theology. It is interesting to note, however, that the attempts of most great Western mystics to relate their mystical experiences to the official dogmas of their respective churches often resulted in teachings which were looked upon askance by the orthodox, if not considered downright heretical.

The psychological facts underlying those religious experiences are accepted by the Buddhist and are well-known to him; but he carefully distinguishes the experiences themselves from the theological interpretations imposed upon them. After rising from deep meditative absorption (*jhāna*), the Buddhist meditator is advised to view the physical and mental factors constituting his experience in the light of the three characteristics of all conditioned existence: impermanence, liability to suffering, and absence of an abiding ego or eternal substance. This is done primarily in order to utilize the meditative purity and strength of consciousness for the highest purpose: liberating insight. But this procedure also has a very important side effect which concerns us here: the meditator will not be overwhelmed by any uncontrolled emotions and thoughts evoked by his singular experience, and will thus be able to avoid interpretations of that experience not warranted by the facts.

Hence a Buddhist meditator, while benefiting from the refinement of consciousness he has achieved, will be able to see these meditative experiences for what they are; and he will further know that they are without any abiding substance that could be attributed to a deity manifesting itself to his mind. Therefore, the Buddhist's conclusion must be that the highest mystical states do not provide evidence for the existence of a personal God or an impersonal godhead.

Buddhism has sometimes been called an atheistic teaching, either in an approving sense by freethinkers and rationalists, or in a derogatory sense by people of theistic persuasion. Only in one way can Buddhism be described as atheistic, namely, in so far as it denies the existence of an eternal, omnipotent, God or godhead who is the creator and ordainer of the world. The word "atheism," however, like the word "godless," frequently carries a number of disparaging overtones or implications, which in no way apply to the Buddha's teaching.

Those who use the word "atheism" often associate it with a materialistic doctrine that knows nothing higher than this world of the senses and the slight happiness it can bestow. Buddhism is nothing of that sort. In this respect it agrees with the teachings of other religions: true lasting happiness cannot be found in this world, nor, the Buddha adds, can it be found on any higher plane of existence, conceived as a heavenly or divine world, since all planes of existence are impermanent and thus incapable of giving lasting bliss. The spiritual values advocated by Buddhism are directed not towards a new life in some higher world, but towards a state utterly transcending the world, namely, Nibbāna. In making this statement, however, we must point out that Buddhist spiritual values do not draw an absolute separation between the beyond and the here-and-now. They have firm roots in the world itself for they aim at the highest realization in this present existence. Along with such spiritual aspirations, Buddhism encourages earnest endeavour to make this world a better place to live in.

The materialistic philosophy of annihilationism (*ucchedavāda*) is emphatically rejected by the Buddha as a false doctrine. The doctrine of kamma is sufficient to prove that Buddhism does not teach annihilation after death. It accepts survival, not of an eternal soul, but of a mental process subject to renewed becoming; thus it teaches rebirth without transmigration. Again, the Buddha's teaching is not a nihilism that gives suffering humanity no better hope than a final cold nothingness. On the contrary, it is a teaching of salvation (*niyyānika-dhamma*) or deliverance (*vimutti*) which attributes to man the faculty to realize by his own efforts the highest goal, Nibbāna: the ultimate cessation of suffering and the final eradication of greed, hate and delusion. Nibbāna is far from being the blank zero of annihilation; yet it also cannot be identified with any form of God-idea, as it is neither the origin nor the immanent ground or essence of the world.

Buddhism is not an enemy of religion as atheism is believed to be. Buddhism, indeed, is the enemy of none. A Buddhist will recognize and appreciate whatever ethical, spiritual and cultural values have been created by God-belief in its long and chequered history. We cannot, however, close our eyes to the fact that the God-concept has served too often as a cloak for man's desire for power, and the reckless and cruel use of that power, thus adding considerably to the ample measure of misery in this world supposed to be an all-loving God's creation. For centuries free thought, free research and the expression of dissident views were obstructed and stifled in the name of service to God. And alas, these and other negative consequences are not yet entirely things of the past.

The word "atheism" also carries the innuendo of an attitude countenancing moral laxity, or a belief that man-made ethics, having no divine sanction, rest on shaky foundations. For Buddhism, however, the basic moral law is inherent in life itself. It is a special case of the law of cause and effect, needing neither a divine law-giver nor depending upon the fluctuating human conceptions of socially-conditioned minor moralities and conventions. For an increasing section of humanity, the belief in God is breaking down rapidly, as well as the accustomed motivations for moral conduct. This shows the risk of basing moral postulates on divine commandments when their alleged source rapidly loses credence and authority. There is a need for an autonomous foundation for ethics, one that has deeper roots than a social contract and is capable of protecting the security of the individual and of human institutions. Buddhism offers such a foundation for ethics.

Buddhism does not deny that there are in the universe planes of existence and levels of consciousness which in some ways may be superior to our terrestrial world and to average human consciousness. To deny this would indeed be provincial in this age of space travel. Bertrand Russell rightly says: "It is improbable that the universe contains nothing better than ourselves."

Yet, according to Buddhist teachings, such higher planes of existence, like our familiar world, are subject to the law of impermanence and change. The inhabitants of such worlds may well be, in different degrees, more powerful than human beings, happier and longer-lived. Whether we call those superior beings gods, deities, devas or angels is of little importance, since it is improbable that they call themselves by any of those names. They are inhabitants of this universe, fellow-wanderers in this round of existence; and though more powerful, they need not be wiser than man. Further, it need not be denied that such worlds and such beings may have their lord and ruler. In all probability they do. But like any human ruler, a divine ruler too might be inclined to misjudge his own status and power, until a greater one comes along and points out to him his error, as our texts report of the Buddha.

These, however, are largely matters beyond the range and concern of average human experience. They have been mentioned here chiefly for the purpose of defining the Buddhist position, and not to serve as a topic of speculation and argument. Such involvements can only divert attention and effort from what ought to be our principal object: the overcoming of greed, hatred and delusion where they are found in the here and now.

An ancient verse ascribed to the Buddha in the *Questions of King Milinda* says:

> Not far from here do you need to look!
> Highest existence—what can it avail?
> Here in this present aggregate,
> In your own body overcome the world!

The Texts

Origin of the Belief in a Creator God

Now, there comes a time, monks, when, sooner or later, after the lapse of a long period, this world-system passes away. And when this happens, beings have mostly been reborn in the World of Radiance, and there they live made of mind, feeding on joy, radiating light from themselves, traversing the air, continuing in glory; and thus they remain for a long period of time.

Now, there comes a time, monks, when, sooner or later, this world-system begins to re-evolve. When this happens, the Palace of Brahmā appears, but it is empty. And some being or other, either because his span of years has passed or his merit is exhausted, falls from the World of Radiance, and comes to life in the Palace of Brahmā. And there also he lives made of mind, feeding on joy, radiating light from himself, traversing the air, continuing in glory; and thus does he remain for a long, long period of time.

Now, there arises in him, due to his living there so long alone, a dissatisfaction and a longing: "O! would that other beings might come to join me in this place!" And, just then, either because their span of years had passed or their merit was exhausted, other beings fall from the World of Radiance, and appear in the Palace of Brahmā as companions to him, and in all respects like him.

On this, monks, the one who was first reborn thinks thus to himself: "I am Brahmā, the Great Brahmā, the Supreme One, the Mighty, the All-Seeing, the Ruler, the Lord of all, the Maker, the Creator, the Chief of all, appointing to each his place, the Ancient of days, the Father of all that are and are to be. These other beings are of my creation. And why is that so? A while ago I thought, 'That they might come!' And on my mental aspiration, behold the beings came."

And those beings themselves too think thus: "This must be Brahmā, the Supreme, the Mighty, the All-Seeing, the Ruler, the Lord of all, the Maker, the Creator, the Chief of all, appointing to each his place, the Ancient of days, the Father of all that are and are to be. And we must have been created by him. And why? Because, as we see, it was he who was here first, and we came after that."

On this, monks, the one who first came into existence there is of longer life and more glorious, and more powerful than those who appeared after him. And it might well be, monks, that some being on his falling from that state, should come hither. And having come hither he might go forth from the household life into the homeless state. And having thus become a recluse he, by reason of ardour, of exertion, of application, of earnestness, of careful thought, reaches such rapture of heart that, rapt in heart, he calls to mind his last dwelling-place, but not the previous ones. He says to himself: "That illustrious Brahmā, the Great Brahmā, the Supreme One, the Mighty, the All-Seeing, the Ruler, the Lord of all, the Maker, the Creator, the Chief of all, appointing to each his place, the Ancient of days, the Father of all that are and are to be, he by whom we were created, he is steadfast, immutable, eternal, of a nature that knows no change, and he will remain so for ever and ever. But we who were created by him have come hither as being impermanent, mutable, limited in duration of life."

This, monks, is the first state of things on account of which, starting out from which, some recluses and brahmans, being eternalists as to some things, and non-eternalists as to others, maintain that the soul and the world are partly eternal and partly not.

From Dīgha Nikāya No. 1:
Brahmajāla Sutta.
Translated by Prof. Rhys Davids.

The Inexplicable God

"Well then, Udāyi what is your own teacher's doctrine?"

"Our own teacher's doctrine, venerable sir, says thus: 'This is the highest splendour ! This is the highest splendour!'"[1]

"But what is that highest splendour, Udāyi, of which your teacher's doctrine speaks?"

"It is, venerable sir, a splendour, greater and loftier than which there is none. That is the highest splendour."

"But, Udāyi what is that splendour, greater and loftier than which there is none?"

"It is, venerable sir, that highest splendour, greater and loftier than which there is none."

"For a long time, Udāyi, you can continue in this way, saying, 'A splendour greater and loftier than which there is none; that is the highest splendour.' But still you will not have explained that splendour.

"Suppose a man were to say: 'I love and desire the most beautiful woman in this land.' And then he is asked: 'Good man, that most beautiful woman whom you love and desire, do you know whether she is a lady from the nobility or from a brahman family or from the trader class or sudra?' And he replies: 'No'—'Then, good man, do you know her name and that of her clan? Or whether she is tall, short, or of middle height, whether she is dark, brunette or golden skinned, or in what village or town or city she dwells?' And he replies, 'No'. And then he is asked: 'Hence, good man, you love and desire what you neither know nor see?' And he answers, 'Yes'—What do you think, Udāyi; that being so, would not that man's talk amount to nonsense?"

"Certainly, venerable sir, that being so, that man's talk would amount to nonsense."

---

1. *Deve devato abhijānāti.* In earlier sections of this discourse, a similar formulation occurs, referring to other terms. In this context, the commentary to our discourse explains (and this applies also to our passage): "Without ignoring [the respective term; here, it is gods, lord of creatures, etc.], he knows it distinctly [*abhijānāti*] as impermanent, liable to suffering, void of self and substance."

"But in the same way, you, Udāyi, say, 'A splendour, greater and loftier than which there is none. That is the highest splendour,' and yet you have not explained that splendour."

From Majjhima Nikāya No. 79:
Cūla-Sakuludāyi Sutta.

Blind Faith

"Is there, Vāseṭṭha, a single one of the brahmans versed in the three Vedas who has ever seen Brahmā face to face?"

"No, indeed, Gotama."

"Or is there, then, Vāseṭṭha, a single one of the teachers of the brahmans versed in the three Vedas, who has seen Brahmā face to face?"

"No, indeed, Gotama."

"Or is there, then, Vāseṭṭha, a single one of the pupils of the teachers of the brahmans versed in the three Vedas who has seen Brahmā face to face?"

"No, indeed, Gotama."

"Or is there then, Vāseṭṭha, a single one of the brahmans up to the seventh generation who has seen Brahmā face to face?"

"No, indeed, Gotama."

"Well then, Vāseṭṭha, those ancient rishis of the brahmans versed in the three Vedas, the authors of the verses, the utterers of the verses, whose ancient form of words so chanted, uttered or composed, the brahmans of today chant over again and repeat, intoning or reciting exactly as has been intoned or recited—to wit, Aṭṭhaka ... and Bhāgu, did even they speak thus, saying: 'We know it. We have seen it: where Brahmā is, whence Brahmā is, whither Brahmā is?'"

"Not so, Gotama."

"Then you say, Vāseṭṭha, that none of the brahmans, nor of their teachers, nor of their pupils, even up to the seventh generation, has ever seen Brahmā face to face. And that even the rishis of old, the authors and utterers of the verses, of the ancient form of words which the brahmans of today so carefully intone and recite precisely as they have been handed down—even they did not pretend to know or to have seen where or whence or whither Brahmā is. So the brahmans versed in the three Vedas have in fact said thus: 'What we know not, what we have not seen, to a state of union with that we can show the way, and can say: "This is the straight path, this the direct way that makes for salvation, and leads him who acts according to it into a state of union with Brahmā."'

"Now, what do you think, Vāseṭṭha? Does it not follow, this being so, that the talk of the brahmans versed in the three Vedas, turns out to be foolish talk?"

"Certainly, Gotama, that being so, it follows that the talk of the brahmans versed in the three Vedas is foolish talk."

The String of Blind Men

"Verily, Vāseṭṭha, that brahmans versed in the three Vedas should be able to show the way to a state of union with that which they do not know, nor have seen—this is not possible!

"Just, Vāseṭṭha, as when a string of blind men are clinging one to the other, neither can the foremost see, nor can the middle one see, nor can the hindmost see—even so, I think, Vāseṭṭha, is the talk of the brahmans versed in the three Vedas but blind talk: the first sees not, the middle one sees not, nor can the last see. The talk, then, of these brahmans versed in the three Vedas turns out to be ridiculous, mere words, a vain and empty thing!"

The Staircase to Nowhere

"Just, Vāseṭṭha, as if a man should make a staircase in the place where four roads cross, to mount up into a mansion. And people should say to him, 'Well, good friend, this mansion, to mount up into which you are making this staircase, do you know whether it is in the east, or in the south, or in the west, or in the north? Whether it is high or low or of middle size?'

"And when so asked he should answer, 'No.' And people should say to him, 'But then, good friend, you are making a staircase to mount up into something—taking it for a mansion—which, all the while, you knew not, neither have seen.'"

Praying for the Beyond

"Again, Vāseṭṭha, if this river Aciravatī were full of water even to the brim, and overflowing. And a man with business on the other side, bound for the other side, making for the other side, should come up, and want to cross over. And he, standing on this bank, should invoke the further bank, and say, 'Come hither, further bank! Come over to this side!'

"Now what think you, Vāseṭṭha? Would the further bank of the river Aciravatī by reason of the man's invoking and praying, and hoping and praising, come over to this side?"

"Certainly not, Gotama."

"In just the same way, Vāseṭṭha, do the brahmans versed in the three Vedas—omitting the practice of those qualities which really make a man a brahman, and adopting the practice of those qualities which really make men non-brahmans—say thus: 'Indra we call upon, Soma we call upon, Varuṇa, Isāna, Pajāpati, Brahmā, Mahiddhi, Yama we call upon.'

"Verily, Vāseṭṭha, that those brahmans versed in the three Vedas—omitting the practice of those qualities which really make man a brahman, adopting the practice of those qualities which really make men non-brahmans—may, by reason of their invoking and praying, and hoping and praising, after the breaking up of the body after death, attain to union with Brahmā; this is not possible."

From Dīgha Nikāya No. 13: Tevijjā Sutta.
Translated by Prof. Rhys Davids.

Revealed Religion

"Again, Sandaka, here some teacher depends on hearsay, takes hearsay for truth, he teaches his doctrine [relying on] legendary lore and scripture. But when, Sandaka, a teacher depends on hearsay, takes hearsay for truth, this he will have heard well and that he will have heard badly, this will be thus and that will be otherwise.

"Herein a wise man will consider: 'This teacher depends on hearsay, takes hearsay for truth, he teaches his doctrine [relying on] legendary lore and scripture. But when a teacher depends on hearsay, takes hearsay for truth, this he will have heard well, and that he will have heard badly this, will be thus, and that will be otherwise.'

"So when he finds that this kind of religious life is unsatisfactory, he becomes disappointed and leaves it. This, Sandaka, is the second unsatisfactory religious life declared by the Blessed One who knows and sees, who is the Arahat, fully enlightened, wherein a wise man certainly would not lead the religious life, or, when leading it, would miss the true path-teaching that is profitable."

From Majjhima Nikāya No. 76:
Sandaka Sutta.

The Buddhist Saint (Arahat) and the God-Idea

Also a monk who is a saint [*arahat*], canker-free, who has lived the life, accomplished his task, laid down the burden, reached the true goal, who has destroyed the fetters to existence, and is liberated through right final knowledge—he too has full knowledge of the gods as gods; and knowing them as such, he does not imagine [anything] about the gods,[2] he does not imagine himself among the gods,[3] he does not imagine himself as [originating] from a god,[4] he does not imagine, "Mine are the gods",[5] and he does not find delight in the gods. And why not? Because this has been comprehended by him; and because he is freed from greed through greed's extinction, freed from hate through hate's extinction, freed from delusion through delusion's extinction.

Also a monk who is a saint, canker-free, who has lived the life, accomplished his task, laid down the burden, reached the true goal, who has destroyed the fetters to existence, and is liberated through right final knowledge—he, too, has full knowledge of the

2. *Deve na maññati.* According to the commentary, the "imagination" (*maññanā*) which he avoids appears in three forms, as craving, conceit and wrong views. These three pertain also to most of the other types of imaginings in this paragraph and in the following ones, with exceptions mentioned in the Commentary (where only one or two apply, which space does not permit us to specify here).

3. *devesu na maññati.*

4. *devato na maññati.*

5. Here we may think, for instance, of tribal deities, of the possessiveness exhibited by fetish worshippers, but also by devotees of higher religions.

lord of creatures as lord of creatures; and knowing him as such, he does not imagine [anything] about the lord of creatures,[6] he does not imagine [the qualities] in the lord of creatures,[7] he does not imagine himself as [originated] from the lord of creatures,[8] he does not imagine, "Mine is the lord of creature,"[9] and he does not find delight in the lord of creatures. And why not? Because this has been comprehended by him; and because he is freed from greed through greed's extinction, freed from hate through hate's extinction, freed from delusion through delusion's extinction.

Also a monk who is a saint, canker-free, who has lived the life, accomplished his task, laid down the burden, reached the true goal, who has destroyed the fetters to existence, and is liberated through right final knowledge—he, too, has full knowledge of Brahmā as Brahmā; and knowing him as such, he does not imagine [anything] about Brahmā, he does not imagine [the qualities] in Brahmā,[10] he does not imagine himself as [originated] from Brahmā,[11] he does

6. In the Commentary, the lord of creatures (*pajāpati*) is identified with Māra who, in Buddhist cosmology, is the ruler over the *Paranimmitavasavatti* Gods, "those who wield power over the creations of others."

7. Namely his permanence, immutability, that in him there is no evil, etc. (Commentary)

8. By creation or emanation. (Commentary)

9. "Thinking, 'He is my Lord and Master.'" (Commentary) The statement of the text may also be applied to the belief that a God-concept adhered to individually, or by one's own religion, can claim exclusive validity or superiority.

10. *Brahmasmiṃ maññati.* The Commentary restricts its explanation to imaginings about the qualities or attributes found in Brahmā (See Note 6). But it appears possible to render the locative case of the Pali term *Brahmasmiṃ* as literally as the commentary does with other terms of the discourse, and to translate by "he imagines himself in Brahmā." This, then, would refer to a mystic union with the deity.

11. *Brahmato maññati.* Here, too, the Commentary explains the ablative case only in the sense of originating from Brahmā by way of creation or emanation (see Note 8 on the previous page). But when explaining the parallel phrase applied to other terms, the Commentary mentions an alternative interpretation of the ablative case, as signifying "different from." The rendering here would then be: "He imagines himself different from Brahmā." This would refer to a strict dualism of God and man. One will also

not imagine, "Mine is Brahmā," and he does not find delight in Brahmā.[12] And why not? Because this has been comprehended by him; and because he is freed from greed through greed's extinction, freed from hate through hate's extinction, freed from delusion through delusion's extinction.

From Majjhima Nikāya, No. 1:
Mūlapariyāya Sutta.

God Belief and Fatalism

There are ascetics and brahmans who maintain and believe that whatever a man experiences, be it pleasant, unpleasant or neutral, all that is caused by God's act of creation. I went to them and questioned them [whether they held such a view], and when they affirmed it, I said:

"If that is so, venerable sirs, then people commit murder, theft and unchaste deeds due to God's act of creation; they indulge in lying, slanderous, harsh and idle talk due to God's act of creation; they are covetous, full of hate and hold wrong views due to God's act of creation."

Those who fall back on God's act of creation, as the decisive factor, will lack the impulse and effort for doing this and not doing that. Since for them, in truth and fact, [a necessity for] action or inaction does not obtain, the designation "ascetic" does not fit them who live without mindfulness and self-control.

From Aṅguttara Nikāya, Book of the Threes, No. 62.

If God is the cause of all that happens, what is the use of man's striving?

From Aśvaghoṣa, *Buddhacarita* 9.53.

---

be reminded here of those Christian theologians who emphasize the deep gulf between the creator and creature.

12. The Commentary says that he delights (in Brahmā) by way of craving (*taṇhā*) and wrong views (*diṭṭhi*), which may be exemplified by the "yearnings for the delights of divine love," and by indulging in theological speculations.

The Transient Deity

As far as suns and moons revolve and the sky's directions brilliantly shine, so far reaches a thousandfold world-system. In that thousandfold world-system, there are a thousand moons, a thousand suns, a thousand Sinerus, a thousand kings of the mountains, a thousand of the four continents, a thousand of the four oceans, a thousand of the heavenly worlds of the sense plane, and a thousand Brahmā-worlds. As far as this thousandfold world-system reaches, so far is the great Brahmā deemed the highest there.

But even in that great Brahmā, monks, there is transformation, there is change. Seeing this, monks, a well-instructed disciple feels disgust even with that. Being disgusted with it, his attachment even to the highest fades away; how much more to what is low!

From Aṅguttara Nikāya, Book of the Tens, No. 29.

The Disillusionment of the Gods

Now there arises in the world the Blessed One, who is holy, fully enlightened, endowed with knowledge and pure conduct, sublime, the knower of worlds, the incomparable leader of men in need of guidance, the teacher of gods and men, enlightened and blessed.

He thus teaches Dhamma: "This is personality; this the origination of personality; this the cessation of personality; this is the way leading to the cessation of personality."

And those gods who are long-lived, resplendent in beauty, who dwell full of happiness and for a long time in lofty heavenly mansions, even they, having heard the Perfect One teaching Dhamma, are mostly beset by fear, agitation and trembling:

"Alas, we who, in fact, are impermanent, believed that we were permanent! We who, in fact, are evanescent, believed that we were ever lasting! We who, in fact, are non-eternal, believed that we were eternal! But, truly, we are impermanent, evanescent, non-eternal, engrossed in personality!"

From Aṅguttara Nikāya, Book of the Fours, No. 33.

Brahmā Admits His Transiency

One there is[13] who thought of posing
The Divinity[14] this question
In Sudhamma Hall in Heaven:
"Is there still in you existing,
Friend, the view that once existed?
Is the radiance of heaven
Clearly seen by you as passing?"

The Divinity gave answer
Truly to my question's order:
"There exists in me no longer,
Sir, the view that once existed;
All the radiance of heaven
I now clearly see as passing;
I condemn my erstwhile claiming
To be permanent, eternal."

From Majjhima Nikāya, No. 50.

God's Responsibility

If there exists some lord all-powerful to fulfil, in every creature, bliss or woe, and action good or ill, that lord is stained with sin. Man does but work his will.

From the Mahābodhi Jātaka,
Jātaka No. 528 (J-a V 238).

He who has eyes can see the sickening sight;
Why does not Brahmā set his creatures right?
If his wide power no limit can restrain,
Why is his hand so rarely spread to bless?
Why are his creatures all condemned to pain?
Why does he not to all give happiness?
Why do fraud, lies, and ignorance prevail?
Why triumphs falsehood—truth and justice fail?

13. Mahā-Moggallāna Thera, a chief disciple of the Buddha.

14. Brahmā.

I count your Brahmā one th'unjust among
Who made a world in which to shelter wrong.[15]

From the Bhūridatta Jātaka,
Jātaka No. 543 (J-a VI 208).

Creation and Cause

The assumption that a God [*īśvara*] is the cause, etc. [of the world] rests upon the false belief in an eternal self; but that belief has to be abandoned if one has clearly understood that everything is [impermanent, and therefore] subject to suffering.

From Vasubandhu, *Abhidharmakoṣa*, 5.8
(vol. IV p. 19); *Sphuṭārtha* p. 445, 26.

Refutation of the Absolute Creator

A certain school holds that there is a *Maheśvara* God who is absolute, omnipresent, and eternal; and that he is the creator of all dharmas [i. e. phenomena].

This theory is illogical. And why?

(a) That which creates is not eternally present, is not eternal, is not omnipresent; that which is not omnipresent is not absolute.

---

15. The above is a poetic and rather free rendering. An alternative, more literal translation is:

If indeed he is the master in the whole world, Brahmā, the lord of many beings, his offspring,

Then why did he create the world in such a miserable way, why didn't he make the world happy?

If indeed he is the master of the whole world, Brahmā, the lord of many beings, his offspring,

Then why did he make the world with unrighteous means, involving deceit, false speech, and madness.

If indeed he is the master of the whole world, Brahmā, the lord of many beings, his offspring,

An unjust lord of beings he is, who, although justness exists, created in an unjust manner.

(b) If he is eternal and omnipresent, and complete with all kinds of capacities, he should, in all times and at all places, produce all of a sudden all *dharmas* [phenomena].

(c) [If they say] that his creation depends upon desire and conditions, then they contradict their own doctrine of "unique cause." Alternatively, we may say that desire and conditions should also all arise of a sudden, since the cause [which produces them] is there always.

From *Vijñaptimātratā Siddhi Śāstra.*[16]

Śāntideva

The creative nature of one who is incomprehensible must likewise be incomprehensible. Why then talk about it?

From *Bodhicaryāvatāra* 9, 121.

If the cause [God] has no beginning, how can the effect [God's creation] have a beginning?

Ibid. 9, 123.

Why did [God] not produce always?[17] There is no other person or thing he need consider. For there is no other person or thing he has not created. Why then, should he thus consider?

Ibid. 9, 124.

If he has to consider the completeness of conditions, then God is not the cause [of the world]. For he is then not free[18] to refrain from creating when that completeness of conditions is present; nor is he free to create when it is absent.

Ibid. 9, 125.

16. A standard work of the Buddhist idealistic school. Translated from the Chinese version by Wong Mow Lam, *The Chinese Buddhist*, Vol. 11, No. 2. Shanghai, 1932.

17. That is, produce the whole creation all at once.

18. Literally, the master, the Lord (*īsā*).

If God acts without wishing it, he creates in dependence upon something else; but if he has the wish, then he will be dependent upon that wish. Hence where is the creator's sovereignty?[19]

Ibid. 9, 126.

Śāntarakṣita

Extracts from the *Tattvasaṃgraha*, *The Compendium of Truth*, with the commentary of Kāmalasīla. Translated by Gaṅganath Jha, *Gaekwads Oriental Series*, Oriental Institute, Baroda.

From Chapter II—Doctrine of God

1. The One and the Many (Paley's "Watchmaker" Argument)

The existence of a being who is eternal, one, and the substratum of eternal all-embracing consciousness—can never be proven .... (Text 72)

... for the simple reason that any corroborative instance that might be cited in the form of a jar and such things, would be lacking in the element of similarity that is essential [the maker of the jar not having all the character that is predicated of God]. (Commentary to Text 72.)

For instance, all such products as houses, steps, gateways, towers and the like definitely known to have been fashioned by makers who have been many, and with fleeting ideas. (Text 73.)

2. The Eternal Cannot be Productive

Eternal things cannot produce any effects, because "consecutive" action and "concurrent" action are mutually contradictory; and if objects are consecutive, there must be the same consecutiveness in their cognitions also. (Text 76.)

19. These arguments and those in the preceding section from the *Vijñaptimātratā* are elaborated in the following extracts from the *Tattvasaṃgraha*.

Only non-eternal things can be productive causes, as it is these alone which go on unceasingly changing their sequential character—of being present now and past at the next moment. Thus it is proven that an intelligent maker must be evanescent and many. (Commentary to Text 76.)

God's cognitions must be consecutive, because they are related to consecutive cognizable things .... (Text 77.)

If God's cognition manifesting itself is produced by objects which are consecutive, then it becomes proven that it must be consecutive; if it is not so produced, then, as there would be no proximate contact [with the object and the cognition], God could not cognize the object at all .... (Commentary to Text 77.)

3. An Unobstructed Divine Cause Requires Simultaneous Creation

God cannot be the cause of born things, because he is himself devoid of birth, like the sky-lotus. Otherwise all things would come into existence simultaneously. (Text 81.)

If the cause were one whose efficiency is never obstructed, then all things would come into existence simultaneously ....

The absurdity [involved in the theist's position] is to be shown in this manner: When the cause is present in its complete form, then the effect must appear as a matter of course; just as it is found in the case of the sprout which appears as soon as the final stage has been reached by the causal conditions conducive to it. Now under the doctrine of the theist, as God, the cause of all things, would always be there and free from defects, all things, the whole world, should come into existence at once.

The following argument might be urged: "God is not the only cause [of all things]; in fact, what he does he does through the help of such auxiliary causes as merit and the rest, God himself being only the efficient [controlling] cause. So that so long as merit and the rest are not there, the cause of things cannot be said to be present there in its efficient form."

This is not valid. If there is help that has got to be rendered to God by the auxiliary causes, then he must be regarded as dependent upon their aid. As a matter of fact, however, God is [said to be] eternal, and as nothing can introduce into him any efficiency that is not there already, there can be no help that he should receive from the auxiliary causes. Why then, should he need such auxiliaries as are of no use to him?

Uddyotakara has argued as follows: "Though the cause of things, named God, is eternal and perfect and always present, yet the producing of things is not simultaneous because God always acts intelligently and purposely. If God has produced things by his mere presence, without intelligence [and purpose], then the objection urged would have applied to our doctrine. As a matter of fact, however, God acts intelligently; hence the objection is not applicable, as God operates towards products solely by his own wish. Thus our reason is not 'inconclusive.'"

This is not valid. The activity and inactivity of things are not dependent upon the wish of the cause; only if it were so, the appearance of all effects would not be possible, even in the constant presence of the untrammelled cause in the shape of God, simply on account of his wish being absent. The fact of the matter is that the appearance and non-appearance of things are dependent upon the presence and absence of due efficiency in the cause. For instance, even though a man may have the wish, things do not appear if he has not the efficiency or power to produce them; and when the cause in the form of seed has the efficiency or faculty to produce the sprout, the sprout does appear, even though the seed has no wish at all. If then the cause called God is always there, fully endowed with the due untrammelled efficiency (as he is at the time of the producing of a particular thing), then why should things stand in need of his wish, which can serve no purpose at all? And the result of this should be that all things should appear simultaneously, at the same time as the appearance of any one thing. Thus alone could the untrammelled causal efficiency of God be shown, if things were produced simultaneously. Nor can God, who cannot be helped by other things, stand in need of anything, for which he would need his wish.

Further, in the absence of intelligence, there can be no desire for anything else, and the intelligence of God is held to be eternally uniform; so that, even if God acted intelligently, why should there not be a simultaneous production of things? Because like God himself, his intelligence is always there. If then, his intelligence be regarded as evanescent, even so it must co-exist with God, and its presence must be as constant as God himself; so that the objection on that score remains in force.

And yet the production of things is not found to be simultaneous; hence the conclusion must be contrary to that desired by the theist.

The argument may be formulated as follows: "When a certain thing is not found to be produced at a certain time, it must be taken to be one whose cause at that time is not untrammelled in its efficiency as it is found in the case of the sprout not appearing while the seed is still in the granary; it is found that at the appearance of one thing the whole world is not produced. Hence what has been stated [by the opponent] as a universal proposition is not found to be true. (Commentary to Text 87.)

From Chapter 6

Doctrine of the Puruṣa (Spirit, Personality) as Cause of the World

Others, however, postulate the *puruṣa* [spirit], similar in character to God, as the cause of the world .... The refutation of this also is to be set forth in the same manner as that of God: for what purpose does this spirit perform such an act [as the creating, of the world]? (Text 155.)

If he does it because he is prompted by another being, then he cannot be self-sufficient [independent]. If he does it through compassion, then he should make the world absolutely happy. When he is found to have created people beset with misery, poverty, sorrow and other troubles, where can his compassion be perceived? (Texts 156–157.)

Further, inasmuch as, prior to creation, the objects of compassion would not be there, there could not be even that compassion through the presence of which the ordainer is assumed. (Text 158.)

Nor should he bring about the dissolution of those beings who would always be prosperous. If in so doing he be regarded as dependent upon the unseen force [of destiny], then his self-sufficiency ceases. (Text 159.)

It might be argued that "He makes people happy or unhappy in accordance with their destiny, in the shape of merit and demerit." That cannot be right, as in that case his self-sufficiency, which has been postulated, would cease. One who is himself endowed with power does not depend upon anything else; if he is wanting in power, then the creation of the world itself might be attributed to that on which he is dependent; and in that case he would cease to be the cause. (Commentary to Text 159.)

Then again, why should he make himself dependent upon that destiny, which is conducive to suffering and pain? In fact, full of mercy as he is, the right course for him would be to ignore that destiny. (Text 160.)

Merciful persons do not seek for such causes as bring about suffering, because the sole motive behind their actions consists in the desire to remove the suffering of others. (Commentary to Text 160.)

The Discourse on the Snake Simile

Alagaddūpama Sutta

with Introduction and Notes

translated by

Nyanaponika Thera

WHEEL PUBLICATION NO. 48/49

Copyright © Kandy: Buddhist Publication Society (1974)

Introduction

The discourse of the Buddha on the Snake Simile (Alagaddūpama Sutta) that is presented here, together with explanatory notes taken mostly from the commentarial literature, is the 22nd text in the "Collection of Discourses of Medium Length" (Majjhima Nikāya).

It is a text rich of contents and graced by many similes. At the very beginning there is a sequence of ten pithy similes on the perils of sense desires; then follows the simile on correctly or wrongly getting hold of a snake (from which our text derives its name); further, and still better known, the parable of the raft; and finally the simile of the vegetation of the Jeta Grove. The evocative power of these similes will strengthen the impact of the sutta's message, in him who ponders on them deeply and repeatedly.

The main concern of this discourse is to warn against misconceptions, misrepresentations and dilution of the Teaching.

While the Buddha repeatedly stressed that his Teaching should be accepted only after due investigation, and uninfluenced by tradition or external authority; while he also advised his monks to make light of praise and blame of the Teaching uttered by outsiders (see here §38f.); the Master was quite firm, and even stern, when misrepresentations of the Teaching occurred on the part of his monks—that is, by those who had accepted the Teaching and had chosen a life devoted to its realization. Our discourse is not the only one where the Buddha had voiced a stern rebuke of monks who misinterpreted essential parts of the Teaching (see, e.g., MN 38). What moved the Buddha to do so was his deep concern that the efficacy of his unique Path of Deliverance should not be impaired, his Teaching not be undermined from within, and the purity of conduct and wisdom not be tarnished. If that were to be, the raft of the Teaching of which the discourse speaks, would be rendered incapable of carrying those across who have placed their confidence in it. The raft would forever be chained to the hither shore by those very fetters from which it is intended to bring release.

Our discourse deals with two chief obstacles which will impede the raft's progress: the affirmation of sense-gratification and the affirmation of ego-belief. If, by misrepresenting the

Teaching, these are admitted entrance in it, in whatever guise and whatever degree of dilution, they will necessarily nullify the effort for final liberation.

It should be noted that it is the *affirmation*, the approval, of those two tendencies that constitutes misrepresentation of the Teaching. These two tendencies themselves—i.e., sensuality and ego-belief—are deeply ingrained in human nature as we find it. They are, in fact, the two tap-roots from which existence and, with it, suffering spring: craving (*taṇhā*) and ignorance (*avijjā*). To weaken them first and finally eradicate them is the difficult task before us which, however, we can face courageously if guided by the methods of the Dhamma which are realistic as well as radical. But if what ought to be overcome is actually affirmed and approved, if hidden or open reservations with regard to either of these two tendencies are maintained, there is obviously no chance for achieving mind's final deliverance from that bondage to craving and ignorance.

The attitude towards dispassion (*virāga*; Skt: *virāgya*) and towards the doctrine of egolessness (*anattā*) is, in fact, a crucial test how far the core of the Teaching has been preserved or impaired or entirely abandoned in those presentations of the Dhamma that appeared after the Master passed away; and some of these developments obviously do not stand the test.

Considering all this, we shall understand and appreciate the grave warning and the firm repudiation expressed in our discourse by the Master wishing for the welfare and progress of those who had confidence in his guidance.

The first section of the discourse deals with the rejection of the views held by the monk Ariṭṭha. His views are not merely a misconception of the Teaching but a direct challenge of some of the Buddha's statements. Ariṭṭha expressly denies that what the Buddha taught as obstructive is an obstruction by necessity. He does not specify the obstructions he means, but from the monks' reply, referring to sense-desires (*kāma*), it is evident that they were well aware of Ariṭṭha's intention: the condoning of sexual indulgence for a monk.

It need hardly be stressed that the Buddha's firm rejection of such condonation was meant for monks only. Of his lay followers he did not expect sexual abstinence. To them he advised restraint and mindfulness, and avoidance of giving excessive nourishment to sex desire. Here, if anywhere, a middle path between unrestrained indulgence and enforced repression was apt. But the Buddha made it clear that full deliverance required full detachment from desire. The gradual progress towards it, however, was left to the degree of insight and self-control possessed and developed by the individual lay follower.

For the monk, however, it was expected that the ardor of his quest for the final goal, the serenity of mind and emotional satisfaction derived from meditation, and his relative freedom from external sense titillation—that all these and other factors should enable him to keep the sex urge well in check and his mind tranquil enough for allowing further progress (or at least effort) on the road to radical detachment. He who could not attain to that degree of self-mastery, was free to leave the Order, and no stigma was attached; and he was also free to return whenever he wanted. But inside the Sangha no compromise could be admitted unless the Buddha was to invite disintegration from within and disrepute from without.

(§§10–12). The instance of Ariṭṭha's wrong view is now used by the Buddha as an opportunity to warn against any other wrong approach to the Teaching, and the misuse of it. He gives here the simile of the wrong grasp of a snake to illustrate the harm and the danger of misconceiving the Dhamma.

The harm done is to the individual's character and his progress on the Path; and the danger is the likelihood of his falling into lower forms of existence, or at the least a rebirth unfavorable to the understanding and practicing of the Dhamma. That such results may follow can be easily understood in the case of Ariṭṭha's views which are an outright reversal and corruption of the Teaching. It may, however, at first sight be surprising to the reader that, in the section now under consideration, the misuse of the Teaching for the verbal wrangles of disputation is likewise regarded as a dangerously wrong grasp of the Dhamma.

Here the danger and harm have more subtle, but no less real, roots. The danger in contentiousness is chiefly twofold. It provides one of the many evasions by which the mind shirks from devoting itself earnestly to the actual practice of the Dhamma. Secondly, under the respectable guise of the advocacy of the Dhamma, the attachment to "I" and "mine" finds an easy outlet. In disputations the ego gets the chance to indulge in self-assertion, superiority feeling, self-righteousness and opinionatedness. Furthermore, the ego may attach itself to the Dhamma in an attitude of possessiveness which sometimes may even resemble the behavior of a dog jealously and angrily defending a morsel of food without having himself the inclination to eat it. We see here the danger that an excessive concern with an argumentative advocacy of the Dhamma may strengthen subconsciously the deeply engrained egotistic impulses. It may even become one of the "grounds (or starting-points) for false views" as described by the Buddha (in §15).[1]

Finally, from indulging in wordy warfare will also spring feelings of partisanship, intolerance, fanaticism and hostility. Truly, we have here a formidable catalogue of detrimental qualities of mind, and from this we can now better understand why the Buddha applied here, too, the metaphor of the dangerously wrong way of grasping a snake.

(§§13–14). He who is so much preoccupied with doctrinal controversy, furnishes, indeed, a fitting illustration of one who carries the raft of the Dhamma on his head or shoulders; and, in his case, this will be not *after* the crossing but before he has done, or even seriously tried, the fording of the stream. In fact, this famous parable of the raft will in most cases apply to those who, in the words of the Dhammapada (v. 85), "run up and down the river's bank" on this side of the stream, without daring or wishing to cross. We find them using the raft for a variety of purposes: they will adorn it and adore it, discuss it, compare it—indeed anything else than use it.

There are, on the other hand, those who wrongly believe that this parable justifies them in jettisoning the raft *before* they have used it, and that it invites them to let go the good teachings along with the false ones, even before they have benefited by the former and fully discarded the latter.

As we see, there are, indeed, many more ways of "grasping wrongly" than of grasping rightly; hence the strong emphasis laid on examining wisely the true meaning and purpose of the Dhamma. And there should be frequent re-examination—lest we forget.

(§§15–17). This section on the "grounds for false views" connects with the mention of "false teachings" in the preceding paragraph (§14).

Here, and in almost all the following sections, up to §41, it is the gravest of all wrong views—the belief in a Self, in an abiding ego-entity—that is dealt with from different angles. Our discourse is one of the most important texts concerned with the *Anattā*-doctrine, the teaching on Not-self. This teaching is the core of the Buddhist doctrine and a singular feature of it. It is of a truly revolutionary nature, and hence it is not easily absorbed by the human mind which, since an unfathomable past, has been habituated to think, and to induce action, in terms of "I" and "mine." But this bias towards egocentricity has to be broken on the intellectual, emotional, and ethical level, if deliverance from suffering is ever to be won. In this task, the repeated and careful contemplation of our discourse can become a valuable aid.

In §15, the Buddha speaks of the sources from which the notion of a self is derived and formed. It is, in the first instance, the identification with any or all of the five aggregates (*khandha*) constituting what is conventionally called the personality. Identification with *the body* (or corporeality) is the "ground" or standpoint for materialism (naïve or philosophical). *Feeling* is seen as the core of Being, in the hedonist's attitude to life, or when, in mystical teachings, the soul is regarded as pure Divine Bliss or Divine Love. The self is identified with *perception* when being is equated with perceiving (*esse est percipi*), when the personality is regarded as "nothing but" a bundle of sensations (Ernst Mach). The *mental formations* contribute to ego-belief when, e.g., the will is regarded as the ultimate essence of self and world; or when any other function of the mind receives an excessive emotional or intellectual emphasis. The aggregate of *consciousness* is circumscribed, in the discourses, by terms denoting the content of consciousness, indicating hereby that the self is here believed to be the totality of mind or consciousness. Included in this view are the conceptions of a Super or Cosmic Consciousness,[2] or any notion of an "Over-self" (*mahātmā, paramātmā*), imagined to exist "beyond the five aggregates."[3]

The view that the self is the unity of all five aggregates is found, for instance, in those religions which believe in a final resurrection of a (re-animated) body or in other forms of survival of the whole personality, body and mind, be it in an eternal heaven or an eternal hell.

The first five "grounds for false views" can be summarized by the following succinct statement of the Buddha: "Those ascetics and brahmans, O monks, who conceive a self in many ways, all those conceive it as the five aggregates or as one of them" (SN 22:47).[4]

As to the sixth "ground for false views," it should be noted that it does not consist in the eternalist view itself (which is covered by the foregoing), but in the strong attachment to that view, up to the degree of full identification with it, as part and parcel of one's individuality: "This (view) is mine, this I am, this is my self." Such a tenacious clinging to the soul-belief has its roots firstly in the deep urge for self-assertion and self-perpetuation; and secondly in the "conditioning" forces of education, environment and tradition. Like the other more common types of "self-defense," this identification with the belief in a self can assume quite a passionate character, with hostility or contempt for those who do not share it.

The persistence of the soul-belief is demonstrated by the fact that from the earliest time of the Teaching up to the present day there have been not only individuals (like Sāti in MN 38), but also groups and sects within the Buddhist fold who believed in a self though they usually relegate it to a realm beyond the five aggregates.

In the next section (§18ff.), it is shown that the belief in "I" and "mine," instead of giving a feeling of security, is, in fact, a cause of anxiety, fear and worry. And even when the faith in an immortal soul breaks down, its after-effect is still so strong that the assumption of a self that can be destroyed still persists, and, through the fear of annihilation, becomes a source of despair. This belief in "I" and "mine," and the passionate attachment to it, is at the root of the existentialist philosopher's "anguish" as well as of the anxiety neuroses that haunt modern man. The belief in unrealities, even if a temporary solace, must ultimately end in disappointment and despair.

Hence the Buddha took great care to question and re-question his monks on this crucial point of soul and self, in order to remove any doubt in this respect. The thorough manner of his inquiry is exemplified in §§22–25 which leave no room for ambiguity on this issue. In §§26–27 all the possible constituents of an alleged self (i.e., the five aggregates) are examined and found to be evanescent, liable to suffering and without a self or any other underlying substance. It should be noted that the statement of the text extends also to the most sublime manifestations of consciousness, be they conceived as internal ("in oneself") or external.

Though the analysis of "the individual and its property," as given in the preceding sections, is placed here in the context of refuting wrong views, this is in no way its intrinsic value and purpose, which rather consists in opening the gateway to liberation. To indicate this, §§28–29 speak of the attainment of final deliverance in sainthood (*arahatta*), brought about by insight that leads to alienation and detachment from all that is transient and void of substance. In the following (§§30–36), there is an impressive metaphorical description of the saint (*arahant*), concluding with the solemn declaration of the "untraceable" (i.e., ineffable) nature of one who has uprooted all craving and ignorance. With express reference to that solemn utterance, the Buddha now rejects emphatically the imputation that a denial of self and soul makes him a nihilist (§37) and he summarizes his teaching in those words of wide renown:

"What I teach now as before, O monks, is suffering and the cessation of suffering."

In the section on "Praise and Blame" (§§38–39), we have a practical application of the *anattā*-doctrine: it frees the mind from elation and pride in the case of praise, and from dejection and anger in the case of blame. The Buddha asks his disciples to emulate him in this respect. To be unshaken in the serene detachment of one's mind by any approval or disapproval by others, this is another benefit bestowed by the deep realization of the truth of *anattā*. Pointing out this additional benefit, the Master makes another earnest appeal to the monks to give up attachment to "what is not yours": the five aggregates constituting the so-called personality (§§40–41). Indeed, if viewed in the single-minded and passion-free detachment of insight-meditation (*vipassanā*), these physical and mental processes, so long regarded as "I" and "mine," will be seen to be as alien as the vegetation of the Jeta Grove to which the Buddha's finger may have pointed while he spoke.

The symphonic rhythm of this great discourse approaches now its finale. It is the majestic voice of uncompromising truth that speaks here in grave tones of crystal-clear penetrative power, without any gentler softening and soothing notes. The teaching as here conveyed, "plain and open, explicit and consistent," was and is a bold challenge of "public opinion." It goes counter to the two mighty currents of sense desire and self-affirmation which make up the "common stream" of mankind. In this discourse, the Buddha rejects repeatedly (in the former case) and excludes carefully (in the latter case) any attempt at compromise in these two respects. Furthermore the Buddha voices here a grave warning that a wrong grasp and misuse of the Dhamma may bring much harm and suffering. All escape routes for circumventing the true purpose and for avoiding the salient truths of the Doctrine were thus envisaged and carefully closed.

In this brief recapitulation, our discourse appears indeed as a rather formidable assemblage of stern messages. Yet, for one who is familiar with the Buddha Word, this will be softened by the fact that in numerous discourses the Buddha spoke of his Teaching as one that offers "gradual training, gradual progress." It is here that the Buddha's gentleness and compassion appears, his forbearance with human frailties, and his wise and patient guidance of men. Our discourse, too, ends on an encouraging note of assurance. Having earlier evoked the inspiring image of the saint (see §30 ff.), the Master now speaks of the fruits and highest summit, the final deliverance in saintship, preceded by the three Noble Paths leading to it, to the access stage of mind's growing maturity for enlightenment, down to those aspirants who, in the indubitable confrontation with the Truth by way of insight-meditation, have won deep faith in the Master and sublime love for him. Of them our discourse says that they are assured of those superhuman realms which are usually called "heaven." But it may well be as the ancients explain, that it is "the heaven on earth" which is meant here: the superhuman bliss experienced when for the first time, and still imperfect, the insight dawns on the meditator that phenomena, being evanescent and coreless throughout, do not and cannot enforce bondage unless we ourselves forge the chains of craving and delusion.

A Bhikkhu who in solitude
has mind's tranquility obtained,
enjoys a super human bliss,
if insight in the Teaching dawns.

Whenever in the aggregates
their rise and fall he clearly notes,
to joy and rapture he attains.
To those who know—
this is the Deathless State.

Dhammapada, vv. 373–374

Thus will a vision stern
Change into freedom's smile...

Nyanaponika Thera

The Snake Simile

1. Thus have I heard. Once the Blessed One lived at Sāvatthī, in Jeta's Grove, in Anāthapiṇḍika's monastery.

Ariṭṭha's Wrong View

2. Now, on that occasion a monk called Ariṭṭha, formerly of the vulture-killers, had conceived this pernicious view: "There are things called 'obstructions'[5] by the Blessed One. As I understand his teaching, those things are not necessarily obstructive for one who pursues them."

3. Several monks, hearing about it, went to the monk Ariṭṭha, formerly of the vulture killers, and asked him: "Is it true, friend Ariṭṭha, that you have conceived this pernicious view: 'There are things called (obstructions) by the Blessed One. As I understand his teaching, those things are not necessarily obstructive for one who pursues them'?"

"Yes, indeed, friends (I do hold that view)."

Then those monks, wishing to dissuade Ariṭṭha from that pernicious view, urged, admonished, questioned and exhorted him thus: "Do not say so, friend Ariṭṭha, do not say so! Do not misrepresent the Blessed One! It is not right to misrepresent him. Never would the Blessed One speak like that. For in many ways, indeed, has the Blessed One said of those obstructive things that they are obstructions, indeed, and that they necessarily obstruct him who pursues them. Sense desires, so he has said, bring little enjoyment and much suffering and disappointment. The perils in them are greater. Sense desires are like bare bones, has the Blessed One said. They are like a lump of flesh, like a torch of straw, like a pit of burning coals, like a dream, like borrowed goods, like a fruit-bearing tree, like a slaughter house, like a stake of swords, like a snake's head, has the Blessed One said.[6] They bring little enjoyment, and much suffering and disappointment. The perils in them are greater."

Yet, though the monk Ariṭṭha was thus urged, admonished, questioned and exhorted by those monks, he still clung tenaciously and obstinately to his pernicious view, saying: "There are things called 'obstructions' by the Blessed One. As I understand his teaching, those things are not necessarily obstructive for one who pursues them."

4. When those monks could not dissuade the monk Ariṭṭha, formerly of the vulture killers, from his pernicious view, they went to the Blessed One, and after respectfully saluting him, they sat down at one side. Being seated, they told the Blessed One (all that had happened), and they said: "Since, O Lord, we could not dissuade the monk Ariṭṭha from his pernicious view, we have now reported this matter to the Blessed One."

5. Then the Blessed One addressed a certain monk thus: "Go, O monk, and tell the monk Ariṭṭha, formerly of the vulture killers, that the Master calls him."—"Yes, Lord," replied the monk. He went to the monk Ariṭṭha and spoke to him: "The Master calls you, friend Ariṭṭha."—"Yes, friend," replied Ariṭṭha and he went to meet the Blessed One. Having arrived, he saluted the Blessed One respectfully and sat down at one side. When he was seated, the Blessed One addressed him thus:

"Is it true, Ariṭṭha, that you have conceived this pernicious view: 'There are things called "obstructions" by the Blessed One. As I understand his teaching those things are not necessarily obstructive for him who pursues them.'?"—"Yes, indeed, Lord, I understand the teaching of the Blessed One in this way that those things called 'obstructions' by the Blessed One, are not necessarily obstructive for him who pursues them."

6. "Of whom do you know, foolish man, that I have taught to him the teaching in that manner? Did I not, foolish man, speak in many ways of those obstructive things that they are obstructions indeed, and that they necessarily obstruct him who pursues them? Sense desires, so I have said, bring little enjoyment, and much suffering and disappointment. The perils in them are greater. Sense desires are like bare bones, have I said. They are like a lump of flesh... they are like a snake's head, have I said. They bring much suffering and disappointment. The perils in them are greater. But you, O foolish man, have misrepresented us by what you personally have wrongly grasped. You have undermined your own (future) and have created much demerit. This, foolish man, will bring you much harm and suffering for a long time."[7]

7. Then the Blessed One addressed the monks thus: "What do you think, O monks: has that monk Ariṭṭha, formerly of the vulture killers, produced any spark (of understanding) in this teaching and discipline?"[8]—"How should that be, Lord? Certainly not, O Lord."

After these words, the monk Ariṭṭha, formerly of the vulture killers, sat silent, confused, with his shoulders drooping and his head bent, brooding and incapable of making a rejoinder.

Then the Blessed One, knowing (his condition), spoke to him: "You will be known, foolish man, by what is your own pernicious view, I shall now question the monks about this."

8. Then the Blessed One addressed the monks: "Do you, O monks, also understand the teaching proclaimed by me, in the same manner as this monk Ariṭṭha does, who misrepresents us by what he personally has wrongly grasped; who has undermined his own (future) and created much demerit?"

"Certainly not, Lord. For in many ways has the Blessed One told us of those obstructive things that they are obstructions indeed, and that they necessarily obstruct him who pursues them..."

"Good, monks. It is good that you thus understand the teaching proclaimed by me.[9] For in many ways have I spoken of those obstructive things that they are obstructions, indeed, and that they necessarily obstruct him who pursues them. Sense desires, so have I said, bring little enjoyment, and much suffering and disappointment. The perils in them are greater. Sense desires are like bare bones, have I said. They are like a lump of flesh, like a torch of straw, like a pit of burning coals, like a dream, like borrowed goods, like a fruit-bearing tree, like a slaughter-house, like a stake of swords, like a snake's head are sense desires, have I said. They bring much suffering and disappointment. The perils in them are greater. But this monk Ariṭṭha, formerly of the vulture killers, misrepresents us by what he personally has wrongly grasped; he undermines his own (future) and creates much demerit. This will bring to this foolish man much harm and suffering for a long time.

9. "Monks, it is impossible indeed, that one can pursue sense gratification[10] without sensual desire,[11] without perceptions of sensual desire, without thoughts of sensual desire."

The Snake

10.[12] "There are here, O monks, some foolish men who study the Teaching—discourses, mixed prose and verse, prose expositions, verses, solemn utterances, sayings, birth stories, marvels, and replies to questions—having studied it, they do not wisely examine the purpose of those teachings. To those who do not wisely examine the purpose, these teachings will not yield insight.[13] They study the Teaching only to use it for criticizing or for refuting others in disputation. They do not experience the (true) purpose[14] for which they[15] (ought to) study the Teaching. To them these teachings wrongly grasped, will bring harm and suffering for a long time. And why? Because of their wrong grasp of the teachings.

"Suppose, monks, a man wants a snake, looks for a snake, goes in search of a snake. He then sees a large snake, and when he is grasping its body or its tail, the snake turns back on him and bites his hand or arm or some other limb of his. And because of that he suffers death or deadly pain. And why? Because of his wrong grasp of the snake.

"Similarly, O monks, there are here some foolish men who study the Teaching; having studied it, they do not wisely examine the purpose of those teachings. To those who do not wisely examine the purpose, these teachings will not yield insight. They study the Teaching only to use it for criticizing or for refuting others in disputation. They do not experience the (true) purpose for which they (ought to) study the Teaching. To them these teachings wrongly grasped, will bring harm and suffering for a long time. And why? Because of their wrong grasp of the teachings.

11. "But there are here, O monks, some noble sons who study the Teaching;[16] and having studied it, they examine wisely the purpose of those teachings. To those who wisely examine the purpose, these teachings will yield insight. They do not study the Teaching for the sake of criticizing nor for refuting others in disputation. They experience the purpose for which they study the Teaching; and to them these teachings being rightly grasped, will bring welfare and happiness for a long time. And why? Because of their right grasp of the teachings.

"Suppose, monks, a man wants a snake, looks for a snake, goes in search of a snake. He then sees a large snake, and with a forked stick he holds it firmly down. Having done so, he catches it firmly by the neck. Then although the snake might entwine with (the coils of) its body that man's hand or arm or some other limb of his, still he does not on that account suffer death or deadly pain. And why not? Because of his right grasp of the snake.

"Similarly, O monks, there are here some noble sons who study the Teaching; and having learned it, they examine wisely the purpose of those teachings. To those who wisely examine the purpose, these teachings will yield insight. They do not study the Teaching for the sake of criticizing nor for refuting others in disputation. They experience the purpose for which they study the Teaching; and to them these teachings being rightly grasped, will bring welfare and happiness for a long time. And why? Because of their right grasp of the teachings.

12. "Therefore, O monks, if you know the purpose of what I have said, you should keep it in mind accordingly. But if you do not know the purpose of what I have said, you should question me about it, or else (ask) those monks who are wise."

The Raft

13. "I shall show you, monks, the Teaching's similitude to a raft: as having the purpose of crossing over, not the purpose of being clung to. Listen, monks, and heed well what I shall say"—"Yes, Lord," replied the monks. And the Blessed One spoke thus:

"Suppose, monks, there is a man journeying on a road and he sees a vast expanse of water, of which this shore is perilous and fearful, while the other shore is safe and free from danger. But there is no boat for crossing nor is there a bridge for going over from this side to the other. So the man thinks: 'This is a vast expanse of water; and this shore is perilous and fearful, but the other shore is safe and free from danger. There is, however, no boat here for crossing, nor a bridge for going over from this side to the other. Suppose I gather reeds, sticks, branches and foliage, and bind them into a raft.' Now, that man collects reeds, sticks, branches and foliage, and binds them into a raft. Carried by that raft, laboring with hands and feet, he safely crosses over to the other shore. Having crossed and arrived at the other shore, he thinks: 'This raft, indeed, has been very helpful to me. Carried by it, laboring with hands and feet, I got safely across to the other shore. Should I not lift this raft on my head or put it on my shoulders, and go where I like?'

"What do you think about it, O monks? Will this man by acting thus, do what should be done with a raft?"—"No, Lord"—"How then, monks, would he be doing what should be done with a raft? Here, monks, having got across and arrived at the other shore, the man thinks: 'This raft, indeed, has been very helpful to me. Carried by it, and laboring with hands and feet, I got safely across to the other shore. Should I not pull it up now to the dry land or let it float in the water, and then go as I please?' By acting thus, monks, would that man do what should be done with a raft?

"In the same way, monks, have I shown to you the Teaching's similitude to a raft: as having the purpose of crossing over, not the purpose of being clung to.

14. "You, O monks, who understand the Teaching's similitude to a raft, you should let go even (good) teachings,[17] how much more false ones!"

Grounds for Views

15. "There are, monks, these six grounds for false views.[18] What are the six? There is here, monks, an uninstructed worldling who has no regard for Noble Ones, who is ignorant of their teaching and untrained in it; who has no regard for men of worth, who is ignorant of their teaching and untrained in it: he considers corporeality thus: 'This is mine, this I am, this is my self';[19] he considers feeling... perception... mental formations thus: 'This is mine, this I am, this is my self'; and what is seen, heard, sensed, and thought;[20] what is encountered, sought, pursued in mind,[21] this also he considers thus: 'This is mine, this I am, this is my self'; and also this ground for views (holding): 'The universe is the Self.[22] That I shall be after death;[23] permanent, stable, eternal, immutable; eternally the same,[24] shall I abide in that very condition'—that (view), too, he considers thus: 'This is mine, this I am, this is my self.'[25]

16. "But, monks, there is here a well-instructed noble disciple who has regard for Noble Ones, who knows their teaching and is well trained in it; who has regard for men of worth, who knows their teaching and is well trained in it: he does not consider corporeality in this way: 'This is mine, this I am, this is my self'; he does not consider feeling... perception... mental formations in this way: 'This is mine, this I am, this is my self'; and what is seen, heard, sensed, and thought; what is encountered, sought, pursued in mind, this also he does not consider in this way: 'This is mine, this I am, this is my self'; and also this ground for views (holding): 'The universe is the Self. That I shall be after death; permanent, stable, eternal, immutable, eternally the same shall I abide in that very condition'—that (view), too, he does not consider thus: 'This is mine, this I am, this is my self.'

17. "Considering thus, he is not anxious about unrealities."[26]

Anxiety about Unrealities

18. When this was said, a certain monk asked the Blessed One:

"Lord, can there be anxiety about unrealities, in the external?"[27]

"There can be, O monk," said the Blessed One. "In that case, monk, someone thinks: 'Oh, I had it! That, alas, I have no longer! Oh, may I have it again! But alas, I do not get it!' Hence he grieves, is depressed and laments; beating his breast, he weeps and dejection befalls him. Thus, monk, is there anxiety about unrealities, in the external."

19. "But, Lord, can there be absence of anxiety about unrealities, in the external?"

"There can be, O monk," said the Blessed One. "In that case, monk, someone does not think thus: 'Oh, I had it! That, alas, I have no longer! Oh, may I have it again! But, alas, I do not get it!' Hence he does not grieve, is not depressed, does not lament; he does not beat his breast nor does he weep, and no dejection befalls him. Thus, monk, is there absence of anxiety about unrealities, in the external."

20. "Lord, can there be anxiety about unrealities, in the internal?"

"There can be, monk," said the Blessed One. "In that case, monk, someone has this view: 'The universe is the Self. That I shall be after death; permanent, stable, eternal, immutable, eternally the same shall I abide in that very condition.' He then hears a Perfect One expounding the Teaching for the removal of all grounds for views, of all prejudices, obsessions, dogmas and biases; for the stilling of all (kamma-) processes, for the relinquishment of all substrata (of existence), for the extirpation of craving, for dispassion, cessation, Nibbāna. He then thinks: 'I shall be annihilated, I shall be destroyed! No longer shall I exist!' Hence he grieves, is depressed and laments; beating his breast, he weeps, and dejection befalls him. Thus, monk, is there anxiety about realities, in the internal."

21. "But, Lord, can there be absence of anxiety about unrealities, in the internal?"

"There can be, monk," said the Blessed One. "In that case, monk, someone does not have this view: 'The universe is the Self... eternally the same shall I abide in that very condition.' He then hears a Perfect One expounding the Teaching for the removal of all grounds for views, of all prejudices, obsessions, dogmas and biases; for the stilling of all (kamma) processes, for the relinquishing of all substrata (of existence), for the extirpation of craving, for dispassion, cessation, Nibbāna. He then does not think: 'I shall be annihilated, I shall be destroyed! No longer shall I exist!' Hence he does not grieve, is not depressed, does not lament; he does not beat his breast nor does he weep, and no dejection befalls him. Thus, monk, is there absence of anxiety about unrealities, in the internal."[28]

Impermanence and Not-self

22. "You may well take hold of a possession,[29] O monks, that is permanent, stable, eternal, immutable, that abides eternally the same in its very condition. (But) do you see, monks, any such possession?"—"No, Lord."—"Well, monks, I too, do not see any such possession that is permanent, stable, eternal, immutable, that abides eternally the same in its very condition."

23. "You may well accept, monks, the assumption of a self-theory[30] from the acceptance of which there would not arise sorrow and lamentation, pain, grief, and despair. (But) do you see, monks, any such assumption of a self-theory?"—"No, Lord."—"Well, monks, I too, do not see any such assumption of a self-theory from the acceptance of which there would not arise sorrow and lamentation, pain, grief and despair."

24. "You may well rely, monks, on any supporting (argument) for views[31] from the reliance on which there would not arise sorrow and lamentation, pain, grief and despair. (But) do you see, monks, any such supporting (argument) for views?"—"No, Lord."—"Well, monks, I too, do not see any such supporting (argument) for views from the reliance on which there would not arise sorrow and lamentation, pain, grief and despair.[32]

25. "If there were a self, monks, would there be my self's property?"—"So it is, Lord."—"Or if there is a self's property, would there by my self?"—"So it is, Lord."—"Since in truth and in fact, self and self's property do not obtain, O monks, then this ground for views, 'The universe is the Self. That I shall be after death; permanent, stable, eternal, immutable; eternally the same shall I abide, in that very condition'—is it not, monks, an entirely and perfectly foolish idea?"—"What else should it be, Lord? It is an entirely and perfectly foolish idea.[33]

The Three Characteristics

26. "What do you think, monks: is corporeality permanent or impermanent?"—"Impermanent, Lord."—"And what is impermanent, is it painful or pleasant?"—"Painful, Lord."—"What is impermanent, painful, subject to change, is it fit to be considered thus: 'This is mine, this I am, this is my self'?"—"Certainly not, Lord."—"What do you think, monks: Is feeling... is perception... are mental formations... is consciousness... permanent or impermanent?"—"Impermanent, Lord."—"And what is impermanent, is it painful or pleasant?"—"Painful, Lord."—"And what is impermanent, painful, subject to change, is it fit to be considered thus: 'This is mine, this I am, this is my self?"—"Certainly not, Lord."

27. "Therefore, monks, whatever corporeality, whether past, future, or present, in oneself or external, gross or subtle, inferior or superior, far or near—all corporeality should with right wisdom, thus be seen as it is: 'This is not mine, this I am not, this is not my self.'

"Whatever feeling... whatever perception... whatever mental formations... whatever consciousness, whether past, future or present, in oneself or external, gross or subtle, inferior or superior, far or near—all... consciousness should, with right wisdom, thus be seen as it is: 'This is not mine, this I am not, this is not my self.'

28. "Seeing this, monks, the well-instructed noble disciple becomes disgusted[34] with corporeality, becomes disgusted with feeling, with perception, with mental formations, with consciousness.

29. "Through his being disgusted, his passion fades away.[35] His passion having faded, he is freed.[36] In him who is freed there is the knowledge of freedom:[37] 'Ceased has rebirth, fulfilled is the holy life, the task is done, there is no more of this to come," thus he knows."

The Arahant[38]

30. "This monk is called one who has removed the crossbar, has filled the moat, has broken the pillar, has unbolted (his mind); a Noble One who has taken down the flag, put down the burden, become unfettered.

31. "And how, monks, is that monk one who has removed the crossbar? Herein the monk has abandoned ignorance, has cut it off at the root, removed it from its soil like a palmyra tree, brought it to utter extinction, incapable of arising again. Thus has he removed the crossbar.

32. "And how, monks, is that monk one who has filled the moat? Herein the monk has abandoned the round of rebirths, leading to renewed existence; he has cut it off at the root, removed it from its soil like a palmyra tree, brought it to utter extinction, incapable of arising again.

33. "And how has he broken the pillar? He has abandoned craving, has cut it off at the root, removed it from its soil like a palmyra tree, brought it to utter extinction, incapable of arising again.

34. "And how has he unbolted (his mind)? He has abandoned the five lower fetters, has cut them off at the root, removed them from their soil like a palmyra tree, brought them to utter extinction, incapable of arising again.

35. "And how is the monk a Noble One who has taken down the flag, put down the burden, become unfettered? He has abandoned the conceit of self, has cut it off at the root, removed it from is soil like a palmyra tree, brought it to utter extinction, incapable of arising again. Thus is the monk a Noble One who has taken down the flag, put down the burden, become unfettered.

36. "When a monk's mind is thus freed, O monks, neither the gods with Indra, nor the gods with Brahma, nor the gods with the Lord of Creatures (Pajāpati), when searching will find[39] on what the consciousness of one thus gone (*tathāgata*) is based. Why is that? One who has thus gone is no longer traceable here and now, so I say."[40]

Misrepresentation

37. "So teaching, so proclaiming, O monks, I have been baselessly, vainly, falsely and wrongly accused by some ascetics and brahmans: 'A nihilist[41] is the ascetic Gotama; he teaches the annihilation, the destruction, the non-being of an existing individual.'[42]

"As I am not as I do not teach, so have I been baselessly, vainly, falsely and wrongly accused by some ascetics and brahmans thus: 'A nihilist is the ascetic Gotama; he teaches the annihilation, the destruction, the non-being of an existing individual.'

"What I teach now as before, O monks, is suffering and the cessation of suffering."

Praise and Blame

38. "If for that (reason)[43] others revile, abuse, scold and insult the Perfect One, on that account, O monks, the Perfect One will not feel annoyance, nor dejection, nor displeasure in his heart. And if for that (reason) others respect, revere, honor and venerate the Perfect One, on that account the Perfect One will not feel delight, nor joy, nor elation in his heart. If for that (reason) others respect, revere, honor and venerate the Perfect One, he will think: 'It is towards this (mind-body aggregate) which was formerly[44] fully comprehended, that they perform such acts.'[45]

39. "Therefore, O monks, if you, too, are reviled, abused, scolded and insulted by others, you should on that account not entertain annoyance or dejection or displeasure in your hearts. And if others respect, revere, honor and venerate you, on that account you should not entertain delight or joy or elation in your hearts. If others respect, revere, honor and venerate you, you should think: 'It is towards this (mind-body aggregate) which was formerly comprehended, that they perform such acts.'[46]

Not Yours[47]

40. "Therefore, monks, give up whatever is not yours.[48] Your giving it up will for a long time bring you welfare and happiness. What is it that is not yours? Corporeality is not yours. Give it up! Your giving it up will for a long time bring you welfare and happiness. Feeling is not yours. Give it up! Your giving it up will

for a long time bring you welfare and happiness. Perception is not yours. Give it up! Your giving it up will for a long time bring you welfare and happiness. Mental formations are not yours. Give them up! Your giving them up will for a long time bring you welfare and happiness. Consciousness is not yours. Give it up! Your giving it up will for a long time bring you welfare and happiness.[49]

41. "What do you think, monks: if people were to carry away the grass, sticks, branches and leaves in this Jeta Grove, or burnt them or did with them what they pleased, would you think: These people carry us away, or burn us, or do with us as they please?"—"No, Lord."—"Why not?" Because, Lord, that is neither our self nor the property of our self."—"So, too, monks, give up what is not yours! Your giving it up will for a long time bring you welfare and happiness. What is it that is not yours? Corporeality... feeling... perception... mental formations... consciousness are not yours. Give them up! Your giving them up will for a long time bring you welfare and happiness."

The Explicit Teaching and Its Fruit

42. "Monks, this Teaching[50] so well proclaimed by me, is plain, open, explicit, free of patchwork.[51] In this Teaching that is so well proclaimed by me and is plain, open, explicit and free of patchwork, for those who are arahants, free of taints, who have accomplished and completed their task, have laid down the burden, achieved their aim, severed the fetters binding to existence, who are liberated by full knowledge, there is no (future) round of existence that can be ascribed to them.

43. "Monks, in this Teaching that is so well proclaimed by me and is plain, open, explicit and free of patchwork, those monks who have abandoned the five lower fetters will all be reborn spontaneously (in the Pure Abodes) and there they will pass away finally, no more returning from that world.

44. "Monks, in this Teaching that is so well proclaimed by me and is plain, open, explicit and free of patchwork, those monks who have abandoned three fetters and have reduced greed, hatred and delusion, are all once-returners, and, returning only once to this world, will then make an end of suffering.

45. "Monks, in this Teaching that is so well proclaimed by me and is plain, open, explicit and free of patchwork, those monks who have abandoned three fetters, are all stream-enterers, no more liable to downfall, assured, and headed for full Enlightenment.

46. "Monks, in this Teaching that is so well proclaimed by me and is plain, open, explicit, and free of patchwork, those monks who are mature in Dhamma, mature in faith,[52] are all headed for full Enlightenment.

47. "Monks, in this Teaching that is so well proclaimed by me and is plain, open, explicit and free of patchwork, those who have simply faith in me, simply love for me,[53] are all destined for heaven."

48. This said the Blessed One. Satisfied, the monks rejoiced in the words of the Blessed One.

Notes

1. This may result from the unwillingness to give up a wrong view advocated in the argument. It may also come under the heading "What is encountered, this he also considers thus: This is mine..."; that is, he identifies himself with a given situation (here the disputation) and with his own stand taken in it.
2. See §27: "Whatever consciousness... gross or subtle."
3. This, too, falls under the fifth of the "grounds," being a mental construction (§15: "what is thought"), and something "sought after and pursued in mind," due to human yearning for permanence.
4. See *The Wheel* No. 11: *Anattā and Nibbāna*, by Nyanaponika Thera, p. 18.
5. **Things called "obstructions"** (*antarāyikā dhammā*). Comy gives here a list of ideas and actions that obstruct either heavenly rebirth or final deliverance or both. Ariṭṭha, so says Comy, being a learned exponent of the Teaching, was quite familiar with most of these "obstructions"; but, being unfamiliar with the Code of Discipline (Vinaya), he conceived the view that sex indulgence was not necessarily an obstruction for a monk. Ariṭṭha is said to have used a rather sophistic argument, saying, "If some of the five sense enjoyments are permissible even for lay adherents who are stream-enterers (*sotāpanna*), etc., why is an exception made as to the visible shape, voice, touch, etc., of women?" According to Comy, Ariṭṭha goes so far as to charge the Buddha with exaggerating the importance of the first grave offence (*pārājikā*) for a monk (i.e., sexual intercourse), saying that the emphasis given to it is like the effort of one who tries to chain the ocean.

The similes about sense-desires, given in the following section of the discourse, seem to support the commentarial reference to sexual intercourse.

6. **The similes about sense-desires.** Of the ten similes, the first seven were explained in detail in the Potaliya Sutta (MN 54; see *The Wheel* No. 79). A summary of these explanations follows here; and after each of these, and also for the remaining three similes, an expansion is given of the one-word explanation found in the Comy to our present text:

(1) **Bare bones,** fleshless, bloodsmeared, are thrown to a starving dog but cannot satisfy the animal's hunger. Similarly, sense-desires give no lasting satisfaction (Comy: *appasādaṭṭhena*).

(2) **A lump of flesh** for which birds of prey fight each other; if the bird that has seized the lump of flesh, does not yield it, it may meet death or deadly pain from the beaks and claws of the other birds. Similarly, the sense-desires are common to many (*bahusādhāraṇa*), i.e., the same sense objects may be claimed by many and may become the cause of deadly conflict.

(3) **A torch of straw** carried against the wind may cause severe burns to the careless man if not quickly discarded. Similarly, sense-desires will severely burn (*anudahana*), i.e., greatly harm him who thoughtlessly, and unaware of the great danger, partakes of them in the belief that they will bring light and joy to his life.

(4) **A pit of burning coals** towards which a man is dragged by others; if he cannot free himself from the grip, he will be thrown into the fire and consumed by it. Similarly, sense-desires are like a vast conflagration (*mahābhitāpa*) into which the victim is dragged by bad company, or by his own deeds, causing his rebirth in miserable states of woe.

(5) **A dream** of a beautiful landscape that vanishes on awakening. Similarly, sense-desires are a brief illusion (*ittara-paccupaṭṭhāna*) like a dream, and disappointing after one awakens from infatuation to reality.

(6) **Borrowed goods** on which the borrower foolishly prides himself in public; but which are withdrawn by the owners when they see the boastful man. Similarly, sense-desires are temporary (*tāvakālika*) and not a true and lasting possession of him who enjoys them, filled with vain glory.

(7) **A fruit tree** climbed by one who craves for the fruits; but another man, likewise greedy for them but unable to climb, chooses another method and fells the tree; and unless the first man quickly descends, he will break his limbs. Similarly, in the blind pursuit of sense pleasures one may "break all one's limbs" (*sabbaṅga-paccaṅga-bhañjana*), may suffer severe injury of body and mind. The Sub-Comy refers also to punishment and torture incurred by reckless deeds to which people are driven by sense infatuation.

(8) **A slaughter house** (or place of execution): because sense-desires are like a butcher's (or executioner's) block (*adhikuṭṭana*). This may mean that sense-desires kill much that is noble in man and cut off his higher development.

(9) **A stake of swords**: sense-desires are piercing (*vinivijjhana*), penetrating deep within, causing wounds where there had been none. Unfulfilled or frustrated desire, or the pains of jealousy, are, indeed, like that ancient torture of the stake of swords.

(10) **A snake's head**: sense-desires are a grave risk and peril (*sasaṅka-sappaṭibhaya*) for the present and future welfare, if one walks unwarily.

7. This first part of the Ariṭṭha episode occurs twice in the Vinaya Pitaka. In the Cūla Vagga (*Kammakkhandaka*) it is followed by announcing the Sangha act of suspension (*ukkhepaniya-kamma*) against Ariṭṭha as he did not give up his wrong views. In the Pācittiya section of the Vinaya, Ariṭṭha's refusal to renounce his wrong view is defined as the monastic offence called "*pācittiya.*"

8. **...produced any spark (of understanding) in this teaching and discipline** (*usmīkato pi imasmiṃ dhammavinaye*). This is a stock phrase in

similar contexts—e.g., in MN 38, where Sāti's misconceptions are rejected. Our rendering follows Comy: "This refers to one who has (not) produced the 'warmth of understanding' (*ñāṇusmā*) that can bring the 'seed of wisdom' (*paññā-bīja*; Sub-Comy) to the maturity required for attaining to the paths and fruitions of sanctity."

9. Comy says that by questioning the other monks the Master wanted to clarify the opinion held by the community of monks; and, on the other hand, leave no doubt in Ariṭṭha that through obstinately clinging to his views, he had separated himself from the community.

10. **Can pursue sense gratification** (*kāme paṭisevissati*). *Kāma* is here *vatthukāma*, the objective aspect of *kāma*, "sensuality," the sense experience. Comy adds: *methunasamācāraṃ samācarissati*, "It is impossible that he can commit the sexual act (without perceptions and thoughts of sense-desire)." Sub-Comy says that also other physical acts expressive of sexual desire, are to be included, as embracing, stroking, etc.

11. *Aññatra kāmehi*: this refers to *kilesa-kāma*, "sensuality as a defilement of mind," i.e., sense desire, the subjective aspect of *kāma*.

12. Comy: After the Master had pointed out Ariṭṭha's wrong views, he continues now by showing the grievous fault that lies in a wrong grasp of what has been learned (i.e., the serious danger inherent in misconceiving and misinterpreting the Teaching).

13. *Dhammā na nijjhānaṃ khamanti*. Comy: The teachings do not become clear, do not come into the range (of understanding); so that one cannot discern whether in the respective place of the exposition, morality is spoken of, or concentration, insight, the paths, the fruits, the round of existence or its ending. Sub-Comy: "That is, one cannot understand that the purpose of morality is the attaining of concentration, the purpose of concentration the winning of insight, etc."

Nijjhāna has here the meaning of "insight" or "comprehension" (Sub-Comy: *nijjhāna-paññakkhamā na honti*). This phrase appears with the same meaning and in the same context, in the Kīṭāgiri Sutta (MN 70) and the Caṅkī Sutta (MN 95), that is, likewise preceded by an "examination of purpose (or meaning)." Also SN 25:1 confirms our rendering: *Yassa kho bhikkhave ime dhammā evaṃ paññāya mattaso nijjhānaṃ khamanti ayaṃ vuccati dhammānusārī.*

14. Comy: That is, the attainment of the paths and fruitions of sanctity.

15. Comy refers this to "the noble sons" mentioned in §11.

16. **The three ways of studying the teaching.** Comy: "They, the noble sons, study the Teaching for the sake of crossing (the ocean of saṃsāric suffering). There are to wit, three manners of studying the Teaching: studying it in the manner of the Snake-simile (*alagadda-pariyatti*); studying it for the sake of

crossing over (*nittharaṇa-pariyatti*); and studying in a treasurer's (or store-keeper's) position (*bhaṇḍāgārika-pariyatti*).

(1) He who studies the Buddha's word for getting robes and other requisites, or for becoming widely known; that is, he who learns for the sake of fame and gain, his study is that of the Snake-simile (i.e., the wrong grasp); but better than such a study would be for him to sleep and not to study at all.

(2) But there is one who studies the Buddha's word, and when morality is the subject, he fulfills morality; when concentration is the subject, he lets it take deep root; when insight is the subject, he establishes himself well in insight; when the paths and fruitions are the subject, he studies with the intention, "I shall develop the path, I shall realize the fruition." Only the studying of such a one is "studying for the sake of crossing over" (as expressed in the simile of the raft; §13).

(3) But the studying by one who (as an arahant, a saint) has extinguished the taints (*khīṇāsavo*), is "studying in the Treasurer's position." For him, indeed, there remains nothing unpenetrated, nothing unrelinquished, nothing undeveloped, and nothing unrealized. [This refers to the 1st, 2nd, 4th, and 3rd Truths, respectively.] He is one who has penetrated the aggregates of existence (*khandha*), who has relinquished the defilements, developed the path and realized the fruition. Hence, in studying the Buddha's Word, he studies it as a keeper of the scriptures, as a guardian of the tradition, as a preserver of the continuity. Thus his study is like (the activity of) a treasurer (or store keeper).

"Now, when those proficient in the books cannot live at one place, being afraid of starvation, etc., if (in such a situation) there is one who, while himself going the alms round with very great fatigue, as an unliberated worldling takes up studies with the thought: 'Lest the exceedingly sweet Buddha-word may perish, I shall keep the scriptures (in mind), shall preserve the continuity and guard the tradition,' in that case, is his study of the Treasurer's type or is it not?—It is not. And why not? Because his study is not applied to his own situation (*na attano ṭhāne ṭhatvā pariyāpunattā*); Sub-Comy: that of (having to) cross over. An unliberated worldling's study [be he a monk or a lay follower] will either be of the type of the Snake-simile, or for the sake of crossing over; while for the seven (noble persons; *ariya-puggala*) who have entered the higher training (*sekha*), the study is only for the sake of crossing over; for the saint (*arahat*) it is only of the Treasurer's type."

17. Comy: "The teachings" (*dhammā*) are tranquility (*samatha*) and insight (*vipassanā*). The Blessed One, indeed, enjoins us to abandon desire and attachment (*chanda-rāga*) concerning tranquility and insight. Where, then, has he enjoined the abandonment of desire and attachment in the case of tranquility? He did so in the following saying: "Thus, Udāyi, do I teach the abandoning even of the sphere of neither-perception-nor-non-perception. Do

you see Udāyi, any fetter fine or coarse, that I did not tell you to discard?" (MN 66). And in the case of insight, the abandoning was enjoined by him as follows: "And to that view thus purified and cleansed, you should not be attached, should not be enamored of it, and should not treasure it." But here, in this present text, he enjoined the abandoning of desire and attachment concerning both (tranquility and insight), by saying: "You should let go even (good) teachings, how much more false ones!" The meaning is this: "I teach, O monks, the abandoning of desire and attachment even for such peaceful and sublime states (as tranquility and insight); how much more so in regard to that ignoble, low, contemptible, coarse and impure thing in which this foolish Ariṭṭha does not see any harm, saying that desire and attachment for the five sense-objects is not necessarily an obstruction! But you, O monks, unlike that Ariṭṭha, should not fling mud and refuse into my dispensation!" In this way, the Blessed One again rebuked Ariṭṭha by this admonition.

18. **Grounds for false views** (*diṭṭhiṭṭhāna*). Comy: By the words "There are, monks, these six grounds for false views," the Master wishes to show this: "He who takes the five aggregates of existence as 'I' and 'mine', by way of a threefold wrong grasp (*tividha-gāha*), he flings mud and refuse into my dispensation, like this Ariṭṭha."

Comy and Sub-Comy: False views themselves are "grounds" (or bases, starting-points) for subsequently arising false views, like personality belief, eternalism, etc. (Comy: *diṭṭhi pi ditthiṭṭhānaṃ*). Further, the "grounds" are the subject-matter (*ārammaṇa*, "object") of the views, i.e., the five aggregates, the visual objects, etc. Finally, they are also the conditioning factors (*paccaya*) of the false views, e.g., ignorance, sense-impression (*phassa*), (faulty) perceptions and thoughts, unwisely directed attention (*ayoniso manasikāra*), bad company, others' speech, etc. [These, with the aggregates as the first, are the eight "grounds for false views," as mentioned in the Paṭisambhidāmagga (Diṭṭhi-kathā). The term *diṭṭhiṭṭhāna* also occurs in the Brahmajāla Sutta (DN 1) and in the commentary to it.

19. **"He considers corporeality thus: 'This is mine'."** Comy: This is wrong grasp (or wrong approach) induced by craving (*taṇhā-gāha*). "This I am": this is wrong grasp induced by conceit (*māna-gāha*). "This is my self": this is wrong grasp induced by false views (*diṭṭhi-gāha*). Here, reference is to craving, conceit, and false views which have corporeality as object; but corporeality cannot be said to be a self. The same holds true for feeling, perception and mental formations.

20. **"What is seen"**: (Comy) the visual sense-object base (*rūpāyatana*); **"heard":** the sound-base; **"sensed"** (*mutaṃ*): the sense-object bases of smell, taste, and touch-sensations; **"what is thought"**: the remaining seven bases, i.e., the mind-object base (*dhammāyatana*) and the six sense-organ bases.

21. **"Encountered"**: (Comy) after having been sought for, or not sought for; **"sought"**: encountered or not encountered (before); **"mentally pursued"** (*anuvicaritaṃ manasā*): resorted to by consciousness (*cittena anusañcaritaṃ*)—what was encountered or not encountered without being sought for.

The terms "thought," "encountered," etc., refer to the fifth aggregate, i.e., consciousness (*viññāṇakkhandha*), which was not mentioned in the first part of §15.

22. **"The universe is the Self,"** lit.: "This (is) the world, this (is) the self" (*so loko so attā*). That, in fact, an identification of the two terms is intended here, will be shown in the following comments. The best explanation of the passage is furnished in the Brahmajāla Sutta (DN 1) where a similar phraseology is used: "There are, monks, some ascetics and brahmans who are eternalists and who proclaim self and world to be eternal" (*sassatavādā sassataṃ attañca lokañca paññapenti*); subsequently the theorist is introduced as stating his view in similar terms: "Eternal are self and world... they exist as eternally the same" (*sassato attā ca loko ca... atthi idheva sassatisamaṃ*). The last term appears likewise in our text; see Note 24. From this we may safely conclude that it is the identity, or unity, of the Self (or soul; *mahātman, paramātman*) with the universe (or the Universal Spirit, Brahman) which is conveyed by our text.

In the Commentary specific to our text, this eternalistic view is rendered and classified in the terminology of the Dhamma. The Commentary says:

"This statement ('The universe is the Self') refers to the (wrong) view 'He considers corporeality, etc., as the self (*rūpaṃ attato samanupassatī' ti ādinā nayena*).'"

The canonical quotation (e.g., in MN 44), included here in the Commentary, has two implications which are of importance for understanding the reason why it was cited in this context:

(1) As very often in the commentaries (e.g., to Satipaṭṭhāna Sutta), the term "world" (*loko*) is explained as truly referring to the five aggregates (*khandhā*, i.e., corporeality, feeling, etc.), singly or *in toto*.

(2) This quotation is the formula for the first of the twenty types of personality-belief (*sakkāya-diṭṭhi*; e.g., in MN 44). In the first five of these twenty, the self is said to be identical with each of the five aggregates (as in the earlier part of §15 of our text). Hence the application of this quote to our textual passage signifies that the theorist conceives the "world" (i.e., corporeality, feeling, etc.) as *identical* with the self.

The double "*So (loko) so (attā)*" in our text, should therefore, be taken as standing for "*yo (loko) so (attā),*" lit.: what is the world that is the self. In the Comy to MN 44 we find a similar phrase: "Someone considers corporeality as self: what is corporeality that is 'I'; what is 'I' that is corporeality. Thus he considers corporeality and self as non-dual' (... *yaṃ rūpaṃ so ahaṃ, yo ahaṃ taṃ rūpan' ti rūpañca advayaṃ samanupassati*)." According to this interpretation the phrase has been translated here by "This universe is the Self."

Mostly, the first five types of personality-belief are explained as referring to the wrong view of annihilationism (*uccheda-diṭṭhi*). [See, e.g., Paṭisambhidāmagga, Diṭṭhikathā, Ucchedadiṭṭhi-niddesa; further Comy to MN 44.]

But their being quoted in our context, shows that they may also apply to eternalism (*sassata-diṭṭhi*). We have come to this conclusion since it is improbable that, in our textual passage two mutually exclusive views should have been combined in a single statement formulating the sixth "ground for false views"; that is, in the first part of that statement, annihilationism, and in the second, eternalism.

23. **"That I shall be after death..."** (*so pecca bhavissāmi*). Comy explains by "*so ahaṃ*," a Pāli idiom, meaning literally "this I." *Pecca*: lit. "having gone," i.e., to the other world.

24. **"Eternally the same"** (*sassati-samaṃ*): an Upanishadic term; see Bṛhadāraṇyaka Upaniṣad 5.10: *sāsvatīḥ samāḥ*.

This entire statement of the sixth 'ground for views' may well have been the original creed of an eternalistic doctrine. The phrasing appears rather vague in the first part, and in general it is rather loosely worded (*so* for *so aham*). To contemporaries, however, the meaning may have been quite clear since it was perhaps the stock formula for teachings that were well known. Hence, in this translation, we have left the first part of the statement in its rather cryptic and ambiguous original form, while giving the interpretations in the notes only.

25. He identifies himself entirely (Sub-Comy: *attānaṃ viya gaṇhāti*) with that eternalist misconception (*gāha*), induced by craving (for self-perpetuation), by false views (tenaciously maintained) and by conceit (deeply ingrained egocentricity). Here one view serves as subject-matter for another view (Comy, Sub-Comy).

26. **"He is not anxious about unrealities"** (*asati na paritassati*); or "about the non-existing" ("I" and "mine"). The verb *paritassati* has, according to Comy, the twofold connotation of fear (*bhaya*) and craving (*taṇhā*). Hence this passage may also be rendered: "he has no fears nor cravings concerning the non-existent." Comy and Sub-Comy to the Brahmajāla Sutta have a long disquisition about the corresponding noun *paritassana*, occurring also in MN 138; SN 22:7, 8, 53, 55.

Comy: "By showing herewith the taint-free saint who has no anxiety at the destruction of his own (lit.: internal) aggregates, the Blessed One concludes his exposition."

27. **"In the external"** (*bahiddhā*): concerning external property which includes also animate possessions, like wife and child, friends, etc.

28. This section deals, according to Comy, with a "four-fold voidness" (*catukoṭikā suññatā*), i.e., absence of self and mine, referring to one who, at the destruction of his own aggregates (i.e., his personality), (1) feels anguish, (2) feels none; and to one who, at the destruction of external property (3) feels anguish, (4) feels none. For another classification of the "four-fold voidness," see *Visuddhimagga* (translated by Ñāṇamoli as *The Path of Purification*), p. 762 f; and SN 22:5, where likewise reference to "anxiety" or "anguish" (*tāso*) is made.
29. *Pariggahaṃ pariggaṇheyyātha*. This links up with §19: the anxiety about external possessions.
30. *Attavādupādānam upādiyetha*. While in most translations the term *upādāna* has been rendered by "clinging," we have followed here a suggestion of the late Bhikkhu Ñāṇamoli, rendering it by "assumption" [see *The Wheel* No. 17: *Three Cardinal Discourses of the Buddha*, p. 19, BPS]. In this context, the word "assumption" should be understood: (1) in the sense of a supposition, (2) in the literal sense of its Latin source: *adsumere*, "to take up," which closely parallels the derivation of our Pāli term: *upa-ādāna*, "taking up strongly." In this sense we have used it when translating the derivative verb *upādiyetha* by "you may accept." *Attavādupādāna* is one of the four types of clinging (see Nyanatiloka's *Buddhist Dictionary*), conditioned by craving (*taṇhā*). This term comprises, according to Comy, the twenty types of personality-belief (*sakkāya-diṭṭhi*).

Quoting this passage of our text, the Ven. Dr. Walpola Rāhula remarks: "If there had been any soul-theory which the Buddha had accepted, he would certainly have explained it here, because he asked the monks to accept that soul-theory which did not produce suffering. But in the Buddha's view, there is no such soul-theory..." (*What the Buddha Taught*, London, 1959; p.58).
31. *Diṭṭhinissayaṃ nissayetha. Nissaya*, lit.: support basis. Comy explains this phrase as the sixty-two false views headed by personality-belief (see DN 1, Brahmajāla Sutta). They form the theoretical or ideological basis, or support, for the various creeds and speculative doctrines derived from them. Sub-Comy: "The view itself is a support for views; because for one with incorrect conceptions, the view will serve as a prop for his firm adherence to, and the propagation of, his ideas." Alternative renderings: You may well place reliance on a view, or may derive conviction from it.

See Satipaṭṭhāna Sutta where, in explanation of *anissito* the Comy mentions *taṇhānissaya* and *diṭṭhinissaya*, "dependence on craving and views."
32. In this section, according to Comy, a "three-fold voidness is shown," i.e., referring to external possessions, self-theory and reliance on speculative views.
33. The two supplementary statements in this section suggest the following implications: The concepts of "I" and "mine" are inseparably linked; so also, in

philosophical terms, are substance and attribute. If there is personality-belief or self-theory, there will be necessarily acquisitiveness or possessiveness in some form or other; at least these views themselves will be held with strong tenacity and be regarded as an "inalienable property" (see Note 25). There is no pure, abstract self or substance without its determination, property or attribute. On the other hand, acquisitiveness and possessiveness—even if of a quite unphilosophical character—cannot be without at least a tacit assumption of a proprietary self; this applies also to materialistic doctrines (annihilationism). Since in truth and fact neither an abiding property (or attribute) can be established nor an abiding self (or substance), either of these terms is left without its essential referent. Hence the conception of individual immortality as formulated in the sixth ground for views, is found to be devoid of any basis and is, therefore, rejected by the Buddha as a fool's doctrine, being outside of serious consideration.

Comy: Here a "two-fold voidness" is shown, that of self (*attā*) and of property (or properties) belonging to a self (*attaniya*).

34. **"He becomes disgusted"** (*nibbindati*). Comy: he is dissatisfied, repelled. This disgust (or "turning away," revulsion; *nibbidā*) signifies the stage of "insight leading to emergence" (*vuṭṭhānagāmini-vipassanā*; Vism XXI.83), which is the culmination of insight, immediately preceding the attainment of the supramundane path (of stream-entry, etc.).

35. **"His passion fades away"** (*virajjati*). This signifies, according to Comy, the attainment of the supramundane path (*magga*); that is the single "moment of entering into one of the four stages of holiness produced by intuitional insight (*vipassanā*) into the impermanency, misery and impersonality of existence, flashing forth and forever transforming one's life and nature" (Nyanatiloka, *Buddhist Dictionary*). It is at that moment that the fetters are finally eliminated.

36. **"He is freed"** (*vimuccati*). This points to the attainment of the supramundane fruition (*phala*), that is "those moments of consciousness which follow immediately after the path-moment as its result, and which under given circumstances may repeat for innumerable times during a lifetime" (*Buddhist Dictionary*).

37. **"Knowledge of freedom"** refers to the stage of reviewing (*paccavekkhana*) the preceding experience of path and fruition, the defilements abandoned, etc. See Vism XXII.19.

38. This section appears also in AN 5:71 & 72/A III 84. Comy explains the metaphorical expressions as follows:

"There are two cities: one is a city of brigands, the other a city of peace. Now, to a great warrior of the city of peace (i.e., a meditator) the following thought occurs: 'As long as this city of brigands (the self-delusion) exists, we shall never be free from danger.' So he dons his armor (of virtue) and goes to the city of brigands. With his sword (of wisdom) he breaks the gate pillar (of craving) together with the door wings, he removes the bolt (of the five lower fetters), lifts the crossbar (of ignorance), fills in the moat (of saṃsāra), and lowers the (enemy's) flag (of self-conceit). Such a saint (a Noble One) has put down for good the burden of the five aggregates (*khandha*), of kamma-producing volitions (*kammābhisaṅkhāra*) and of the defilements (*kilesa*); has fully liberated himself from the round of existence."

39. **When searching will (not) find out** *(anvesaṃ nādhigacchanti).* The same phrase is used in the Godhika Sutta (SN 4:23/S I 122) by Māra: *anvesaṃ nādhigacchāmi*, "Searching I cannot find"—i.e., the consciousness of the monk, Godhika who, at the moment of committing suicide, had attained sainthood (*arahatta*). About him the Buddha declares that he "has passed away finally with a consciousness that no longer gives a footing" (for a rebirth; *apatiṭṭhena viññāṇena parinibbuto*).

40. *Diṭṭh'ev'āhaṃ bhikkhave dhamme Tathāgataṃ ananuvejjo'ti vadāmi.* Comy: The term *tathāgato* (lit.: "thus-gone") may refer either to a being (*satto*) or to the greatest man (*uttamo puriso*; the Buddha) and a taint-free saint (*khīṇāsavo*). *Ananuvejjo** means either "non-existing" (*asaṃvijjamāno*) or "not traceable" (*avindeyyo*). If *tathāgato* is taken as "a being" (in the sense of an abiding personality), the meaning "non-existing" applies; if in the sense of a taint-free saint, the meaning "not traceable" is apt. The intention implied in the first case, is: "O bhikkhus, even of a taint-free saint during his lifetime, here and now, I do not declare that he is 'a being, a personality' (in the sense of an abiding entity); how, then, should I declare it of a taint-free saint who has finally passed away, without any future rebirth? One thus-gone is untraceable; because in the ultimate sense (*paramatthato*), there is no such thing as 'a being' (*satto*). Searching for the basis of consciousness of such a non-existing (being) how can they find it, how can they obtain it?" In the case of the second explanation, the intention is this: "I say that Indra and other gods cannot trace a taint-free saint by way of consciousness (*viññāṇavasena*). For the gods who are with Indra and other deities, even if they make a search, cannot know about the consciousness of insight or that of the supramundane path or fruition (of sainthood; *arahatta*) that 'it proceeds based on such or such an object.' How, then, could they know it in the case of one who has finally passed away (*parinibbuto*), and has not been born again?" [Sub-Comy: "The consciousness of insight (*vipassanā-citta*) that aims at the attainment of the highest fruition (i.e., *arahatta*) leaps forward to the unconditioned element (*Nibbāna*) in the thought: "Non-origination is safety. Non-origination is safety!"] (* The Burmese Sixth Council edition reads *ananuvajjo.*)

41. **"A nihilist"** *(venayiko).* Comy: *satta-vināsako*, "destroyer of a being's (personality)"; a denier of individuality.

42. **"The annihilation of an existing creature"** (*sato sattassa ucchedaṃ*). Sub-Comy: "One who speaks of doing away with a being that has existence in the ultimate sense (*paramatthato*), would actually be one who teaches the destruction of a being. But I am speaking of what does not exist in the ultimate sense. I am using that (term 'being') only in the conventional sense as done in common parlance (*yathā loke voharati*)."
43. **"For that"** i.e., for proclaiming the Four Truths (Comy).
44. Comy: "**Formerly**, that is when still in the environ of the Bodhi tree before turning the Wheel of the Dhamma; and also from the time of turning the Wheel when teaching Dhamma, it was only the Four Truths that I proclaimed." In our sentence, the term "suffering" includes also its roots, the origination; and the term "cessation" also the path that leads to the cessation.

Sub-Comy: "There is no teaching of the Master that is unrelated to the Four Truths. By saying, 'What I teach now as before, is suffering and the cessation of suffering,' the Blessed One indicates this: 'Never do I teach a self that is annihilated or destroyed, nor do I teach that there is any kind of self'."
45. *Evarūpā kārā karīyanti*. Some Burmese texts and the paraphrase in Comy have *sakkāra*; then to be translated: "that they pay such respect."
46. In the ultimate sense, praise and blame do not refer to a self or ego, but to that five-fold aggregate (*pañcakkhandhakaṃ*) which was comprehended by the Buddha as an evanescent combination of material and mental processes, void of an ego-entity. Hence there is no reason for elation or dejection. A passage similar to Sections 38–39 is found at the beginning of DN 1.
47. **"Not yours"** (*na tumhākaṃ*) is also the title of a section of suttas in the Saṃyutta Nikāya (SN 22:33ff.).
48. Comy stresses that it is the attachment to the five aggregates, the desire for them (*chanda-rāga*) which should be given up; it is not so that the five aggregates themselves should be, as it were, "torn to pieces or pulled out" (*na uppāṭetvā luñcitvā vā*).
49. Sub-Comy: "Only corporeality, feeling and the other aggregates are the basis for the wrong concept of a self, since apart from them there is nothing else to be craved for."
50. **"This Teaching"**: these words refer, according to Comy, to the entire exposition beginning with §26.
51. **"Free of patchwork"** (*chinna-pilotika*); lit., "devoid of the nature of a patched cloth." Comy: *Pilotika* is a torn rag cloth patched up with stitches and knots which are similar to hypocrisy and other deceptions. Sub-Comy: substituting assumed attitudes (*iriyapatha-santhapana*) for an actually, in that individual, non-existing practice of meditation and insight. *Pilotika* means also "refuse," referring to false and unworthy monks who do not have any footing in the Buddha's dispensation.

This phrase *chinna-pilotika* seems, however, to point to the inner consistency of the Teaching which, like a new cloth (Comy: *ahata-sātaka*), is of one piece and is not in need of patching up contradictions, by artificial attempts of reconciling inconsistencies. Hence the term may freely be rendered by the single word "consistent."

52. *Dhammānusārino saddhānusārino.* These two terms refer to those whose minds are in the process of ripening towards stream-entry (*sotāpatti*), either by way of strengthening the wisdom-faculty (*paññindriya*) through the contemplation of no-self (in the case of the *dhammānusāri*), or by way of strengthening the faith-faculty (*saddhindriya*) through the contemplation of impermanence (in the case of the *saddhānusāri*). When they actually reach the path of stream-entry (*sotāpattimagga*), they are called "mature in Dhamma" and "mature in faith."

53. **Those who have simply faith in me.** Comy: This refers to persons devoted to the practice of insight-meditation (*vipassaka-puggalā*). When monks are seated after having got a firm footing in insight-meditation, there arises in them a unique and fully absorbing faith in, and love for, the Master of the Ten Powers (i.e., the Buddha). (Sub-Comy: because in pursuance of their insight-meditation they have received proof that "the Dhamma is well-proclaimed.") Through that faith and love they are as if taken by the hand and transported to heaven. They are said to be of assured destiny (*niyatagatika*), i.e., of the final attainment of Nibbāna. The Elder Monks of old say that such bhikkhus are lesser stream-enterers (*cūla-* or *bāla-sotāpanna*; Vism XVIII.27).

Knowledge and Conduct

Buddhist Contributions to
Philosophy and Ethics

Prof. O. H. de A. Wijesekera
Dr. K. N. Jayatilleke
Prof. E. A. Burtt

WHEEL PUBLICATION NO. 50

Copyright © Kandy: Buddhist Publication Society (1963, 1977)

Preface

The Buddhist Publication Society, which is continuing its unremitting service in the worthy cause of the propagation of the Dhamma, deserves the commendation of all seekers of the Truth for the publication of this volume of Buddhist essays as an enlarged issue of the fiftieth number of their Wheel Series. The Society's publications are well known in every part of the world and there is no doubt that this volume will help a large number of readers to probe deeper into the Buddhist attitude to problems of knowledge and conduct—the two essentials of the religion (*sāsana*)—traditionally known as *pariyatti* and *paṭipatti* comprehension and practice of the Dhamma.

This number includes two essays dealing with Buddhist thought: the one by Prof. Burtt attempts to outline the four basic ideas which are important for the assessment of Buddhist philosophy, and the other by Dr. Jayatilleke is devoted to a discussion of the Buddhist method of comprehending Truth. The third presents an examination of the moral problems that arise in the practice of the Dhamma. Thus the reader will be fortunate to have within the compass of this single volume a critical treatment of the basic principles and essentials of Buddhist thought and Buddhist conduct.

A compendium of this nature has been a long-felt need and the Buddhist Publication Society must be congratulated on the initiative shown in bringing out this handy volume to satisfy both the critical student of the subject and the average reader.

O. H. Dr. A Wijesekera
University of Ceylon, Peradeniya, Ceylon,
February, 1963.

Buddhist Ethics

Prof. O. H. de A. Wijesekera

It will be realised by careful students of Buddhism, particularly in its earliest form as preserved in the *Dīgha Nikāya, Majjhima Nikāya, Sutta Nipāta,* etc., that most of the dialogues are entirely devoted to ethical discussions. This will be found to be especially the case with the *Majjhima Nikāya,* as well as the Mahāvagga of the *Suttanipāta,* while a good many of the Suttas in the *Dīgha Nikāya* are also ethical in character. Thus it will be seen that an exhaustive examination of all the data is necessary for a complete study of this important subject, and this has to be said in spite of the useful treatise *The Ethics of Buddhism* by Dr. Tachibana of Tokyo; for, as it was pointed out in the Introduction to the Colombo edition of that work, he has only classified the moral categories of Buddhism without entering upon any discussion of the main problems of ethics in relation to the Buddhist view. It is hoped that the present discussion will, at least to some extent, indicate the lines along which such a study must be conducted, and lead students of the subject to a critical appreciation of its main problems.

It is universally recognised that Buddhism can claim to be the most ethical of religio-philosophical systems of the world. No less an authority than Professor Radhakrishnan himself calls it "Ethical Idealism" and says that the Buddha gave an "ethical twist" to the thought of his time. "We find in the early teaching of Buddhism," he remarks, "three marked characteristics: an ethical earnestness, an absence of any theological tendency and an aversion to metaphysical speculation."[1] Even Albert Schweitzer, a leading Western philosopher and one of the most astute critics of Indian thought has not grudged the Buddha the honour of being "the creator of the ethic of inner perfection." He writes: "In this sphere he gave expression to truths of everlasting value and advanced the ethics not of India alone but of humanity. He was one of the greatest ethical men of genius ever bestowed upon the

1. *Indian Philosophy,* vol. 1 p. 858

world."[2] Professor T. W. Rhys Davids who spent a lifetime in the study of Buddhism has admirably brought out in his *American Lectures* the importance of the study of Buddhist ethics in modern life and thought: "The point I stand here to submit to your consideration is that the study of ethics and especially the study of ethical theory in the West has hitherto resulted in a deplorable failure through irreconcilable logomachies and the barrenness of speculation cut off from actual fact: The only true method of ethical inquiry is surely the historical method ... and I cannot be wrong in maintaining that the study of Buddhism should be considered a necessary part of any ethical course and should not be dismissed in a page or two but receive its due proportion in the historical perspective of ethical evolution."[3] Oswald Spengler, who perhaps ranks as the greatest philosophical student of world culture, believes that Buddhism, which for him expresses "the basic feeling of Indian civilization," and "rejects all speculation about God and the cosmic problems; only self and the conduct of actual life are important to it."[4]

Such statements as these emphasising the ethical importance of the Buddha's teaching can be quoted from numerous other authorities. But to any unbiased and careful student of religion or philosophy it would be needless to stress this importance too much, for, as we shall attempt to show in this paper, Early Buddhism—by which term we generally refer to the doctrines as found in the dialogues of the major *Nikāyas*—presents a unique synthesis of ethics and philosophy, of morality and knowledge, of action and thought.

To estimate correctly the greatness and the universality of the Buddha's ethics one has to obtain a mental picture of the moral ferment and the spiritual unrest that prevailed in India just before the appearance of the Buddha. Traditional religion as professed by the theologians and the metaphysicians of the Upaniṣads was being undermined by the constant and vehement attacks of materialists and sceptics. Therefore, before we turn to the actual ethical system of Early Buddhism it is essential to discuss as briefly

2. *Indian Thought and its Development*, p. 117
3. *Buddhism*, pp. 185–186
4. *Decline of the West*, Pt. I, p. 356

as possible the development of the moral consciousness during the time of the pre-Buddhist Upaniṣads as well as the attitude to the moral problem of the various heretical philosophical schools such as those promulgated by the numerous *titthiyas* and *ājīvakas*.

There were some Upaniṣadic thinkers who had discovered and formulated the main principles of moral behaviour in conformity with their respective views of life. Earlier, Brahmanism had established a rigid and dreadfully static morality by its insistence on the universality of the ritual act (*karma*=*yañja*). Hence the actual morality inculcated did not go beyond what was practically necessary in the conduct and successful performance of the sacrifice. Thus evolved a conception of "dharma," originally "ritualistic duty," and its ethical correlates such as "*śraddhā*," the faith needed in bestowing gifts (*dakṣinā*) and alms (*dāna*) to the priesthood who were the meditators between man and his gods. Such was the moral code of the ritualistic religion. The earliest Upaniṣads carry out these very moral tendencies and thus it cannot be said that they had completely transcended the ethical externalism of the Brahmanic religion. When Sākalya in the Bṛhadāraṇyaka Upaniṣad (3.9) asked Yājñavalkya: "And on what is sacrifice based?" "On gifts to the priests," replied Yājñavalkya. "And on what are the gifts to the priests based?" "On faith (*śraddha*), for when one has faith one gives gifts to the priests. Verily, on faith are gifts to the priests based." Similarly, Chāndogya Upaniṣad (2.23) enumerates three branches of duty: "Sacrifice, study of the Vedas, alms-giving, that is the first; austerity, indeed, is the second; a student of sacred knowledge (*brahmacārin*) dwelling in the house of a teacher is the third."

Though Upaniṣadic ethics start with such compromises to ritualism, an attempt is progressively made to conceive a higher kind of morality. For example, the Upaniṣadic thinkers attribute the highest power to truth (*satya*) in contrast to untruth (*anṛta*). Speakers of falsehood were put to the test by the ordeal of the heated axe. Says the Chāndogya Upaniṣad (6.16): "Speaking untruth he covers himself with untruth; he seizes hold of the heated axe and is burned: Speaking truth he covers himself with truth; he seizes hold of the heated axe and is not burned." It is important to observe here that what is true is held to be in conformity with the natural order of things, the cosmic law (*ṛta*), and that what was untrue was what went against that order (*anṛta*). It is to the credit of Indian culture that at a very early period in its history from the cosmological conception of world-order (*ṛta*) they had derived a notion of an ethical order in man. Thus the gradual development of a practical code of ethics is seen in these Upaniṣads. Quarrelsomeness, tale-bearing (*pisunā*), slander (*upavāda*) are regarded as evil traits tending to make people small (*alpāḥ*) of character. The threefold offspring of *Prajāpati* gods, men, and *asuras* are respectively taught by him (Brh. Up., 5.2) that to restrain (*damyata*), to give (*datta*), and to be compassionate (*dayadhvam*) are the three greatest virtues. There was also a certain conception of social ethics as is implied in the declaration of Aśvapati Kaikeya:

> "Within my realm there is no thief,
> no miser, nor a drinking man,
> none altarless, none ignorant,
> no man unchaste, no wife unchaste."
>
> (Ch. Up., 5.11).

It is important to students of Buddhist ethics to find the Chāndogya Upaniṣad (8.4,5) condemning to rebirth in the form of small creatures those who commit theft, drink liquor, invade the teacher's bed, kill brahmins, as well as those who consort with them: "*Brahmacarya*" which generally means "the chaste life of a student of sacred knowledge" is extolled and its goal is set forth as the Brahma-world. In the very next paragraph this life of abstinent religious duty (*brahmacarya*) is said to include all other forms of moral behaviour such as sacrifice, silent asceticism, fasting, and hermit life in the forest.

There are many passages in the Upaniṣads establishing as the highest moral ideal or goal of the spiritual life the Brahma-world which is identified with immortality (*amṛtam*). It is also necessary to point out that the *raison d'etre* of ethics in the Upaniṣads is derived from metaphysics: "Verily, O Gargi at the command of that Imperishable (*akśarasya praśāsane*) men praise those who give, the gods are desirous of a sacrificer, and the fathers (are desirous) of the Manes-sacrifice" (Bṛh. Up., 3.8). Further, according to the Upaniṣads, the criterion of moral judgment is merely conventional, being nothing other than the practice of elderly and learned brahmins: "Now, if you should have doubt concerning an act, or doubt concerning conduct, if there should be these Brāhmaṇas, competent to judge, apt, devoted, not harsh, lovers of virtue (*dharma*)—as they may behave themselves in such a case, so should you behave yourself in such a case (Tait. Up., 1.11).

In the last phase of the development of Upaniṣadic thought morality dwindles into insignificance. This results from the static conception of spiritual life as is inevitable from the identity of the human soul as it is with the highest ideal, Brahman, sometimes referred to as the highest Self (*ātman*). This metaphysical abstraction naturally removes all urgency and necessity for any ethic, for, if man as he is, is already one with his ideal, what would be the need for spiritual effort, why worry about a moral life at all! "Whoso were to know me (*ātman*)," teaches the Kauśītaki Upaniṣad (3.2), "not by any action of his can the world be injured; not by murdering his mother or his father, not by stealing or by killing the embryo..." This overemphasis of the Ātman-knowledge and the consequent disregard of the moral life discloses the inner weakness of the absolutist pantheism of the Upaniṣads: Two of the most critical Hindu students of Upaniṣadic thought, Ranade and Belvalkar, regard this as the worst trait of the philosophy of absolutism: "Here, indeed, is touched what may be called the danger line of Upaniṣadic ethics. To say that the *ātman* dies not is legitimate. To say that weapons cannot cut him nor fire burn him is also a legitimate variation of the phrase. But to argue that, therefore, the murderer is no murderer, and there is nobody really responsible for his action is to carry this *śāśvata* or *akriyā* doctrine to a point which, if seriously preached, would be subversive of all established social institutions and religious sacraments".[5]

These considerations not only indicate to us that the absolutism of the Upaniṣads inevitably ended in a kind of amoralism, but also that there could be a dangerous side to religious and spiritual conservatism. It was as a reaction against such dogmatism in philosophy and ethics that there arose several heterodox philosophies which not only denied the authority of the conservative ethics of the Upaniṣads, but even went to the extent of declaring moral scepticism, moral nihilism and moral

5. *History of Indian Philosophy*, IT, p. 399

anarchism. It is significant that our earliest sources for the study of these doctrines are the Buddhist *Nikāyas* themselves. There was a strong school of philosophical opinion which encouraged a downright ethical nihilism (*natthikavāda*):

> "There is no such thing as alms, sacrifice or oblation; good and bad actions bear no fruit or consequence; there is no (distinction between) this world and the next; there is no (moral obligation towards) father or mother; there are no beings of spontaneous generation, and there are no recluses and brahmins in this world of virtuous conduct who with insight (*abhiññā*) have realised and proclaimed (the true nature of) this world and the next." This moral nihilism was based on a crass materialism in philosophy: "Man as he '*is*' is constituted out of the four elements; when he dies earth combines with earth, water with water, heat with heat and air with air; the sense functions are merged in the ether and all that is left of him are his greyish bones after the cremation; the value of the alms-giving is merely in the imagination of the giver and to affirm the moral consequences of the act is a hollow assertion; both the foolish and the wise are annihilated and completely cut off at death."[6]

This was the doctrine that Ajita Kesakambalī, among others, is reported to have professed.

Then there were others who denied moral causation (*ahetuvādins*). Their main thesis was as follows:

> "There is no cause or reason for the depravity of beings; they become depraved without cause or reason; they become pure without cause or reason; there is no such thing as self-agency or the agency of another or human effort; there is no such thing as power or energy or human strength or human endeavour; all animals, all creatures, all beings and all living things are without initiative, without power and strength of their own; they just evolve by fate, necessity and fortuitous concatenation of events; and it is according to their peculiar nature as belonging to one of the six classes that they experience ease or

6. M I 515

pain, and it is only at the end of the appointed period—after one has passed through the 84,00,000 periods of wandering in saṃsāra—that there shall be an end of pain; thus there is no such thing as that one should experience the result of kamma and thereby put an end to it either through virtuous conduct or precept, asceticism or *'brahmacariya'*; consequently there is neither spiritual growth nor decline; neither depravation nor exaltation, inasmuch as in saṃsāra pain and pleasure are determined and circumscribed. As automatically as a ball of thread thrown up rolls along unreeling itself, so do both the foolish and the wise reach their salvation at the termination of their appointed course in *saṃsāra*".[7]

The foremost leader of this school was Makkhali Gosāla, and from the importance attached to the refutation of his theories in the early Buddhist books we may infer that he had a large following.

He roundly denied all initiative and choice in man, being rigidly deterministic. The only redeeming feature of this philosophy was its belief in some form of moral ideal, however wrongly the process of its accomplishment was conceived. Therefore, the Buddhist books disparagingly call this the "purity through saṃsāra" (*saṃsārasuddhi*), because the theory postulated that purity occurred just by saṃsāric evolution over which man had no control. This was further condemned as *"akiriyavāda"* or "theory of non-action".

Another teacher, Purāṇa Kassapa, held the opinion that the act had no moral consequences, that merit (*puñña*) did not result from good action and demerit (*pāpa*) from bad action; giving, generosity, restraint, self-control, and truth-speaking did not conduce to merit".[8] This doctrine, too, is condemned as *"akiriyavāda"* or a denial of the efficacy of the act.

Another school professed a fatalistic pluralism and the most prominent teacher of this doctrine was Pakudha Kaccāyana:

"The following seven things are neither made nor commanded to be created; they are barren (and so nothing is produced out of them), steadfast as a mountain peak, as a pillar firmly fixed.

7. D I 54
8. D I 52

They move not, neither do they vary, they trench not one upon the other, nor avail aught as to ease or pain or both. And what are the seven? The four elements—earth, water, fire, air—and pleasure and pain, and the soul as the seventh. So there is neither slayer nor causer of slaying, hearer or speaker, knower or explainer. When one with a sharp sword cleaves a head in twain, no one thereby deprives anyone of life; a sword has merely penetrated into the space between seven elementary substances."[9]

As this doctrine is obviously based on the Upaniṣadic concept of the indestructibility and the unchangeability of the *"ātman"* it has been called *"sassatavāda"* or eternalism. In ethics it also leads to an *"akiriyavāda"* or amoralism like the previous philosophies.

Then there was the ethical scepticism of the agnostic philosopher, Sañjaya Bellaṭṭhiputta, who refused to pass final judgment on any such metaphysical problem as the existence of a future world or on any ethical question. When questioned about the moral consequences of good and bad acts, he would resort to the four-membered formula of prevarication and refuse to set down a definite opinion.[10]

The doctrines of these rival teachers not only led to clashes with the dogmatism and orthodoxy of the Upaniṣadic moralists but also resulted in interminable conflicts among themselves, thus creating that state of moral ferment to which we referred earlier and which characterised Indian religion just before the advent of the Buddha. It was a critical epoch in the history of Indian religion and the Buddha with his principle of the golden mean (*majjhima paṭipadā*) brought sanity and a sense of poise to a society harassed by ideological disturbances and shaken about by heated metaphysical wranglings and ethical disputations.

Apart from these doctrines that led to a moral upheaval, there was the Jaina system of ethics with its rigid formalism and externalism frequently criticised in the Buddhist books. Nigaṇṭha Nātaputta emphasized the external act in preference to the mental act.[11]

---

9. M I 517
10. D I 58
11. M I 372ff

In addition to all these ethical doctrines the *Dīgha* and *Majjhima Nikāyas* make constant reference to the inevitable moral upshot of philosophical materialism in general, referred to as the perverted philosophy (*viparīta-dassana*) that denied all morality; it is branded as the heresy *par excellence* (*micchādiṭṭhi*), the evil doctrine (*pāpakaṃ diṭṭhigataṃ*), and moral nihilism (*natthikavāda*).[12] This view which is prominently attributed to a prince known as Payāsi-rājañña asserted the following three propositions:

(1) There is no world beyond;
(2) There are no beings reborn otherwise than from parents;
(3) There is no result or consequence of good or bad acts.[13]

As opposed to this *micchādiṭṭhi* early Buddhism sets forth *sammādiṭṭhi* or the correct view of life on which it bases its ethics. Let us now turn to an examination of that fundamental philosophical basis of Buddhist morality.

According to Early Buddhism man's appearance in this world is clearly not due to a mere concatenation of physical factors. Many statements in the dialogues make it clear that a non-physical factor is necessary for successful conception.[14] Such concatenation is due to *upadhisaṅkhāras* generated by previous saṃsāric experiences[15] and it is precisely in this context that it is affirmed that the reborn individual is neither the same nor another (*na ca so na 'ca añño*).[16] It may be observed, that in the latter portion of this statement (*na ca añño*) moral responsibility is definitely asserted. Life thus come into being is said to be characterised by several marks (*lakkhaṇa*) such as impermanence, unsatisfactoriness, liability to disease and corruption, extraneousness, subjection to dissolution, voidness, and insubstantiality.[17]

These characteristics are sometimes brought under the three headings of *anicca, dukkha* and *anattā*, or *anicca, dukkha* and

12. M I 130, 287, 401; D II 316
13. D II 316, 317
14. M I 265; D II 63
15. Suttanipāta, 728
16. Cf. S III 20
17. M I 435

viparināmadhamma.[18] Thus is set forth the Noble Truth of the unsatisfactoriness (*dukkha-sacca*) of saṃsāric existence (*bhava*), which is sometimes analysed as threefold *dukkhatā* (*dukkhadukkha, saṅkhāra-dukkha* and *viparināma dukka*).[19]

Such unsatisfactoriness is due to the continuous change or becoming that is saṃsāra.[20] This very dynamic nature of saṃsāric life with its self-generated potentialities tends to a continuation of individuality (*nāma-rūpa*) or personality (*attabhāva*). Thus it is asserted in Early Buddhism that there is a life beyond (*atthi paro loko*),[21] which is proved by the supernormal experience of the Perfect Ones (*arahants*) who are perceivers of the world beyond (*paralokaviduno*) by virtue of their having acquired the faculties of recollecting past births (*pubbenivāsānussati*) and observing the passing away and rebirth of beings (*sattānaṃ cutūpapātañāṇa*),[22] the latter being also termed the super-normal vision (*dibbacakkhu*). Buddha himself exercised this power on several occasions when requested to explain the rebirth (*gati*) of his departed disciples.[23]

The Early Buddhist conviction of this fact of saṃsāric continuity is, therefore, beyond doubt and it is no wonder that those who refused to admit a life beyond were dubbed *micchādiṭṭhika*. It is clear then on what foundation the ethical system of Early Buddhism rests. Once this saṃsāric continuity with all its attendant *dukkha* is granted, the ideal of man's perfection turns out to be the release (*nissaraṇa*) therefrom. This is the Goal of Buddhist ethics which consequently is conceived as the cessation of becoming (*bhava-nirodha*) or the ending of *dukkha*, generally called Nibbāna. Thus we discover that the *raison d'etre* of Buddhist ethics is the fundamental fact of saṃsāric *dukkha*. Hence the essential basis of the Buddhist moral life (*brahmacariya*) lies not in some metaphysical hypothesis conceived by *a priori* reasoning, but, as Buddha pointed out to Māluṅkyaputta, on the conviction that, "Verily there is birth, there is decay, there is

18. M I 232
19. D III 216
20. Suttanipāta 742
21. M I 403
22. D I 82
23. See DN 16, 18, 19

death, etc.," of which the destruction is declared to be possible in this very life.[24]

Thus the mere speculation on metaphysical problems, usually referred to as ten, is condemned as unprofitable. Similarly, the Buddha tells Udāyi that such ultimate questions as those that concern the beginning (*pubbanta*) and the end (*aparanta*) of things, being solvable only by developing the higher faculties (*vijjā, abhiññā*) but not by the exercise of mere reason. It becomes imperative for man to accomplish the ethical process which alone could lead to the acquirement of such faculties.[25] Therefore, the importance of the ethical process for the realization of Nibbāna is unquestionable, and, as Dhammadinnā points out to Visākha, the moral life finds its apex, goal and consummation in Nibbāna.[26]

The foregoing discussion of the fundamental basis of the Buddhist ethic, its *raison d'etre* and its goal, will help the student of Buddhism and the student of ethics to appreciate the important bearing that the Buddhist view of morality has to the burning questions of ethics such as the problem of evil, and the problem of ethical relativity: To an unbiased student of Buddhism it appears that Early Buddhism offers definite solutions to these problems and as such it has a claim to serious consideration in this respect.

Our brief presentation of the philosophical basis of Buddhist ethics will have stressed the extreme urgency of the problem of evil for Early Buddhism as well as its all-embracing and profound nature as indicated by its saṃsāric context. The concept of evil as discussed by Western thinkers, pertaining as it does to merely this visible life, covers only a minute aspect of the problem, but it can be seen that fundamentally there is no difference between the two issues, for as Early Buddhism viewed it "*dukkha-dukkhatā,*" which is defined as man's conflict with his environment is only one aspect of the general unsatisfactoriness of saṃsāric becoming (*bhava-dukkha*). Thus it is to be expected that a thinking person (*viññu puriso*) cannot but be impressed by the obtrusiveness of evil or *dukkha* around him.

But this was exactly the point on which Professor Joad

24. M I 431
25. M II 31, 32, 38
26. M I 304

condemned Buddhism in his book, *Matter, Life and Value* (p. 369, publ. 1929) in which he complained that "for Buddhism as for Job man is born to trouble as sparks fly upward" and declared: "I differ, therefore, from the dominant philosophy of the East in not despising the ordinary life of struggle and enjoyment of effort and reward." It is ironically significant, however, that after the lapse of only thirteen years he was compelled to radically alter his opinion, for in his later book, *God and Evil* (1942), he was forced to admit: "I conclude that attempts which are made to show that evil is not a real and fundamental principle belonging to the nature of things, are unsuccessful." Such coincidence as this between Early Buddhism and Western philosophy on the problem of evil will necessarily remain partial in so far as such philosophers confine their observations merely to the experience of the individual in this visible existence. But as we have attempted to show above, what is specially characteristic of the Buddhist Weltanschauung (worldview) is the undeniable fact that this short span of a few score of years on earth is not the whole of one's empirical existence, but only a temporary manifestation of a saṃsāric process that extends for innumerable lives in the past and may also extend for an indefinable period in the future.

Now, since this deeper significance of the general unsatisfactoriness of saṃsāric life and also the possibility of release therefrom has to be accepted on the validity of the experiences of the Perfect Ones, Early Buddhism recommends *saddhā* or the reliance on the experience of such arahants who have realised the higher vision and on their statements, after adequate investigation, as to their worth.[27] Hence *saddhā* is held up to be the basis of the ethical process which ultimately leads to the realisation of the highest truth (*parama sacca*) and therewith the goal.[28] Thus in practical ethics *saddhā* comes to be regarded as one of the five good things to be cultivated (*paricaritabbaṃ*), although the definite warning is given that mere faith in the teacher is not sufficient for complete ethical progress.[29] The faith (*saddhā*) we have previously referred is considered to be mere blind faith (*amūlikā saddhā*),

27. M I 173
28. M II 171
29. M II 94

and is consequently condemned by the Buddha in a talk with the brahmin Bhāradvāja.[30] It is on account of this that *saddhā* in Early Buddhism is said to be twofold, the faith that may be empty, void and false in its fruition, and the faith that is bound to lead to genuine consequences.[31] We cannot escape the conclusion that the *saddhā* encouraged in Early Buddhism is only the result of an inference from the realisation of arahants as to the possibility of one's own realisation of the goal. Hence the only kind of faith that is advocated, if it could be called faith at all, is what is designated "logical faith" (*ākāravatī saddhā*).[32] The conversion of laymen to the belief that it was necessary to lead the higher moral life under the Buddha or his disciples was always prompted by this kind of *saddhā*, a fact attested to at numerous places in the Canon.

The layman who thus takes up the spiritual life through his reliance (*uddissa*) on such a teacher is said to have started his career (*paṭipanna*) along the Path (*magga, paṭipadā*) to Nibbāna. This Path is said to consist of three stages or parts usually called the three *sampadās* or the three *khandhas*. The first of these stages is *sīla* or ethical conduct, and practical morals have a meaning for the disciple only till such time as he arrives at the fourth stage of the Path, namely, concentration (*samādhi*). But the goal is not reached even then; and a still higher stage of development must be gone through and this is technically known as wisdom (*paññā*). What is generally believed to be the Eightfold Path in Buddhism is included within these three stages as the learned Dhammadinnā explained to Visākhā.[33] How far, then, practical morality is of significance to one aspiring for the Buddhist goal becomes clear when it is considered that *sīla* forms only the initial stage of such process. In fact, Early Buddhism administers a warning to the aspirant to master morality but not allow morality to get the better of him, and it is clearly laid down that even virtuous conduct has to be transcended at one stage. It need not, therefore, appear paradoxical when it is asserted in the same context that the disciple should try to put a final end to meritorious forms of good

30. M II 170
31. MN 95
32. M I 401
33. M I 301

conduct.[34] Thus, for Buddhism morality is not an end in itself. It is considering these features of the Path which, it is obvious, transcend ethical perfectionism as is understood by Western moralists, and also the metaphysical perfection implied in the Upaniṣads, that it is claimed that the Exalted One is the originator and proclaimer of a unique Way.

It is to be observed that in the spiritual evolution as indicated in this Path the question of happiness as the ideal of morality finds a perfect solution. It is said that in the stage of concentration when the aspirant reaches the fourth *jhāna* both happiness and its opposite cease to concern him for he becomes indifferent to both pleasurable and painful feeling (*vedanā*). Up to that moment the aspirant is to experience inner happiness. This inner form of happiness is clearly differentiated from worldly happiness which is called "low, vulgar, and ignoble" inasmuch as such happiness depends on the senses.

It is expressly stated that this latter form of material happiness is to be shunned[35] and hence to classify Buddhism as any form of hedonism, as Dr. Pratt has done in his *Pilgrimage of Buddhism* (p. 20), is quite unjustifiable.

Over and above this sensuous happiness which has an erotic basis (*kāma*) as well as the inner *jhānic* happiness which is non-erotic (*nekkhamma*) is placed Nibbāna, as even this *jhānic* happiness is not final (*analaṃ*), for it is only in the ultimate state of spiritual attainment (*saññāvedayitanirodha*) that happiness assumes its most perfect form. This state, which is the *summum bonum* of Buddhism, can be styled happiness only in an exceptional sense. Yet, Buddha persists in calling it happiness in the face of the criticism of heretics, for, as he once explained to Ānanda, he did not regard a state as happy just because of pleasurable feeling, and also because he considered that there could be levels of "happiness" relative to the stage of spiritual evolution. Thus, if in the ideal state of Nibbāna the aspirant transcends the subtlest forms of happiness and is not tinged by them, it would not be quite apposite to identify the Early Buddhist ideal in ethics with that of Eudaemonism. But this does not deny the fact that for

34. M II 27
35. M III 230, 233

Buddhism just as for modern psychology and biology man, as well as other living beings, by nature seeks for pleasure and avoids pain (*sukhakāmo dukkhapaṭikkūlo*).

It can now be seen that there is a sense in which we may assert that the ethical process of Buddhism is intended to release man from the miseries of saṃsāric existence (*dukkha*) and take him to the ultimate happiness or the good (*attha*) that is Nibbāna. In this, Buddhism does not go against the basic psychology of man's nature, but endeavours to bring about its refinement and sublimation until it totally transcends the level at which it is found in saṃsāric existence. Thus Nibbānic happiness must be considered as the ideal for every living being. Hence is derived also the criterion of moral judgment according to the ethical philosophy of Early Buddhism which we have attempted to outline above. This criterion of Buddhist ethics is emphasised in several places and seeks to determine whether a particular act would obstruct or not oneself or others in the attempt to win this release (*nissaraṇa*) from *dukkha* or saṃsāric Evil. In his admonition to Rāhula, Buddha makes it perfectly clear that "whatever act tends to the obstruction or harm (*vyābādha*) of oneself and others (on the Path) is to be considered bad (*akusala*) as its upshot is pain and its result evil."[36] It is significant that the word "*vyābādha*" means both harm to the individual concerned and obstruction to spiritual progress. Therefore; subjectively an act (*kamma*) becomes good (*kusala*) or bad (*akusala*) according as it promotes or hinders spiritual progress, and objectively it is considered to be meritorious (*puñña*) or demeritorious (*apuñña*) according as it is beneficial (*hita*) or harmful (*ahita*) to the similar progress of others. Sir Edward Arnold in his *Light of Asia* has beautifully summed up this idea.

> *"Kill not—for pity's sake—and lest ye slay*
> *The meanest thing upon its upward way."*

To inflict pain, for instance, either on oneself or others is to cause distraction of mind by inciting evil and harmful emotions which cannot be but an obstacle on the "upward way." Thus the ethical content of an act is psychological and its source is volitional.

---

36. M I 415

Accordingly, Early Buddhism considers as ethical only those acts which are volitional (*sañcetanika*).[37] *Thus the Aṅguttara Nikāya* (III 415) attributes to the Buddha the statement that the real act (*kamma*) as an act of volition (*cetanā*). This is natural inasmuch as the intensity of the act depends on the extent to which it is committed deliberately (*sañcicca*).[38] For instance, it is pointed out that an infant who is not conscious even of his own body cannot commit any sin. In technical language this would mean that all acts are not ethically significant but only those that are voluntary, that is to say, willed by the agent. This being the fundamental sense in which an act is conceived in Buddhist ethics what we do and say have only an indirect ethical significance, whereas what we think or will is directly ethical.

In a conversation with the Jain Dīghatapassī Buddha emphasises the greater ethical importance, of the mental or volitional act (*mano-kamma*) as compared with the verbal (*vacī-kamma*) or the physical act (*kāya-kamma*).[39] Hence the Buddha's emphasis on the elimination of the cardinal evils of attachment (*rāga, lobha*), ill-will (*dosa*) and infatuation (*moha*), for they directly affect the nature of our volitions, while other evil acts such as meat-eating and drinking of liquor, etc., affect the mind only indirectly. Therefore, while the distinction between absolute and relative moral values seems meaningless and unnecessary according to the Buddha, there appears to be some sense in which we may divide voluntary acts or ethically significant acts into *direct* and *indirect* according as they affect the main ethical purpose of leading to the release from *saṃsāric* existence.

It thus becomes clear that for the Buddha moral judgments are not to be based on some *a priori* conceptions of objectively real values like goodness, truth and beauty, as is usually held by idealistic philosophers, nor are they to be regarded as subjective or relative from all points of view as asserted by most scientific and materialistic thinkers.

According to Mr. Bertrand Russell it would seem that ethics are a mere matter of taste. "If two men differ about values," he

37. M III 207, cp. I 377
38. M I 523, II 103
39. M I 373

says summing up his ethical doctrine, "there is not a disagreement as to any kind of truth but a difference of taste"[40] Similarly, Professor Edward Westermarck, for whom all ethical judgments have an emotional basis, is the leading exponent of a theory of ethical relativity, which, however, adds that moral phenomena are not made meaningless just because they happen to fall within the subjective sphere of experience. For him, nevertheless, ethics remain still relative because moral judgments depend on economic, social and psychological (emotional) circumstances.[41] According to the Buddha, however, moral judgments assume a permanent value in so far as they are based on the point of view of the end which, as we have stressed above, is the release from *saṃsāric* evil. But we may add that there is a sense in which moral values are relative even for the Buddha, and this derives only from the existence of levels of spiritual experience corresponding to the respective stages of the Path to which we have already referred.

The above discussion should make it clear that the ethics of the Buddha is prompted by one motive, viz., the desire for release and relies on no external sanctions such as God, Church or State, but is pre-eminently autonomous in character.[42] In fact, the desire for release and the psychological observation that attachment, hate and infatuation directly affect the nature of our volitions, sum up the motives and sanctions of Buddhist morality. In this discussion, however, we have taken for granted the most important fact of the freedom of the human will. We regarded man as intrinsically a morally free agent who had within him the power to choose between alternative courses of action. Is this justifiable according to the Buddha's doctrine? Certainly, yes. There is, in fact, no more important conviction in the whole of Buddha's philosophy than the idea that within this individuality (*nāma-rūpa*) there is the potentiality of release if only man wills that way.[43] Therefore, in spite of the fact that there is in a sense determinism to the

40. *Religion and Science*, p. 237

41. *The Origin and Development of Moral Ideas*, pp. 4, 18, 19; *Ethical Relativity*, p. 220

42. See my Introduction to Tachibana's *Ethics of Buddhism* (Colombo 1961, Bauddha Sahitya Sabha)

43. S I 62

extent that empirical existence is admittedly conditioned and thus is obviously subject to the vicissitudes of birth, decay and death, there is in man the power (*balaṃ, viriyaṃ*)[44] to overcome all this by the strength of will (*chando*).[45] Human life is regarded by the Buddha as in every way the best suited for this effort, and birth among the animals, etc., is consequently deprecated, for it is only in man that the power to will exists in such a high degree with infinite capacity to develop higher by self-discipline and meditation.

Early Buddhism does not deny the importance of environmental factors in the moulding of man's conduct, but, on the other hand, it does not in the least subscribe to any theory that man's conduct is merely a set of reactions to external stimuli or unconscious tendencies, or that it is determined by social and economic factors alone, for it would be admitted even by the most adverse critics of the Buddha that no one raised man and his noblest gift, the human reason or will, to such dignity as that greatest of ethical teachers born in the philosophically rife atmosphere of India twenty-five centuries ago.

44. M I 407
45. M I 313

The Buddhist Conception of Truth

by K. N. Jayatilleke,
M A (Cantab), Ph.D. (London).

Buddhism is the first missionary religion in the history of humanity with a universal message of salvation for all mankind. The Buddha after His Enlightenment sent out sixty-one disciples in different directions asking them to preach the doctrine for the weal and welfare of mankind. He is said in one of the earliest texts to have been born for the good and happiness of humanity" (*manussaloke hitasukhatāya jāto*, Sn 683). Addressed as "the King of kings" (*rājābhirāja*, Sn 553), He says: "I am a King, the supreme King of Righteousness, with righteousness do I extend my kingdom, a kingdom which cannot be destroyed." (Sn 554)

The era in which the Buddha was born marks a turning point in history, for everywhere in the world from Greece to China we notice a new awakening and a quest for truth. A historian says: This sixth century BCE was, indeed, one of the most remarkable in all history. Everywhere ... men's minds were displaying a new boldness ... It is as if the race had reached a stage of adolescence—after a childhood of 20000 years.[46] To the east of India, in China, appeared the great religious teachers Lao Tze and Confucius, the founders of Taoism and Confucianism, respectively. To the west there was Zarathustra in Persia, the founder of Zoroastrianism, Prophet Isaiah in Israel and Pythagoras in Greece. A student of religion observes: "It was in these days, rather than in those which made Bethlehem of Judea famous, that the principle of 'peace on earth, goodwill to men' first began to sweep across the world like a cleansing wind."[47]

Buddhist legends say that at this time the world over people were looking forward to the birth of a Supremely Enlightened One, an event which happens very rarely (*kadāci karahaci*) in history. With an air of expectancy Prophet Isaiah says: "For unto

---

46. H. G. Wells, *A Short History of the World*, Penguin Books, 1945, p. 90
47. Ed. Robert O. Ballou. *The Pocket World Bible*, London. 1948, p. 3

us a child is born, unto us a son is given ... and his name shall be called Wonderful, Councellor, The Mighty God, The Everlasting Father, The Prince of Peace." It is a strange coincidence that almost contemporaneous with this prophecy[48] was born the Buddha to whom all these titles have been given within a few centuries of his birth, for he has been called the *Acchariya puggala,* the Wonderful Person; *sattha devamanussānaṃ,* the Councellor of gods and men; *Brahmātibrahmā* (also *Devātideva*) the God among gods, *Ādipitā*—the eternal Father and *Santirāja*—the Prince of Peace.

In India men prayed and longed for the Truth:

"From the unreal lead me to the real!
From darkness lead me to light !
From death lead me to immortality!"

Bṛh. Up. 1.3:28 (c. 700 BCE).

Thus appeared many sages who claimed to have discovered as many paths to immortality and some of these are described in the Upaniṣads and the scriptures of the Ājīvikas and Jains. Then appeared the Buddha who announced in unmistaken terms.

"Open to them are the doors of immortality;
Those who have ears, let them send forth faith."

M I 169 (c. 528 BCE).

The Truth of Nibbāna that Buddha discovered is called in the Canon "the Truth" (*sacca*) and the fundamental doctrines that he proclaimed are summed up in the "Four Noble Truths" (*cattāri ariyasaccāni*). We do not propose in this article to describe or explain any of these "truths" but shall concern ourselves with the more prosaic task of examining what is meant by the term "truth." This is a purely philosophical investigation and the reader may wonder as to what such academic philosophy has to do with the religion of the Buddha.

Here it is necessary to draw attention to another unique feature of the religion of the Buddha, namely that it is the only religion of any religious teacher which is the outcome of a

48. "... Gautama Buddha, who taught his disciples at Benares in India about the same time that Isaiah was prophesying among the Jews in Babylon ...", H. G. Wells, op. cit., p.90

consistent philosophy, which claims to tell us about the ultimate facts of existence and reality. The religion of the Buddha is a way of life resulting from the acceptance of a view of life, which is said to be factual (*yathābhutaṃ*). His philosophy is not without an epistemology or an account of the nature of knowledge. A detailed examination of this epistemology or theory of knowledge is outside the scope of this brief essay[49] and we shall, therefore, take up this problem of what is meant by the term "truth" as explained and understood in the Canonical texts.

We use the term "truth" to characterise statements or more exactly to characterise what is expressed by statements, namely, propositions. To take an example: we say, for instance, that the statement "There is an artificial lake in Kandy" expresses a truth. Not all true statements have a relevance for religion. The above statement about the Kandy lake has no bearing on religion. But the statement that "life is impermanent and insecure" has a relevance for religion, for the religious quest (*brahmacariyesanā*) or the noble quest (*ariyapariyesanā*) is the quest for security and permanence.

The Four Noble Truths state the following propositions: (i) life within the Cosmos, being infected with impermanence and insecurity, is subject to unhappiness, however "happy" we may be in a relative sense even for very long periods of time; (ii) this unhappiness is caused by the operation of the unsatisfied desires for sensuous gratification, for selfish pursuits and for destruction, which continually seek satisfaction; (iii) the cessation of these desires, which cannot be brought about by violent means (suicide) but only by self-development, coincides with the realisation of supreme happiness; (iv) the total development of the moral, intuitive and spiritual-intellectual aspects of one's personality culminates in this final real realisation and enlightenment. These propositions which are claimed to be true are also said to be useful (*atthasaṃhitaṃ*) in the sense that they are relevant to our weal and welfare and a knowledge of these helps us to attain the goal of all human (and divine) spiritual development. At the same time

49. The author has made a comprehensive study of the epistemology of Buddhism in a book entitled *Early Buddhist Theory of Knowledge* (Motilal Banarsidass, pp. 550).

there are propositions which do not serve such a purpose and are useless in the above sense. Propositions also may be agreeable and pleasant to hear as well as the reverse. If we tabulate the possibilities in terms of propositions, which may be true or false, useful or useless, pleasant or unpleasant, we get the following possibilities:

1.	True	useful	pleasant
2.	True	useful	unpleasant
3.	True	useless	pleasant
4.	True	useless	unpleasant
5.	False	useful	pleasant
6.	False	useful	unpleasant
7.	False	useless	pleasant
8.	False	useless	unpleasant.

In the Abhayarājakumāra Sutta, it is said that the Buddha asserts propositions of the types one and two and that he does not assert propositions of the types three, four, seven and eight. The possibilities five and six are omitted, probably, because it was considered that they did not, in fact, exist. The passage reads: "the Tathāgata does not assert a statement which he knows to be untrue, false, useless, disagreeable and unpleasant to others (8). He does not assert a statement which he knows to be true, factual, useless, disagreeable and unpleasant to others (4). He would assert at the proper time a statement which he knows to be true, factual, useful, disagreeable and unpleasant to others (2). He would not assert a statement which he knows to be untrue, false, useless, agreeable and pleasant to others (7). He would not assert a statement which he knows to be true, factual, useless, agreeable and pleasant to others (3). He would assert at the proper time a statement which he knows to be true, factual, useful, agreeable and pleasant to others (1)." (M I 395)

So the Buddha makes assertions which are true and useful and either pleasant or unpleasant. In the Suttanipāta it is said that "one should say only what is pleasant." (Sn 452). This is, no doubt, the general rule, though exceptionally one may say what is unpleasant as well, for the good of an individual, just as out of love for a child one has to cause a certain amount of pain in order to remove something that has got stuck in its throat (M I 394, 5). Even the truth, it should be noted, should be stated only "at the proper time." We normally make unpleasant statements when we are motivated by anger, jealousy, envy, malice or hatred and we try to rationalise what we do by imagining that our utterances are being made from the best of motives for the good of others. This is the reason why we should be extremely suspicious when we make such unpleasant statements.

What is the defining characteristic of truth? The words commonly used in the Pali to denote "truth" mean "what has taken place" (*bhūtaṃ*), "what is like that" (*tacchaṃ*) and "what is not otherwise" (*anaññathā*). It is the object of knowledge. "One knows what is in accordance with fact" (*yathābhutaṃ pajānāti*; D I 83). These usages suggest the acceptance of what is called in philosophy the correspondence theory of truth. According to this theory, truth is "what accords with fact" and falsity "what discords with fact." True and false beliefs, conceptions, and statements are defined in this manner in the *Apaṇṇaka sutta*: "When, in fact, there is a next world, the belief occurs to me that there is a next world, that would be a true belief. When, in fact, there is a next world, if one thinks that there is a next world, that would be a true conception. When, in fact, there is a next world, one asserts the statement that there is a next world, that would be a true statement" (M I 403). Similarly for falsity: "When, in fact, there is a next world, the belief occurs to me that there is no next world, that would be a false belief ... " (M I 402).

While truth is thus defined in terms of correspondence with fact, consistency or coherence is also considered a criterion of truth. The Canonical texts are quite aware of the principle of contradiction. In one place it is stated that "if P (a certain statement) is true, not-P is false and if not-P is true P is false" (S IV 298–99). But we also find in the texts statements of the following sort:

(i) S is both P and not-P., e.g., the universe is both finite and infinite;

(ii) S is neither P nor not-P., e.g., the universe is neither finite nor infinite.

These statements appear to be self-contradictory to people who are acquainted only with Aristotelian logic.

How can a universe be both finite and infinite when according to the law of contradiction it cannot be both finite and infinite? And how can a universe be neither finite nor infinite, when according to the law of excluded middle it must be either finite or infinite? Western scholars completely misunderstood the nature of these assertions and what they misunderstood they attributed to the idiocy of the Indians. The French scholar, De la Vallee Poussin, makes the following observations about this logic: "Indians do not make a clear distinction between facts and ideas, between ideas and words; they have never clearly recognised the principle of contradiction. Buddhist dialectic has a four-branched dilemma: *Nirvana* is existence or non-existence or both existence and non-existence or neither existence nor non-existence. We are helpless."[50]

Today with the discovery of many-valued logics and the consequent realisation that Aristotelian logic is only one of many possible systems, the significance of this Buddhist logic of four alternatives (*catuskoṭi*) could be better understood. Briefly, this is a two-valued logic of four alternatives, unlike Aristotelian logic, which is a two-valued logic of two alternatives. It is two-valued since it asserts that all propositions are either true (*saccaṃ*) of false (*musā*). Also according to this logic we say that something either is the case or is not the case; there is no other possibility, but in actual conversation in certain situations we make statements of the form "both is and is not" (i.e., "he is both bald and not bald") or "neither is nor is not." The Buddhist logic uses these statements as descriptive of these classes of situations. A discussion of the precise nature of this system of logic would lead us into discussions of a technical nature, but an example would make it clear as to what is meant by the third and fourth possibilities, which are logically impossible according to the Aristotelian scheme. If we talk about the extent of the universe we find for instance, that we can think of four and only four possible mutually exclusive alternatives viz:

(i) The universe is finite in all respects, i.e., it is finite and spherical (*parivaṭuma*);

(ii) The universe is infinite in all dimensions;

(iii) The universe is finite in some, dimensions and infinite in other dimensions; this is what is meant by saying that "the universe is both finite and infinite;"

50. *The Way to Nirvana*, Cambridge University Press, 1917, p. iii.

(iv) If the universe was unreal or space was subjective, then we cannot predicate spatial attributes like "finite" or "infinite" of the universe. In such a situation we may say, "the universe is neither finite nor infinite."

We see from the above that the alternatives three and four are not self contradictory, as Western scholars sometimes back in their ignorance of the true nature of logical systems. According to this fourfold Buddhist system of logic, the above four alternative views about the extent of the universe are seen as four possible alternatives. (It may also be seen that only one and not more than one alternative may be true). According to the Aristotelian system, on the other hand, we can only make the statements "the universe is finite" and "the universe is not finite." By the latter statement it is not clear whether we are stating that the universe is not finite in all dimensions or in one or some dimensions only (views ii and iii). The fourth alternative cannot even be stated since according to the law of excluded middle the above two are the only alternatives possible and one of them must necessarily be true. The Buddhist fourfold logic makes it possible to state the four alternative theses clearly as mutually exclusive and together exhaustive possibilities. It is no more true or false than the Aristotelian and its merits should be judged by its adequacy for the purposes for which it is used.

The propositions of a specific or general character which can be thus stated in the form of the four alternatives belong to the class of statements which concern the events in the space-time-cause world. Statements about Nibbāna or the Super-cosmic, which is a reality that is non-spatio-temporal and unconditioned (*na paṭiccasamuppanna*), fall outside the scope of logical discourse (*atakkāvacara*).

That consistency is held to be a criterion of truth is clear from the fact that the Buddha very often appeals to this principle in arguing with his opponents. He uses dialectical arguments in Socratic fashion to show that some of the theories held by his opponents were false. He starts with one of the assumptions of his opponents and proceeds step by step until at a certain stage in the discussion he is able to show that "his (opponent's) later statement is not compatible with the former nor the former with the later" (*na kho te sandhīyati purimena vā pacchimaṃ pacchimena vā purimaṃ*, M I 232). It is assumed that a theory is false unless it was consistent.

In the Suttanipāta, referring to diverse mutually contradictory theories, the question is asked: "Claiming to be experts, why do they put forward diverse theories—is truth many and at variance?" (Sn 885). The answer given is: "Truth, verily, is not multiple and at variance" (Sn 886). In this context the statement is made that "truth is one without a second" (*ekaṃ hi saccaṃ na dutiyaṃ atthi;* Sn 884). The presence of logical coherence and compatibility in all the statements of a theory and the absence of contradiction is clearly recognised as a criterion of truth.

Now, although consistency is accepted as a criterion of truth, it need not necessarily be the case that a consistent theory is true. A true theory must be consistent but consistency alone is no infallible or sufficient criterion of truth. Consistency, no doubt, lends plausibility to the truth of a theory but we must not forget that it is also possible for a person to lie consistently and thereby present an appearance of truth. A religious philosophy like that of Spinoza's, which is founded on *a priori* reasoning may appear to be true if it is consistent but it would nevertheless be false if it does not correspond with fact. There could be mutually inconsistent theories each of which was internally consistent.

It is a remarkable fact that the Canonical texts recognise this fact. The *Sandaka* Sutta refers to religions based on pure reasoning and speculation, as being unsatisfactory (*anassāsikaṃ*) and not necessarily true; even when the reasoning is sound. The Buddha says that one should not accept a view on the basis of pure reasoning (*mā takka-hetu*), for there could be either mistakes in logic (*sutakkitaṃ pi hoti duttakkitaṃ pi hoti*, M I 520) or even otherwise the findings of such reasoning may or may not be true of external reality (*tathā pi hoti aññathā pi hoti*, ibid.). This is, in fact, a very modern view.

But it is important to note that there is another sense of consistency recognised in the Canonical texts. This is the consistency between the behaviour of a person and his statements. In this sense it is claimed that the Buddha "practised what he preached and preached what he practised" (*yathāvādī tathākārī, yathākārī tathāvādī*, It 122). One does not normally speak of this kind of consistency as logical consistency, but when Toynbee says that "the Buddha was an illogical evangelist"[51] and speaks of his "sublime inconsistency" (op. cit. p. 64) or "sublimely illogical practice" (op. cit., p. 73) he is using "illogical" in this novel sense. Toynbee's conclusions are based on a faulty understanding of the Canonical texts and—as we have shown elsewhere—some of his criticisms have already been forestalled and met in the Pali Canon itself.[52]

There is also a reference to "partial truths" (*pacceka-sacca*) in the Canon. Some religious teachers, it is said, comprehend part of the nature of man and his destiny in the universe and mistakenly assume that this is the whole truth. For instance, according to the description given of the origin of a theistic religious philosophy in the Brahmajāla Sutta, a person from the world of Brahmā (one believed to be a Personal Creator God) is born on earth, lives a homeless life, practises meditation and sees the heavenly world from which be came but does not see beyond. He concludes that heaven and earth and all in it was created by the person who is adored as "God, the Mighty God, the Omnipotent, the All-seeing, the Ruler, the Lord of All, the Maker, the Creator, the Most High, the Ordainer, and Almighty Father of beings that are and are to be" (D I 18) This is cited as a typical case where the partial and limited experience of a mystic forms the basis of a generalisation applied to all reality. The conclusions are said to be wrong but the limited value and validity of the experience is not denied. The diversity of religious theories is attributed to the universalisation of limited experiences valid in their own sphere. The parable of the blind men and the elephant is narrated to illustrate this fact. A number of men born blind are assembled by the king who instructs that they be made to touch an elephant. They touch various parts of the elephant such as the forehead, ears, tusks, etc. They are then asked to describe the elephant and each reports, mistaking the part for the whole, that the elephant was like that portion of the elephant which was felt by them (Udāna 68).

So truth is what corresponded with fact and was consistent, although whatever is consistent is not necessarily true; for a pack

51. A. Toynbee, *An Historian's Approach to Religion*, O.U.P., 1956, p. 77

52. *Vide* K. N. Jayatilleke, "A Recent Criticism of Buddhism" in *Aspects of Buddhist Social Philosophy*, Wheel No. 128/129

of lies could very well be consistent. Partial truths had a partly factual basis.

The Buddhist conception of truth has also been called pragmatic. Poussin says[53]: "*Nous avons defini l'ancienne dogmatique comme une doctrine essentiallement 'pragmatique'...*" (We have defined the ancient teaching as a doctrine essentially "pragmatic"). But it is necessary to clarify the sense in which it is pragmatic. It is not pragmatic in the narrow utilitarian sense of the word for although in the classification of different types of propositions no mention is made of propositions which are both false and useful; true propositions could be either useful or useless in the Buddhist sense of the term as being "conducive to one's spiritual welfare" or not.

Man should give ear to true propositions which are useful in this sense and not fritter away his energies in trying to solve metaphysical questions, pertaining to the origin and extent of the universe, for instance, which have no bearing on the moral and spiritual life. The parable of the arrow illustrates this well when it says that a man struck with a poisoned arrow should be concerned with removing the arrow and getting well rather than be interested in purely theoretical questions (about the nature of the arrow, who shot it, etc.), which have no practical utility. In the *Siṃsapā* forest, the Buddha takes a handful of leaves and says that what he has taught is as little as the leaves in his hand and that what he knew but did not teach is like the leaves in the forest (S V 43,7). He did not teach these things because "they were not useful, not related to the fundamentals of religion and not conducive to revulsion, passion, cessation, peace, higher knowledge, realisation and Nibbāna." (M I 431). The parable of the raft has the same motive and is intended to indicate the utilitarian character of the truths of Buddhism in a spiritual sense. The Buddha says, "I preach you a Dhamma comparable to a raft for the sake of crossing over and not for the sake of clinging to it ..." (M I 134). A person intending to cross a river and get to the other bank, where it is safe and secure, makes a raft and with its help safely reaches the other bank; but however useful the raft may have been, he would throw it aside and go his way without carrying it on his shoulders; so it is said

53. *Bouddhisme*, Third Ed., Paris, 1925. p.129

that "those who realise the Dhamma to be like a raft should discard the Dhamma as well, not to speak of what is not Dhamma" (M I 135). The value of the Dhamma lies in its utility and it ceases to be useful though it does not cease to be true when one has achieved one's purpose with its help by attaining salvation.

While moral and spiritual truths are useful (*atthasaṃhitaṃ*) and truth is not defined in terms of utility, it seems to have been held that the claim of a belief to be true was to be tested in the light of personally verifiable consequences. Thus the truth of rebirth is to be verified by developing the memory of pre-existence (*pubbenivāsānussati*). Verifiability in the light of experience, sensory and extra-sensory, is considered a characteristic of truth but what is thus claimed to be true is considered to be true only by virtue of its correspondence with fact (*yathābhutaṃ*). Thus verifiability is a test of truth but does not itself constitute truth.

Many of the important truths of Buddhism are considered to lie between two extreme points of view: extreme realism, which says that "everything exists" (*sabbaṃ atthīti*), is one extreme and extreme nihilism, which asserts that "nothing exists" (*sabbaṃ natthīti*), is the other extreme—the truth lies in the middle (S II 76). The view of personal immortality (*sassatadiṭṭhi*) is one extreme and the dogma of annihilationism (*ucchedadiṭṭhi*) is the other (S III 60). Similar antinomies are the materialist conception that the body and the soul are not different and the dualist conception that they are different (S II 60), the determinist thesis that everything is conditioned by past factors (*sabbaṃ pubbekatahetu*) and the indeterminist thesis that nothing is due to causes and conditions (*sabbaṃ ahetu appaccaya*, A I 173), the view that we are entirely personally responsible for our unhappiness and the opposite view that we are not at all responsible for our unhappiness (S II 20), extreme hedonism (*kāmasukhallikānuyoga*) and extreme asceticism (*attakilamath-ānuyoga*) (S IV 330). In all these instances it is said that the Buddha, without falling into these two extremes, taught the Dhamma in the middle, and thus the mean between two extremes is held to be true. The "middle way" (*majjhimā paṭipadā*), which is mean both in the matter of belief as well as of goal is said to "make for knowledge ... and bring about intuition and realisation" (M I 15) That these truths lie in the middle seems to be a contingent fact to be discovered empirically.

A distinction that gained currency in the scholastic period but which has its origin in the Canon itself is the contrast between conventional truth (*sammuti sacca*) and absolute truth (*paramattha sacca*). It is said that "just as much as the word 'chariot' is used when the parts are put together in order, there is the conventional use (*sammuti*) of the term 'being' when the psycho-physical constituents are present" (S I 135). The statement "there is a being" is true in reference to a person only in the conventional sense, for there is no entity or substance (soul), in reality corresponding to the word "being." Therefore, it would be false, or meaningless, to say "there is a being" in an absolute sense. The reality of the empirical individual is not denied. The Buddha is quite emphatic on this point. In the *Poṭṭhapāda Sutta,* where the question is discussed, he approves of his interlocutor's statement: "I did exist in the past, not that I did not, I will exist in the future, not that I will not, and I do exist in the present, not that I do not" (D I 200). Only it does not make sense to speak of a substantial soul or entity in the absolute sense since such a soul or entity is not verifiable. We can compare this distinction with the contrast that is sometimes made by scientists between the conventional commonsense point of view and the scientific point of view. As a scientist says, "the kitchen sink, like all the objects surrounding us, is a convenient abstraction."[54]

54. Sherman K. Stein, *Mathematics*, W.H. Freeman & Co., San Francisco and London, 1963.

The Contribution of Buddhism to Philosophic Thought

Prof. E. A Burtt,
Sage Professor of Philosophy, Cornell University.

Ten or fifteen years from now, if I am still in the land of the living, I shall hope to write something more substantial on this topic. To do so would require that one achieve a broad perspective on the history of thought in the West and in the East, and that one adequately assess the long-run significance of Buddhism with its various schools when viewed in such a perspective. What I offer in this paper is my best present surmise as to the main conclusions that more sustained and mature reflection would approve.

In developing this anticipatory surmise I shall sketch four ideas, each of which seems to me highly likely to play an important part in such an assessment. With one partial exception, I believe that these ideas were present in Gautama's own philosophy. And, so far as I can tell, they were original with him in the form in which I shall describe them and in their significant challenge to philosophy. I do not wholly agree with all of them; what I mean in emphasizing them is that philosophers, especially in the West, need to ponder them with utmost seriousness; no philosophy which has failed to understand them and to meet their challenge can hope to stand.

I

The first of these ideas is that philosophy, in its investigations, its analyses, and its explanations, must start from where we are rather than from somewhere else. Now, when expressed in such a general form, this idea is far from unique with Buddhism. Much Chinese thinking, especially in the Confucian tradition, assumes this principle, and what the West calls "empirical" philosophy has consciously accepted it. One of the questions confidently asked by empiricists through the centuries is: "Where else can we start than from experience?"

But human experience is so defective and untidy in so many ways, that keen thinkers in every age have been sorely tempted to start with something else, something neater, simpler, more rational, more perfect and to conceive experience as the product of this something else. Different schools of thinkers succumb to this temptation in different ways; let us briefly review a few of them.

Religious thinkers wish to begin (and also to end) with God, or Brahman. Convinced as they are that he alone is eternally real and that all else in existence depends on him, this seems to them the only reasonable conclusion to draw. It is presumptuous, they will admit, for man in his finitude to assume that he can see things from the standpoint of the Ultimate; yet, since an explanation from that standpoint would alone be true, one must make the best attempt that one can. Thinkers who incline toward materialism wish to start with the atoms—the simple units which are the building blocks of the physical universe—together with the modes of their combination. These, they are sure, last forever, while all the experienced-compounds that arise from them sooner or later pass away. Thinkers who find their haven in the realm of logic and mathematics wish to start with the abstract entities and the fully rational laws there revealed. They do not see how the world of experience can be analyzed or explained in any other way than in terms of this logical structure.

Nonetheless, is there any reason to suppose that experience must submit to any of these demands? It is what it is, and if we wish to understand we must avoid imposing any dubious requirements upon it, however reasonable those requirements might seem to be.

It is at just this point that the Buddha's interpretation of the principle: "Let us start from where we are," is peculiarly challenging. Chinese acceptance of the axiom never quite worked free from limitations due to the Chinese cultural heritage; it was frankly or subtly pervaded by the conviction that experience as we now confront it is a lapse from the Golden Age of Yao and Shun and needs to recover that lost ideal. Western philosophies of experience have been haunted by provincial and transitory notions of what sort of process experience is. Hume—the most influential empirical thinker of the past—thought it must be a temporal sequence of "impressions" and "ideas," as he conceived those mental phenomena. More recent empiricists have reduced experience to "sense data" in their relational patterns, boldly assuming all that is involved in this complex and questionable concept.

As I interpret him, Gautama realized quite clearly that "starting where we are" cannot be a purely passive principle like that of Western empiricism, but must express an active interpretation of experience. He realized also that if it is to give effective guidance it must be freed so far as possible from any limitations of time or place. Experience must be conceived in universal human terms—in terms of factors that are basic in the daily living of people everywhere and always. What this meant concretely in his mind was twofold. On the one hand, we must approach experience as an uniqualifiedly dynamic affair incapable of being understood in relation to any static goal or any fixed structural forms. On the other hand, we must approach it as a process in which men and women are groping toward the conditions of stable and secure well-being, away from the confused mixture of suffering, numbness, frustration, and transitory happiness in which they now exist. He was confident that sound axioms of analysis and of explanation would grow out of the confrontation of experience in these terms, and in no other way.

I am sure that the challenge of this idea has by no means been fully appreciated, either by the philosophies of the East or by those of the West. So far as the West is concerned, the notion of starting where we are has been so deeply affected by the assumptions of empirical science that attempts to conceive experience in any richer and more inclusive way have faced almost insuperable handicaps. So far as India is concerned, it has been impossible for most of her philosophic minds to escape from domination by the fixed conviction that since Brahman is the only unqualified reality, experience must somehow be explained or construed in relation to it. Many among them will admit that this quest cannot hope to succeed—all our categories of interpretation apply within the phenomenal world but not to the relation between that world and the transcendent reality. They will also admit that even if it could succeed, the explanation reached would have meaning only to the saints who have realized union with Brahman; but they need no explanation, they have left behind the state in which searching for a logical system to encase the world is an insistent demand. It is not a bold conclusion then that the Buddha's position will continue to exert a profound challenge until both Western and Eastern philosophies have taken its claims more soberly into account than they thus far have.

II

The second of these four ideas is the one usually referred to as Buddha's agnosticism with respect to metaphysical problems—his deep conviction that one should avoid attachment to any particular solution of these issues, and that when we need to refer to what lies beyond present experience it should be in terms of its contrast with what experience discloses rather than in terms of supposedly common factors.

The very provocative challenge of this idea is brought out most sharply when one considers it in relation to the points of view in Western thought that have most nearly filled a similar role—namely, the agnosticism of the last seventy-five years, the skepticisms of earlier philosophy, and the doctrine that in view of the limits of rational knowledge some form of faith is ultimately valid. .

Late nineteenth century agnosticism, as represented by T. H. Huxley, was a consequence of assuming the exhaustive competence of empirical science so far as knowledge is concerned. The only knowledge man can attain (so it was firmly believed) is the knowledge that is verifiable by science; hence in the case of metaphysical and theological questions, that by their very nature lie beyond such verification, the only justifiable position is to hold that we cannot know which answer to them is the true one. The positivism of our century rests on the same foundations, but adopts the more extreme contention that these questions are not merely unanswerable but are even senseless. A question whose scientific verification is impossible is no genuine question; it is just a series of words. As for the skeptics of ancient and of early modern times, they did not restrict their drastic criticism to trans-empirical matters; the more redoubtable among them, at least, believed it possible to undermine any conclusions drawn by reason. And in their case there seems to have been no positive insight to which this devastating criticism was expected to lead. With those who have been eager to limit rational knowledge so as to leave room for religious faith, there is the necessity of facing a difficult dilemma. Either the faith is entirely discontinuous with the operations of reason, in which case the acceptance of one form of faith, rather than another, would seem to be a purely blind commitment; or also it is continuous with them, in which case the positive relation between faith and knowledge needs to be clearly defined. Religious thinkers in the West have found it very hard to formulate a persuasive position with regard to this dilemma. The Buddha's agnosticism, I believe, is different from any of these viewpoints and avoids the specific difficulties that each of them confronts.

I find no adequate support for the conclusion that Gautama condemned speculative thinking as such. His agnosticism was the expression of three fundamental convictions. First, here was the conviction implied by the major idea above described, that beliefs about questions lying beyond experience are irrelevant to the real problems of life, and if our minds worry about them attention is inevitably distracted from the issues on which we crucially need a solution. We need to understand ourselves in our aspiration to end suffering and to find the dependable conditions of well-being; it will take all the intellectual energy we possess to carry out successfully this task. He was sure, therefore, that he must discourage those whose keenness of mind tempts them into metaphysical speculation from wasting their precious powers in this fashion.

Second, there was the conviction, constantly confirmed by observation, that those who become attached to this or that metaphysical doctrine tend to make dogmatic claims for it and to engage in argumentative wrangling with those who hold a different position. Now, on the one hand, it seemed to him clear that this unhappy outcome is unavoidable, once one devotes oneself to answering these questions; thinkers will be enticed by different theories about them, and since they are trans-empirical there is no way of establishing objectively one proposed solution as against others. On the other hand, it was clear that this outcome, far from leading toward release from self-centred craving, reveals an unfortunate form of bondage to it. Such a situation shows that metaphysical doctrines are intrinsically incapable of being asserted in serenity and compassion, and if this is the case they should not be asserted at all. Only the truth that can be spoken in love—the truth that ends discord rather than fosters it is really truth.

Third, there was the final conviction that even when these difficulties are avoided any attempt to refer in positive terms to that which transcends our present experience is bound to be misleading, and to show effects which will obstruct our quest for liberation. A person who is fully thinking of starting from where we are, and is also ready to centre his intellectual powers on the real problem of life, finds that at one point he will need to speak of that which lies beyond experience, and to relate it in the most clarifying fashion he can to experience as we now find ourselves immersed in it. He will need a term by which to refer to the goal toward which spiritual growth is leading; he must answer questions as to what it is that will have been achieved when the process of liberation is complete. But even at this point serious difficulties arise if such questions are answered in positive terms. Shall he say that peace will have been achieved, or joy, or love? To say this would be true, not false. However, to say it would be misleading—and perhaps seriously so. Anyone to whom it is said will inevitably interpret the meaning of these words in the light of his experience to date. But if he is still in bondage to blind and selfish craving the meaning he will give them is infected throughout by that bondage. He will think of peace as the hoped-for quiescence achieved when his longings have been satisfied; he will imagine joy as the pleasurable concomitant of such a state; love will mean his devoted attachment to this or that person whose help he needs in the quest for these satisfactions. The radically different qualities that these words would denote to one who has achieved liberation are completely beyond him. But what would happen if, under these circumstances, he were encouraged to dwell hopefully on these words, and to indulge freely in the images they suggest to his mind? He would try more zealously than ever to satisfy his immature desires and thus to realize these goals as he now pictures them, instead of being inspired to strive toward the superior state that can be achieved only when such desires are laid aside. For this reason the true goal must be described in negative terms—it is *Nirvāna.* Not *Nirvāna* in the sense of utter extinction, but *Nirvāna* as the state in which the blind, demanding turmoil that has enslaved the person seeking liberation has been rooted out.

On Buddha's carefully considered presuppositions there is no escape from a thoroughgoing agnosticism in this form. Perhaps the philosophic world will find that he was right.

III

The third of these ideas grows directly out of this agnosticism. I shall put it in the form of a paradoxical question. Is the only sound philosophy a form of no-philosophy? So far as I can tell, nothing quite comparable to this idea has appeared in the West. The ancient skeptics, who exemplified something verbally similar, did not share the further insight that is essential to this idea in its Buddhist guise; nor does Ludwig Wittgenstein, who in his famous *Tractatus* holds that all one can really do in relation to other philosophers is to wait till they say something and then show that they have actually said nothing.[55] And, so far as I can tell also, this idea was not definitely adopted by Gautama himself. In him we meet an approach to it in the silence that he sometimes maintained in the presence of metaphysical questionings—at least when the meaning of that silence is considered in relation to his readiness to deal with all inquirers on their own ground. This readiness betokened a remarkable capacity to probe their perplexities in full awareness of individual differences and thus in a way most likely to be helpfully clarifying to each person. The idea comes before us, fully grown and articulate only in the *Madhyamika* Philosophy of Nāgārjuna and his great successors.

Granted the basic Buddhist assumptions, what is the real task of philosophy? It cannot be, of course, what most philosophers have supposed, namely to reach solutions to speculative questions. In general terms the answer is that its function is to contribute, in the way systematic intellectual analysis can, to the guidance of seekers for ultimate liberation. But how should it do this with specific reference to the great issues that philosophers perennially raise? As I interpret the *Madhyamika* thinkers, they are confident that they understand the reason for his way of dealing with metaphysical questions and are revealing it more fully than he did. Their crucial conviction here is a very simple one. It is that

55. *Tractatus Logico-Philosophicus*, London, 1922, P. 187f

the quest for a positive answer to puzzles about the nature of reality is not an expression of the aspiration towards spiritual perfection; however subtle the disguise may be, it is an exhibition of compulsive demands that need to be overcome, not satisfied. These demands are characteristic of intellectually keen minds; they represent the kind of obstruction to the full achievement of liberation to which such minds are peculiarly apt to succumb.

What then should be done about these speculative cravings? Essentially, to discourage those who are seduced by them from expecting their satisfaction, and to entice them to seek instead the kind of spiritual insight that needs no rational articulation and is, indeed, capable of none. This, of course, cannot be accomplished by a hostile attack on their transcendental searching, so natural to persons of great logical power, nor by a refutation of their major conclusions which rests on some alternative set of theoretical assumptions. Such attacks would only provoke them to a more ardent attachment to the obstructive notions that symbolize and express their enslavement. What this programme calls for is, rather, that one compassionately places oneself within the framework in which one's self-deceptive thinking moves, and show, by a fuller logical unfolding of their premises than because of their bondage they could achieve, that there are inherent contradictions in all the explanatory categories that they confidently employ.

To carry out such a task of internal criticism requires that the thinker pursuing it, on the one hand, shows himself as competent in systematic philosophical analysis as those whom he is criticizing, and that, on the other hand, having attained a deeper level of spiritual insight, so that his radical criticisms may express the loving understanding without which their constructive promise would be lost. And it means also, that, in intent at least, he is setting up no alternative philosophical system in place of the refuted systems of others. Were he to do this he would himself have fallen prey to the temptations that have misled those whose doctrines and hopes he has swept away.

I can think of no more searching challenge to philosophers of the West than is contained in this idea; and thinkers of the East also need to square themselves more profoundly with it than most of them as yet have done.

IV

The fourth of these ideas is one which underlies each of the other three, and hence may be stated quite briefly. This is the idea that theoretical inquiry is not independent of practical action, as keen thinkers are prone to suppose, but is itself one factor in human action—the factor in virtue of which any action can be consciously guided instead of expressing a purely blind urge.

Now the West has produced pragmatic philosophers who have stressed this principle, and Eastern thought has been influenced by it to a very large extent. But I believe that in his way of conceiving it Gautama caught a rather distinctive insight, which not too many even among His own followers have fully shared. The pragmatism of John Dewey, a generation ago in the West, expressed a clear insistence that theory is one aspect of practice, whose role is to give it intelligent guidance, but in Dewey this insight, reflected the limitations of his time and place. Especially was it confined by the orientation of Western empirical science and by the social reforms that in Dewey's mind constitute the only sound goals of practical action. In the East this kind of limitation has, of course, been absent. Nonetheless, most non-Buddhist modes of thought, and not a few Buddhist ones, have been captive to traditional Eastern notions as to what sort of thing practical action must be and how intellectual inquiry is related to it.

It seems to me that Gautama's insight here included two features, one of which was expressed in clearer and more radical form than his predecessors had given it, and the other was probably original with him. As for the former, I am thinking of the thoroughly dynamic conception of experience, and, therefore, of human action that has already been mentioned. One consequence of this conception was that intellectual searching itself is interpreted in terms of this dynamic framework; far from being the halting expression within finite experience of a changeless transcendent consciousness, it exhibits the interaction of the same combining and separating forces that other modes of action reveal.

As for the latter feature, I believe Gautama must have apprehended a principle whose implications for a theory of truth are, at least, equally radical. Certainly his own compassionate action, in relation to inquirers who came to him, was constantly guided by this principle. It grows out of the recognition that whatever one says to another person, whether one is aware of it or not, has practical effects in the experience and action of that person. In particular, it either has the effect of eliciting his constructive capacities and fostering his growth toward spiritual freedom, or the contrary effect of confusing his emotions, dulling his aspiration, and stimulating his attachment to deceptive beliefs. Now so far as a speaker has gained liberation himself, he will be alertly aware of these effects, and his dominant motive will be so to speak, in everyone's presence, as to express a compassionate concern for the listener's dynamic growth toward unfettered well-being. All his philosophic thinking and every item in its verbal expression will be guided by this concern; it will be a part of the discovering, exploring, creative action which his whole experience in relation to every living creature will exemplify.

This idea is the most searching and challenging of the four I have sketched. Its drastic implication for philosophy may be succinctly stated in the principle that truth must be a dynamic and loving truth if it is to be truth at all.

In conclusion, I do not feel sure at present what qualification in the case of each of these ideas are needed if they are to enter into the enduring deposit of man's philosophic reflection. But I do feel sure that such qualifications will only be accurately formulated when thinkers, both Eastern and Western, have pondered these ideas with the deepest sensitivity and the most adventurous vision of which they are capable.

Paper read at a Symposium on "Buddhism's Contribution to Art, Letters and Philosophy," arranged in November, 1956, by the Working Committee for the 2500th Buddha Jayanthi Government of India, in collaboration with the UNESCO, to commemorate the 2500th anniversary of the Parinirvāna of the Buddha. Reprinted from "The Mahā Bodhi," December, 1956.

Taming the Mind

Discourses of the Buddha

Edited by

Nyanaponika Thera

WHEEL PUBLICATION NO. 51

Copyright © Kandy: Buddhist Publication Society
(1963, 1973, 1983)

1. No Other Single Thing

(Aṅguttara, Ones)

"Monks, I know not of any other single thing so intractable as the untamed mind. The untamed mind is indeed a thing untractable.

"Monks, I know not of any other single thing so tractable as the tamed mind. The tamed mind is indeed a thing tractable.

"Monks, I know not of any other single thing so conducive to great loss as the untamed mind. The untamed mind indeed conduces to great loss.

"Monks, I know not of any other single thing so conducive to great profit as the tamed mind. The tamed mind indeed conduces to great profit.

"Monks, I know not of any other single thing that brings such woe as the mind that is untamed, uncontrolled, unguarded and unrestrained. Such a mind indeed brings great woe.

"Monks, I know not of any other single thing that brings such bliss as the mind that is tamed, controlled, guarded and restrained. Such a mind indeed brings great bliss."

Gradual Sayings (*Aṅguttara Nikāya*)
The Book of the Ones, Ch. IV
Translated by F. L. Woodward[1]

---

1. We are obliged to the Pali Text Society, London for kind permission to reproduce the translations collected here, excepting the last item which has been taken from Bhikkhu Buddharakkhita's rendering of the Dhammapada, published by the Maha Bodhi Society, Bangalore (India).

2. Discourse to Gaṇaka-Moggallāna

(Majjhima Nikāya No. 107)

Thus I have heard: At one time the Lord was staying near Sāvatthī in the palace of Migāra's mother in the Eastern Monastery. Then the brahmin Gaṇaka-Moggallāna approached the Lord; having approached he exchanged greetings with the Lord; having conversed in a friendly and courteous way, he sat down at a respectful distance. As he was sitting down at a respectful distance, Gaṇaka-Moggallāna the brahmin spoke thus to the Lord: "Just as, good Gotama, in this palace of Migāra's mother there can be seen a gradual training, a gradual doing, a gradual practice, that is to say as far as the last flight of stairs;[2] so, too, good Gotama, for these brahmins there can be seen a gradual training, a gradual doing, a gradual practice, that is to say in the study [of the Vedas];[3] so too, good Gotama, for these archers there can be seen a gradual ... practice, that is to say in archery; so too, good Gotama, for us whose livelihood is calculation[4] there can be seen a gradual training, a gradual practice, that is to say in accountancy. For when we get a pupil, good Gotama, we first of all make him calculate: 'One one, two twos, three threes, four fours, five fives, six sixes, seven sevens, eight eights, nine nines, ten tens,' and we, good Gotama, also make him calculate a hundred. Is it not possible, good Gotama, to lay down a similar gradual training, gradual doing, gradual practice in respect of this Dhamma and discipline?"

"It is possible, brahmin, to lay down a gradual training, a gradual doing, a gradual practice in respect of this Dhamma and discipline. Brahmin, even a skilled trainer of horses, having taken

---

2. A seven-storied palace is not to be built in one day [Commentary].

3. It is not possible to learn the three Vedas by heart in one day [Commentary].

4. *Gaṇanā*—from this profession, the appellation Gaṇaka is added to the brahmin's name. Moggallāna later became Mahāmoggallāna, one the chief disciples of the Buddha and teacher of the Sangha [Ed., *The Wheel*].

on a beautiful thoroughbred first of all gets it used to the training in respect of wearing the bit. Then he gets it used to further training — even so brahmin, the Tathāgata, having taken on a man to be tamed, first of all disciplines him thus:

Morality

"'Come you, monk, be of moral habit, live controlled by the control of the Obligations, endowed with (right) behaviour and posture, seeing peril in the slightest fault and, undertaking them, train yourself in the rules of training.' As soon, brahmin, as the monk is of moral habit, controlled by the control of the Obligations, endowed with (right) behaviour and posture, seeing peril in the slightest fault and, undertaking them, trains himself in the rules of training, the Tathāgata disciplines him further saying:

Sense-control

"'Come you, monk, be guarded as to the doors of the sense-organs; having seen a material shape with the eye, do not be entranced with the general appearance, do not be entranced with the detail; for if one dwells with the organ of sight uncontrolled, covetousness and dejection, evil, unskilful states of mind, may flow in. So abide controlling it; guard the organ of sight, achieve control over the organ of sight. Having heard a sound with the ear... Having smelt a smell with the nose... Having savoured a taste with the tongue... Having felt a touch with the body... Having cognised a mental state with the mind, do not be entranced with the general appearance, do not be entranced with the detail. For if one dwells with the organ of mind uncontrolled, covetousness and dejection, evil, unskilful states of mind, may flow in. So abide controlling it; guard the organ of mind, achieve control over the organ of mind.'

Moderation in eating

"As soon, brahmin, as a monk is guarded as to the doors of the sense-organs, the Tathāgata disciplines him further, saying: 'Come you, monk, be moderate in eating; you should take food reflecting carefully, not for fun or indulgence or personal charm or beautification, but taking just enough for maintaining this body and keeping it going, for keeping it unharmed, for furthering the Holy Life,[5] with the thought: Thus will I crush out an old feeling, and I will not allow a new feeling to arise, and then there will be for me subsistence and blamelessness and abiding in comfort.'

Vigilance

"As soon, brahmin, as a monk is moderate in eating, the Tathāgata disciplines him further, saying: 'Come you, monk, dwell intent on vigilance; during the day while pacing up and down, while sitting down, cleanse the mind of obstructive mental states; during the middle watch of the night, lie down on the right side in the lion posture, foot resting on foot, mindful, clearly conscious, reflecting on the thought of getting up again; during the last watch of the night, when you have risen, while pacing up and down, while sitting down, cleanse the mind of obstructive mental states.'

Mindfulness and clear consciousness

"As soon, brahmin, as a monk is intent on vigilance, the Tathāgata disciplines him further, saying: 'Come you, monk, be possessed of mindfulness and clear consciousness, acting with clear consciousness whether you are approaching or departing, acting with clear consciousness whether you are looking ahead or looking round, acting with clear consciousness whether you are bending in or stretching out (the arms), acting with clear consciousness whether you are carrying the outer cloak, the bowl or robe, acting with clear consciousness whether you are eating, drinking, munching, savouring, acting with clear consciousness whether you are obeying the calls of nature, acting with clear consciousness whether you are walking, standing, sitting, asleep, awake, talking or being silent.'

Overcoming of the five hindrances

"As soon, brahmin, as he is possessed of mindfulness and clear consciousness, the Tathāgata disciplines him further, saying:

5. *Brahmacariya*—this refers to the pure life of a celibate recluse [Ed., *The Wheel*].

'Come you, monk, choose a remote lodging in a forest, at the root of a tree, on a mountain slope, in a glen, a hill cave, a cemetery, a woodland grove, in the open, or on a heap of straw.' On returning from alms-gathering after the meal, the monk sits down cross-legged, holding the back erect, having made mindfulness rise up in front of him. He, getting rid of covetousness for the world, dwells with a mind devoid of covetousness, he cleanses the mind of covetousness. Getting rid of the taint of ill-will, he dwells benevolent in mind; compassionate and merciful towards all creatures and beings, he cleanses the mind of ill-will. Getting rid of sloth and torpor, he dwells without sloth or torpor; perceiving the light, mindful and clearly conscious he cleanses the mind of sloth and torpor. Getting rid of restlessness and worry, he dwells calmly; the mind inward tranquil, he cleanses the mind of restlessness and worry. Getting rid of doubt, he abides free from doubt; unperplexed as to the states that are wholesome,[6] he cleanses his mind of doubt.

Jhāna

"He, by getting rid of these five hindrances[7] which are defilements of the mind and deleterious to intuitive wisdom, aloof from pleasures of the senses, aloof from unskilled states of mind, enters and abides in the first meditation which is accompanied by initial thought and discursive thought, is born of aloofness and is rapturous and joyful. By allaying initial thought and discursive thought, his mind subjectively tranquillised and fixed on one point, he enters and abides in the second meditation which is devoid of initial thought and discursive thought, is born of concentration and is rapturous and joyful. By the fading out of rapture, he dwells with equanimity, attentive and clearly conscious, and experiences in his person that joy of which the ariyans[8] say: 'Joyful lives he who has equanimity and is mindful,' and he enters and abides in

6. *Kusala*—sometimes translated as "skilled, salutary, profitable, kammically wholesome." [Ed., *The Wheel*].

7. On these, see *The Wheel* No. 26.

8. *Ariyā* refers here, according to the *Visuddhi Magga*, to the Enlightened Ones.

the third meditation. By getting rid of anguish, by the going down of his former pleasures and sorrows, he enters and abides in the fourth meditation which has neither anguish nor joy, and which is entirely purified by equanimity and mindfulness.

"Brahmin, such is my instruction for those monks who are learners who, perfection being not yet attained, dwell longing for the incomparable security from the bonds. But as for those monks who are perfected ones, the cankers destroyed, who have lived the life, done what was to be done, shed the burden, attained to their own goal, the fetters of becoming utterly destroyed, and who are freed by perfect profound knowledge — these things conduce both to their abiding in ease here and now as well to their mindfulness and clear consciousness."

When this had been said, the brahmin Gaṇaka-Moggallāna spoke thus to the Lord:

"Now, on being exhorted thus and instructed thus by the good Gotama, do all the good Gotama's disciples attain the ultimate goal[9] — Nibbāna or do some not attain it?"

"Some of my disciples, brahmin, on being exhorted and instructed thus by me, attain the ultimate goal — Nibbāna; some do not attain it."

"What is the cause, good Gotama, what the reason that, since Nibbāna does exist, since the way leading to Nibbāna exists, since the good Gotama exists as adviser, some of the good Gotama's disciples on being exhorted thus and instructed thus by the good Gotama, attain the ultimate goal — Nibbāna, but some do not attain it?"

"Well then, brahmin, I will question you on this point in reply. As it is pleasing to you, so you may answer me. What do you think about this, brahmin? Are you skilled in the way leading to Rājagaha?"

"Yes, sir, skilled am I in the way leading to Rājagaha."

"What do you think about this? A man might come along here wanting to go to Rājagaha. Having approached you, he might speak thus: 'I want to go to Rājagaha, sir; show me the way to this Rājagaha.' You might speak thus to him: "Yes, my good man, this road goes to Rājagaha; go along it for a while.

9. *Accantaniṭṭhā—accanta* means "utmost, culminating, supreme."

When you have gone along it for a while you will see a village; go along for a while; when you have gone along for a while you will see a market town; go for a while. When you have gone along for a while you will see Rājagaha with its delightful parks, delightful forests, delightful fields, delightful ponds.' But although he has been exhorted and instructed thus by you, he might take the wrong road and go westwards. Then a second man might come along wanting to go to Rājagaha... (*as above*) '... you will see Rājagaha with its delightful... ponds.' Exhorted and instructed thus by you he might get to Rājagaha safely. What is the cause, brahmin, what the reason that, since Rājagaha does exist, since the way leading to Rājagaha exists, since you exist as adviser, the one man, although being exhorted and instructed thus by you, may take the wrong road and go westwards while the other may get to Rājagaha safely?"

"What can I, good Gotama, do in this matter? A shower of the way, good Gotama, am I."

"Even so, brahmin, Nibbāna does exist, the way leading to Nibbāna exists and I exist as adviser. But some of my disciples, on being exhorted and instructed thus by me attain the ultimate goal – Nibbāna, some do not attain it. What can I, brahmin, do in this matter? A shower of the way, brahmin, is a Tathāgata."

When this had been said, the brahmin Gaṇaka-Moggallāna spoke thus to the Lord:

"Good Gotama, as for those persons who, in want of a way of living, having gone forth from home into homelessness without faith, who are crafty, fraudulent, deceitful, who are unbalanced and puffed up, who are shifty, scurrilous and of loose talk, the doors of whose sense-organs are not guarded, who do not know moderation in eating, who are not intent on vigilance, indifferent to recluseship, not of keen respect for the training, who are ones for abundance, lax, taking the lead in backsliding, shirking the burden of seclusion, who are indolent, of feeble energy, of confused mindfulness, not clearly conscious, not concentrated but of wandering minds, who are weak in wisdom, drivellers – the good Gotama is not in communion with *them*. But as for those young men of respectable families who have gone forth from home into homelessness from faith, who are not crafty, fraudulent or deceitful, who are not unbalanced or puffed up, who are not shifty, scurrilous or of loose talk, the doors of whose sense-organs are guarded, who know moderation in eating, who are intent on vigilance, longing for recluseship, of keen respect for the training, who are not ones for abundance, not lax, shirking, backsliding, taking the lead in seclusion, who are of stirred up energy, self-resolute, with mindfulness aroused, clearly conscious, concentrated, their minds one-pointed, who have wisdom, are not drivellers — the good Gotama is in communion with *them.* As, good Gotama, black gum is pointed to as chief of root-scents, as red sandalwood is pointed to as chief of pith-scents, as jasmine is pointed to as chief of flower scents — even so is the exhortation of the good Gotama highest among the teachings of today. Excellent, good Gotama, excellent, good Gotama. As, good Gotama, one might set upright what had been upset, or disclose what had been covered, or show the way to one who had gone astray, or bring an oil-lamp into the darkness so that those with vision might see material shapes — even so in many a figure is Dhamma made clear by the good Gotama. I am going to the revered Gotama for refuge and to Dhamma and to the Order of monks. May the good Gotama accept me as a lay-follower going for refuge from today forth for as long as life lasts."

From *Middle Length Sayings*
Translated by I. B. Horner
(Pali Text Society, London)

3. Vijitasena's Verses

(Theragāthā vv. 355-359)

I shall fasten you, mind, like an elephant at a small gate. I shall not incite you to evil, you net of sensual pleasure, body-born.

When fastened, you will not go, like an elephant not finding the gate open. Witch-mind, you will not wander again, and again, using force, delighting in evil.

As the strong hook-holder makes an untamed elephant, newly taken, turn against its will, so shall I make you turn.

As the excellent charioteer, skilled in the taming of excellent horses, tames a thoroughbred, so shall I, standing firm in the five powers, tame you.

I shall bind you with mindfulness; with purified self shall cleanse [you]. Restrained by the yoke of energy you will not go far from here, mind.

Translated by K.R. Norman
The Elders' Verses I, P.T.S. 1969

4. Discourse on the "Tamed Stage"
Dantabhūmi sutta

(Majjhima Nikāya No. 125)

Thus have I heard: At one time the Lord was staying near Rājagaha in the Bamboo Grove at the squirrels' feeding place. Now, at that time the novice Aciravata was staying in the Forest Hut.[10] Then prince Jayasena,[11] who was always pacing up and down, always roaming about on foot, approached the novice Aciravata; having approached he exchanged greetings with the novice Aciravata; having exchanged greetings of friendliness and courtesy, he sat down at a respectful distance. While he was sitting down at a respectful distance, Prince Jayasena spoke thus to the novice Aciravata:

"I have heard, good Aggivessana, that if a monk is abiding here diligent, ardent, self-resolute, he may attain one-pointedness of mind."

"That is so, prince; that is so, prince. A monk abiding here diligent, ardent, self-resolute, may attain one-pointedness of mind."

"It were good if the reverend Aggivessana were to teach me Dhamma as he has heard it, as he has mastered it."

"I, prince, am not able to teach you Dhamma as I have heard it, as I have mastered it. Now, if I were to teach you Dhamma as I have heard it, as I have mastered it, and if you could not understand the meaning of what I said, that would be weariness to me, that would be a vexation to me."

"Let the reverend Aggivessana teach me Dhamma as he has heard it, as he has mastered it. Perhaps I could understand the meaning of what the good Aggivessana says."

"If I were to teach you Dhamma, prince, as I have heard it, as I have mastered it, and if you were to understand the meaning of

---

10. A hut in a secluded part of the Bamboo Grove for the use of monks who wanted to practice striving, *padhāna* — [Commentary].

11. A son of King Bimbisāra.

what I say, that would be good; if you should not understand the meaning of what I say, you must remain as you are: you must not question me further on the matter."

"Let the reverend Aggivessana teach me Dhamma as he has heard it, as he has mastered it. If I understand the meaning of what the good Aggivessana says, that will be good; if I do not understand the meaning of what the good Aggivessana says, I will remain as I am; I will not question the reverend Aggivessana further on this matter."

Then the novice Aciravata taught Dhamma to Prince Jayasena as he had heard it, as he had mastered it. When this had been said, Prince Jayasena spoke thus to the novice Aciravata:

"This is impossible, good Aggivessana, it cannot come to pass that a monk abiding diligent, ardent, self-resolute, should attain one-pointedness of mind." Then Prince Jayasena, having declared to the novice Aciravata that this was impossible and could not come to pass, rising from his seat, departed.

And soon after Prince Jayasena had departed, the novice Aciravata approached the Lord; having approached and greeted the Lord, he sat down at a respectful distance. As he was sitting down at a respectful distance, the novice Aciravata told the Lord the whole of the conversation he had with Prince Jayasena as far as it had gone. When this had been said, the Lord spoke thus to the novice Aciravata:

"What is the good of that, Aggivessana? That Prince Jayasena, living as he does in the midst of sense-pleasures, enjoying sense-pleasures, being consumed by thoughts of sense-pleasures, burning with the fever of sense-pleasures, eager in the search for sense-pleasures, should know or see or attain or realise that which can be known by renunciation, seen by renunciation, attained by renunciation, realised by renunciation — such a situation does not exist. It is as if, Aggivessana, among elephants or horses or oxen to be tamed, two elephants, two horses or two oxen are well tamed, well trained, and two are not tamed, not trained. What do you think about this, Aggivessana? Would these two elephants or horses or oxen that were to be tamed and that were well tamed, well trained — would those on being tamed reach tamed capacity, would they, being tamed, attain a tamed stage?"

"Yes, revered sir."

"But those two elephants or horses or oxen that were to be tamed but that were neither tamed nor trained — would these, not being tamed, attain a tamed stage as do the two elephants or horses or oxen to be tamed that were well tamed, well trained?"

"No, revered sir."

"Even so, Aggivessana, that Prince Jayasena, living as he does in the midst of sense-pleasures... should know or see or attain or realise that which can be known and realised by renunciation — such a situation does not exist. It is as if, Aggivessana, there were a great mountain slope near a village or a market-town which two friends, coming hand in hand from that village or market-town might approach; having approached the mountain slope one friend might remain at the foot while the other might climb to the top. Then the friend standing at the foot of the mountain slope might speak thus to the one standing on the top: 'My dear, what do you see as you stand on the top of the mountain slope?' He might reply: 'As I stand on the top of the mountain slope I, my dear, see delightful parks, delightful woods, delightful stretches of level ground, delightful ponds.' But the other might speak thus: 'This is impossible, it cannot come to pass, my dear, that, as you stand on the top of the mountain slope, you should see... delightful ponds.' Then the friend who had been standing on top of the mountain slope having come down to the foot and taken his friend by the arm, making him climb to the top of the mountain slope and giving him a moment in which to regain his breath, might speak to him thus: 'Now, my dear, what is it that you see as you stand on the top of the mountain slope?' He might speak thus: 'I, my dear, as I stand on the top of the mountain slope, see delightful parks... delightful ponds.' He might speak thus: 'Just now, my dear, we understood you to say: This is impossible, it cannot come to pass that, as you stand on the top of the mountain slope, you should see delightful... ponds. But now we understand you to say: 'I, my dear, as I stand on the top of the mountain slope, see delightful parks... delightful ponds.' He might speak thus: 'That was because I, my dear, hemmed in by this great mountain slope, could not see what was to be seen.'

"Even so but to a still greater degree, Aggivessana, is Prince Jayasena hemmed in, blocked, obstructed, enveloped by this mass of ignorance. Indeed, that Prince Jayasena, living as he does in the midst of sense-pleasures, enjoying sense-pleasures, being consumed by the thoughts of sense-pleasures, burning with the fever of sense-pleasures, eager in the search for sense-pleasures, should know or see or attain or realise that which can be known... seen... attained... realised by renunciation — such a situation does not exist. Had these two similes occurred to you, Aggivessana, for Prince Jayasena, Prince Jayasena naturally would have trusted you and, having trust, would have acted in the manner of one having trust in you."

"But how could these two similes for Prince Jayasena have occurred to me, revered sir, seeing that they are spontaneous, that is to say to the Lord, and have never been heard before?"

"As, Aggivessana, a noble anointed king addresses an elephant hunter saying; 'You, good elephant hunter, mount the king's elephant and go into an elephant forest. When you see a forest elephant, tie him to the neck of the king's elephant.' And, Aggivessana, the elephant hunter having answered: 'Yes, sire,' in assent to the noble anointed king, mounts the king's elephant and goes into an elephant forest. Seeing a forest elephant, he ties him to the neck of the king's elephant. So the king's elephant brings him out into the open. But, Aggivessana, the forest elephant has this longing, that is to say for the elephant forest. But in regard to him the elephant hunter tells the noble anointed king that the forest elephant has got out into the open. The noble anointed king then addresses an elephant tamer, saying: 'Come you, good elephant tamer, tame the forest elephant by subduing his forest ways, by subduing his forest memories and aspirations, and by subduing his distress, his fretting and fever for the forest, by making him pleased with the villages and by accustoming him to human ways.'

"And, Aggivessana, the elephant tamer, having answered 'Yes, sire,' in assent to the noble anointed king, driving a great post into the ground ties the forest elephant to it by his neck so as to subdue his forest ways... and accustom him to human ways. Then the elephant tamer addresses him with such words as are gentle, pleasing to the ear, affectionate, going to the heart, urbane, pleasant to the manyfolk, liked by the manyfolk. And, Aggivessana, the forest elephant, on being addressed with words that are gentle... liked by the manyfolk, listens, lends ear and bends his mind to learning. Next the elephant tamer supplies him with grass-fodder and water. When, Aggivessana, the forest elephant has accepted the grass-fodder and water from the elephant tamer, it occurs to the elephant tamer: 'The king's elephant will now live.' Then the elephant tamer makes him do a further task, saying: 'Take up, put down.' When, Aggivessana the king's elephant is obedient to the elephant tamer and acts on his instructions to take up and put down, then the elephant tamer makes him do a further task, saying: 'Advance, retreat… a further task, saying: 'Get up, sit down.' When, Aggivessana, the king's elephant is obedient to the elephant tamer and acts on his instructions to get up and sit down, then the elephant tamer makes him do a further task known as 'standing your ground': he ties a shield to the great beast's trunk; a man holding a lance is sitting on his neck, and men holding lances are standing surrounding him on all sides; and the elephant tamer, holding a lance with a long shaft, is standing in front. While he is doing the task of 'standing your ground' he does not move a foreleg nor does he move a hind-leg, nor does he move the forepart of his body, nor does he move the hindpart of his body, nor does he move his head, nor does he move an ear, nor does he move a tusk, nor does he move his tail, nor does he move his trunk. A king's elephant is one who endures blows of sword, axe, arrow, hatchet, and the resounding din of drum and kettle-drum, conch and tam-tam, he is [like] purified gold purged of all its dross and impurities, fit for a king, a royal possession and reckoned as a kingly attribute.

Acquisition of faith

"Even so, Aggivessana, does a Tathāgata arise here in the world, a perfected one, fully Self-Awakened One, endowed with right knowledge and conduct, well-farer, knower of the worlds, the matchless charioteer of men to be tamed, the Awakened One, the Lord. He makes known this world with the *devas,* with Māra, with Brahma, the creation with its recluses and brahmins, its *devas* and men, having realised them by his own super-knowledge. He teaches Dhamma which is lovely at the beginning, lovely in the middle, lovely at the ending, with the spirit and the letters; he proclaims the Holy Life,[12] wholly fulfilled, quite purified. A

12. *Brahmacariya:* the pure life of a celibate recluse [Ed., *The Wheel*].

householder or a householder's son or one born in another family hears that Dhamma. Having heard that Dhamma he gains faith in the Tathāgata. Endowed with this faith that he has acquired, he reflects in this way: 'The household life is confined and dusty, going forth is in the open; it is not easy for one who lives in a house to practise the Holy Life wholly fulfilled, wholly pure, polished like a conch-shell. Suppose now that I, having cut off hair and beard, having put on saffron robes, should go forth from home into homelessness?' After a time, getting rid of his wealth, be it small or great, getting rid of his circle of relations, be it small or great, having cut off his hair and beard, having put on saffron robes, he goes forth from home into homelessness. To this extent, Aggivessana, the ariyan disciple gets out into the open.

Morality

"But, Aggivessana, *devas* and mankind have this longing, that is to say, for the five strands of sense-pleasures. The Tathāgata disciplines him further, saying: 'Come you, monk, be moral, live controlled by the control of the Obligations[13], possessed of [right] behaviour and posture, seeing danger in the slightest faults; undertaking them, train yourself in the rules of training.'

Sense-Control

"And when, Aggivessana, the ariyan disciple is moral, lives controlled by the control... undertaking them, trains himself in the rules of training, then the Tathāgata disciplines him further, saying: 'Come you, monk, be guarded as to the doors of the sense-organs. Having seen a material shape with the eye... (*as above*). Having cognised a mental state with the mind, be not entranced by the general appearance, be not entranced by the detail. For, if you were to dwell with the organ of mind uncontrolled, covetousness and dejection, evil unskilful states of mind, might flow in. So practise control, guard the organ of mind, achieve control over the organ of mind.'

---

13. *Patimokkha*: the code of disciplinary rules for Buddhist monks.

Moderation in eating

"And when, Aggivessana, the ariyan disciple is guarded as to the doors of the sense-organs, then the Tathāgata disciplines him further, saying: 'Come you, monk, be moderate in eating... (*as above*)... abiding in comfort.'

Vigilance

"When, Aggivessana, the ariyan disciple is moderate in eating, the Tathāgata disciplines him further, saying: 'Come you, monk, abide intent on vigilance... (*as above*)... you should cleanse the mind of obstructive mental states.

Mindfulness and clear consciousness

"And when, Aggivessana, the ariyan disciple is intent on vigilance, then the Tathāgata disciplines him further, saying: 'Come you, monk, be possessed of mindfulness and clear consciousness. Be one who acts with clear consciousness... (*as above*)... talking, silent.'

Overcoming of the five hindrances

"And when, Aggivessana, the ariyan disciple is possessed of mindfulness and clear consciousness, then the Tathāgata disciplines him further, saying: 'Come you, monk, choose a remote lodging in a forest, at the root of a tree, on a mountain slope, in a wilderness, a hill-cave, a cemetery, a forest haunt, in the open or on a heap of straw.' He chooses a remote lodging in the forest... or on a heap of straw. Returning from alms-gathering, after the meal, he sits down cross-legged, holding the back erect, having made mindfulness rise up in front of him, he, by getting rid of coveting for the world, dwells with a mind devoid of coveting, he purifies the mind of coveting. By getting rid of the taint of ill-will, he dwells benevolent in mind, compassionate for the welfare of all creatures and beings, he purifies the mind of the taint of ill-will. By getting rid of sloth and torpor, he dwells devoid of sloth and torpor; perceiving the light, mindful, clearly conscious, he purifies the mind of sloth and torpor. By getting rid of restlessness and worry, he dwells calmly the mind subjectively tranquillized, he purifies the mind of restlessness and worry. By getting rid of doubt, he dwells doubt-crossed, unperplexed as to the states that are skilful, he purifies the mind of doubt.

The four applications of mindfulness

"He, by getting rid of these five hindrances, which are defilements of the mind and weakening to intuitive wisdom, dwells contemplating the body in the body, ardent, clearly conscious [of it], mindful [of it] so as to control the covetousness and dejection in the world. He dwells contemplating the feelings... the mind... the mental states in mental states, ardent, clearly conscious [of them], mindful [of them] so as to control the covetousness and dejection in the world.

"As, Aggivessana, an elephant tamer, driving a great post into the ground, ties a forest elephant to it by his neck so as to subdue his forest ways, so as to subdue his forest aspirations, and so as to subdue his distress, his fretting and fever for the forest, so as to make him pleased with villages and accustom him to human ways – even so, Aggivessana, these four applications of mindfulness are ties of the mind so as to subdue the ways of householders and to subdue the aspirations of householders and to subdue the distress, the fretting and fever of householders; they are for leading to the right path, for realising Nibbāna.

"The Tathāgata then disciplines him further, saying: 'Come you, monk, abide contemplating the body in the body, but do not apply yourself to a train of thought connected with the body; abide contemplating the feelings in the feelings... the mind in the mind... mental states in mental states, but do not apply yourself to a train of thought connected with mental states.'

Jhāna

"He by allaying initial thought and discursive thought, with the mind subjectively tranquillized and fixed on one point, enters on and abides in the second meditation[14] which is devoid of initial and

14. It is noteworthy that the section on the Four Applications of Mindfulness (*satipaṭṭhāna*) is here followed by the *second* meditation (*jhāna*) without mention of the first. This may either refer to a meditator who, already

discursive thought, is born of concentration and is rapturous and joyful. By the fading out of rapture, he dwells with equanimity, attentive and clearly conscious, and experiences in his person that joy of which the ariyans say: 'Joyful lives he who has equanimity and is mindful,' and he enters and abides in the third meditation. By getting rid of joy, by getting rid of anguish, by the going down of his former pleasures and sorrows, he enters and abides in the fourth meditation which has neither anguish nor joy, and which is entirely purified by equanimity and mindfulness.

The three knowledges (tevijjā)

1. Recollection of former habitations

"Then with the mind composed thus, quite purified, quite clarified, without blemish, without defilement, grown pliant and workable, fixed, immovable, he directs his mind to the knowledge and recollection of former habitation: he remembers a variety of former habitations, thus: one birth, two births, three... four... five... ten... twenty... thirty... forty... fifty... a hundred... a thousand... a hundred thousand births, and many an eon of integration and many an eon of disintegration and many an eon of integration-disintegration: 'Such a one was I by name, having such a clan, such and such a colour, so was I nourished, such and such pleasant and painful experiences were mine, so did the span of life end. Passing from this, I came to be in another state where such a one was I by name, having such and such a clan, such and such a colour, so was I nourished, such and such pleasant and painful

---

previously, has attained to the first *jhāna,* or, which seems more probable, it is meant to indicate that the intensive practice of Satipaṭṭhāna which, through emphasis on bare observation, tends to reduce discursive thought, and enables the meditator to enter directly into the second *jhāna,* which is free from initial and discursive thought (*vitakka-vicāra*). This latter explanation is favoured by the facts that (1) in our text, the practice of Satipaṭṭhāna is preceded by the temporary abandonment of the five Hindrances, which indicates a high degree of concentration approaching that of the *jhāna;* (2) in our text, the meditator is advised not to engage in the *thought about* the body, feelings, etc. — that is, in discursive thinking, which is still present in the first *jhāna.* [Ed., *The Wheel*].

experiences were mine, so did the span of life end. Passing from this, I arose here.' Thus he remembers divers former habitations in all their modes and details.

2. The Divine Eye

"Then with the mind composed, quite purified, quite clarified, without blemish, without defilement, grown pliant and workable, fixed, immovable, he directs his mind to the knowledge of the passing hence and the arising of beings. With the purified *deva*-vision surpassing that of men, he sees beings as they pass hence or come to be; he comprehends that beings are mean, excellent, comely, ugly, well-going, ill-going, according to the consequence of their deeds, and he thinks: Indeed these worthy beings who were possessed of wrong conduct in body, who were possessed of wrong conduct of speech, who were possessed of wrong conduct of thought, scoffers at the ariyans, holding a wrong view, incurring deeds consequent on a wrong view — these, at the breaking up of the body after dying, have arisen in a sorrowful state, a bad bourn, the abyss, Niraya hell. But these worthy beings who were possessed of good conduct in body, who were possessed of good conduct in speech, who were possessed of good conduct in thought, who did not scoff at the ariyans, holding a right view, incurring deeds consequent on a right view — these, at the breaking up of the body, after dying, have arisen in a good bourn, a heaven world.

3. Destruction of Cankers: Sainthood

"Then with the mind composed... immovable, he directs his mind to the knowledge of the destruction of the cankers.[15] He understands as it really is: This is anguish,[16] this is the arising of anguish, this is the stopping of anguish, this is the course leading to the stopping of anguish. He understands as it really is: These are the cankers; this is the arising of the cankers; this is the stopping of the cankers; this is the course leading to the stopping of the cankers. Knowing thus, seeing this, his mind is freed from the canker of sense pleasures, is freed from the canker of becoming,

15. *āsava.*

16. *dukkha:* usually rendered by "suffering" or "ill" [Ed., *The Wheel*].

freed from the canker of ignorance. In freedom the knowledge came to be: I am freed; and he comprehends: Destroyed is birth, brought to a close is the Holy Life, done is what was to be done; there is no more of being such or such.

"That monk is able to endure, heat, cold, hunger, thirst, the touch of mosquitoes, gadflies, wind, sun and creeping things, abusive language and unwelcome modes of speech: he has grown to bear bodily feelings which as they arise are painful, acute, sharp, severe, wretched, miserable, deadly. Purged of all the dross and impurities of attachment, aversion and confusion,[17] he is worthy of oblations, offerings, respect and homage, an unsurpassed field of merit in the world.

"If, Aggivessana, a king's elephant dies in old age, untamed, untrained, the king's old elephant that has died is reckoned as one that has died untamed. And so, Aggivessana, of a king's elephant that is middle-aged. And too, Aggivessana, if a king's elephant dies young, untamed, untrained, the king's young elephant that has died is reckoned as one that has died untamed. Even so, Aggivessana, if a monk who is an elder dies with the cankers not destroyed, the monk who is an elder that has died is reckoned as one that has died untamed. And so of a monk of middle standing. And too, Aggivessana, if a newly ordained monk dies with the cankers not destroyed, the newly ordained monk that has died is reckoned as one that has died untamed. If, Aggivessana, a king's elephant dies in old age, well tamed, well trained, the king's old elephant that has died is reckoned as one that has died tamed. And so, Aggivessana of a king's elephant that is middle-aged. And too, Aggivessana, if a king's elephant dies young, well tamed, well trained, the king's young elephant that has died is reckoned as one that has died tamed. Even so, Aggivessana, if a monk who is an elder dies with the cankers destroyed, the monk who is an elder that has died is reckoned as one that has died tamed. And so, Aggivessana, of a monk of middle standing. And too, Aggivessana, if a newly ordained monk dies with cankers destroyed, the newly ordained monk that has died is reckoned as one that has died tamed."

Thus spoke the Lord. Delighted, the novice Aciravata rejoiced in what the Lord had said.

---

17. *rāga, dosa, moha.*

5. Dantikā's Verses

(Therīgāthā vv. 48-50)

Coming from noonday rest on Vulture's Peak
I saw an elephant, his bathing done,
Forth from the river issue.

And a man, taking his goad,
bade the great creature stretch his foot:
"Give me your foot."

The elephant obeyed,
and to his neck the driver sprang.
I saw the untamed tamed,
I saw him bent to master's will;
and marking inwardly,
I passed into the forest depths and there
In faith I trained and ordered all my heart.

From *Psalms of the Sisters*
Translated by C.A.F. Rhys Davids

6. The Goad

Aṅguttara-Nikāya, Fours, No. 113

"Monks, these four goodly thoroughbred steeds are found existing in the world. What four?

"In this case, monks, we may have a certain goodly thoroughbred steed which at the very sight of the shadow of the goad-stick is stirred, feels agitation [thinking:] 'What task, I wonder, will the trainer set me today? What return can I make him?'[18] Here, monks, we may have such a steed, and this is the first sort of goodly thoroughbred steed found existing in the world.

"Then again, monks, we may have a certain goodly thoroughbred steed which is not stirred at the mere sight of the goad-stick's shadow, feels no agitation, but when his coat is pricked with the goad, he is stirred, feels agitation [thinking:] 'What task, I wonder...' This is the second sort...

"Then again, monks, we may have a certain goodly thoroughbred steed which is not stirred... at the sight of the goad-stick's shade, nor yet when his coat is pricked with the goad, but when his flesh is pierced, he is stirred, he feels agitated [thinking:] 'What task, I wonder...' This is the third sort...

"Once more, monks, we may have a goodly thoroughbred steed which is stirred neither at the sight of the goad-stick's shade nor when his coat is pricked, nor yet when his flesh is pierced by the goad-stick; but when he is pierced to the very bone, he is stirred, feels agitation [thinking:] 'What task, I wonder, will the trainer set me today? What return can I make him?' Here we have such a goodly thoroughbred steed... This is the fourth sort.

"Thus, monks, these four goodly thoroughbred steeds are found existing in the world.

"Just in the same way, monks, these four goodly thoroughbred men are found existing in the world. What four?

"In this case, monks, we may have a certain goodly thoroughbred man who hears it said that in such and such a village or township is a woman or a man afflicted or dead. Thereat he is stirred, he feels agitation. Thus agitated he strictly applies himself. Thus applied he both realises in his own person the supreme truth, and sees it by penetrating it with wisdom. Just as, monks, that goodly thoroughbred steed on seeing the shadow of the goad-stick is stirred, feels agitation, even so using this figure do I speak of this goodly thoroughbred man. Such in this case is the goodly thoroughbred man. This is the first sort...

"Again, monks, here we may have a goodly thoroughbred man who does not hear it said that in such a village or township is

---

18. *Kiṃ paṭikaromi* seems to mean that the horse intends to do his best in return for the training. (Translator)—Alternative rendering: 'Should I not respond (or: obey him)?'

a woman or a man afflicted or dead, but with his own eyes beholds such. Thereupon he is stirred, he feels agitation (*as above*)... Just as, monks, that goodly thoroughbred steed on having his coat pricked with the goad stirred... even so using this figure do I speak of this goodly thoroughbred man... Such in this case is... This is the second sort...

"Then again, monks, here we may have a goodly thoroughbred man who does not hear it said... nor yet with his own eyes beholds a woman or a man afflicted or dead, but his own kinsman or blood-relation is afflicted or dead. Thereupon he is stirred... just as, monks, that goodly thoroughbred steed on having his flesh pierced is stirred... even so using this figure do I speak of this goodly thoroughbred man... Such in this case... This is the third sort.

"Once more, monks, here we may have a goodly thoroughbred man who neither hears it said... nor yet with his own eyes beholds... nor is his own kinsman or blood-relation afflicted or dead, but he himself is stricken with painful bodily feelings, grievous, sharp, racking, distracting, discomforting, that drain the life away. Thereat he is stirred, he feels agitation. Being so stirred he strictly applies himself. Thus applied he both realises in his own person the supreme truth, and sees it by penetrating it with wisdom. Just as, monks, that goodly thoroughbred steed on being pierced to the very bone is stirred, feels agitation, even so using this figure do I speak of this goodly thoroughbred man. Of such a sort, monks, is the goodly thoroughbred man in this case. This is the fourth sort.

"These, monks, are the four sorts of thoroughbreds among men found existing in the world."

From *Gradual Sayings*, The Book of the Fours,
Translated by F.L. Woodward. (Pali Text Society, London)

7. The Chapter on the Mind

(Dhammapada)

Just as a fletcher straightens an arrow, so does the wise man straighten his mind which is fickle and unsteady and difficult to guard and difficult to restrain. (33)

Just as a fish taken out of its watery abode and cast on land, quivers and throbs, so does the mind. (Hence) should the realm of Passions be shunned. (34)

It is good to restrain the mind which is difficult to subdue and is swift-moving and which seizes whatever it desires. A mind thus tamed brings happiness. (35)

Difficult to grasp and extremely subtle is this mind, seizing on whatever it desires; let the wise guard it. A guarded mind brings happiness. (36)

This mind wanders afar, is solitary, formless, and rests in the cave (of the heart). Those who subdue it are freed from the bonds of Māra. (37)

He whose mind is not steadfast and who knows not the Good Teaching and whose faith wavers, the wisdom of such a man never becomes perfect. (38)

He whose mind remains untouched by lust, and unaffected by hatred, and who has discarded both good and evil, for such a vigilant one there is no fear. (39)

Knowing this body to be as fragile as a clay pot and fortifying this mind like a well-fortified city, let a man fight Māra with the sword of wisdom; and let him guard his conquest and remain unattached (to it). (40)

Ere long alas! will this body lie upon the earth, unheeded and lifeless, even as a useless log. (41)

Whatever an enemy may do to an enemy or a hater to a hater, an ill-directed mind would do one a greater injury. (42)

Neither mother nor father nor any other relative can do a person greater good than what his well-directed mind can do. (43)

Dhammapada, Citta Vagga
Translated by Bhikkhu Buddarakkhita

Pathways of Buddhist Thought

Four Essays

by

Ñāṇamoli Thera

WHEEL PUBLICATION NO. 52/53

Copyright © Kandy: Buddhist Publication Society (1963, 1983)

Preface

The essays presented here have been collected from the posthumous papers of the late English Bhikkhu, the Venerable Ñāṇamoli. They are issued in commemoration of his premature death on 8th March 1960, aged 55. A short biographical sketch of the author may be found in a memorial booklet issued by this Society on the occasion of his death.

Since the publication of that memorial booklet, the following translations from the pen of Ñāṇamoli Thera have been issued by the Pali Text Society in London: *Minor Readings and Illustrator (Khuddakapāṭha and Commentary)*, 1960; *The Guide (Nettippakaraṇa)*, 1962; *Piṭaka-Disclosure (Peṭakopadesa)*, 1964; and *Path of Discrimination (Paṭisambhidāmagga)*, 1982.

While his translations bear witness to the Venerable Author's mature scholarship, the essays here show other aspects of his rich personality. Here is a mind at work that was not satisfied with facile answers, a mind of rare penetrative insight and clarity. It is hoped that these pages will prove stimulating and helpful to the thoughtful reader.

Buddhist Publication Society

Buddhism: a Religion or a Philosophy?

Sometimes the question is heard: "Is Buddhism a religion or a philosophy?" And sometimes the answer comes readily: "It is a religion." "But why?" "Well isn't religion a matter of observances? And the Eightfold Path is largely observance, with Right Speech and so on. So Buddhism is a religion, like any other." Or it may come just as readily: "It is not a religion; it is a philosophy." "Why?" "Because it doesn't rely on blind faith but emphasises understanding. It is the way of Reason. And isn't Right View philosophy?" Or someone may say: "It is neither a religion nor a philosophy; it is an ethico-philosophical system." Who is right? Are they all right, some right, or none?

We may have read somewhere that religion is a matter of emotions and that philosophy is rational. If we fly to the dictionaries for help, we may well come away in this case more uncertain than before, as to define "Buddhism," "religion," and "philosophy" from the dictionaries is no easy matter. (But if we once begin to inquire from them what exactly the word "is" implies, we shall soon find ourselves in a pretty tangle, as anyone can see for themselves if they would like to try.)

But if we are not sure what we mean by religion or philosophy (let alone the word "is"), can we attempt to answer the question at all? Suppose we do agree on a meaning for those two words; are we right in supposing that the question is rightly put, and put in such a way that some correct answer is possible if it can be found?

Are, in fact, all religions and philosophies each just *a* religion and *a* philosophy among a crowd, and is Buddhism *necessarily* one among this crowd? What then would be the unique Olympian point of view, able to survey all those religions and philosophies, and able to class them and pigeon-hole them so readily and neatly?

There used to be a recognized type of question in ancient Greece which committed the answerer equally, whether he replied affirmatively or negatively. One was "Do you use a thick stick when you beat your wife? Answer yes or no." Now, whether the answer was "Yes" or "No," the retort was "So you *do* beat your wife, then." There are many questions of that type, and some of them not at all evidently so.

Why not pause (there is no hurry) before plumping for a one-sided answer, and take a quick glance at the way in which the Buddha handles and presents his whole teaching.

One thing among many others to be noticed here is that he is careful to spread a net with which to intercept all speculative views. This is the *Brahmajāla*, the "Divine Net," which as the first discourse of the whole Sutta Piṭaka forms as it were a kind of filter for the mind; or to change the analogy, a tabulation by whose means (if rightly used) all speculative views can be identified, traced down to the fallacy or unjustified assumption from which they spring, and neutralized. This Net, in fact, classifies all possible speculative views (rationalist or irrationalist) under a scheme of sixty-two types.

These 62 types are not descriptions of individual philosophies of other individual teachers contemporary with the Buddha (a number of those are mentioned as well elsewhere in the Suttas), but are the comprehensive net (after revealing the basic assumptions on which these speculative views all grow) with which to catch *any* wrong viewpoints that can be put forward. (Ultimately, these must all be traceable to the contact of self-identification in some form, however misinterpreted, but that cannot be gone into here.)

But why bring in this here, it may well be asked. Because, instead of accepting the question "Is Buddhism a religion or a philosophy?" and attempting an answer straight off, we can step back for a moment. We can ask ourselves if, by replying "It is a philosophy," we may not be making out that the Buddha was actually teaching one of the types of wrong view catchable in the Divine Net, against which that net should protect us. Then the Buddha denounces ritualism (*sīlabbata-parāmāsa*) as a vain waste of time bound to lead to disappointment. If we take practice of rites to be a religion, or unjustified and unverifiable emotional beliefs, to then say "Buddhism is a religion" is to imply that Buddhism teaches the very rite-ridden blindness of gullible credulity that the Buddha himself so plainly denounces.

There is, of course, no end to the arguments that can be churned out on both sides. The dialectic goes on oscillating with no resolution, till cut short by sheer weariness, or till some eloquent plea lulls us into thinking the matter is settled once and for all. Or we may just accept one side and forget about it for the time. But it will be reopened again for sure sooner or later, and the dialectic will resume its pendulum-swing. With the best will in the world, though, and the most tireless patience and brilliant dialectic skill, is there really anywhere to go, any solution to be found, on these lines? What are we to do, then?

In the Aṅguttara Nikāya, the Buddha divides questions into four kinds. Some can be answered unilaterally (yes or no). Some have to be analysed before answering. Others must be dealt with by a counter-question (making the questioner produce material out of himself that shows him how things are). And lastly there are some that cannot be answered at all. (They are like the one above about thick and thin sticks, for they make the answerer affirm an assumption, whatever he replies.) These must be entirely set aside.

Now a question, as long as it remains a question, is a dialectic; and when it is answered, the dialectic is unilaterally resolved.

In his fourfold classification of questions (dialectics), the Buddha may be taken to be communicating how to treat dialectics. There are two forms of communication. They have been called the "didactic" and the "existential." The first says, "This is like this; this is what has to be done," while the second tends to set forth the basic elements of a situation and leave it to the other to discover for himself the act-of-discovery that can be made on the basis of those elements set forth. Didactically one can tell someone how to cook a dish by communicating the recipe, but the satisfying of hunger, the discovery of cooking, and how good the dish is in the eating, can only be communicated existentially. It must be lived.

Now to return to the four types of questions and ways of communicating answers, as communicated to us by the Buddha: first, any question is a dialectic. The first type of question is answerable didactically. It is the kind of dialectic where both sides are already evident, which can and ought to be resolved by a unilateral answer (the authority for such a resolution being always accurate observation without forgetting what has been accurately observed). Examples of such unilateral decisions would be: choosing giving and not avarice; choosing kindness, not hate or anger; choosing unilateral keeping of the five precepts unbroken (since the Buddha observed that breaking them entails pain, such being the observable nature of existence for a Buddha who sees how it is), and so on. The highest form in which this unilateral decision is expressed is in the form of the Noble Eightfold Path, in choosing the Right and rejecting the Wrong. (Regarded in this way, the Path appears not as an observance, a rationalist scheme or a duty, but as a practical way to end suffering.) This is a didactic communication which communicates the unilateral resolution of a dialectic for a clear reason without mystification.

The second type of question (that answerable after analysis) can be regarded as a dialectic, one side of which is hidden or partly hidden, both sides of which need bringing clearly to light, and one whose ambiguity should be displayed didactically. Whether it can then be answered, or partly answered, unilaterally is here of secondary importance. The important thing is not to "buy a pig in a poke" by answering unilaterally a question one has not yet fully understood. The doubleness of the dialectic involved, until it has been brought to light by analysis, lurks concealed, can be harmful, and mislead. Such a question would be "Does the Buddha condemn all asceticism?" Before answering, the main debatable points involved should be clearly displayed.

The third type has to be dealt with by a counter-question. It makes the questioner dig out of his own mind the elements that prompt him to ask it. These, when thus brought to light by himself, give him the opportunity to discover how he went wrong in formulating his question. He can discover for himself that the supposed dialectic of his question is fictitious and that the truth lies elsewhere. This is not a didactic communication at all but an existential one. The questioner is not told didactically what to do; he is existentially given the opportunity to discover for himself. (What is discovered may be didactically communicable, but the act-of-discovery is not.) The Buddha's teaching (that of the Four Truths together) is at heart an existential communication in this sense. (An example would be the "Gaṇaka Moggallāna Sutta," MN 107.)

The fourth type of question, which must be avoided, is that which traps the answerer, either purposely or unwittingly, into affirming an unjustifiable assumption, whether he answers negatively or affirmatively. (It is well recognized in logic how a denial necessarily implies the prior affirmation of what is denied or negated.) The best examples of such questions are this set of four: "Does the Tathāgata exist after death?" "Does he not exist after death?" "Does he both exist and not exist after death?" "Does he neither exist nor not exist after death?" None of these the Buddha consented to answer. "Was it because he was an agnostic?" some people have asked. But that very question shows that the existential communication has failed in the questioner. For besides the fact that to describe the Buddha (the Awakened One) as agnostic is rather a quaint contradiction, the point is overlooked that the four questions about the Tathāgata existing after death or not all contain an assumption which the answers yes and no alike affirm: they are all ultimately begged questions.

We may seem to have by now wandered rather far from the original query: "Is Buddhism a religion or a philosophy?" But two things have come to light. The first is that if we answer in too much of a hurry one way or the other, we may unwittingly be making out that Buddhism "is" either one of the speculative views which are caught by the Buddha's own Divine Net (the *Brahmajāla*), or that it "is" one of the ritualistic observances of blind faith condemned by the Buddha as bound to disappoint. The second is that, before undertaking to answer, we may ask ourselves which of the four types of questions this one falls under.

Yet before we start doing that, which might well involve us again deeply in dialectics, let us take another look at the way the Buddha sometimes gives his teaching. He was, in fact, asked a question whose essentials were much the same though the details were different. It was the night of the Buddha's Parinibbāna, and the wanderer Subhadda went to him and asked: "Master Gotama, there are these monks and divines with their congregations, teachers of congregations, famous philosophers whom many regard as saints....Have they all direct acquaintance of what they claim, or none of them, or have some and some not?" The Buddha's reply was this: "Enough, Subhadda. Let that be. I shall teach you the Dhamma." And he went on to expound the Eightfold Path. Now the Noble Eightfold Path is one of the Four Noble Truths. The Noble Truth of Suffering, the Noble Truth of the Origin of Suffering (which is need), the Noble Truth of the Cessation of Suffering (which is cessation of need), and the Noble Truth of the Way leading to cessation of suffering (which is the Eightfold Path). These four Truths (termed "truth" (*sacca*) because they do not deceive, are founded on actual experience and nothing else, and cannot disappoint) are called the "teaching peculiar to Buddhas" (*Buddhānaṃ sāmukkaṃsika-desanā*), since it is precisely this teaching by which a Buddha is recognizable and distinguished.

Religion tends to rely upon faith alone, and philosophy on understanding alone. But the Buddha, in his teaching of the Truths, stresses the even balancing of five faculties. They are those of faith, energy, mindfulness, concentration, and understanding. While mindfulness can never be overdone, the others, if one-sidedly overdeveloped or repressed, may distort the character, outlook, and spiritual health that resides in their even balancing. Faith alone is blind credulity and gambles against disappointment. Over-exerted energy agitates and distracts. Too much concentration tends to sleep and quietism, while understanding unsupported by the others degenerates into craftiness and cunning. When all are being properly managed, faith functions as confidence in the ability of the others to resist opposition and to reach their fulfilment in liberation from suffering.

All the five are perfectly familiar because they are present to some extent, however small, in everyone. No one can act at all without at least faith that his act will bring the desired result. Everyone has the energy to show life. Without mindfulness nothing at all could ever be remembered or recognized. Every time we hold a thought for the shortest space of time we concentrate. And no one could ever place their faith at all, however strong or weak, without making some judgment, however bad, where to place it. Such are these five faculties at their bare inescapable minimum. And these same faculties, the Buddha says, "end in the Deathless," which is the end of greed, hate, and delusion, the end of suffering. They are with us always.

The Eightfold Path has eight factors: right view, right intention, right speech, right action, right livelihood, right effort, right mindfulness, and right concentration. The five faculties are (to repeat) faith, energy, mindfulness, concentration, and understanding. What has the one set to do with the other? Faith (which is faith in the other four faculties) undertakes the three path factors that constitute virtue, namely right speech, action and livelihood; for these are first undertaken (like any other action) in the faith that they will lead to the development of the rest and to the ending of suffering. Energy is right effort. Mindfulness is right mindfulness. Concentration is right concentration. Understanding is right understanding and right intention. In this way, the five faculties correspond to the Eightfold Path. They are the Path's raw material. In this way too the Eightfold Path is clearly not faith alone, and so is not adequately or rightly described as an observance (observance of ritual), that is, as a religion. It is equally clearly not understanding alone, and so is not adequately or rightly described as purely rationalistic in the sense of limited to logic (suffering is not a logical category, nor is liberation), that is, a philosophy. Again, while it certainly has its ethical and philosophical aspects (the first steps in the Path are right intention, speech, action, and livelihood; the second, mundane right view), and is certainly systematic, not chaotic or incoherent, yet it is not adequately or rightly to be pigeonholed as an ethico-philosophical system. The Buddha said, "I teach only suffering and the liberation from suffering," and he said, "As the ocean has only one taste, that of salt, so my teaching has only one taste, that of liberation." That seems hardly a mere system.

But is Buddhism a religion or philosophy? Would the reader not like to deal with this for himself?

Does Saddhā Mean Faith? Part I

Sheer ignorance, gullibility, credulity, belief, faith, trust, confidence, certainty, knowledge—set out like that, the words seem to form a sort of spectrum with faith (most disputed of all the shades) somewhere in the middle.

Perhaps it is that very middle aspect of faith which makes it so liable to distortions in opposite directions; for not only is it in the middle in that sense, and not only is it an essential mediating relation between subject and object, but also it stands in between lack of knowledge and the need to know. So some see it only as pure limpid spontaneity of Truth and the noblest Human Faculty, for which no price is too high to pay, while others deride it as a wretched, even worthless, substitute for knowledge. Many try a hand at defining it, arriving at oddly diverse conclusions.

Bewildered from time to time in this way by his betters, some ordinary man (whose knowledge is limited and who wants to believe something) may ask, "But what does the word 'faith' mean? What are we talking about?" At once the extremists chip in again: "Faith is the Noblest Attribute of Man," "Faith is a drug for fools," "It must be cherished for ever," "It wants chucking out good and proper," they cry. Then the ordinary man, looking for a compromise, mostly uses his native faith in order, ostrich-like, to hide his head in a dune of euphemisms, saying perhaps something about "needing confidence." But "You can't always trust your own ears," he mutters incredulously to himself.

Others less procrustean may say (driving wedges between words) "To believe only in possibilities is not faith" (Sir Thomas Browne after Tertullian), or (making specious definitions of the faculty itself) "Belief, like any other moving body, follows the path of least resistance" (Samuel Butler), or (attempting to define its object) "The essential characteristic of a materialist doctrine is 'belief in something not dependent on our knowledge of it'" (W.W. Carington, quoting Prof. J.B.S. Haldane, in *Mind, Matter and Meaning*), or else (painting word-pictures) "I've caught belief like a disease; I've fallen into belief like I fell in love" (Graham Greene), and so on. Fanned by these doldrum gusts, the ordinary man drifts this way and that; he doubts here, puts his faith there, and sometimes he is right and often wrong.

Now a dispassionate glance into matters of the heart is notoriously difficult. But, if the effort is made, it can be perceived that exclamations about "Noblest Attributes" and "wretched substitutes" are just evocative haranguings, ways of trying to push people into thinking as one does oneself, or as one thinks they ought to think (as the case may be), perhaps with the best of motives. They appear as an aspect of human behaviour telling quite a lot about the speaker's personal attitude, but precious little about faith considered as a component of experience: whether it is, for example, good or bad in itself or unavoidable. Tending covertly as they do to the extremes of rationalism or irrationalism, none of them (not even the subtle ones) examine experience or even attempt an inquiry into why the ordinary man does not just gullibly do as he is told. Why does he not? Is it because, when pushed too far, his common sense tells him that he can't?

Let us look a little closer. Let us consider for a moment the question of action (of doing, or even saying or thinking, something). An ordinary man sees the past as decided ("What's done can't be undone."), but the future as semi-foreseeable though undecided ("You can never be sure how it will turn out."). So when he acts purposively, intending to do what he does (which always happens now), he seems to do so guided by what he remembers of the past and by some measure of faith (or expectation) that his present acts will not have a too inappropriate result in the rather uncertain future. Still he can never be quite sure: doubts haunt him constantly.

That indeed is the pattern of the ordinary human situation: a state of being committed in a changing scene, of (moral) certainty about a definite-seeming past, of present knowledge of acts by restricted free choice which there is no escaping, and of guessing at a more or less indefinite future potentiality, which one hopes (with a grain of justification) to influence because one believes that things will go on happening roughly as they have done. That too is the pattern which makes life valuable and tolerable for the gambler. And who never gambles in his heart?

On that basis, if such a very rough sketch is provisionally accepted, faith (or call it what you will—give a dog a bad name and hang it, but a rose by any other name is just as sweet) as a chancy expectation of results is, it seems, inevitably present in some form in every act done; there would be no doing anything without it. While one has knowledge of what one is doing now, even if it is only that one is sitting still and doubting, faith alone can cope with the unknown future (as it is apprehended) and decide why one does what one does. Such humdrum faith as that neither needs any special advertising as "noble" nor can it be "chucked out." It is simply a commonplace necessity.

So it is that parents send children to school in the faith that what is taught there will help the children to make a living. Those same children, when adults, delegate some of their influence by vote to governments in the faith that society will thus cater better for their needs. Through faith in the order of Nature those same adults, when old, sense death edging nearer: an impending ambivalent catastrophe that as surely blots out from their certainty all form of the future as it seems an inescapable plunge into it.

Faith is left a free hand here though men have a general intellectual certainty that their physical death will take place (regardless of any considerations of immortality). Other people's bodies are seen to die, but, it is pointed out by Freud, the Unconscious, while accepting that, absolutely rejects its own mortality. Though material bodies only too publicly die and disintegrate, at the same time no materialist theory is capable of proving (in any sense of that word) that physical death is the end, or physical birth the beginning, of conscious activity. Hence the ambivalence of the catastrophe. Hence too the fact that faith is forced willy-nilly to exercise a free hand here.

Faith normally manifests itself as one of three particular types of belief, that is, it must absolutely take on one of them so long as there is ignorance and action. It is, (1) a dogma asserting that something of them will survive the catastrophe, or (2) a dogma asserting that nothing of them at all will survive, or (3) radical agnosticism denying that any knowledge beforehand is possible. Depending on which of the types of belief people assume (and one of the three apparently must be assumed) their behaviour will vary. Any act whatsoever, then, involves (where there is ignorance) one of these three assumptions indirectly or directly. To be born is to die, and to live as the ordinary man does is to act; to be in space-time is to be unsure of a future one is sure to encounter.

The reservation "where there is ignorance" has been made, for ignorance, as we shall see, has an organic relation with faith (which is what the ignorant have to rely on in the acts they are obliged to perform). Will anyone deny that the ordinary man is constantly bothered by immediate ignorance (about the weather tomorrow; the contents of an examination paper; what the person he is talking to is thinking; the price of goods next week; whether his memory can be trusted or not; what will happen to him), or that he is ever without some measure of it, let alone ignorance of what is going on beyond his horizons, and may burst into his world? Then since he cannot avoid doing things ("But what are we going to do, if something happens?"), he has to take risks, to supplement by faith his lack of certain knowledge, to act as if the weather will be such and such tomorrow, and this kind we may call first-degree ignorance, which goes with simple faith. "Take what you will, but pay the price," says Emerson.

But the ordinary man is also subject to desires, needs, fear, and pain. Because he attaches importance to the results of his acts, the lack of certainty inherent in faith is often odious to him (for all that he may like a gamble now and then). Whenever facts do not prohibit his doing so, his desires prompt him to treat the faith, by which he acts, as if it were knowledge ("It's a dead cert!"), and he may well quite honestly forget that he does not know. His defence against fear and pain is forgetting (a mode of ignorance, which, at its deepest, takes the form of death). But if he cannot quite forget, if his forgetting mechanism fails him, he may dope himself with self-deception, refusing both to question his faith and to test its object. This we may call second-degree ignorance, which loses sight not only of the limits of knowledge but of truth as well. With that, his faith has become bad faith. "If bad faith is possible at all," says a modern writer, "it is because it is an immediate and constant threat to every human project; it is because consciousness hides within its very being a permanent risk of bad faith." Bad faith, however, is not a lie, since the essence of a lie implies that the liar is completely aware of the truth which he dissembles. "One no longer lies when one deceives oneself." Bad faith, in short, both refuses to face all one knows and vetoes any investigation into whether the faith is well placed or not. "O take the cash and let the credit go," says Omar Khayyam's translator. (And if the cash runs out, they'll sure let us live on time!)

At any time an ordinary man may become fed up with the consequences of misplacing his own faith or by seeing the silly things other people sometimes do out of faith. Blaming the faith instead of the misplacing of it, he may decide to throw it overboard altogether (away with all bath water and babies too), and become a Cynic or a Rationalist. But has he not merely deceived himself once more in fancying it can be jettisoned like that, for he still has ignorance and still has to act? Even despair is no more than a mode of bad faith: faith that the situation is irremediable with refusal to seek an escape. The self-gulling goes on, and so does the risk of disappointment, anger and frustration. If he is healthy, young, and lucky, perhaps he can forget about it and begin all over again. Forgetting is a very useful kind of ignorance: it wipes the bad sums off our slates.

What is the answer, then? Must one either leave the baby unbathed or bottle the bath water? Surely not. The first thing to be done is to reduce ignorance to the "first degree," to become aware that one is ignorant and how one is ignorant, facing up to it courageously and remembering it, regardless of hopes and fears. That is enough for the Goal, isn't it? What more can be done? After all, faith has been shown to be a practical necessity for the ordinary man. Without it indeed all profitable and unprofitable action, as well as all possibility of remedying suffering, must be paralysed. And how richly it ennobles! It is the source of all inspiration. The rapturous leap of faith at Great Moments exhilarates, uplifts, and transfigures. Faith attends all good things. Faith that the very ground will receive one's foot prevents the vertiginous sensation of falling into a chasm every time one steps forward. Faith is Life, and it must be good in itself. How can it be otherwise? If the right dogma can be found, is not that the answer, the realistic answer? Why cry for the moon?

True, faith is a practical necessity for the ordinary man. That is indeed what we have been trying to show. But how can the Right Dogma ever be found, and can it be absolutely trusted without a grain of bad faith as we have described it? And is faith then to be the goal, in which case is ignorance to remain with us for evermore? Examination of what both the theists and the atheist materialists have offered as dogma from the dawn of history down to the present day, a long time and a wide choice, is far from encouraging (consoling, doubtless but utterly inconclusive). The rather arid alternative seems to be Radical Agnosticism, which is what is usually meant by the phrase "no faith"; no faith, that is, in the heaven the theists offer only after death, or in the substance of matter here and now which the materialists admit can inherently never be known at all and doesn't matter after death anyway.

Why bother, though? Perhaps the world is not such a bad place after all. They say there is plenty of good in it if you look, so forget about the unpleasant side of it. Agnosticism tomorrow, then, and dogma today. "Gather ye roses while ye may," as luck may be on our side.

Dogma or agnosticism. But before we choose, before we risk our faith going bad on us, let us take one more look.

(Editor's Note: The following paragraph in handwriting was found among the late author's papers, together with this essay and carrying the note "above at the end of Pt. 1." Since the insertion of it would have necessitated adjustments in the given manuscript, it was preferable to reproduce this paragraph separately. Its fitting place would be before the second last paragraph of the above text.)

Then if neither dogma nor agnosticism will do, why not be satisfied with some form of the critical humanism of 18th to 19th century Europe? Criticism has been incalculably productive, and we owe to it all the material advances we enjoy today. It is criticism that has allowed science a free hand to question and experiment. Granted that Criticism (as Inquiry) merits all that praise and far more. But that is as a means. If Criticism is to be made the goal, the summum bonnum, against what can it be tested? A fundamental weakness always remains in the position of the critic: if he discloses his own standpoint, that standpoint is open to criticism from some other. That is why it is rare that the academic scholar, who employs the so-called "higher criticism" can afford to state his own position in positive terms. When the English Prime Minister Disraeli was asked what his religion was, it is said that he replied "My religion is that of all wise men." "But what is that, Mr. Disraeli?" "Wise men never say." Criticism requires that the critic be uncommitted, that he is, or pretends he is, outside what he criticises. The professional critic's very being depends on dialectics, the food that keeps him alive is other people's standpoints. As a means this may be invaluable; as an end it can never amount to more than an ordered form of agnosticism.

Does Saddhā Mean Faith? Part II

To "Gather ye roses while ye may," would be fine if there were "roses, roses all the way." But will our simple faith really stretch that far? Hardly.

Soon after the Buddha had attained enlightenment he surveyed the world with the new vision he had achieved. He did not see only roses. He uttered this exclamation: "This world is racked by exposure to the contact [of pain]. Even what the world calls self is in fact ill; for no matter upon what it bases its conceit [of self], the fact is ever other than these [which the conceit conceives]. To be is to become: but the world has committed itself to being, delights only in being; yet wherein it delights brings fear, and what it fears is pain. Now this Life Divine is lived to abandon pain" (Ud 3.10). He was not alone in this estimation of the world: "Here, bhikkhus, some clansman goes forth out of faith [*saddhā*] from the home life into homelessness [considering] 'I am a victim of birth, ageing and death.... I am exposed to pain. Surely an end to this whole aggregate mass of suffering is described?" (MN 29).

Now in this situation how does the Buddha show the function of faith? "One who has faith [*saddhā*] succeeds, Mahānāma, not one who has no faith" (AN 11:12).

Here the question at once intrudes: Is the translation of "*saddhā*" by "faith" justified? Let us try it out and see, for the contexts in which it appears will be the test. We shall be strictly consistent in our renderings. The Buddha speaks of five Faculties, or human potentialities, through whose means an ignorant ordinary man may emerge from ignorance to right understanding, and so from suffering to its cessation. They are faith (*saddhā*), energy, mindfulness, concentration, and understanding (as "mother wit" to start with). If they can be maintained in being against opposition, they are called Powers (SN 48:43). Managed by reasoned attention (*yoniso manasikāra*, awareness of the organic structure of experience), and carefully balanced, they build each other up. Maintained in being and cultivated, they merge into the Deathless (SN 48:57).

The Buddha speaks of faith as one of the seven noble treasures (AN 7:4), one of the seven true ideas (DN 33), one of the five factors of endeavour (MN 8), as an idea "on the side of enlightenment"

(SN 48:51), as a fount of great merit (Aṅguttara Ṭīkā 41), as one of the three forms of growth (Aṅguttara Ṭīkā 48), which "brings five advantages" (AN 5:38).

And then, "Where is the faith faculty to be met with? Among the four Factors of Stream-entry." (SN 48:8). "A Stream-enterer [of whom more below] has absolute confidence [*pasāda*] in the Enlightened One, in the True Idea [the Dhamma], and in the Community, and he has the virtue beloved of Noble Ones" (SN 55:1). Four other factors of Stream-entry are frequenting True Men, hearing the True Idea, reasoned attention, and the putting into practice of ideas that are in accordance with the True Idea (SN 55:5).

"What is the faith faculty? Here a noble disciple who has faith places his faith in a Tathāgata thus: 'This Blessed One is such since he is accomplished and fully enlightened, perfect in true knowledge and conduct, sublime, knower of worlds, incomparable leader of men to be tamed, enlightened, blessed.'" (SN 48:9) "If these five faculties are absolutely perfected, they make an Accomplished One [Arahant]; if a little weaker, a Non-returner; if a little weaker still, a Once-returner; if a little weaker still, a Stream-enterer; if a little weaker still, One Mature in Faith or One Mature in the True Idea" (SN 48:12). "Those who have not known, seen, found, realized, touched with understanding, may go by faith in others that [these five faculties] when maintained in being and developed merge in the Deathless ... but on knowing, seeing, finding, realizing, and touching with understanding, there is no more doubt or uncertainty that when maintained in being and developed they merge in the Deathless" (SN 48:44).

But then, does not the Buddha say in the Kālāma Sutta, "Come, Kālāmas, [do] not [be satisfied] with hearsay-learning or with tradition or with legendary lore or with what has come down in scripture or with conjecture or with logical inference or with weighing evidence or with choice of a view after pondering it or with someone else's ability or with the thought 'The monk is our teacher'"? Is not that an injunction to have nothing to do with faith, to "throw away your books," as Marcus Aurelius says, and listen to no one at all?

If that statement of the Buddha's is taken as a general instruction to disregard instruction, it is then impossible to carry out. For then one could only carry it out by not carrying it out (a well-known logical dilemma). But that is not what is intended, as is shown by the rest of the passage: " ... or with the thought 'The monk is our teacher.' When you know in yourselves 'Certain ideas are unprofitable, liable to censure, condemned by the wise, being adopted and put into effect, they lead to harm and suffering,' then you should abandon them .... When you know in yourselves 'Certain ideas are profitable, not liable to censure, commended by the wise, being adopted and put into effect, they lead to welfare and happiness,' then you should abide in the practice of them" (Aṅguttara Ṭīkā 65).

The ordinary man is affected by ignorance, and he cannot dispense with simple faith, though in good faith he may grossly misplace it, or dissipate it, and be said to have no faith (*asaddhā*). But if he places it honestly and reasonably, he is called faithful (*saddhā*). In the Buddha's words, "A bhikkhu who possesses understanding founds his faith in accordance with that understanding" (SN 48:45), to which words may be added also those of the venerable Sāriputta: "There are two conditions for the arising of right view: another's speech and reasoned attention" (MN 43). From this it emerges that an ordinary man has need of a germ of "mother wit" in order to know where to place his faith and a germ of unsquandered faith in order to believe he can develop his understanding. That is the starting position.

Faith thus begins to appear as a fusion of two elements: confidence (*pasāda*), and what the confidence is placed in. Faith as confidence is elsewhere described as a clearing of the mind, like water cleared of suspended mud by a water-clearing nut, or as a launching out (*pakkhandana*), like a boat's launching out from the near bank to cross a flood to the further bank, or as a hand that resolutely grasps. (A grain of "mother wit" is needed to recognize the nut, to avoid launching out into a flood that has no other shore, to refrain from grasping a red-hot poker as a stick to lean on). Just as "Seeing is the meaning of the understanding as a faculty," so also "Decision [*adhimokkha*] is the meaning of faith as a faculty." (*Paṭisambhidā Ñāṇakatha*). When faith is aided by concentration, "The mind launches out [to its object] and acquires confidence, steadiness and decision" (MN 122).

Choice of a bad object will debauch faith by the disappointment and frustration it entails. Craving and desire can corrupt it into bad faith by the self-deception that it is not necessary to investigate and test the object, and then, as well as error, there is disregard of truth. In one of his great discourses on faith the Buddha says, "Bhāradvāja, there are five ideas which ripen in two ways [expectedly and unexpectedly] here and now. What are the five? They are faith, preference, hearsay-learning, weighing evidence, and choice of a view after pondering it [compare the Kālāma Sutta quoted above]. Now [in the case of faith] something may have faith well placed in it [*susadahita*] and yet it may be hollow, empty and false; and again, something may have no faith placed in it, and yet it may be factual, true and no other than it seems. In such circumstances it is not yet proper for a wise man to make the conclusion without reserve 'Only this is true, anything else is wrong.' ... If a man has faith, then in such circumstances as these he preserves truth when he says, 'My faith is thus'; but then too he still does not, on that account alone, make the conclusion without reserve, 'Only this is true, anything else is wrong.' He preserves truth in that way too" (MN 95). The other four cases are similarly treated, after which it is shown how "preserving of truth" can be developed successively into "discovery of truth" (path of Stream-entry) and "arrival at truth" (fruit of the path of Stream-entry). The element of confidence has then become absolute because its object has been sufficiently tested by actual experience for the principal claims to be found justified. Another discourse concludes by showing how the value of rightly placed faith serves (as the means rather than the end) in the progress from ignorance to liberation: "Bhikkhus, I say that true knowledge and deliverance have a condition, are not without a condition. What is their condition? The seven factors of enlightenment [mindfulness, interest in the True Idea, energy, happiness, tranquillity, concentration, and onlooking equanimity] .... What is the condition for these? The four foundations of mindfulness [contemplation of the body, of feelings, of cognizance, and of ideas] .... What is the condition for these? The three kinds of good conduct [of body, speech and mind] .... What is the condition for these? Mindfulness and full awareness .... What is the condition for these? Reasoned attention .... What is the condition for that? Faith .... What is the condition for that? Hearing the True Idea [the true object of faith, the *saddhamma*] .... What is the condition for that? Frequenting the company of True Men [*sappurisa*]" (AN 10:62).

This shows plainly the need for a reliable guide. How is he to be found? One should be an inquirer (*vīmaṃsaka*) and make the Tathāgata the object of research and tests in order to judge whether confidence in him is rightly placed. The Buddha says "Now bhikkhus, if others should ask a bhikkhu [who is an inquirer] 'What are the evidences and certainties owing to which the venerable one says "The Blessed One is fully enlightened, the True Idea is well proclaimed, the Community has entered upon the good way"?' then, answering rightly, he would answer thus: 'Here, friends, I approached that Blessed One for the sake of hearing the True Idea [Dhamma]. The teacher showed me the True Idea at each successively higher [level], at each superior [stage], with the dark and bright counterparts. According as he did so, by arriving at direct knowledge here of a certain idea [namely, one of the four paths] among the ideas, [taught] in the True Idea, I reached my goal: then I had confidence [*passaddhi*] in the teacher thus: "The Blessed One is fully enlightened, the True Idea is well proclaimed, the Community has entered on the good way."' When anyone's faith in a Tathāgata is planted and rooted and established with these evidences, these phrases and these syllables, then his faith is called supported by evidence, rooted in vision, sound, and invincible by Monk or Divine or Māra or Divinity or anyone in the world" (MN 47).

Faith as the indispensable means, but not the goal, transparent in itself, is debased or ennobled by the mode of its employment and by its goal. As understanding grows, it approximates to knowledge, while the risk of its degenerating into bad faith diminishes with the diminishing of craving.

But there are still two problems. First, it was argued earlier that faith involves not knowing the future. So if faith becomes knowledge, does that not imply that the future can all be known and is therefore predetermined? Second, with craving unabated would not knowledge of everything be unbearable; would it not be Hell itself? How does craving diminish?

The key to these two locks on the gate of liberation lies in the Contemplation of Impermanence. Let us take the second problem first. It is part of the constraint imposed by ignorance and craving together that an ordinary man is led to speculate on time and permanence, and to ask such questions as, "What was I?," "What shall I be?," "What am I?" (MN 2), unanswerable questions to which philosophers go on furnishing many an unquestionable answer, disproving each other as they do. But progress towards liberation from ignorance transforms and transfigures the world. One who is liberated asks no more questions (*akathaṃkathī*). The Buddha tells his listeners, "Bhikkhus, material form [and likewise feeling, perception, determinations, and consciousness] are impermanent, changing and altering. Whoever decides about, and places his faith in, these ideas in this way is called 'mature in faith.' He has alighted upon the certainty of rightness. He has alighted upon the plane of true men and left behind the plane of ordinary men. He can no more perform action capable of causing his rebirth in the animal world or in the realm of ghosts and he cannot complete his time in this life without realizing the fruition of Stream-entry" (SN 25:10). Such faith decides in advance that nothing arisen can reveal any permanence at all, however brief. Since all subsequent evidence supports the decision, if that evidence is not forgotten, craving is progressively stultified in the impossibility of finding any arisen thing worth craving for, and is progressively displaced by the joy of liberation. The first problem, though, that of time, is properly a matter for insight (*vipassanā*) and can only be dealt with here by hints and pointers because of lack of space. As has already been said, the ignorant man questions, but one who is liberated does not. The Buddha tells his listeners, "Let not a man trace back a past or wonder what the future holds .... Instead with insight let him see each idea[1] presently arisen" (MN 131). He includes the contemplation of impermanence under the four foundations of mindfulness: "He trains thus: 'I shall breathe in ... breathe out contemplating impermanence'" (MN 10).

Now, it is in the very nature of ignorance to perceive the bare conditions for consciousness in terms of things, persons and hypostases, and to project upon these percepts a varying degree of permanence, a misperception which it is the task of true vision and mindfulness to correct. During the period of transition, while

1. Dhamma: "thing" or phenomenon, material or mental. (Editor)

understanding that "to be is to be otherwise" is still immature and helped out by faith in the impermanence of everything that is, the faith must be tested and the outcome of the tests remembered. This needs concentration and energy.

"When one gives attention to impermanence, the faith faculty is outstanding." And in the cases of attention to pain and not-self the faculties of concentration and understanding are outstanding respectively. These are called the "Three Gate-Ways to Liberation," which "lead to the outlet from the world" (*Paṭisambhidā Vimokkhakathā*). When the Stream-entry path is reached, a new, supramundane faculty, the I-shall-come-to-know-the-unknown faculty (*anaññātaññassāmītindriya*) appears, to be subsequently followed by the new and supramundane final-knowledge and final-knower faculties (*aññindriya, aññātāvindriya*). These are gained in this life with the attainment of Arahantship.

Meanwhile, however, "The characteristic of impermanence does not become apparent [as universal] because, when the constant rise and fall of determinations[2] [things] is not given attention, it is concealed by continuity" (*Visuddhimagga* Ch. 21). In fact the Buddha said, "There is no matter or feeling, perception, determinations, or consciousness whatever that is permanent ... not inseparable from the idea of change[3]..." Taking a small piece of cow dung in his hand, the Blessed One said, "If there were even that much ... that were permanent ... not inseparable from the idea of change[4] ... the living of the Life Divine[5] could not be described as for the exhaustion of suffering. It is because there is not ... that it is so described" (SN 22:96).

Now that statement can be taken to imply that if time were an absolutely independent objective reality, there would be no liberation.

Permanence and impermanence on the one hand, and time on the other, are but two modes of the same view. The appearance of

---

2. *Saṅkhāra* is usually translated as "formations," or, in the case of the 5 Aggregates, "mental formations." (Editor)

3. *Viparināmadhamma*, usually translated as "subject to change." (Editor)

4. Ibid.

5. *Brahmacariya* is usually translated as "Holy Life" or "Life of Purity." (Editor)

the three new supramundane faculties signals profound changes in the apprehension of permanence and impermanence, that is, of time, and consequently in actual experience itself.

To question the objectivity of time is not new even to Western philosophy. While objective reality of time and space still remains one of the assumptions made by scientists for which they have no proof, Immanuel Kant argued irrefutably for the pure subjectivity of both. But almost a millennium and a half before him, Ācariya Buddhaghosa wrote, "What is called 'time' is conceived in terms of such and such dhammas ... But that [time] should be understood as only a mere conceptual description, since it is non-existent as to any individual essence of its own." (*Atthasālinī.* Space is analogously treated elsewhere.) A century or two later it was observed that "Nibbāna [extinction] is not like other dhammas. In fact because of its extreme profundity it cannot be made the object of consciousness by one who has not yet reached it. That is why it has to be reached by change-of-lineage cognizance [*gotrabhū*], which has profundity surpassing the three periods of time" (*Mūlaṭīkā*). When the seen, heard, sensed and cognized (see Ud 1.10), are misperceived to be this that I see ... that I think about, is that man, so-and-so, that thing of mine, to have temporal endurance and reality, it is because the three periods of time, these three modes by which we subjectively process our raw world in perceiving it, have been projected outwards by ignorance on the raw world and misapprehended along with that as objectively real. That is how we in our ignorance come to perceive things and persons and action.

These fragments are merely pointers. The contemplation of impermanence, which, when fully and unreservedly developed, necessitates the contemplations of suffering (pain) and not-self, involves the whole field of insight. (There is no space to deal with it here.) However, the inquiry has already led us away from the apparent either-or choice between faith in dogma-as-the-goal or agnosticism. By establishing a structural interdependence between faith and ignorance, it has opened up a new line. In the pursuit of that line it has uncovered an unexpected association between faith and the temporal mirage of permanence and impermanence. And so it has been possible to sketch a practical outline of the way to end here and now this whole aggregate mass of suffering. The adventure is waiting to be tested.

"Fruitful as the act of giving is ... yet it is still more fruitful to go with confident heart for refuge to the Buddha, the Dhamma, and the Sangha, and undertake the five precepts of virtue .... Fruitful as that is ... yet it is still more fruitful to maintain loving-kindness in being in the heart for only as long as the milking of a cow .... Fruitful as that is ... yet it is still more fruitful to maintain perception of impermanence in being for only as long as the snapping of a finger" (AN 9:20).

But does *saddhā* really mean faith? Let the reader judge for himself.

Cessation of Becoming

(With a Note on Faith)

Why do normal people normally react with panic and horror to the idea of cessation of becoming, or cessation of consciousness? There are at least two reasons. There is first the failure to see both sides of life, the negative/destructive as well as the positive/constructive, which are (as it were) the obverse and reverse of each piece of experience. It is a refusal to face the ambivalence of experience, and a putting on of blinkers to shut out, as far as one can, what is disturbing. It is by this that life is made to look nice, and appears tolerable. The process is largely automatic and subconscious, so it is seldom ever enquired into. With the blinkers on one does not see what is unwelcome and one quickly forgets the unwelcome that intrudes.

And here I want to distinguish two kinds of suffering: (1) enjoyable suffering and pain (the arduousness of exhausting sports, self mortification, "being ill," masochism and sadism, etc.), which are not properly suffering because they are enjoyed and welcomed; and (2) horror or nausea, which is all those things (whatever they may be, and they vary with different people) that produce horror, nausea, and vertigo, because they are absurd and menace the core and pattern of our personal existence. Everyone knows that border across which he cannot go, even in thought, and it is that, not the former, that people automatically shut out and cannot face. Yet one knows at times (in the middle of the night, perhaps, when one is sleepless, or on encountering some revolting experience) that this horror haunts every form of experience (always and ever), and hastily one readjusts the blinkers that had slipped. Put the beautiful before you and the horror behind you. Yes, but then I shall not dare to turn round.

The world is a bad place. Is it? But it seems that this haunting, this self-delusion by wearing blinkers, is not an attribute of the world. The haunting is in consciousness itself, in its very nature. Just as when I set up any object in the sunlight a shadow is cast (because it is the nature of sunlight to cast shadows), so anything that comes into the light of consciousness casts a shadow of the unknown. It is in the unknown that the horror resides in the dark of knowledge where the patterns can no longer be traced, where chaos resides, and whence utterly hostile systems may emerge, devour, and digest us.

Again this insecurity resides in consciousness because it cheats. It lives between the past and the future like a reflection between two opposing mirrors. I put my head between the opposing mirrors and I see the reflection of the reflection of the reflection ... which suggests recession to infinity. But I cannot see that infinity because (even if the glasses were clear enough) my head and its reflections are in the way. But then if I slightly displace one mirror so that my head is no more in the way then the series of reflections passes out of the field of the mirrors at some stage of the reflections which it must now do (unless the mirrors are made of infinite size). So I am forced by this set of experiences to infer an infinity of which the very circumstances deny the possibility of my experiencing. That is one essential aspect of consciousness: it cheats.

Another example is the moon. I see as an experience an existent crescent, an existent half-moon, or full moon, and there are perceptions of existents that are repeated (which are in fact over and done with as soon as experienced). Consciousness groups together these repeated experiences and forms a concept that transcends all these possible existents, and which it presents as "the moon." But "the moon" can never be experienced, and even when visualized it is only as one of its aspects. It is a fake. This concept "the moon" is then projected upon the objective world where it appears to lurk behind existence as Kant's "*Ding an sich*," or, say, Eddington's "reality," that the physicists are trying to discover behind what they investigate. Suppose a man gets lost in a desert and he wanders all night. When the sun comes up he may see lots of tracks in the sand all pointing the way he is going. He thinks, "Marvellous! I am on the high road. Lots of people have gone this way already. I am alright." So he follows them. They are, in fact, his own tracks made in the night by his walking in circles (which people actually do). If he does not stop to consider and goes on following them, he will get nowhere. He will die. If he put aside his assumption and looked about him, it is possible he might find the way of escape.

This is what I mean by the failure to see both sides of life, to see things and ourselves as they and we really are, in their relationship. This is what Māra (if we like personification) tries his utmost to keep us from seeing, for it is by this that we can slip out of his clutches. Māra is Death, but he is also Life, for "all that is subject to arising is subject to cessation," "all that is born and lives dies." Byron said somewhere:

> Sorrow is knowledge: they who know the most
> Must mourn the deepest o'er the fatal Truth.
> The Tree of Knowledge is not that of life.

But it is Māra that makes us mourn because he makes his living by that, just as a rubber estate owner makes his living by the trees that he cultivates and bleeds, and cuts down when they are old.

But there is another, equally fundamental, reason that makes people shy away from the notion—their notion—of cessation. This is a very deep-rooted double misconception: (1) there is the idea that by "cessation," by "extinction," something "good" and "valuable" and "lasting" will be "lost forever," and (2) there is an uncritical assumption that consciousness will somehow continue to survive—will be "there"—to be aware of this as an "everlasting privation." "Does all this" they say "only end in extinction? But a state of nothingness is horrible!" and there the whole double misconception lies like a pair of Siamese Twins in a bed. But there is, in the last analysis, no "entirely good" and "lasting" individual thing or state discoverable anywhere. Whatever appears good melts away in the end. The subconscious cheating of the mind seizes on the good, rejects and forgets it, and it melts away. By a "sleight of mind" that is one of consciousness's essential functions, the idea is presented that it is possible to skim the good off the world, like cream on a bowl of milk, and live in that cream in "eternal bliss." But, alas, like the cream, the bowl of heavenly bliss is not permanent. Such is the "good" that is supposed to be "lost." And then there is the instinctive feeling, the uncritical automatic reaction that takes cessation somehow to mean a survival of conscious awareness of that loss, in spite of the fact that the proposition was in the first place "cessation of consciousness." This is the verbal-mental subconscious cheating that has only to be examined fearlessly to see it as a mere self-contradiction. If consciousness ceases and with it its objects, there is no question of conscious awareness of privation. If there is awareness of loss and privation, consciousness has not ceased, and it is not such cessation that is being talked about. This misconception (often enough believed in due to uncritical acceptance) is often used to deride Buddhists without seeing that it hurts only him who uses it. And not only Buddhists, for Saṅkāra in his commentary to the Bṛhadāraṇyaka Upaniṣad says: "The Buddhists themselves do not deny the existence of gods and heavens [or hells]—they are not atheists—but only that the gods are omnipotent or everlasting: they change and die, let one down, make one let oneself down, because they cannot help it, because consciousness and its objects, with its disease of impermanence, are there too."

Consciousness without object is impossible, not conceivable, and objects without consciousness, when talked about, are only a verbal abstraction. One cannot talk or think about objects that have no relation to consciousness. The two are inseparable and it is only a verbal abstraction to talk about them separately (legitimate of course in a limited sphere).

But it is in the consideration of this cessation as the goal that the real comfort and safety are to be found. There is no cheating here, and no anxiety to exclude haunting opposites. All else, however good it seems, is only temporary, because there is consciousness there to know and to change. So there is no permanent safety of attack or harm, and there is no permanent safety from one's being led to do harm, even if that harm is merely changing.

Regarding the matter of faith, it is commonly felt and often stated that faith is a weakness, a mere substitute for knowledge, a "blind belief in dogma" and "unnecessary." But the point overlooked is that there is an element of faith in every conscious act. It is another of the false aspects inherent in all consciousness: the presenting of objects in such that the perception of them necessitates inference about what is hidden. This is in fact an aspect of faith. Without this faith nothing can be done at all, viz. faith that things will repeat themselves and happen as one expects. But the case is most clearly seen in the case of death. Death is an obvious fact. Described in terms of life, it is meaningless (like a blank featureless wall, or a black chasm to vision), but nevertheless by its very existence, by its basis in experience, necessitates inference about it. The three main inferences are that life of some sort continues after death, that it does not, or plain agnosticism. Whichever I adopt is a matter of pure faith (I leave out "evidence" for and against other alternatives here). But I cannot avoid adopting one of the three.

On the other hand, faith about, say, "phoenixes rising from their own ashes" is simply this same universal attribute of consciousness applied to a fantasy, an assumption (the phoenix) that has no basis in experience. What is unnecessary here is not the faith but the assumption. Now many faiths place faith in baseless assumptions. And when people discover this, they not only reject the assumption (rightly), but, because they fail to discriminate, they deceive themselves into thinking that they can do without the faith too. All that has happened to them, though, is that they have transferred their faculty of faith to the basis of experience and have simultaneously forgotten that they are using it. Now, to forget that one has a sharp knife in one's hand is dangerous.[6]

6. Here the manuscript ends. This undated fragment (which in the manuscript, follows immediately after the preceding essay) may have stimulated the author to treat the subject more fully in the essay "Does Saddhā mean Faith?" included in this publication. (Editor)

Consciousness and Being

What follows will have to be stated in terms of ordinary speech, though that necessarily involves the word "is" and logical constructions, because speech is hardly possible without them. Nevertheless they have to be regarded here as a makeshift, and the whole of what follows tends to undermine the ultimate value of speech, retaining it, however, as a necessity for communication in conditions where separateness and individuality predominate.

The word "consciousness," it seems to me, can only refer to what one might define provisionally as "the knowing that cannot know itself without intermediary and that cannot function in experience (of which it is an indispensable component) except negatively."

To the question "What is consciousness," then, a low level provisional answer might be "It is the pure subjective" or "It is the bare knowing of what it is not that constitutes (orders) experience and allows it being." It must be added that, when consciousness is, it seems to be individualized by what it knows. But on another (higher) level the "is" in the question has still to be questioned, and so the low-level (and logical) answer is only a conventional makeshift, a conventional view, nothing more. And this qualification applies not only to logically inductive and deductive statements necessitating use of the word "is," but also to descriptive statements that appear in "logical" form, using that term, or any equivalent.

When I ask myself, "What does the verbal expression 'universal consciousness' refer to?," I confess to be unable to find an answer, because, in spite of its "attractive" form, I cannot distinguish it from non-consciousness (see below). So I seem to have no alternative but to regard the phrase as one of those abstract expressions that appear on the surface to mean something, but when more closely examined, do not. (This, I know, may seem shocking, but I am more interested here in finding the facts than in avoiding shock.)

The more I examine and observe experience (What else can one do? Build castles?), the more I find that I can only say of consciousness (and in this I find a notable confirmation in the Pali

Suttas) that it seems only describable (knowable) "in terms of what it arises dependent upon" (i.e. seeing-cum-seen ... mind-knowing-cum-mind, known or mind cum-ideas), that is, negatively as to itself. And so, instead of being said to appear, it should rather be called that negativeness or "decompression of being" which makes the appearance of life, movement, behaviour, etc., and their opposites, possible in things and persons. But while life, etc. cannot be or not be without the cooperation of the negative presence of consciousness, which gives room for them (and itself) to "come to be" in this way (gaining its own peculiar form of negative being, perhaps from them)—the only possible way of being—they are, by ignorance, simultaneously individualized in actual experience. Unindividualized experience cannot, I think, be called experience at all. Thus there appears the positive illusion also of individual consciousness: "illusion" because its individuality is borrowed from the individualness of (1) its percepts, and (2) the body seen as its perceiving instrument.

Unindividualized perception cannot, any more, I think, be called perception at all. The supposed individuality of consciousness (without which it is properly inconceivable) is derived from that of its concomitants. This illusory individualization of consciousness, this mirage, manifests itself in the sense both of "my consciousness" and of "consciousness that is not mine" (as e.g. in the sensation of being seen when one fancies or actually finds one is caught, say, peeping through a keyhole, and from which the abstract notion of universal consciousness develops). The example shows that the experience of being seen does not necessarily mean that another's consciousness is seeing one, as one may have been mistaken in one's fancy owing to a guilty sense (though the experience was just as real at the time), before one found no one was there. To repeat: my supposed consciousness seems only distinguishable from the supposed consciousness that is not mine on the basis of the particular non-consciousness (i.e. material body, etc.) through which its negativity is manifested and with which it is always and inevitably associated in some way. It is impossible, I think, to overemphasize the importance of this fact. So of the concept, "universal consciousness," I at present think that the word "universal" misleads. (Perhaps some hidden desire for power to "catch all consciousness in the net of one's understanding," and so escape the horrors of the unknown, seduces one to catch at this seemingly attractive term.)

Again it may be asked: What knows universal consciousness? Would not individual consciousness (if the "universal" is accepted) be held inadequate to judge it? And how can it know itself, or what are the means by which it can know itself and distinguish itself from non-consciousness and individual consciousness? I can find no answer to that and so I conclude that, if I ask it, that is simply because I must have started out with an unjustified assumption about the nature of consciousness (which, platitudinous as it may seem, is horribly difficult to understand and handle in view of its negativity; when one talks about "consciousness" normally, one finds on examination that one has not been talking about it at all but about the positive things like pleasure and pain, action, perception, etc., that always accompany and screen it). Is the question then really necessary? Consciousness, of course, cannot be denied as a necessary constituent of experience, but the trouble starts when we begin to ask what consciousness (or its nature) is. We have assumed the individuality of consciousness, apparently unjustifiably, because of the observed individuality of the objective part of experience through which we say it is manifested; and the assumption of its individuality logically leads to the further assumption of some universal form. Why?

Now, as I said earlier, when I begin to ask what something is (is, say, consciousness individual, universal, both, or neither?), we have taken being for granted and failed to examine the nature of a part of my question. In one sense consciousness seems correctly describable as functioning (that is in its true negativity) by putting everything in question: What is this? What am I? What is life? What is consciousness? What is being? Now here the emphasis must be removed from "what" and "this" and placed squarely on "is." Suppose I suggest this: for "is" read "belief-attitude" (as a mode of craving combined with ignorance). In other words, it is the nature of consciousness to make be (with the aid of desire--for-being and of ignorance-of-how-anything-comes-to-be) and the nature of being to depend on consciousness. The multiplicity and the contradictoriness of the answers normally given to these questions ought to be sufficient evidence for something of the sort, or at least for the suspicion, that all the methods of answering them in the way normally done are radically wrong in some way. In fact the contradictory answers in all their variety, as usually given, each bolstered up by logic, betray, it seems to me, just that form of ignorance-craving combination which make perception/non-perception, change/immortality, time/eternity, life/death, action/inaction, choice/fatality, unity/variety, individuality/universality, seem not only possible but real. (It then seems necessary or "right" [here we have craving] to determine what among these is [here we have ignorance] real and what is not.) And the trouble begins again: I begin asserting "I am this, I am not that," "This is that," "A is B," "Consciousness is life," "Truth is beauty," "Life is good," "Killing is right," "The end is the justification of the means," "I am," "God is," etc., all of which others may deny. Perhaps we get angry and come to blows. How many more people in history have been killed for the sake of opinions about what is and what is not than have been killed for the sake of facts? Viewpoints, interpretations, and opinions about the raw material of experience differ, less or more, from individual person to individual person. The more consistent and logically strengthened any moral, religious, or philosophical system becomes, the more possible it becomes for it to be contradicted by an opposing system. And then bare craving has to arbitrarily choose and bash the opponent on the head if it can. That is why Buddhism (especially Nāgārjuna, but also Theravada) favours a dialectic that pulls down all such positivistic-negativistic systems (the positive is always haunted by the negative, and so there is really no true *via negativa* or *via positiva* in any absolute sense). It pulls them down using their own premises.

Of whatever I can say that it is, by that very fact I imply that it is not: It is this, is not that. It then is in virtue of what it is not, being so constituted by the consciousness that determines it thus. But the consciousness on which its being depends is negative, whose negativity appears in objective things as their temporality and change, the change in their being. But while the being of whatever is objective to it appears as positive, even though it may change, its own being appears as a negation of itself and a denial, flight or movement, the temporalizing of the temporalized objective world.

Now, perhaps, you will understand why it is really impossible for a Buddhist to answer the questions, "Does Buddhism teach the extinction of consciousness? Is nibbāna the extinction of consciousness?" On the basis of what has been said above, could it be answered yes or no without examining each term of the question?

There is, of course, another, different approach to the analysis of (not the answer to) that question: Why should consciousness (however conceived) seem preferable to cessation-of-consciousness (however conceived)? Consciousness of deprivation, of an "abyss of nothingness," is not cessation of consciousness. Would not any preference (absolute one-sided choice) for one over the other show craving in the aim if that were set up as the ultimate aim? The desire-to-end-craving, as I see it, is a provisional measure adopted while craving is still present in order to use craving to terminate itself, while the aim is absence-of-craving and consequently ending of suffering. Use of the word is (which implies presence of ignorance) in this way is also use of present ignorance to terminate itself, while the aim is (to me in this state) liberation from ignorance.

Second, suppose a state of consciousness without suffering. Would it not have to be entirely without change since the slightest change in the state must imply a degree of suffering intruding. But can a state of consciousness absolutely without change be distinguished at all from absence of consciousness? I do not see how it can. However a mixture of longing for the incompatible (craving) and fear of or disinclination to face the facts of the association and complexity which are inseparable from conscious experience (ignorance) can make it seem as possible and realizable as the catching of the red in a rainbow with a butterfly net. So out we go with our butterfly nets chasing colour ... and get wet instead. Craving and ignorance persist in heaven, though suffering may be suspended there for a time.

That is how I see Emerson's "Take what you will but pay the price," viz. "Pay death as the price of life," or "Pay suffering as the price of consciousness." May get it on loan, but if one does not pay up when the bill comes in, the bailiffs distrain. But that does not mean that I think one should counter with undiminished craving and ignorance and use them to denounce life, consciousness, etc. I say one should take them as they are and develop understanding of them. That, as I see it, and only that, along with the sharing of it, is the true source of joy, not joy of life haunted by fear of loss-of-consciousness, and so on. This you know, so I am not saying anything new.

If I ask myself "Is it possible for me to end consciousness?" I have to reply to myself that I see no possibility at present. (What might happen if I succeeded in ending craving and ignorance, of which I see no prospect at present, is, of course, hard to say!) If the possibility were available now, I at present see no sound reason why I should not avail myself of it. Pure speculation! Yes, but at least it prevents me coming down one-sidedly in favour of consciousness or in favour of non-consciousness in the crude mode. I do regard death (my life's end, murder, or suicide) as the ending of consciousness: to presume that conscious continuity (negativity) ends because a particular continuity of its material objective world (including its body) ends seems to me a pure assumption whose opposite is just as valid, with possibly better logical arguments in favour of it if the evidence is observed without bias. However, what happens to me at death cannot be known. Consequently I am at liberty to assume (since I cannot avoid assuming something about it) what seems most reasonable. Death seems above all to be forgetting. I do not know. But since I have to believe something about it whether I like it or not, I do not believe that consciousness ends with death. Memory may well do so. I don't, however, know that this is what I want not to believe.

It is, I think, rather important to bear in mind one thing in regard to what has been said above. With this view there are two scales of value (not so much divorced as crossing at right-angles) which must be carefully discriminated. The physical world of consciousness-being-action in which we live and are, biased by ignorance and propelled by craving, is governed by perception of being and the practical values based on that. But any positive metaphysical system, whether based only logically or emotionally on it, which is founded on that, is haunted by the shadows that it cannot avoid casting and that it cannot itself see (like the Sun). It acts in virtue of cause and effect and its thought is logical by its dependence on the word "is." As far as we live in this world we have to live its mode and by its values, or we risk falling into wells through star-gazing. But none of its laws are made absolute (without divorcing idea from experience). The Void, of which it cannot be said that it is or is not, nor that it has consciousness or has none, while it denies absoluteness to any experiential value (alike to being and to consciousness) cannot be identified. And that is the doctrine of not-self (*anattā*) as I see it in one aspect at present. This voidness cannot be "is-ed" and so introduced into the worldly scheme, except as the denial of absoluteness of all particular values. It has no more effect on ordinary life than the theory of relativity. But just as that theory completely alters calculation of enormous speeds, so, as I see it, this void-element completely alters calculations of extraordinary situations, of death (as killing, suicide or the partner of old age).

Written in June 1957

The Mirror of the Dhamma

A Manual of Buddhist Chanting and Devotional Texts

by

Nārada Thera

and

Bhikkhu Kassapa

Revised By

Bhikkhu Khantipālo

WHEEL PUBLICATION NO. 54 A/B

Copyright © Kandy: Buddhist Publication Society
(1963, 1970, 1980, 1984, 2003)

Preface to the Revised Edition

This booklet has now quite a long history, having gone through seven editions and two impressions since it was originally printed in 1926. With the permission of Ven. Nārada Mahāthera, this new edition has been thoroughly revised and a slight rearrangement of material made, a few things being added and others dropped.

The aim has been to give English translations of Pali devotional passages and verses which can be used by themselves. There are now many Buddhists throughout the world who have not had the chance to learn Pali but who would welcome some devotional element in their practice. The English verse translations here are an attempt to supply this need. The references to the texts from which the Pali passages and verses come, have also been added. All passages and verses which are the words of the Buddha are prefixed by an asterisk so that they can be distinguished from the later compositions.

Chanting has been used traditionally as an aid to meditation, usually as a preparation for it, as has been explained in *Lay Buddhist Practice*, Wheel No. 206–207. May this small selection of texts be a help for stilling the mind and bring both calm and insight!

Bhikkhu Khantipālo
Wat Buddha Dhamma Temple,
Wisemans Ferry, N. S. W., Australia.

From the Preface to the Fifth Edition

The Mirror of the Dhamma was first published by the *Servants of the Buddha* (Colombo) in 1926 as a special number of their publication *The Blessing*. It was edited by Dr. Cassius A. Pereira, later ordained as Bhikkhu Kassapa. The Pali stanzas contained herein were versified by him, except those following the formula of the virtues of the Triple Gem which were by the English Thera, Ānanda Metteyya.

Nārada
Vajirarama, Colombo, Ceylon.
Vesak, 2500/1956.

The Pāli Alphabet

Vowels

a, ā, i, ī, u, ū, e, o

Consonants

k, kh, g, gh, ṅ
c, ch, j, jh, ñ
ṭ, ṭh, ḍ, ḍh, ṇ
t, th, d, dh, n
p, ph, b, bh, m
y, r, l, v, s, h, ḷ, ṃ

Pronunciation of Letters

a	as	u	in	but	ṭ	as	t	in	cat
a	“	a	“	art	ḍ	“	d	“	bad
i	“	i	“	pin	ḍh	“	d-h	“	red-hot
ī	“	i	“	seed	ṇ	“	n	“	hint
u	“	u	“	put	p	“	p	“	lip
ū	“	u	“	rule	ph	“	ph	“	uphill
e	“	a	“	fate	b	“	b	“	rib
o	“	o	“	note	bh	“	bh	“	abhorrence
k	“	k	“	key	m	“	m	“	him
h	“	ckh	“	blockhead	y	“	y	“	yard
g	“	g-h	“	pig-head	r	“	r	“	rat
ṅ	“	ng	“	ring	l	“	l	“	sell
c	“	ch	“	rich	v	“	v	“	vile
h	“	ch-h	“	witch-house	s	“	s	“	sit
j	“	j	“	judge	h	“	h	“	hut
jh	“	dge-h	“	sledge-hammer	ḷ	“	l	“	felt
							ng		sing
ñ	“	gn	“	Mignon	ṭh	“	t-h	“	cat-head

The Mirror of the Dhamma

Homage
(*Vandanā*)

Namo tassa Bhagavato Arahato Sammāsambuddhassa

Homage to Him, the Blessed One, the Worthy One, the Fully Enlightened One. (Three times)

Formula asking for the Refuges and Precepts

A. *Ahaṃ*[1] *bhante tisaraṇena saha pañcasīlāni yācāmi*[1].
Dutiyampi, ahaṃ bhante tisaraṇena saha pañcasīlāni yācāmi.
Tatiyampi, ahaṃ bhante tisaraṇena saha pañcasīlāni yācāmi.

I, Venerable Sir, request the Three Refuges with the Five Precepts.
For the second time, I, Venerable Sir, request the Three Refuges with the Five Precepts.
For the third time, I, Venerable Sir, request the Three Refuges with the Five Precepts.
In Sri Lanka, the following formula is used:

B. *Okāsa, ahaṃ bhante tisaraṇena saddhiṃ pañcasīlaṃ dhammaṃ yācāmi, anuggahaṃ katvā sīlaṃ detha me bhante.*

Dutiyampi, okāsa, ahaṃ bhante tisaraṇena saddhiṃ pañcasīlaṃ dhammaṃ yācāmi, anuggahaṃ katvā sīlaṃ detha me bhante..

Tatiyampi, okāsa, ahaṃ bhante tisaraṇena saddhiṃ pañcasīlaṃ dhammaṃ yācāmi, anuggahaṃ katvā sīlaṃ detha me bhante.

Permit me, Venerable Sir, I request the five Precepts together with the Threefold Refuge, Out of kindness, Venerable Sir, grant me the Precepts.

For the second time... For the third time...

---

1. If asking on behalf of many people, use *mayaṃ* (we) and *yācāma* (request, 1st person plural).

The Three Refuges
(*Tisaraṇa*)

Buddhaṃ saraṇaṃ gacchāmi
Dhammaṃ saraṇaṃ gacchāmi
Saṅghaṃ saraṇaṃ gacchāmi
Dutiyampi Buddhaṃ saraṇaṃ gacchāmi
Dutiyampi Dhammaṃ saraṇaṃ gacchāmi
Dutiyampi Saṅghaṃ saraṇaṃ gacchāmi
Tatiyampi Buddhaṃ saraṇaṃ gacchāmi
Tatiyampi Dhammaṃ saraṇaṃ gacchāmi
Tatiyampi Saṅghaṃ saraṇaṃ gacchāmi

To the Buddha I go for Refuge
To the Dhamma I go for Refuge
To the Saṅgha I go for Refuge
For the second time to the Buddha I go for Refuge
For the second time to the Dhamma I go for Refuge
For the second time to the Saṅgha I go for Refuge
For the third time to the Buddha I go for Refuge
For the third time to the Dhamma I go for Refuge
For the third time to the Saṅgha I go for Refuge

The Five Precepts
(*Pañca Sīla*)

1. *Pāṇātipātā veramaṇī sikkhāpadaṃ samādiyāmi*
2. *Adinnādānā veramaṇī sikkhāpadaṃ samādiyāmi*
3. *Kāmesu micchācārā veramaṇi sikkhāpadaṃ samādiyāmi*
4. *Musāvādā veramaṇī sikkhāpadaṃ samādiyāmi*
5. *Surā-meraya-majja-pamādaṭṭhānā veramaṇī sikkhāpadaṃ samādiyāmi*

    1. I undertake the training-rule to abstain from killing living creatures.
    2. I undertake the training-rule to abstain from taking what is not given.
    3. I undertake the training-rule to abstain from wrong conduct in sexual desires.
    4. I undertake the training-rule to abstain from false speech.

5. I undertake the training-rule to abstain from intoxicants (such as those) distilled and fermented causing carelessness.

The Eight Precepts
(*Aṭṭhaṅga Sīla*)

The same formula as before is repeated in asking for the Eight and Ten Precepts but substituting *aṭṭhaṅga-sīlāni* and *dasa-sīlāni* respectively, for *pañca-sīlāni.*

1. *Pāṇātipātā veramaṇī sikkhāpadaṃ samādiyāmi*
2. *Adinnādānā veramaṇī sikkhāpadaṃ samādiyāmi*
3. *Abrahmacariyā veramaṇi sikkhāpadaṃ samādiyāmi*
4. *Musāvādā veramaṇī sikkhāpadaṃ samādiyāmi*
5. *Surā-meraya-majja-pamādaṭṭhānā veramaṇī sikkhāpadaṃ samādiyāmi*
6. *Vikāla-bhojanā veramaṇī sikkhāpadaṃ samādiyāmi*
7. *Nacca-gīta-vādita-visūkadassanā-mālāgandha-vilepana dhāraṇa-maṇḍana-vibhūsanaṭṭhānā veramaṇī sikkhāpadaṃ samādiyāmi*
8. *Uccāsayana-mahāsayanā veramaṇī sikkhāpadaṃ samādiyāmi*

    1. I undertake the training-rule to abstain from killing living creatures.
    2. I undertake the training-rule to abstain from taking what is not given.
    3. I undertake the training-rule to abstain from unchaste conduct.
    4. I undertake the training-rule to abstain from false speech.
    5. I undertake the training-rule to abstain from intoxicants (such as those) distilled and fermented causing carelessness.
    6. I undertake the training-rule to abstain from eating beyond the time.[2]
    7. I undertake the training-rule to abstain from dancing, singing, music, seeing entertainments; from wearing garlands, smartening with perfumes and beautifying with cosmetics.

2. After midday until the light of dawn.

8. I undertake the training-rule to abstain from using high or large beds.[3]

The Ten Precepts (*Dasa Sīla*)

For the first six, see Eight Precepts, Then:

7. *Nacca-gīta-vādita-visūkadassanā veramaṇī sikkhāpadaṃ samādiyāmi*
8. *Mālā-gandha-vilepana-dhāraṇa-maṇḍana-vibhūsanaṭṭhānā veramaṇī sikkhāpadaṃ samādiyāmi*
9. *Uccāsayana mahāsayanā veramaṇī sikkhāpadaṃ samādiyāmi*
10. *Jāta-rūpa-rajata-paṭiggahaṇā veramaṇī sikkhāpadaṃ samādiyāmi*

    7. I undertake the precept to abstain from dancing, singing, music and seeing entertainments.
    8. I undertake the precept to abstain from wearing garlands, smartening with perfumes and beautifying with cosmetics.
    9. I undertake the precept to abstain from high and large beds.
    10. I undertake the precept to abstain from accepting gold and silver (money).

Homage to the Buddha

Iti pi so bhagavā: arahaṃ, sammāsambuddho, vijjācaraṇa sampanno, sugato, lokavidū, anuttaro purisadammasārathi, satthā devamanussānaṃ, buddho, bhagavā'ti.

> Thus, indeed, is that Blessed One: he is the Holy One, fully enlightened, endowed with clear vision and virtuous conduct, sublime, the knower of worlds, the incomparable leader of men to be tamed, the teacher of gods and men, enlightened and blessed.

Namo tassa Sammāsambuddhassa

> Homage to that Perfectly Enlightened One!

---

3. Neither soft nor large enough for two.

Ye ca buddhā atītā ca—ye ca buddhā anāgatā
Paccuppannā ca ye buddhā—ahaṃ vandāmi sabbadā

Those Buddhas of the ages past,
Those of the times to come,
Those Buddhas of the present time,
Forever do I reverence.

Natthi me saraṇaṃ aññaṃ—buddho me saraṇaṃ varaṃ
Etena saccavajjena—hotu me jayamaṅgalaṃ

No other refuge do I seek,
The Buddha is my refuge true:
By the speaking of this Truth
May peaceful victory be mine!

Uttamaṅgena vande'ham—pāda-paṃsu varuttamaṃ
Buddhe yo khalito doso—buddho khamatu taṃ mamaṃ

I revere with my head
The dust on his holy feet;
If the Buddha I have wronged
May the Buddha bear with me.

Buddhaṃ jīvitapariyantaṃ saraṇaṃ gacchāmi

Until life's end, to the Buddha I go for Refuge.

Homage to the Dhamma

Svākkhāto bhagavatā dhammo, sandiṭṭhiko, akāliko, ehipassiko, opanayiko paccattaṃ veditabbo viññūhī'ti.

The Dhamma of the Blessed One is perfectly expounded; to be seen here and now, not delayed in time[4], inviting one to come and see; onward leading (to Nibbāna); to be known by the wise, each for himself.

Namo tassa niyyānikassa dhammassa

Homage to that Dhamma leading out (of suffering)!

---

4. The Supramundane Path is immediately followed by the Supramundane Fruit.

Ye ca dhammā atītā ca—ye ca dhammā anāgatā
paccuppannā ca ye dhammā—ahaṃ vandāmi sabbadā

The Dhamma of the ages past,
The Dhamma of the times to come,
The Dhamma of the present time,
Forever do I reverence.

Natthi me saraṇaṃ aññaṃ—dhammo me saraṇaṃ varaṃ
Etena saccavajjena—hotu me jayamaṅgalaṃ

No other Refuge do I seek,
The Dhamma is my Refuge true;
By the speaking of this Truth
May peaceful victory be mine!

Uttamaṅgena vande'haṃ—dhammañ ca tividhaṃ varaṃ
Dhamme yo khalito doso—dhammo khamatu taṃ mamaṃ

I revere with my head
The triple Dhamma true.[5]
If Dhamma I have wronged—
May Dhamma bear with me.

Dhammaṃ jīvitapariyantaṃ saraṇaṃ gacchāmī

Until life's end to the Dhamma I go for Refuge.

Homage to the Saṅgha

Supaṭipanno bhagavato sāvakasaṅgho, ujupaṭipanno bhagavato sāvakasaṅgho, ñāyapaṭipanno bhagavato sāvakasaṅgho, sāmīcipaṭipanno bhagavato sāvakasaṅgho, yadidaṃ cattāri purisayugāni aṭṭhapurisapuggalā esa bhagavato sāvakasaṅgho āhuneyyo, pāhuneyyo, dakkhiṇeyyo, añjalikaraṇīyo, anuttaraṃ puññakkhettaṃ lokassā'ti.

The Saṅgha of the Blessed One's disciples has entered on the good way; the Saṅgha of the Blessed One's disciples has entered on the straight way; the Saṅgha of the Blessed One's

5. The true or supreme Dhamma as (1) virtue, (2) meditation, and (3) insight-wisdom.

disciples has entered on the true way; the Saṅgha of the Blessed One's disciples has entered on the proper way, that is to say: the Four Pairs of Men,[6] the Eight Types of Persons;[7] the Saṅgha of the Blessed One's disciples is fit for gifts, fit for hospitality, fit for offerings, and fit for reverential salutation, as the incomparable field of merit for the world.

Namo tassa aṭṭha-ariyapuggala-mahāsaṅghassa

Homage to that Great Community of the Eight Noble persons.

Ye ca saṅghā atītā ca—ye ca saṅghā anāgatā
Paccuppannā ca ye saṅghā—ahaṃ vandāmi sabbadā

The Saṅghas of the ages past,
Those of the times to come,
The Saṅghas of the present time,
Forever do I reverence.

Natthi me saraṇaṃ aññaṃ—saṅgho me saraṇaṃ varaṃ
Etena saccavajjena—hotu me jayamaṅgalaṃ

No other Refuge do I seek.
The Saṅgha is my Refuge true,
By the speaking of this Truth
May peaceful victory be mine!

Uttamaṅgena vande'haṃ—saṅghañ ca tividh'uttamaṃ
Saṅghe yo khalito doso—saṅgho khamatu taṃ mamaṃ

I revere with my head
The Saṅgha peerless in three ways,[8]

---

6. The four Pairs of Persons are the four kinds of Noble (*ariya*) disciples who have attained the four Paths and the four Fruits of Nobility in Dhamma namely, Sotāpatti (Stream-Winner), Sakadāgāmi (Once-Returner), Anāgāmi (Non-Returner) and Arahatta (One of supreme worth).

Though the word 'men' is used, the meaning is 'human beings (and devas) who have won one of the above Noble Paths and Fruits'.

7. The above four Pairs become eight when the Paths and Fruits are regarded separately.

8. It is difficult to think how the Saṅgha is "peerless in three ways". The Thai version reads "in two ways" (*duvidhuttamaṃ*): those who are in the

If the Saṅgha I have wronged
May the Saṅgha bear with me.

Saṅghaṃ jīvitapariyantaṃ saraṇaṃ gacchāmi

Until life's end, to the Saṅgha I go for Refuge.

The Triple Gem (*Tiratana*)

Yo vadataṃ pavaro manujesu
Sakyamunī bhagavā katakicco
Pāragato bala-viriya-samaṅgi
Taṃ sugataṃ saraṇatthaṃ-upemi.

"Who is the Foremost Speaker 'mongst mankind,
Sakya Sage, O Holy One, whose task is done,
Gone beyond, possessed of power and energy;
To you, the Welcome One, I go for Refuge!"[9]

Rāgavirāgam-anejam-asokaṃ
Dhammam-asaṅkhatam-appaṭikūlaṃ
Madhuram-imaṃ paguṇaṃ suvibhattaṃ
Dhammam-imaṃ saraṇatthaṃ-upemi.

"Exempt from lust—from craving, sorrow-free,
Law unconditioned and delectable,
Sweet, potent, profoundly analytic,
To this very Dhamma I go for Refuge!"

Yattha ca dinna-mahapphalam-āhu
Catusu sucīsu purisayugesu
Aṭṭha ca puggala dhammadāsā te
Saṅghamimaṃ saraṇatthamupemi.

"Whate'er is given bears great fruit 'tis said,

---

higher training (*sekha*, referring to the first three Noble Persons), and those beyond training (*asekha*)—the Arahants.

9. Translated by ex-Bhikkhu Ānanda Metteyya. These three verses were taught by the Buddha to young Chatta who was later killed by robbers. See the 53rd story in the Vimānavatthu (The Stories of the Mansions, in *Minor Anthologies of the Pali Canon* IV, P.T.S. 1974).

To four Pure Pairs of Persons; and these Eight
Are people who have realized the Truth;
To this very Saṅgha I go for Refuge!"

Flower-Offering

Vaṇṇagandha-guṇopetaṃ—etaṃ kusuma-santatiṃ
Pūjayāmi munindassa—sirīpāda-saroruhe.

With these flowers, as long as they last,
Colourful, fragrant and excellent,
The Sacred Feet on the lotus
Of the Lord of sages, I revere.

Pūjemi buddhaṃ kusumenanena
Puññena-metena ca hotu mokkhaṃ
Pupphaṃ milāyati yathā idam-me
Kāyo tathā yāti vināsabhāvaṃ.

The Buddha I revere with varied flowers
By this, my merit, may there be Release.
Even as this flower fades away
So will my body be destroyed.

Idāni pupphāni vaṇṇenapi suvaṇṇaṃ, gandhenapi sugandhaṃ, saṇṭhānenapi susaṇṭhānaṃ, khippameva dubbaṇṇaṃ duggandhaṃ dussaṇṭhānaṃ pappoti.
Imameva kāyaṃ suvaṇṇaṃ sugandhaṃ susaṇṭhānaṃ, khippameva dubbaṇṇaṃ duggandhaṃ dussaṇṭhānaṃ pappoti.
Ayampi kho kāyo evaṃ dhammo evaṃ bhāvi evam anatīto'ti.

These flowers, bright and beautiful, fragrant and good-smelling, handsome and well-formed, soon indeed discoloured, ill-smelling and ugly they become. This very body, beautiful, fragrant and well-formed, soon indeed discoloured, ill-smelling and ugly it becomes.
This body of mine too is of the same nature, will become like this, and has not escaped from this.

Offering of Light

Ghanasārappadittena—dīpena tamadaṃsinā

Tiloka-dīpaṃ sambuddhaṃ—pūjayāmi tamonudaṃ

With lights of camphor brightly shining
Destroying darkness here,
The three world's light, the Perfect Buddha,
Dispeller of darkness, I revere.

Offering of Perfume

Sugandhikāyā vadanaṃ—anantaguṇa-gandhinaṃ
Sugandhinā'ham gandhena—pūjayāmi tathāgataṃ

Fragrant of voice and form,
Fragrant with virtues infinite,
The Fragrant One, Tathāgata,
With fragrance I revere.

Offering of Incense

Gandhasambhāra-yuttena—dhūpenāhaṃ sugandhinā
Pūjaye pūjaneyyaṅtaṃ—pūjābhājanamuttamaṃ

With this incense sweetly scented
Prepared from blended fragrances
Him I revere who is rightly revered,
Worthy of highest reverence.

For Recitation at the Bodhi-Tree

Yo sannisinno varabodhimūle
Māraṃ sasenaṃ sujitaṃ jinitvā
Sambodhim-āgacchi anantañāṇo
Lokuttamo taṃ paṇamāmi buddhaṃ
Aṭṭhaṅgiko ariyapatho janānaṃ
Mokkhappavesāya ujū ca maggo
Dhammo ayaṃ santikaro paṇito
Niyyāniko taṃ paṇamāmi dhammaṃ
Saṅgho visuddho varadakkhiṇeyyo
Santindriyo sabbamalappahīno
Guṇehinekehi samiddhipatto
Anāsavo taṃ paṇamāmi saṅghaṃ

Iccevam-accanta-namassa-neyyaṃ
Namassamāno ratanattayaṃ yaṃ
Puññabhisandaṃ vipulaṃ alatthaṃ
Tassānubhāvena hatantarāyo.

Seated serene at the Sacred Bodhi's root
Having conquered Mara and his serried hosts,
Attained to Sambodhi, with wisdom that is infinite,
Highest in the Universe, that Buddha I revere.
Eight-factored Noble Path for people everywhere.
For those seeking Freedom, the Way that is straight,
This Dhamma fine and subtle, making for peace,
Leading out of dukkha, that Dhamma I revere.
Right worthy of gifts is the Saṅgha purified,
With pacified senses, all mental stains removed,
One quality alone with which all powers won:
Gone beyond desire, that Saṅgha I revere.
Thus indeed the Highest which is the Triple Gem
Should be venerated as revered by me,
And then by the power of this vast amount of merit,
Very beneficial, may danger be destroyed.

Homage to the Three Symbols

Vandāmi cetiyaṃ sabbaṃ—sabbaṭṭhānesu patiṭṭhitaṃ
Sārīrika-dhātu-mahābodhiṃ—buddharūpaṃ sakalaṃ sadā

All the stupas in every place
Wherever they are found,
The bodily relics, the great Bo-tree,
And Buddha-images I revere.

Concluding Homage to the Triple Gem

Imāya dhammānudhamma-paṭipattiyā buddhaṃ pūjemi.
Imāya dhammānudhamma-paṭipattiyā dhammaṃ pūjemi.
Imāya dhammānudhamma-paṭipattiyā saṅghaṃ pūjemi.

By practising Dhamma according with Truth the Buddha I revere.
By practising Dhamma according with Truth the Dhamma I

revere.
By practising Dhamma according with Truth the Saṅgha I revere.

Dedication of Good Kamma to Devas, etc.

Ākāsaṭṭhā ca bhummaṭṭhā—devā nāgā mahiddhikā
Puññaṃ taṃ anumoditvā[10]*—ciraṃ rakkhantu sāsanaṃ*[11]

May beings who dwell in space, on earth,
Devas and Nāgas of wondrous might,
Rejoice now with this merit made
And long protect the Sāsana!

Ettāvatā ca amhehi—sambhataṃ puñña-sampadaṃ
Sabbe satt'ānumodantu—sabba-sampatti-siddhiyā.

So much of merits made
A fortune stored by us,
May beings all rejoice
and so obtain all happiness.

Dedication of Good Kamma to the Departed

Idaṃ no ñātīnaṃ hotu sukhitā hontu ñātayo.

Let this be for our relatives, and may they be happy!

Aspiration (*Patthanā*)

Iminā puññakammena—mā me bāla-samāgamo,
sataṃ samāgamo hotu—yāva Nibbāna-pattiyā.

By virtue of this wholesome act
Never may I live with fools
But with the wise have company
Until Nibbāna's won.

---

10. Also recited as "*Puññaṃ no anumodantu.*"

11. For *sāsanaṃ* (Religion) substitute *desanaṃ* (Teaching) or *me garu* (my teachers) and *maṃ paraṃ* (me and others) in other stanzas. On suitable occasions, the words, *te sadā* (you constantly) may be substituted for *maṃ paraṃ*.

Contemplation of Unattractiveness of the Body (*Asubha-bhāvanā*)

(i) *Imameva kāyaṃ uddhaṃ pādatalā adho kesamatthakā tacapariyantaṃ pūrā nānappakārassa asucino. Atth'imasmiṃ kāye:*

l. kesā, 2. lomā, 3. nakhā, 4. dantā, 5. taco, 6. maṃsaṃ, 7. nahāru, 8. aṭṭhī, 9. aṭṭhimiñjaṃ, 10. vakkaṃ, 11. hadayaṃ. 12. yakanaṃ, 13. kilomakaṃ, 14. pihakaṃ, 15. papphāsaṃ, 16. antaṃ, 17. antaguṇaṃ, 18. udariyaṃ, 19. karīsaṃ, 20. matthaluṅgaṃ,[12] *21. pittaṃ, 22. semhaṃ, 23. pubbo, 24. lohitaṃ, 25. sedo, 26. medo, 27. assu, 28. vasā, 29. kheḷo, 30. siṅghāṇikā, 31. lasikā, 32. muttan'ti.*

In this very body from the soles of the feet up, from the crown of the head down, surrounded by skin, full of these various mean impurities, there are in this body:

1. hair of the head, 2. hair of the body, 3. nails, 4. teeth, 5. skin, 6. flesh, 7. sinews, 8. bones, 9. marrow, 10. kidneys, 11. heart, 12. liver, 13. membranes, 14. spleen, 15. lungs, 16. large gut, 17. small gut, 18. gorge, 19. dung, 20. brain, 21. bile, 22. phlegm, 23. pus, 24. blood, 25. sweat, 26. fat, 27. tears, 28. skin-grease 29. spittle, 30. snot, 31. oil of the joints, 32. urine.

(ii) *Aṭṭhī, maṃsaṃ, taco—taco, maṃsaṃ, aṭṭhī.*

Bones, flesh and skin—skin, flesh and bones.

12. This is not in most lists.

For Contemplation Everyday

Atthi kho tena bhagavatā jānatā passatā arahatā sammāsambuddhena pañca ṭhānāni sammadakkhātāni, yāni abhiṇhaṃ paccavekkhitabbāni itthiyā vā purisena vā gahaṭṭhena vā pabbajitena vā. Katamāni pañca?

1. *Jarādhammo 'mhi jaraṃ anatīto*
2. *Byādhidhamm 'mhi byādhiṃ anatīto*
3. *Maraṇadhammo 'mhi maraṇaṃ anatīto*
4. *Sabbehi me piyehi manāpehi nānābhāvo vinābhāvo*
5. *Kammassako 'mhi kammadāyādo kammayoni kammabandhu kammapaṭisaraṇo, yaṃ kammaṃ karissāmi, kalyāṇaṃ vā pāpakaṃ vā, tassa dāyādo bhavissāmi.*

Five things have been well taught by the Blessed One who knows and sees, the Purified One, Perfectly Enlightened by himself, that is, the subjects for daily recollection by women and men, monks and householders. What are the five?

1. I am of the nature to decay, I have not got beyond decay.
2. I am of the nature to be diseased, I have not got beyond disease.
3. I am of the nature to die, I have not got beyond death.
4. All that is mine, dear and delightful, will change and vanish.
5. I am the owner of my kamma, heir to my kamma, born of my kamma, related to my kamma, abide supported by my kamma. Whatever kamma I shall do, whether good or evil, of that I shall be the heir.

Contemplation of Death (*Maraṇassati*)

(i) *Aniccā vata saṅkhārā—uppāda-vaya-dhammino*
Uppajjitvā nirujjhanti—tesaṃ vūpasamo sukho[13]

Formations truly they are transient,
It is their nature to arise and cease,

13. This famous verse is found in many places in the Pali Canon. Notably it occurs in the account of the Buddha's Parinibbāna, see *The Last Days of the Buddha*, p. 79 (Wheel 67–69).

Having arisen, then they pass away,
Their calming and cessation—happiness.

Sabbe sattā maranti ca—mariṃsu ca marissare
Tathevāhaṃ marissāmi—natthi me ettha saṃsayo

In the present every being dies,
They will die in future, always died,
In the same way then I shall surely die.
There is no doubt in me regarding this.

(ii) *Addhuvaṃ jīvitaṃ, dhuvaṃ maraṇaṃ avassaṃ, mayā maritabbaṃ, maraṇa-pariyosānaṃ me jīvitaṃ. Jīvitameva aniyataṃ, maraṇaṃ niyataṃ, maraṇaṃ niyataṃ.*

Uncertain is life, certain is death. I shall surely die. Death will be the termination of my life. Life is indeed unsure, but death is sure, death is sure![14]

(iii) *Aciraṃ vata'yaṃ kāyo—paṭhaviṃ adhisessati*
Chuddho apetaviññāṇo—niratthaṃ va kaliṅgaraṃ

Not long, alas! and it will lie
upon the earth! This body here,
Rejected, void of consciousness
And useless as a rotten log.[15]

Contemplation on the Death of a Dear One

Anabbhito tato āga—ananuññāto ito gato
Yathā gato tathā gato—tattha kā paridevanā?

Uncalled he hither came,
Unbidden soon to go;
Even as he came, he went,
What cause is here for woe?[16]

---

14. From the Story of the Weaver's Daughter (Dhammapada Commentary). See *Buddhist Legends*, Vol. III, p.14 (Pali Text Society, London).

15. Dhammapada verse 41.

16. See Jātaka 354 (Uraga Jātaka) in *Jātaka Stories* III, P.T.S. London, 1973.

Contemplation on the Loss of Children, Wealth, Etc.

Puttā m'atthi dhanaṃ m'atthi—iti bālo vihaññati
Attā hi attano natthi—kuto puttā kuto dhanaṃ?

"Sons have I, wealth have I"
Thus the fool worries:
He himself is not his own,
How then are sons, how wealth?[17]

Contemplation on Non-Self for Fostering Fearlessness, Cultivating Detachment, Enduring Pain, Etc.

N'etaṃ mama; n'eso 'hamasmi: na me so attā.

This is not mine; I am not this: this is not myself (soul).[18]

Contemplation of Loving-Kindness (*Mettā*)

(i) 1. *Attūpamāya sabbesaṃ—sattānaṃ sukhakāmataṃ*
Passitvā khamato mettaṃ—sabba-sattesu bhāvaye

Having seen that like oneself
All beings seek for happiness
Patiently then cultivate
Love for beings all

2. *Sukhī bhaveyyaṃ niddukkho—ahaṃ niccaṃ ahaṃ viya*
Hitā ca me sukhī hontu—majjhattā'tha ca verino

Ever happy may I be,
May I from dukkha ever be free
With friends and neutral ones also,
May my foes be happy too.

17. Dhammapada verse 62.

18. Craving is eradicated by insight (*vipassanā*) into the first phrase, with the second conceit, while the third tends to eradicate the false notion of selfhood (or soul). These are the Buddha's words spoken on many occasions.

3. *Imamhi gāmakkhettamhi—sattā hontu sukhī sadā*
Tato parañ ca rajjesu—cakkavāḷesu jantuno

Within the boundaries of this town,
May beings ever happy be,
Likewise those from foreign lands
And men from other galaxies.

4. *Samantā cakkavāḷesu—sattānantesu pāṇino*
Sukhino puggalā bhūtā—attabhāvagatā siyuṃ

From all around the galaxies,
All creatures and all breathing things,
All persons and all entities
Be happy in their destinies.

5. *Tathā itthī pumā c'eva—ariyā anariyā pi ca*
Devā narā apāyaṭṭhā—tathā dasa-disāsu cā'ti

Likewise women, men as well,
The Noble Ones, the unawake,
Devas, men, unhappy ones,
Who in the ten directions dwell.

(ii) *Ye keci pāṇabhūt'atthi—tasā vā thāvarā vā anavasesā*
Dīghā vā ye mahantā vā—majjhimā rassakāṇukathūlā

Whatever living beings there may be,
No matter whether frail or strong,[19]
With none excepted, long or large
Or middle-sized or short or small,

Diṭṭhā vā yeva adiṭṭhā—ye ca dūre vasanti avidūre
Bhūtā vā sambhavesī vā—sabbe sattā bhavantu sukhitattā

Or thick, those seen or those unseen,
Or whether dwelling far or near
That are, or that yet seek to be,
May creatures all be of a blissful heart!

19. Meaning: "unenlightened" or "enlightened". The translation of this and the following verse is by Ven. Ñāṇamoli Thera. See his *Minor Readings and Illustrator* (Pali Text Society, London); and *The Practice of Loving Kindness* (The Wheel No. 7).

(iii) *Ahaṃ avero homi*
Abyāpajjho homi
Anīgho homi
Sukhī attānaṃ pariharāmi

May I be free from enmity!
May I be free from distress!
May I be free from affliction!
May I live happily!

Sabbe sattā averā hontu
Sabbe sattā abyāpajjhā hontu

Whatever beings there are: May they be free from enmity!
Whatever beings there are: May they be free from distress!

Sabbe sattā anīghā hontu
Sabbe sattā sukhī attānaṃ pariharantu

Whatever beings there are: May they be free from affliction!
Whatever beings there are: May they live happily!

(iv) *Sabbe puratthimāya disāya sattā ... pāṇā ... bhūtā ... puggalā ... attabhāva-pariyāpannā ... sabbā itthiyo... sabbe purisā... sabbe ariyā... sabbe anariyā... sabbe devā... sabbe manussā... sabbe vinipātikā abyāpajjā anīghā sukhī attānaṃ pariharantu. Sabbe pacchimāya ... uttarāya ... dakkhiṇāya disāya ... puratthimāya anudisāya ... pacchimāya anudisāya ... uttarāya anudisāya ... dakkhiṇāya anudisāya ... heṭṭhimāya disāya ... uparimāya disāya ... averā abyāpajjā anīghā sukhī attānaṃ pariharantu.*

(iv) May all beings ... all breathing things ... all creatures ... all persons ... all entities ... women ... men ... the Noble Ones ... those who are not noble ones ... gods ... humans ... beings in the realms of deprivation in the east ... west ... north ... south ... above ... below ... and all around be free from enmity, free from distress, free from affliction, live happily!

The Four Divine Abidings

(Loving-kindness—*mettā*)

Sabbe sattā sukhitā hontu
Sabbe sattā averā hontu
Sabbe sattā abyāpajjhā hontu
Sabbe sattā anīghā hontu
Sabbe sattā sukhī attānaṃ pariharantu

Whatever beings there are: May they be happy!
Whatever beings there are: May they be free from enmity!
Whatever beings there are: May they be free from distress!
Whatever beings there are: May they be free from affliction!
Whatever beings there are: May they live happily!

(Compassion—*karuṇā*)

Sabbe sattā sabba-dukkhā pamuccantu

Whatever beings there are: May they be free from all suffering!

(Joy with others—*muditā*)

Sabbe sattā mā laddha-sampattito vigacchantu

Whatever beings there are: May they not be parted from the fortune obtained by them!

(Equanimity—*upekkhā*)

Sabbe sattā kammasaka kammadāyādā kammayonī kammabandhū kammapaṭisaraṇā, yaṃ kammaṃ karissanti kalyāṇaṃ vā pāpakaṃ vā tassa dāyādā bhavissanti.

Whatever beings there are: they are the owners of their kamma, heirs to their kamma, born of their kamma, related to their kamma, abide supported by their kamma; whatever kamma they will do, whether good or evil, of that they will be the heirs.

Contemplation on Equanimity (*Upekkhā*)

Selo yathā ekaghaṇo—vātena na samīrati
Evaṃ nindā-pasaṃsāsu—na samiñjanti paṇḍitā

Just as a one-piece rock
Shakes not with the wind,
So the wise are not disturbed
Either by praise or blame.[20]

Sukhe patte na rajjāmi, dukkhe homi na dummano.
Sabbattha tulito homi, esā me upekkhā-pāramī

I cling not in the case of happiness,
Depressed I am not in the grip of pain,
Balanced I am in every chance,
This is my perfect equipoise.

Some Notes on Mindfulness of Breathing (*Ānāpānasati*)

Ānāpāna Sati is mindfulness on respiration. *Ānā* means inhalation and *apāna*, exhalation.

Concentration on the breathing process leads to one-pointedness of the mind and ultimately to Insight which enables one to attain Arahatship (Freedom or Perfection). The Buddha also practised concentration on respiration before He attained Enlightenment; but this beneficial meditation may be practised by any person irrespective of religious beliefs.

Adopt a comfortable posture but keep the body erect. Place the right palm over the left palm. Eyes may be closed or half-closed.

Easterners generally sit cross-legged with the body erect. They sit placing the right foot on the left thigh and the left foot on the right thigh. This is the full lotus position. Sometimes they adopt the half-lotus, that is, by simply placing the right foot on the left thigh, or the left foot on the right thigh. The body is balanced upon the triangular position of buttocks with both knees on the ground.

20. Dhammapada verse 81.

It feels firm and unshakeable. Those who find a cross-legged posture too difficult may sit comfortably on a chair or any other support sufficiently high to rest the feet on the ground. It is not important which posture one adopts provided the position is easy and relaxed. The head should not be drooping, while the neck should be straightened so that the nose may be in a perpendicular line with the navel.

Buddhas usually adopt the full lotus position as one may see from Buddha images. They sit with half-closed eyes looking not more than a distance of three and half feet.

Before the practice, stale air from the lungs should be breathed out slowly through the mouth which should then be closed.

Now inhale through the nostrils normally, without strain, without force. Mentally count one. Exhale and count two. Inhale and count three. Count up to ten, constantly concentrating on the breathing process without thinking of anything else. While doing so the mind may wander, but one should not be discouraged. When a wandering thought is detected begin again from one. Eventually one will be able to reach ten without stray thoughts, and then many series of ten.

Later, one may inhale and pause for a moment, concentrating merely on inhalation without counting. Exhale and pause for a moment. Thus inhale and exhale concentrating on respiration. Some prefer counting as it aids concentrating while others prefer not to count. What is essential is concentration and not the counting, which is just an aid to practice.

When one practises this concentration, one feels very peaceful, light in mind and body. After practising for a certain period, a day may come when one realizes that this seemingly solid body is supported by mere breath and that the body perishes when breathing ceases. One fully realizes impermanence. Where there is change there cannot be a permanent self or immortal soul. Insight can then be developed to attain Arahatship.

It should be clear that the object of this concentration on respiration is not only to gain one-pointedness of mind but also to cultivate Insight for deliverance from suffering.

In some Discourses of the Buddha this simple and beneficial method of respiration is described as follows:

"Mindfully he inhales; mindfully he exhales."

1. "When breathing in long, he knows: 'I breathe in long'; when breathing out long, he knows: 'I breathe out long.'"
2. "When breathing in short, he knows: 'I breathe in short'; when breathing out short, he knows:'I breathe out short.'"
3. "Experiencing the entire breathing process (i.e. the beginning, middle and end), 'I shall breathe in': thus he trains himself; experiencing the entire breathing process, 'I shall breath out': thus he trains himself."
4. "'I shall inhale, calming the respiration', thus he trains himself; 'I shall exhale, calming the respiration,' thus be trains himself."[21]

Contemplation of the Ten Perfecting Qualities (*Dasa Pāramī*)

May I be generous and helpful (*dāna pāramī*)!
May I be pure, virtuous and well-disciplined (*sīla pāramī*)!
May I not be selfish and self-possessive but selfless and self-sacrificing (*nekkhamma pāramī*)!
May I be wise and be able to give the benefit of my knowledge to others (*paññā pāramī*)!
May I be strenuous, energetic, and persevering (*viriya pāramī*)!
May I be patient! May I be able to bear and forbear the wrongs of others (*khanti pāramī*)!
May I be honest and truthful (*sacca pāramī*)!
May I be firm and resolute (*adhiṭṭhāna pāramī*)!
May I be kind, compassionate and friendly (*mettā pāramī*)!
May I be humble, calm, quiet, unruffled and serene (*upekkhā pāramī*)!
May I serve to be perfect; may I be perfect to serve!

21. For this subject in detail see *Mindfulness of Breathing*, Ñāṇamoli Thera, B.P.S.

Contemplation of Dependent Origination

(*Paṭicca-samuppāda*)

Avijjā-paccayā saṅkhārā; saṅkhārā-paccayā viññāṇa; viññāṇa-paccayā nāmarūpaṃ; nāmarūpa-paccayā saḷāyatanaṃ; saḷāyatana-paccayā phasso; phassa-paccayā vedanā; vedanā-paccaya taṇhā; taṇhā-paccayā upādānaṃ; upādāna-paccayā bhavo; bhava-paccayā jāti; jāti-paccayā jarāmaraṇa soka-parideva-dukkha-domanass-upāyāsā sambhavanti. Evametassa kevalassa dukkhakkhandhassa samudayo hoti.

Avijjāya-tveva asesa-virāga-nirodhā saṅkhāra-nirodho; saṅkhāra-nirodhā viññāṇa-nirodho; viññāṇa-nirodhā nāmarūpa-nirodho; nāmarūpa-nirodhā saḷāyatana-nirodho:saḷāyatana-nirodhā phassa-nirodho; phassa-nirodhā vedanā-nirodho; vedanā-nirodhā taṇhā-nirodho; taṇhā-nirodhā upādāna-nirodho; upādāna-nirodhā bhava-nirodho; bhava-nirodhā jāti-nirodho; jāti-nirodhā jarāmaraṇa-soka- parideva-dukkha-domanassupāyāsā nirujjhanti. Evametassa kevalassa dukkhakkhandhassa nirodho hotī'ti.

Dependent on ignorance arises kamma-formations (moral and immoral);
Dependent on kamma-formations arises (rebirth) consciousness;
Dependent on (rebirth) consciousness arises mind and body;
Dependent on mind and body arise the six sense spheres;
Dependent on the six sense spheres arises contact;
Dependent on contact arises feeling ;
Dependent on feeling arises craving;
Dependent on craving arises grasping;
Dependent on grasping arises becoming;
Dependent on becoming arises birth;
Dependent on birth arises decay, death, sorrow, lamentation, pain, grief and despair.
Thus arises this whole mass of suffering.
With the complete, passionless cessation of ignorance there is cessation of kamma-formations;
With cessation of kamma-formations there is cessation of (rebirth) consciousness;

With cessation of (rebirth) consciousness there is cessation of mind and body;
With cessation of mind and body there is cessation of the six sense spheres;
With cessation of the six sense spheres there is cessation of contact;
With cessation of contact there is cessation of feeling;
With cessation of feeling there is cessation of craving;
With cessation of craving there is cessation of grasping;
With cessation of grasping there is cessation of becoming;
With cessation of becoming there is cessation of birth;
With cessation of birth there is cessation of decay, death, sorrow, lamentation, pain, grief and despair.
Thus ceases this whole mass of suffering.

Contemplation on the Three Characteristics (of Existence) (*Ti-lakkhaṇa*)

1. Anicca (Impermanence)

Sabbe saṅkhārā aniccā'ti—yadā paññāya passati
Atha nibbindati dukkhe—esa maggo visuddhiyā.

Impermanent, all that is conditioned;
When with wisdom one sees this,
Then one tires of dukkha—
This is the path to purity.

2. Dukkha (Unsatisfactoriness)

Sabbe saṅkhārā dukkhā'ti—yadā paññāya passati
Atha nibbindati dukkhe—esa maggo visuddhiyā.

Dukkha, all that is conditioned
When with wisdom one sees this,
Then one tires of dukkha—
This is the path to purity.

3. *Anattā (Non-self, or not soul)*

Sabbe dhammā[22] *anattā'ti—yadā paññāya passati*
Atha nibbindati dukkhe—esa maggo visuddhiyā.

All the dhammas, not one's self;
When with wisdom one sees this,
Then one tires of dukkha—
This is the path to purity.[23]

Great Peaceful Victory Verses (Benedictory) (*Mahājayamaṅgala Gāthā*)

1. *Mahākāruṇiko nātho—hitāya sabbapāṇinaṃ*
pūretvā pāramī sabbā—patto sambodhimuttamaṃ
etena saccavajjena—hotu me[24] *jayamaṅgalaṃ.*

The Lord of Great Compassion
for benefit of beings all
completed all perfections
and won Awakening's peak;
by speaking of this truth
may peaceful victory be mine.

2. *Jayanto bodhiyā mūle—sakyānaṃ nandivaddhano*
Evaṃ mayhaṃ jayo hotu[25]*—jayassu jayamaṅgalaṃ*

He, victorious at the Bodhi-tree,
enhanced the Sakya's happiness,
so, victorious may I be,
may I win peaceful victory.

3. *Sakkatvā buddharatanaṃ—osadhaṃ uttamaṃ varaṃ*
hitaṃ devamanussānaṃ—buddhatejena sotthinā
nassant' upaddavā sabbe—dukkhā vūpasamentu me.[26]

---

22. In the third verse the Buddha used the term *dhammā* instead of *sankhārā* in order to include both conditioned things and the unconditioned (= Nibbāna).
23. Dhammapada verses 277–279.
24. When repeated for the benefit of others, use *te* (you).
25. For others, use *Evaṃ tvaṃ vijayo hohi*, and *jayamaṅgale* in the next line.
26. For others, use *te*.

The Buddha-Gem have I revered
truly, best of medicines,
benefit for gods and men
by Buddha's might may safety be,
may all distresses be destroyed
and all my pain be stilled.

4. *Sakkatvā dhammaratanaṃ—osadhaṃ uttamaṃ varaṃ*
pariḷāhūpasamanaṃ—dhammatejena sotthinā
nassant' upaddavā sabbe—bhayā vūpasamentu me.[26]

The Dhamma-Gem have I revered
truly, best of medicines,
calmer of heated passions;
by Dhamma's might may safety be,
may all distresses be destroyed
and all my fears be stilled.

5. *Sakkatvā saṅgharatanaṃ—osadham uttamaṃ varaṃ*
āhuneyyaṃ pāhuneyyaṃ—saṅghatejena sotthinā
nassant' upaddavā sabbe—rogā vūpasamentu me.[26]

The Saṅgha-Gem have I revered
truly, best of medicines,
worthy are they of gifts and alms
by Saṅgha's might may safety be,
may all distresses be destroyed
and all my ills be stilled.

6. *Yaṃ kiñci ratanaṃ loke—vijjati vividhā puthū*
ratanaṃ buddhasamaṃ natthi—tasmā sotthī bhavantu me.[26]

Whatever the many kinds of gems
in the world found here and there,
no gem is Buddha's peer indeed
and so in safety may I be.

7. *Yaṃ kiñci ratanaṃ loke—vijjati vividhā puthū*
ratanaṃ dhammasamaṃ natthi—tasmā sotthī bhavantu me.[26]

Whatever the many kinds of gems
in the world found here and there,
no gem is Dhamma's peer indeed
and so in safety may I be.

8. *Yaṃ kiñci ratanaṃ loke—vijjati vividhā puthū*
ratanaṃ saṅghasamaṃ natthi—tasmā sotthī bhavantu me.[26]

Whatever the many kinds of gems
in the world found here and there,
no gem is Saṅgha's peer indeed
and so in safety may I be.

9. *Natthi me saraṇaṃ aññaṃ—buddho me saraṇaṃ varaṃ*
Etena saccavajjena—hotu me[26] *jayamaṅgalaṃ.*

No other refuge do I seek,
The Buddha is my refuge true;
By the speaking of this Truth
May peaceful victory be mine!

10. *Natthi me saraṇaṃ aññaṃ—dhammo me saraṇaṃ varaṃ*
Etena saccavajjena—hotu me[26] *jayamaṅgalaṃ.*

No other refuge do I seek,
The Dhamma is my refuge true;
By the speaking of this Truth
May peaceful victory be mine!

11. *Natthi me saraṇaṃ aññaṃ—saṅgho me saraṇaṃ varaṃ*
Etena saccavajjena—hotu me[26] *jayamaṅgalaṃ*

No other refuge do I seek.
The Saṅgha is my refuge true,
By the speaking of this Truth
May peaceful victory be mine!

12. *Sabbītiyo vivajjantu—sabbarogo vinassatu*
Mā me26 bhavatvantarāyo—sukhi dīghāyuko ahaṃ.[27]

May all distresses be averted,
may all diseases be destroyed,
may no dangers be for me,
may I be happy living long.

13. *Bhavatu sabbamaṅgalaṃ—rakkhantu sabbadevatā*
sabbabuddhānubhāvena—sadā sotthī bhavantu me.

---

27. For others, use *sukhi dīghāyuko bhava.*

May there be for me all blessings,
may all the devas guard me well,
by the power of all the Buddhas
ever in safety may I be.

14. *Bhavatu sabbamaṅgalaṃ—rakkhantu sabbadevatā*
sabbadhammānubhāvena—sadā sotthī bhāvantu me.

May there be for me all blessings,
may all the devas guard me well,
by the power of all the Dhammas
ever in safety may I be.

15. *Bhavatu sabbamaṅgalaṃ—rakkhantu sabbadevatā*
sabbasaṅghānubhāvena—sadā sotthī bhavantu me.

May there be for me all blessings,
may all the devas guard me well,
by the power of all the Saṅghas
ever in safety may I be.

The Buddha's Peaceful Victory Verses (*Buddhajayamaṅgala Gāthā*) (*Benedictory*)

1. *Bāhuṃ sahassam-ābhinimmita-sāvudhantaṃ*
Grīmekhalaṃ udita-ghora-sasenamāraṃ
Dānādidhamma-vidhinā jitavā munindo
Tan-tejasā bhavatu me jayamaṅgalāni

The Lord of Māras conjured up a thousand-armed form
While riding on his elephant Girimekhala
Brandishing in every hand a weapon fit to kill
Surrounded by his soldier-hosts shrieking frightfully:
The Lord of Munis conquered him by Generosity and the rest.
By the power of that victory may I win all success!

2. *Mārātirekam-abhiyujjhita-sabba-rattiṃ*
Ghoram-panāḷavakam-akkhama-thaddha-yakkhaṃ
Khantī-sudanta-vidhinā jitavā munindo
Tan-tejasā bhavatu me jayamaṅgalāni

Āḷavaka, the demon fierce with heart as hard as stone
All night he came and went again until the dawn appeared.
Although he had more power than the arms of Māra's might
Small was his endurance when he fought against the Lord:
The Lord of Munis conquered him, by patience was he tamed.
By the power of that victory may I win all success!

3. *Nālāgiriṃ gajavaraṃ atimatta-bhūtaṃ*
Dāvaggi-cakkamasanīva sudāruṇantaṃ
Mettambuseka-vidhinā jitavā munindo
Tan-tejasā bhavatu me jayamaṅgalāni

A great beast Nālāgiri was a mighty elephant.
Consuming fiery brew became fierce as a forest fire
Ferocious as the flaming disk which Vishnu hurls to kill
Or fearsome as the thunderbolt that out of heaven strikes;
The Lord of Munis conquered him: He poured out friendliness.
By the power of that victory may I win all success!

4. *Ukkhitta-khaggam-atihattha-sudāruṇantaṃ*
Dhāvan-tiyojana-pathaṅgulimālavan-taṃ
Iddhībhisaṅkhatamano jitavā munindo
Tan-tejasā bhavatu me jayamaṅgalāni

The robber called Aṅgulimāla or "finger-garlanded"
Who near a thousand men had slain, a terror of the land,
Who skilful with his weapons had eluded every search
With sword in hand, three yojanas did he pursue the Lord:
The Lord of Munis conquered him by magic of the mind.
By the power of that victory may I win all success!

5. *Katvāna kaṭṭham-udaraṃ iva gabbhinīyā*
Ciñcāya duṭṭha-vacanaṃ janakāya majjhe
Santena soma-vidhinā jitavā munindo
Tan-tejasā bhavatu me jayamaṅgalāni

Pretending to be pregnant she, the woman Ciñcā called,
Upon her belly tied with string a rounded piece of wood,
And then amidst the crowds who came to listen to the Lord
Accused him foully face to face speaking what was false:
The Lord of Munis conquered her, equitable and calm,
By the power of that victory may I win all success!

6. *Saccaṃ vihāya matisaccakavādaketuṃ*
Vādābhiropita-manaṃ ati-andhabhūtaṃ
Paññā-padīpa-jalito jitavā munindo
Tan-tejasā bhavatu me jayamaṅgalāni

The wanderer called Saccaka though blinded to the truth
When arguing would cunningly raise up his twisted views
As high as flaunts the victor's flag, although the truth was lost,
And proud, he thought to win debate, to overcome the Lord,
The Lord of Munis conquered him by wisdom's shining lamps.
By the power of that victory may I win all success!

7. *Nandopananda-bhujagaṃ vibudhaṃ mahiddhiṃ*
Puttena thera-bhujagena damāpayanto
Iddhūpadesa-vidhinā jitavā munindo
Tan-tejasā bhavatu me jayamaṅgalāni

The Nāga-king of potency, Nandopananda named,
Of power and perverted views, the Lord permission gave
His son the elder Moggallāna to tame in Nāga-form,
And he so tamed perceived his faults, by magic taught the way:
The Lord of Munis conquered him through Moggallāna's might.
By the power of that victory may I win all success!

8. *Duggāha-diṭṭhi-bhujagena sudaṭṭhahatthaṃ*
Brahmaṃ visuddhi-jutim-iddhi-bakābhidhānaṃ
Ñāṇāgadena vidhinā jitavā munindo
Tan-tejasā bhavatu me jayamaṅgalāni

Baka Brahma luminous, entertained these views:
"The Lord am I, the One who Makes, Father of the World.
I flourish from my purity," but he had wrongly grasped
The views which wrapped around him as tight as serpents' coils:
The Lord of Munis conquered him, by knowledge he was cured.
By the power of that victory may I win all success!

9. *Etāpi buddhajayamaṅgala-aṭṭha-gāthā*
Yo vācako dinadine sarate matandī
Hitvān-aneka-vividhāni-cupaddavāni
Mokkhaṃ sukhaṃ adhigameyya naro sapañño.

The man sincere of wisdom sure will recollect each day
These stanzas eight of victories won by the Buddha's might
And chanting them he will avoid all dangers, accidents,
To come at last to happiness when liberation's found.[28]

Maṅgala Sutta

Evaṃ me sutaṃ: ekaṃ samayaṃ bhagavā sāvatthiyaṃ viharati jetavane Anāthapiṇḍikassa ārāme. Atha kho aññatarā devatā abhikkantāya rattiyā abhikkantavaṇṇā kevalakappaṃ jetavanaṃ obhāsetvā yena bhagavā ten'upasaṅkami. Upasaṅkamitvā bhagavantaṃ abhivādetvā ekamantaṃ aṭṭhāsi. Ekamantaṃ ṭhitā kho sā devatā bhagavantaṃ gāthāya ajjhabhāsi.

1. *Bahū devā manussā ca—maṅgalāni acintayuṃ*
Ākaṅkhamānā sotthānaṃ—brūhi maṅgalam-uttamaṃ

2. *Asevanā ca bālānaṃ—paṇḍitānañ ca sevanā*
Pūjā ca pūjanīyānaṃ—etaṃ maṅgalam-uttamaṃ

3. *Paṭirūpadesavāso ca—pubbe ca katapuññatā*
Atta-sammāpaṇidhi ca—etaṃ maṅgalam-uttamaṃ

4. *Bāhu-saccañca sippañ-ca—vinayo ca susikkhito*
Subhāsitā ca yā vācā—etaṃ maṅgala uttamaṃ

5. *Mātāpitu upaṭṭhānaṃ—puttadārassa saṅgaho*
Anākulā ca kammantā—etaṃ maṅgalam-uttamaṃ

6. *Dānañ ca dhamma-cariyā ca—ñātakānañca saṅgaho*
Anavajjāni kammāni—etaṃ maṅgalam-uttamaṃ

7. *Ārati virati pāpā—majjapānā ca saññamo*
Appamādo ca dhammesu—etaṃ maṅgalam-uttamaṃ

8. *Gāravo ca nivāto ca—santuṭṭhī ca kataññutā*
Kālena dhammasavanaṃ—etaṃ maṅgalam-uttamaṃ

---

28. This paraphrase or expanded translation first appeared in *Visakha Puja*, the annual publication of The Buddhist Association of Thailand.

9. *Khantī ca sovacassatā—samaṇānañca dassanaṃ*
Kālena dhammasākacchā—etaṃ maṅgalam-uttamaṃ
10. *Tapo ca brahmacariyañ-ca—ariyasaccānadassanaṃ*
Nibbānasacchikiriyā ca—etaṃ maṅgalam-uttamaṃ
11. *Phuṭṭh'assa lokadhammehi—cittaṃ yassa na kampati*
Asokaṃ virajaṃ khemaṃ—etaṃ maṅgalam-uttamaṃ
12. *Etādisāni katvāna—sabbattham-aparājitā*
Sabbattha sotthiṃ gacchanti—taṃ tesaṃ maṅgalam-uttaman'ti.

The Discourse on Blessings

Thus have I heard:
On one occasion the Exalted One was dwelling at the monastery of Anāthapiṇḍika, in Jeta's grove, near Sāvatthī. Now when the night was far spent a certain deity, whose surpassing splendour illuminated the entire Jeta Grove, came to the presence of the Exalted One, and drawing near, respectfully saluted Him and stood at one side. Standing thus, he addressed the Exalted One in verse:

1. Many deities and men wishing to know what is good, have pondered on Blessings.[29] Pray, tell me the Highest Blessing!
2. Not to associate with fools, to associate with the wise, and to honour those who are worthy of honour—this is the Highest Blessing.
3. To reside in a suitable locality, to have done meritorious actions in the past, and to set oneself in the right course—this is the Highest Blessing.
4. Great learning, good workmanship, a highly trained discipline, and pleasant speech—this is the Highest Blessing.
5. The support of father and mother, the cherishing of wife and children, and peaceful occupations—this is the Highest Blessing.
6. Liberality, righteous conduct, the helping of relatives, and blameless actions—this is the Highest Blessing.

29. *Maṅgala*—this word in the ordinary worldly meaning covers the ideas of blessing, luck, auspicious signs, omens, ceremonies (in Hinduism, such as marriage). See Wheel No. 254/256 *Life's Highest Blessings* in which this Sutta is explained.

7. To cease and to abstain from evil, refraining from intoxicants, and steadfastness in virtue—this is the Highest Blessing.
8. Reverence, humility, contentment, gratitude and the timely hearing of Dhamma—this is the Highest Blessing.
9. Patience, obedience, the sight of the Samaṇas (those who have calmed themselves), and religious discussions at the right time—this is the Highest Blessing.
10. Self-control, the Holy life, perception of the Noble Truths and the realisation of Nibbāna—this is the Highest Blessing.
11. He whose mind is not shaken by the worldly conditions[30] sorrowless, stainless, and secure—this is the Highest Blessing.
12. Having done such things as these, everywhere they're undefeated, everywhere they go in safety—these are the Highest Blessings.

Ratana Sutta

1. *Yānīdha bhūtāni samāgatāni—bhummāni vā yāni vā antalikkhe*
   Sabb'eva bhūtā sumanā bhavantu—atho'pi sakkacca suṇantu bhāsitaṃ.
2. *Tasmā hi bhūtā nisāmetha sabbe—mettaṃ karotha mānusiyā pajāya*
   Divā ca ratto ca haranti ye baliṃ—tasmā hi ne rakkhatha appamattā.
3. *Yaṃ kiñci vittaṃ idha vā huraṃ vā—saggesu vā'yaṃ ratanaṃ paṇītaṃ*
   Na no samaṃ atthi tathāgatena—idampi buddhe ratanaṃ paṇītaṃ
   Etena saccena suvatthi hotu!
4. *Khayaṃ virāgaṃ amataṃ paṇitaṃ—yadajjhagā sakya-muni samāhito*
   Na tena dhammena sam'atthi kiñci—idampi dhamme ratanaṃ paṇītaṃ
   Etena saccena suvatthi hotu!

30. Gain and loss, honour and dishonour, praise and blame, happiness and sorrow. See Wheel No. 208–211 *Aṅguttara Nikāya, An Anthology*, Part 11, page 96 f.

5. *Yaṃ buddhaseṭṭho parivaṇṇayī suciṃ—samādhim-ānantarikaññam-āhu*
Samādhinā tena samo na vijjati—idampi dhamme ratanaṃ paṇītaṃ
Etena saccena suvatthi hotu!

6. *Ye puggalā aṭṭha sataṃ pasaṭṭhā—cattāri etāni yugāni honti*
Te dakkhiṇeyyā sugatassa sāvakā—etesu dinnāni mahapphalāni
Idampi saṅghe ratanaṃ paṇītaṃ—etena saccena suvatthi hotu!

7. *Ye suppayuttā manasā daḷhena—nikkāmino gotama-sāsanamhi*
Te pattipattā amataṃ vigayha—laddhā mudhā nibbutiṃ bhuñjamānā
Idampi saṅghe ratanaṃ paṇītaṃ—Etena saccena suvatthi hotu!

8. *Yath'indakhīlo paṭhaviṃ sito siyā—catubbhi vātehi asampakampiyo*
Tathūpamaṃ sappurisaṃ vadāmi—yo ariya-saccāni avecca passati
Idampi saṅghe ratanaṃ paṇītaṃ—Etena saccena suvatthi hotu!

9. *Ye ariya-saccāni vibhāvayanti—gambhīra-paññena sudesitāni*
Kiñcā'pi te honti bhusappamattā—na te bhavaṃ aṭṭhamaṃ ādiyanti
Idampi saṅghe ratanaṃ paṇītaṃ—etena saccena suvatthi hotu!

10. *Sahāvassa dassana-sampadāya—tayassu dhammā jahitā bhavanti*
Sakkāyadiṭṭhi vicikicchitañ-ca—sīlabbataṃ vāpi yadatthi kiñci
Catuh'apāyehi ca vippamutto—cha chābhiṭhānāni abhabbo kātuṃ
Idampi saṅghe ratanaṃ paṇītaṃ—etena saccena suvatthī hotu!

11. *Kiñcāpi so kammaṃ karoti pāpakaṃ—kāyena vācā uda cetasā vā*
Abhabbo so tassa paṭicchādāya—abhabbatā diṭṭhapadassa vuttā
Idampi saṅghe ratanaṃ paṇītaṃ—etena saccena suvatthi hotu!

12. *Vanappagumbe yathā phussitagge—gimhāṇamāse paṭhamasmiṃ gimhe*
Tath'ūpamaṃ dhammavaraṃ adesayi—nibbānagāmiṃ paramaṃ hitāya
Idampi buddhe ratanaṃ paṇītaṃ—etena saccena suvatthi hotu!

13. *Varo varaññū varado varāharo—anuttaro dhammavaraṃ adesayi.*
Idampi buddhe ratanaṃ paṇitaṃ—etena saccena suvatthi hotu!

14. *Khīṇaṃ purāṇaṃ navaṃ natthi sambhavaṃ—virattacittā'yatike bhavasmiṃ*
Te khīṇabījā avirūḷhicchandā—nibbanti dhīrā yathāyam-padīpo
Idampi saṅghe ratanaṃ paṇitaṃ—etena saccena suvatthi hotu!

15. *Yānīdha bhūtāni samāgatāni—bhummāni vā yāni vā antalikkhe*
Tathāgataṃ deva-manussa-pūjitaṃ—buddhaṃ namassāma suvatthi hotu!

16. *Yānīdha bhūtāni samāgatāni—bhummāni vā yāni ya antalikkhe*
Tathāgataṃ deva-manussa-pūjitaṃ—dhammaṃ namassāma suvatthi hotu!

17. *Yānīdha bhūtāni samāgatāni—bhummāni vā yāni vā antalikkhe*
Tathāgataṃ deva-manussa-pūjitaṃ—saṅghaṃ namassāma suvatthi hotu!

The Discourse on Jewels

1. Whatever beings are assembled here, whether on earth or whether celestial, may they all be happy! Moreover, may they listen attentively to my words!
2. Accordingly give good heed, all ye beings! Show your love to the human beings, who, day and night, bring offerings to you. Therefore guard them zealously.
3. Whatever treasure there is here or in the world beyond, whatever precious jewel in the heavens—none is there comparable with the Accomplished One. Truly, in the Buddha is this precious jewel. By this truth may there be happiness!
4. The tranquil Sage of the Sakyas realised that Cessation, Passion-free, Deathlessness Supreme. There is nought comparable with this Dhamma. Truly, in the Dhamma is this precious jewel. By this truth may there be happiness
5. That Purity praised by the Buddha Supreme is described as "concentration without interruption". There is nought like that Concentration. Truly in the Dhamma is this precious jewel. By this truth may there be happiness!

6. Those Eight Persons, praised by the virtuous, constitute four pairs. To them—worthy of offerings, the disciples of Welcome One—gifts given yield abundant fruit. Truly, in the Saṅgha is this precious jewel. By this truth may there be happiness!
7. With steadfast mind, applying themselves thoroughly in the Dispensation of Gotama, exempt (from passion), they have attained to "that which should be attained," and, plunging into the Deathless, they enjoy Peace obtained without price. Truly, in the Saṅgha is this precious jewel. By this truth may there be happiness!
8. Just as a firm post, sunk in the earth, cannot be shaken by the four winds; even so do I declare him a righteous person who thoroughly perceives the Noble Truths. Truly, in the Saṅgha is the precious Jewel. By this truth may there be happiness!
9. Those who comprehend clearly the Noble Truths, well taught by Him of wisdom deep, do not, however exceedingly heedless they may be, undergo an eighth birth. Truly, in the Saṅgha is the precious Jewel. By this truth may there be happiness!
10. For him with the acquisition of Insight, three things are abandoned—namely, the view of selfhood, doubt, and indulgence in (wrongful) rites and vows, whatever there are. From the four states of misery, he is absolutely freed, and incapable of committing the six heinous crimes. Truly, in the Saṅgha is this precious Jewel. By this truth may there be happiness!
11. Whatever evil action he does, whether by body, speech or mind, he is incapable of hiding it; for it has been said that such an act is impossible for one who has seen the Path. Truly, in the Saṅgha is this precious Jewel. By this truth may there be happiness!
12. Like woodland groves with blossoming treetops in the first heat of the summer season, has the sublime doctrine, that leads to Nibbāna, been taught for the Highest Good. Truly, in the Buddha is this precious Jewel. By this truth may there be happiness!
13. The unrivalled Excellent One, the Knower, the Giver, and the Bringer of the Excellent has expounded the excellent Doctrine. Truly, in the Buddha is this precious Jewel. By this truth, may there be happiness!

14. Their past is extinct, a fresh becoming is not, their minds are not attached to a future birth, their desires grow not—those wise ones go out even as this lamp. Truly, in the Saṅgha is this precious Jewel. By this truth may there be happiness!
15. We beings here assembled, whether of earth or whether celestial, salute the Buddha, the Tathāgata honoured by gods and men. May there be happiness!
16. We beings here assembled, whether of earth or whether celestial, salute the Dhamma, the Tathāgata honoured by gods and men. May there be happiness!
17. We beings here assembled, whether of earth or whether celestial, salute the Saṅgha, the Tathāgata honoured by gods and men. May there be happiness!

Karaṇīya Metta Sutta

1. *Karaṇīyam-atthakusalena—yan-taṃ santaṃ padaṃ abhisamecca*
   Sakko ujū ca sūjū ca—suvaco c'assa mudu anatimānī
2. *Santussako ca subharo ca—appakicco ca sallahukavutti*
   Santindriyo ca nipako ca—appagabbho kulesu ananugiddho
3. *Na ca khuddaṃ samācare kiñci—yena viññū pare upavadeyyuṃ*
   Sukhino vā khemino hontu—sabbe sattā bhavantu sukhitattā
4. *Ye keci pāṇabhūt'atthi—tasā vā thāvarā vā anavasesā*
   Dīghā vā ye mahantā va—majjhimā rassakānukathūlā.
5. *Diṭṭhā vā yeva adiṭṭhā—ye ca dūre vasanti avidūre*
   Bhūtā vā sambhavesī vā—sabbe sattā bhavantu sukhitattā
6. *Na paro paraṃ nikubbetha—nātimaññetha katthaci naṃ kañci*
   Byārosanā paṭighasaññā—nāññamaññassa dukkham-iccheyya
7. *Mātā yathā niyaṃ puttaṃ—āyusā ekaputtaṃ anurakkhe*
   Evampi sabbabhūtesu—mānasaṃ bhāvaye aparimāṇaṃ
8. *Mettañ ca sabba-lokasmiṃ—mānasaṃ bhāvaye aparimāṇaṃ*
   Uddhaṃ adho ca tiriyañca—asambādhaṃ averaṃ asapattam
9. *Tiṭṭhaṃ caraṃ nisinno vā—sayāno vā yāvat'assa vigatamiddho*
   Etaṃ satiṃ adhiṭṭheyya—brahmam etaṃ vihāraṃ idhamāhu
10. *Diṭṭhiñca anupagamma sīlavā—dassanena sampanno*
    Kāmesu vineyya gedhaṃ—na hi jātu gabbhaseyyaṃ punar eti'ti.

The Discourse on Loving-Kindness which should be practised

1. He who is skilled in his good and who wishes to attain that state of calm should act (thus:)
   He should be able, upright, perfectly upright, obedient, gentle and humble.
2. Contented, easily supportable, with few duties, of light livelihood, controlled in senses, discreet, not impudent, not be greedily attached to families.
3. He should not commit any slight wrong such that other wise men might censure him. (And he should think:)
   "May all beings be happy and secure; may their hearts be happy!

4–5. Whatever living beings there are—feeble or strong, long, stout, or medium, short, small or large, seen or unseen, those dwelling far or near, those who are born and those who are to be born—may all beings, without exception, be happy-hearted!

6. Let not one deceive another nor despise any person whatever in any place. In anger or ill will let one not wish any harm to another.
7. Just as a mother would protect her only child even at her own life's risk, so let him cultivate a boundless heart towards all beings.
8. Let his heart of boundless love pervade the whole world: above, below and across—with no obstruction, no hatred, and no enmity.
9. Whether he stands, walks, sits or lies down, as long as he is awake, he should develop this mindfulness. This, they say, is Divine Abiding here.
10. Not falling into views, virtuous and endowed with Insight, he gives up attachment to sense-desires. Truly, he does not come again for conception in a womb.

Sabbe Sattā Sukhitā Hontu!
May All Beings Be Happy!

The Five Precepts

Collected Essays

Essays by

**Dr. Paul Dahlke, Bhikkhu Sīlācāra,
L.R. Oates, G. Constant Lounsbery**

WHEEL PUBLICATION NO. 55

Copyright © Kandy: Buddhist Publication Society (1963, 1975)

The Five Precepts
Pañca Sīla

1. *Pāṇātipātā veramaṇī, sikkhāpadaṃ samādiyāmi.*
2. *Adinnādānā veramaṇī, sikkhāpadaṃ samādiyāmi.*
3. *Kāmesu micchācārā veramaṇī, sikkhāpadaṃ samādiyāmi.*
4. *Musāvādā veramaṇī, sikkhāpadaṃ samādiyāmi.*
5. *Surāmeraya majja pamādaṭṭhānā, sikkhāpadaṃ samādiyāmi.*

   1. I undertake to observe the precept to abstain from killing living beings.
   2. I undertake to observe the precept to abstain from taking what is not given.
   3. I undertake to observe the precept to abstain from sexual misconduct.
   4. I undertake to observe the precept to abstain from false speech.
   5. I undertake to observe the precept to abstain from intoxicating drinks and drugs causing heedlessness.

The Precepts in Buddhism

Dr. Paul Dahlke

There are five precepts in Buddhism which are binding on all who call themselves Buddhists. They are:

1. Not to take the life of any living being.
2. Not to take what is not given.
3. Abstaining from sexual misconduct.
4. Abstaining from wrong speech.
5. Abstaining from intoxicants.

These precepts are not commandments in the Christian sense. There is no divine law-giver who raises a threatening finger from behind the clouds. These precepts are self-given rules of conduct, which the individual voluntarily accepts and endeavours to keep—not to please a God, but for bringing himself morally into conformity with the results of his thinking.

Hence the precepts begin with the following words: "I take upon myself the rule of training to abstain ..." This is repeated for each of these rules.

The Judaeo-Christian commandment "Thou shalt not kill" reads in Buddhist formulation: "*I take upon myself the rule of training to abstain from taking the life of living beings.*" From the wide domain of hair-splitting casuistry and theorizing we arrive here at a quite unambiguous mental fact: whether some act of taking life constitutes, morally, legally or conventionally, "killing" or "murder," this may be a matter of argument, and sometimes of a vain argument. But the phrase "Taking the life of living beings" is unambiguously clear. Whether the individual can observe that precept in all situations of life is another question. But if he cannot do it, he will, in any case, know that he has transgressed a self-given rule: he will have a bad conscience and will again and again endeavour to do better in future.

The Judaeo-Christian commandment "Thou shalt not steal" runs in its Buddhist version as follows: "*I take upon myself the rule of training to abstain from taking what is not given.*" What we said about the first commandment applies here too. Whether any appropriation of another's possessions can be called "stealing" may be arguable. But if we say, "Not to take what is not given," that is clear and anybody knows what it implies. The bonds in which that injunction holds him are strict but unambiguous.

The Judaeo-Christian commandment "Thou shalt not commit adultery" reads in its Buddhist formulation: "*I take upon myself the rule of training to abstain from sexual misconduct.*" Here, too, the self-given rule of the Buddhist is much broader and more definite. Someone may refrain from adultery and yet he may not be avoiding any other kind of sexual misconduct and be very far from a pure life. And it is that purity which alone matters if the concern is not only with setting up social barriers and protected fences, but to elevate morality in general.

The Judaeo-Christian commandment "Thou shalt not lie" is formulated in Buddhism as: "*I take upon myself the rule of training to abstain from false speech.*" What was said about the first and second precept holds good here also. What an enormously ambiguous thing is the concept of "telling lies"! But any hair-splitting about it has lost its ground as soon as one no longer clings to the concept, but adheres to the facts. Everyone knows what it means: not to use false speech that is not in accordance with the facts. Present social conditions, however, have made enormously difficult the strict observance of this precept in particular. The so-called "conventional" or "white" lie has for almost all of us become a kind of expedient for protecting us against the brutalities of modern life. Even he who endeavours to lead a good Buddhist life will sometimes find it very hard to do without that expedient; but it makes a great difference whether one does something with a good or a bad conscience. If it is done with a bad conscience, one will constantly fight against it; and if one's social conditions are such that this inner fight does not yield an external success, then one will try to change these circumstances by returning to more simple conditions of life which do not require such an elaborate apparatus of conventional untruths. But if that too proves impossible, one will at least cherish a longing for those simpler and more truthful conditions. Much is gained for inner progress if a man is dissatisfied with himself; and this will be the case when he knows that his life is not in harmony with his self-given rules of conduct.

As to the fifth precept "*I take upon myself the rule of training to abstain from intoxicants*," there is no equivalent of it in the Judaeo-Christian code of morality. Christianity in particular shows in this respect a truly astounding indifference, the result being a laxity of morals as has never prevailed in any other religion.

The grape was one of the most important products of ancient Palestine, and wine a necessary part of the daily meal. Though Christ censured gluttony, he did not see anything wrong in drinking wine. He himself set the example of wine-drinking in one of the most important acts of his career. Hence it is not surprising that already in the early Middle Ages, monasteries were prominent in grape cultivation and later in the manufacture of special liquors and spirits.

To repeat: Buddhism has no commandments or prohibitions with a God as authority or prime mover, but self-given precepts which are a necessity for everyone who knows life as it really is and who has the courage to draw the moral consequences from that knowledge. If I have understood life as it really is, I have also understood that I am committed to those self-given precepts. For any act of violence towards other living beings, any appropriation of what is not given, any unchastity, any false speech, and any partaking of intoxicants, debases and contaminates my own conditions of existence, gives undesirable stimuli, and imparts impulses for a downward path; in brief, it does harm to myself. Whether through an evil act I am doing harm to another, I cannot always know. If this were to be the measure of our actions, there would sometimes be excuses for violence, untruth, theft, unchastity and gluttony, and under certain circumstances, they may even be regarded as praiseworthy. But this is not what matters. The moral needs of the world would be fully satisfied if everyone would measure one's actions with the consequences one has for oneself, and not for others. To be able to do that, one must have a realistic philosophy of life. And to have that, one must be a Buddhist. Being a Buddhist, one will soon understand: even if the good or bad results of my deeds take effect nowhere else, they will take effect in me, the doer, necessarily and unavoidably. For, I do not *have* these actions as a quality of mine, but I *am* these actions myself, and am nothing but my actions. Hence I myself shall become the result of those actions, shall grow myself into these results.

This will have to be comprehended well for enabling one to put into practice a morality that is in accordance with actuality and with the ethical postulates resulting from actuality. Even if one does not possess the inner strength to live up to these ethical postulates, one's comprehension will have removed the possibility of having a good conscience in the violation of the precepts. Through that fact alone much is gained for one's future development, and by patience, earnest aspiration, and repeated attempts at perfecting one's morality, some progress will be attained in times to come.

The goal stands before us: clear, sure and definite, independent of a God's acts of grace and compassion, a goal worthy of man's dignity and attainable by man's effort. If I make progress, it is by virtue of my own strength, because I have thought intelligently and have put these thoughts into practice energetically. If I do not make progress and slide back, it is because I have thought unintelligently and acted accordingly. If I realize that this is so, then I must just try to do better in future. That is all.

Abridged translation from the German *Neu-Buddhistische Zeitschrift, Sommerheft* 1918

Exhortation

Dr. Paul Dahlke

My dear friends, you are so very keen on doing something good for the world, for mankind! But why not, for once, do something good for yourselves? To be sure, what is good always remains good, must always show itself to be good, irrespective whether you practise it towards others or towards yourself. The only difference is that you cannot be always sure what is good for others; but you can quite well know what is good for yourself.

You ask: "Why should I be so much concerned with doing good just for myself?"

I answer: Firstly, because doing something good to yourself is the safest way of doing something good for the world; and secondly, because by that you prepare for yourself a good death and a favourable rebirth. the here and now harbours much more than the here and now. This life of ours contains more than just this limited life span. As a father by providing for himself also provides for his son, so man by providing for this life also provides for the next.

And how can man do good for himself?

He refrains from taking the life of living beings and from using force against them, even if intended for those beings' own best. Even though you who wish to do something good for that being by force or coercion, you cannot know what is actually good for it. But you can know for sure that an attempt to bring force to bear upon another being will do harm to yourself, the user of force. Hence give it up for your own and for others' sake!

He refrains from taking, that is from making his own, what has not been given to him. Theft is here included, but the rule goes much further than that.

He refrains from blindly indulging his sensuality. To be sure, a normal healthy person has a measure of sensuality, and will, at times, yield to it. In moments of gratification, as far as the act itself is concerned, he will be on the same level with the lecher. But there is a great difference in the way how one yields to lust: One might associate with a set of people because one likes them and feels attracted to them; and one might associate with them reluctantly, by force of circumstances, remaining ever mindful of making one's escape from that company. Similarly one can willingly seek the company of one's lustful desires because one is attracted by them; or one may associate with lust reluctantly, and remain constantly mindful of trying to escape from the bondage. He, who yields to lust but remains mindful of the escape, will even when yielding to lust still continue his fight against it, and if he patiently persists, the urge to escape will finally vanquish the urge to yield. But happy is he who, without yielding any more, is strong enough to make his steep and straight ascent of the Path.

He refrains from false speech. This includes telling lies, but again, this precept has a wider range.

He refrains from the use of intoxicants. He will do so because, for one who regards thinking as man's highest faculty, it is a veritable sin to impair the clarity of thought.

These are all prohibitions. But there is also that great postulate of Buddhism, that of Giving.

Give as much as you can, and foremost give in the service of the Teaching, in the service of those who serve the Teaching! The Buddha spoke of his monks as "the incomparable field of merit." To plant seeds in that field means to secure a good harvest. To give means giving a gift that yields interest. He who gives in the service of the Teaching does the very best for himself. He who becomes poorer in the service of the Teaching becomes richer within himself. To give for the Dhamma is the most worthy and the most profitable gift.

Translated from the German *Neu-Buddhistische Zeitschrift, Sommerheft* 1919

Taking the Precepts

Bhikkhu Sīlācāra

When on Uposatha days the Buddhist layman goes to the monastery and having offered his gifts (*dāna*), repeats after the Bhikkhu the words of the pledge to abstain from killing and stealing, from lewdness and lying, from the drinking of intoxicating liquors, it means that he impresses upon his memory once more the Rule by which he is to conduct his daily life. When Uposatha day is over, he is once more back in the midst of worldly duties and occupations. To 'take the precepts' on Uposatha days, or on any other day, means to remind oneself afresh of what the world's pressure of business and pleasure is so apt to make man forget, namely, the course of conduct which leads to the surest happiness in this and in all worlds, and brings him a little nearer to that which is far better than any other happiness this or any other world can give—the great peace of Nibbāna. The precepts, in short, are no magical formula or spell by the mere utterance of which great and miraculous results are to be achieved. They are purely and simply a reminder to the layman of what he must do as he mixes in the life of the great world, so that he may avoid putting any obstacles or hindrances on his path towards the Beyond-of-Life.

If, however, after 'taking the precepts', he goes off and immediately forgets all about them until next time he visits the monastery, obviously, for all the good they do him, he might just as well never have 'taken' them at all. For it cannot be too often insisted that it is not the mere 'taking the precepts', repeating the words of the vows as the Bhikkhu utters them, which leads to happiness here and to Nibbāna when all lives are ended; it is the keeping of these precepts in practice, the fulfilling of the vow in daily life and conduct.

In this matter, it is with Sīla, as it is with Dāna (giving). No one is considered to have made *Dāna* who only gives a promise to provide breakfast for the Bhikkhus, or simply says that he will furnish so many thousand bricks to help to build a new Pagoda. It is only when a man actually does what he has promised to do that it is considered Dāna; until then it is not Dāna at all, but only so many vain words. It is exactly the same with Sīla, the precepts of Right Conduct, the next stage after *Dāna*, which the layman is recommended to follow upon the highroad to Nibbāna pointed out by our Lord Buddha. Until these precepts of Good are kept, acted upon in daily life in lesser or greater degree, there is no Sīla in the matter at all but only idle talk about Sīla.

Sīla, in short, means the *practice of Sīla,* and in this understanding of the word, it may perhaps be compared to a railway train, which conveys passengers to a certain destination. In taking advantage of such a train, the first thing to be done is to get a ticket, and afterwards to enter the train. So doing, in due time, a man will reach the town or village for which he is bound.

But if, after purchasing his ticket, instead of going into the train, a man goes away home or sets about to some other business, will he reach the place to which he wishes to go? There can be only one reply: he will not, even though he should buy a hundred tickets. They are, all of them, useless to bring him to the desired destination if the train is not entered. Though a ticket is necessary, indeed indispensable, it is not the ticket but the train that actually does the work of conveying the passenger to his destination.

Now, 'taking the precepts' from a bhikkhu, is only taking the ticket for the Buddha's train, Sīla, which carries all who will avail themselves of it to Nibbāna, or to at least a certain stage of it. But not in this case, any more than in the other, can any one get to the desired destination by merely taking a ticket. What is needed in addition is to *use* the ticket after it has been taken, to get into the train of the practice of Sīla; then and then only is it certain that the destination will be reached. But then it *is* certain. For there are no accidents or breakdowns on this railway; everything is ordered and regular and sure. What a man does, of that he cannot fail to reap the ripened fruit.

Yet there are many people, in other respects quite sensible, who seem to imagine that all they need is to take the ticket for this train, that everything then is settled, and that they have done all they need do in the matter. And so they go to the monastery and take their ticket—yea, week after week, take ticket after ticket, until they must have accumulated quite a huge number of them; but they never enter the train, never try to practise the Sīla. Will such persons ever reach Nibbāna? Assuredly not. For all their ticket-taking they will not be one inch nearer to Nibbāna than they were at the beginning. And why not? Because they have never taken their seats in the train.

Or, to put it another way, our Lord Buddha has provided us with a map of the road that leads towards Nibbāna. It is a good map, a reliable map, the best map of the Nibbāna road in existence; for it has been planned out, drawn and coloured by One who has been over all the ground, surveyed the whole route Himself. On this map, the Sīla part of that road is clearly and distinctly marked, so that none can mistake it. But what are we to say of a person who sits down by the wayside and passes hours in looking at and admiring this map, in thinking what a fine, correct map it is, how superior to any other map that can be had, supremely satisfied at the thought that this so excellent map is his? Will this man ever get to his destination by this sitting and looking at it as it is marked there on the map? Assuredly not, even though he should look at it till his eyes grow dim with looking, and can look no more. For the thing that brings one to any given destination is not the looking at how one may get there, but the act of going. However long and earnestly he may give himself to such consideration of ways and means, at the end of it all a man is just in the same place he was in at the beginning, still sitting in one spot, not an inch nearer to the desired goal. And meanwhile other travellers along the same road, who perhaps do not possess such a good map as he has, or perhaps have not got one at all, but have only been told of the road by some person who has, are manfully stepping out along the highway and get to the journey's end long before he does. And why? Because they are walking the road.

In much the same fashion, it is to be feared, there are many calling themselves followers of the Lord Buddha and proud to call themselves such, proud that they possess his so excellent chart of the way to Nibbāna who yet do not follow him at all but just sit still by the roadside admiring the splendid chart with which He has provided them, the chart where every byroad and fork that might lead them astray is clearly marked out, so that they may avoid it. Meanwhile, on the highroad of Sīla, Christians, Hindus, Mohammedans, and many other fellow pilgrims with charts of the road not nearly so complete and so accurate as his own, and some with no charts at all, are all steadily passing along, stoutly following the road. Will these reach the end of the road before the man with the superior chart? There is very much probability that they will. Nay, it is certain that they will if he continues to sit still, admiring his chart and himself as the owner of it; for it is not the chart that brings one to the city, but the following of the road marked on it. Those others with their inferior charts may at times go astray from the direct road and for want of a perfectly accurate guide to it take a wrong turning; yet they are always moving. Once they have found that they have taken the wrong turning, they can retrace their steps and look for the right turning, find that right turning, follow it, and so come to their destination, even with all that loss of time, long before the Buddhist who is content to take a few listless steps when the mood seizes him and then sits down again to admire anew his fine chart and himself as the fortunate, much-to-be-envied owner of it.

But the road to Nibbāna is a very long one, and it is not a few fitful steps now and again that will bring one to it within any reasonable time. On that long journey nothing avails but a resolute and continuous stepping out along the road shown to us, the road of Sīla. 'Taking the precepts' is only taking another look at the map of that road to refresh the memory, to remind ourselves of the existence of the depicted side-paths and alleys that might otherwise cause us to wander from it. What remains to do, when we have so refreshed our memory, is to get upon our feet, and, staff in hand, the staff of courage and constancy, fare forth along that grand highway, with the sure confidence that if only we keep on, we shall inevitably reach its glorious end. "*Appamādena sampādetha*" said He who first thoroughly explored and travelled and made known that road, the world-honoured Buddha. *"Appamādena sampādetha!"*: "By diligence attain the goal!"

The Role of the Precepts

L. R. Oates

All religions, as well as the more practical philosophies, have their codes of ethics intended to give some guidance as to the everyday conduct expected of their adherents. Christianity has its Ten Commandments and the Golden Rule; Islam its Five Commandments; Taoism its Three Treasures of Love, Moderation, and Humility; Confucianism its Three Principles of Kindliness, Justice, and Courage; and Brahmanism its complex rules laying down the life prescribed for each caste. It is noteworthy that this last-named tradition does not envisage a uniform ethical system for all castes. For instance, members of the warrior caste may take life under certain circumstances without guilt, while the other castes may not do so. Buddhism, however, resembles the other world religions in that its precepts are regarded as universally applicable, at least under the conditions of human existence.

These precepts are usually formulated as five, which in certain cases, especially in Northern Buddhism, are expanded to a more detailed list of ten. The five, it may be recalled, are defined as abstinence from taking life, from theft, from sexual misconduct, from falsehood, and from intemperance. As an amplification of their true significance, it is worth enumerating the ten, consisting of abstinence from the three bodily evils (taking life, theft, and sexual misconduct), the four verbal evils (falsehood, abuse, slander, and idle gossip), and the three mental evils (greed, hatred, and wrong views). All possible activities come under these three classes of the bodily, the verbal, and the mental, so even when only the usual five are mentioned, the implication is that wrong mental states are at the root of all wrong conduct.

It has often been noted that however much the doctrinal theories of religions may differ, their ethical formulations are remarkably similar, even in detail. For example, by way of comparison with the Christian Golden Rule, we have the Confucian rule of reciprocity, and the Buddhist principle of "likening yourself to others" (*Attānaṃ upamam katvā*), as in verse

129 of the Dhammapada. The reason why so many parallels occur in ethical systems throughout the world is doubtless because all religions have had to adopt a social role as well as a personal one, and whatever the underlying theory might be, it is necessary to solve similar social problems in similar ways. The Buddha recognized this, because in the ethical field he only claimed to confirm what the wisest teachers had always taught. The distinctive part of his doctrine lies in the reasons which he gives for ethical conduct.

This is the main question, as other religious teachers would probably agree. There should not be much dispute that the theistic religions, notably Christianity and Islam, adopt a certain line of action, not for its own sake, but because it is pleasing to the Creator, whose service is held to be the only reason for existence. A certain weakness in this attitude, however, is apparent from the history of these two religions, because in practice certain authorities have taken it upon themselves to define the Divine will, and if these declared that the slaughter of heretics, or the plunder of the heathen, was also pleasing to the Creator, their followers have felt free to do so. This attitude has gone far to undermine the high standards which the founders sought to establish.

Turning further eastward, Confucianism tries to justify its ethical code by an appeal to the interests of the social order, conceived partly as an end in itself and partly as founded on a grander cosmic order, which, however, it is beyond the scope of the human mind to define. Taoism reverses this scheme in an interesting way, since, believing that the social order is entirely dependent on the cosmic order it advises that the best way is to interfere as little as possible with the ultimate law so as to retain the balance and harmony of all things. In its attempt to awaken to ultimate reality and harmonize with it, Taoism approaches the Buddhist spirit more closely than any other philosophy.

The Buddha justified the ethical principles taught by him on two main grounds: firstly, that they form the foundation of all progress towards enlightenment and deliverance from all sorrow, and secondly, that in the interval before this final consummation, they are the basis for the happiest conditions possible in the realm of birth and death. The most concise definition of his teaching was that it concerned "suffering and the end of suffering." By suffering is meant the indefinite series of cycles of birth and death, driven by wrong desires, bred under the sway of illusion. By its end is meant the dispersion of illusion by wisdom, with consequent emancipation from birth and death in the realization of the changeless Real.

So the role of ethics is twofold, first as the initial practical step towards final emancipation, and second as condition for greater happiness during the interval while we are working towards that goal (which, depending on our state of development, may still take many lives to reach). Let us consider the second reason first, as it concerns the preparatory stage which we must enter to begin with. Before awakening to the need of ethical conduct our thoughts and acts are basically conditioned by three forces: greed, aversion, and delusion. The first pair is the attraction and repulsion arising from the mind's deluded discrimination of things as pleasant and painful, lovable or hateful, with the resultant struggle to be united with the pleasant and separated from the painful.

These struggles can never reach any final conclusion because of the perpetual and universal change that pervades the entire universe. Nowhere is there any security from separation from the loved and union with the unloved, yet many of us never seem to see things as they are. Those two forces, greed and aversion, are made possible by the third, delusion. This more specifically means that, although surrounded by the ocean of ceaseless change, we fail to perceive that this change operates according to an unalterable law: that what we sow we reap. It is not easy to overcome this obtuseness, because the causes that produced today's fruits may have been set in motion too long ago for easy recall, either in this life, or in earlier ones in a past whose beginning is beyond conception. But as long as the blindness persists, we will have the urge to injure those we hate, to steal what we covet, to lie to conceal our aims, and so forth, not realizing that these deeds will rebound and frustrate our designs not only in this life but in others to come.

On the other hand, to the extent we become awakened to the law of moral causality proclaimed by the Master, we come to see where our highest good lies. It is true that most of us do not habitually break the precepts in a flagrant way because, for mutual protection, human society has evolved restraints of law and custom which are difficult to challenge too directly. So outwardly, there may not seem to be much difference between the conduct of Buddhists and those without any real ethical convictions. But inwardly there is a great difference.

Those whose conduct is restrained not by conviction but by the fear of the law are never at peace. Their thoughts are full of suppressed passions and hatreds which allow them no contentment, and if (as too often happens) social restraint breaks down through war or other dislocation the hidden passions burst out in savage fury. It is otherwise with a convinced Buddhist. He keeps the precepts willingly and contentedly without any wish to transgress them. So he is at peace within, and can dedicate his conduct to the goal to which the Master pointed the way.

That is why, in Buddhist services, the precepts are not taken for their own sake, but as the corollary of taking refuge in the Triple Gem: the Buddha, the Teaching and the Order. This means that we keep the precepts not for purely temporal reasons alone, but because the Buddha adopted them as the foundation of his Teaching (the Path to Awakening), and because they have always prepared the way for the Order of the Enlightened of all ages, the community of all those who have realized the goal.

The relationship of the precepts to the Threefold Refuge was described by the Zen Master Dogen in these words: "We take refuge in the Buddha because he is the supreme teacher. We take refuge in the Doctrine because it is the best medicine. We take refuge in the Order because its members are our excellent friends. It is through taking the Threefold Refuge that we become the Buddha's disciples. Whatever precepts we take, we should first take the Threefold Refuge and then the precepts. That is to say, the taking of the precepts is based on the Threefold Refuge." This brings us to the consideration of the ultimate reason behind the precepts, the fulfillment of the life of enlightenment.

Even from the beginning this is, of course, always a factor. It is not possible to refrain from wrong conduct without putting something in its place. The merely negative method of repression is full of psychological dangers. It leads to a tendency to brood on our past mistakes and weaknesses, and if these continue to occupy our thoughts, we cannot be freed from them. That is why the Buddha said the holy life is like a serpent which, if grasped wrongly is more dangerous than when left alone. Our thoughts must not be suppressed, but liberated and turned to worthier ends.

In the traditional life of Buddhist monks or anchorites, the main preoccupation has been meditation, which opens up a world of subtle experience so satisfying that all yearning for gross mundane attachments dies away of itself. It is not easy, however, for lay Buddhists to develop the art of meditation deeply enough for their thoughts to be wholly transformed in this way. This needs a great deal of time and (in most cases) expert guidance which may not be easy to obtain. That is no reason, of course, why we should not try to cultivate the habit of meditation to the extent we find possible, but at the same time it is desirable to supplement it with other desirable habits. For instance it may be found profitable to develop an interest in Buddhist literature. Although its extent and variety may seem bewildering at first, its exploration will reveal inexhaustible treasures of beauty and wisdom, which will not only give good exercise to the intellect, but will prove a fruitful source of practical hints on the art of living.

The same applies to Buddhist art. Japanese Buddhism has been particularly fruitful in devising means of expressing the Buddhist spirit in many diverse fields such as the tea ceremony, landscape gardening, architecture, calligraphy, archery, and many others, each of which represents a form of expression completely free from egoism. The only motive behind them is to forget the self by losing it in a wider harmony with everything around us, inanimate or animate. They can, therefore, if rightly practised give a certain foretaste of the meaning of ultimate awakening, when the self-illusion is forgotten and sorrow is at an end.

From *Mettā, The Journal of the Buddhist Federation of Australia*, Vol. II, No. 2.

The Importance of Pañca Sīla

G. Constant Lounsbery,
B. Sc. President "Les Amis du Bouddhisme," Paris.

How easy it is to repeat the precepts, how simple they seem as we say: '*Okāsa ahaṃ Bhante, tisaraṇena saddhiṃ pañcasīlaṃ yācāmi*'. But how many reflect on the significance of these five abstentions: from evil and foolish living; from those ordinary ways of life which create suffering for ourselves and others (individuals, nations, animals, all forms of sentient life).

In fact modern life, consciously or unconsciously, violates these precepts continuously. It is difficult indeed to live a harmless life; to do so it is necessary to have acquired a certain amount of *Sammā diṭṭhi* (right views), views that are not steeped in ignorance of the Four Noble Truths, etc.

Now, to acquire right views we must have learned to practise right attention (*Sammā sati*), vigilant observation of the phenomena around and about us, and to have also acquired the habit of observing internal mental phenomena. He who does not see the suffering that is bound up with sentient existence and the perpetual change of phenomena, has not learned to practise right attention, nor understood why we take these precepts. Therefore when we say "*give* me the precepts," we should say "*teach* me the precepts." Teach me the meaning and the practical application which will lead to the experience of purifying the mind and of establishing a certain harmless way of life, *a different attitude towards life, seen intelligently and compassionately.* Having acquired this attitude these simple precepts, when applied daily, will diminish the suffering for us and for others. *The significance of the precepts is of wide social importance.*

We should reflect that the first precept, that of abstaining from taking life, *any and all life,* will awaken and increase the sentiment of *mettā*. It will establish friendliness between man and man, and man and beast. In this precept is embodied intelligent, all-embracing compassion and goodwill. It alone could save humanity from destruction.

If a large body of men followed this precept they would be peaceful and they would abjure war. No mere lip service of course could so pacify the savage instinct of killing this or that. Life to the savage, as to the proud scientist, is not held sacred; some slay for greed of food, some for greed of power, some for mere sport, others for mere curiosity "to see how the wheel goes round." Scientific curiosity often prefers the wickedness of willful destruction to the peaceful wisdom that is compassionate and protective of life.

> Who has ceased from all hurt to any living thing,
> active or still;
> Who neither slays nor causes to slay—
> him do I call Brahmin.
>
> (Dhammapada 405)

So we see that the observance of the first precept could change our hearts and pacify the lives of multitudes of men. But our social structure is based on ignorant strife rather than on intelligent compassion. Men really believe that the jungle law of "slay or be slain" is a normal and inevitable way of life.

Then again the second precept affirms the necessity of fair play. It renounces greed and grasping unfair competition that, at any cost, leads one to acquire and accumulate riches by ruining others (as well as by flagrant thieving). The first and second precepts, as *social obligations*, would lead to a friendly co-operation instead of fierce competition. However, war justifies pillage and plunder and even the theft of life itself is considered commendable. Slaughter of man and of beast characterizes our "civilization."

The third precept also is of great social importance. It implies self-control and would avoid sensual exaggeration. It would establish fidelity in the married life. It would curb physical excesses. The danger of certain contaminations would be eliminated. Health and family and society would benefit.

Who will deny that *musāvādā* leads to corruption of mind, one's own mind, and causes hurt to others. Lying and slandering are forms of cheating. Stealing a man's good character may be more harmful than stealing his purse. When nations treacherously, fraudulently, fail to keep their treaties with other nations, we understand the social catastrophe of dissimulation.

Now when the drug habit or the drink habit has weakened the moral stamina of a man, society at large suffers. Just as the repetition of good action establishes *Kusala Kamma*, so the repetition of indulgence in poisons becomes a social evil.

Not one of these precepts can be persistently broken without causing social as well as mental harm. For how can the slayer, the greedy, the sensualist, the deliberate liar or he who is poisoned by drink or drugs be pacified, control his senses, purify his mind, quench his passions and "come to coolness"? How could he consciously meditate, cultivate and develop the Four Illimitables, those sentiments that make for happiness when mind dwells peacefully, and happily radiates *mettā, karunā, muditā* and *upekkhā*?

In the temple and the school we "take" these civilizing precepts, but that is not enough; they must "take" us, "get us" as the popular saying is, live in us, live by and through us, and help to make and mould a peaceful society.

We count on our bhikkhus to be living examples of the harmless life. By example and by explanation we should come to understand that only by abstaining from evil can we gain good, and establish the good life that leads beyond suffering.

From *The Bosat,* Vol. XVIII No. 4.

The Five Rules

More is the treasure of the Law than gems;
Sweeter than comb its sweetness: its delights
Delightful past compare. Thereby to live
Hear the *Five Rules* aright:—

Kill not—for pity's sake—and lest you slay
The meanest thing upon its upward way.

Give freely and receive, but take from none
By greed, or force, or fraud, what is his own.

Bear not false witness, slander not, nor lie;
Truth is the speech of inward purity.

Shun drugs and drinks which work the wit abuse;
Clear minds, clean bodies, need no Soma juice.

Touch not thy neighbour's wife, neither commit
Sins of the flesh unlawful and unfit.

Edwin Arnold
The Light of Asia

Ordination in Theravada Buddhism

An Early Account of an Ordination Ceremony in Sri Lanka

By

J. F. Dickson, F.L. Woodward

Edited, with an Introduction and Notes by

Piyadassi Thera

Ordination of a Bhikkhu in Kandy

By

F. L. Woodward

WHEEL PUBLICATION NO. 56

Copyright © Kandy: Buddhist Publication Society (1963, 1983)

Introduction

This general introduction briefly explains the history of the Novice Ordination (*pabbajjā* or "going forth"), the Higher Ordination (*upasampadā*) and the functions of a novice (*sāmaṇera*) and a monk (*bhikkhu*), in Theravāda Buddhism.

The article that follows gives a graphic account of a Higher Ordination ceremony as witnessed by Mr. J. F. Dickson at Malwatta monastery, Kandy, Sri Lanka, in 1872. A few shortcomings and errors in the essay have been corrected.

The followers of the Buddha are fourfold: monks, nuns, laymen and laywomen (*bhikkhu, bhikkhunī, upāsaka, upāsikā*). The Bhikkhunī Sāsana or the Order of the Nuns has ceased to exist, and in the absence of a Buddha and the bhikkhunīs the Order cannot be resuscitated. Today, however, we are left with the Bhikkhu Order and the laity.

To know the origin of the Bhikkhu Order we should go back twenty five centuries when at the Deer Park, at Isipatana (modern Sarnath), near Vārānasi in India, the Buddha Gotama on a full moon day of July, addressed the five ascetics, his former friends, and revealed unto them the Right Way, the Noble Eightfold Path, which leads to calm, realization, enlightenment and Nibbāna. This is known as setting in motion the matchless Wheel of Truth (*Dhammacakka*).

The five ascetics were convinced and became followers of the Buddha. With the proclamation of the Dhamma, for the first time, and with the conversion of the five ascetics, the Deer Park became the birth place of the Buddha's dispensation (Buddha-sāsana) and of the Saṅgha, the community of monks, the ordained disciples.

Before long fifty-five others headed by Yasa, a young man of wealth, joined the Order of the Saṅgha. Now there were sixty disciples altogether. Their Novice Ordination and Higher Ordination were granted by the Buddha in these words: "Come monks, well proclaimed is the Dhamma. Live the noble life (*brahmacariyaṃ*) for the complete ending of suffering (*dukkha*)." When the vassa, the rainy season of three months, July-October, ended, the Master addressed his sixty disciples, the Accomplished Ones (Arahats), and said:

"Released am I, monks, from, all ties whether human or divine. You also are delivered from fetters whether human or divine. Go now and wander for the welfare and happiness of gods and men. Let not two of you proceed in the same direction. Proclaim the Dhamma that is excellent in the beginning, excellent in the middle, excellent in the end, possessed of meaning and the letter and utterly perfect. Proclaim the life of purity, the holy life consummate and pure. There are beings who will understand the Dhamma. I shall go to Uruvelā, to Senānigama, to teach the Dhamma."

In accordance with this admonition, the disciples walked the highways and byways of India spreading the Dhamma, the new message of wisdom and compassion. Men and women from different walks of life who listened to the message of the Master manifested their willingness to follow the Buddha and his teaching. Among them there were those who wished to enter the Order of the Saṅgha. The monks brought these followers to the Master for ordination from various districts. The long journeys, however, fatigued both the monks and the seekers for ordination. To avoid this hardship and inconvenience, the Buddha allowed the monks to ordain the followers in any district. The manner of ordination was explained to the monks by the Buddha himself in this wise:

"The hair and beard must be shaved first, and then the saffron robe put on. Adjusting his robe on one shoulder (the left), the seeker for ordination should pay homage to the monks, and squatting (if this is inconvenient one can kneel) before them with hands raised and palms together, he should say:

Buddhaṃ saraṇaṃ gacchāmi
Dhammaṃ saraṇaṃ gacchāmi
Saṅghaṃ saraṇaṃ gacchāmi

Dutiyampi Buddhaṃ saraṇaṃ gacchāmi
Dutiyampi Dhammaṃ saraṇaṃ gacchāmi
Dutiyampi Saṅghaṃ saraṇaṃ gacchāmi

Tatiyampi Buddhaṃ saraṇaṃ gacchāmi
Tatiyampi Dhammaṃ saraṇaṃ gacchāmi
Tatiyampi Saṅghaṃ saraṇaṃ gacchāmi

I go for refuge to the Buddha (the Teacher)
I go for refuge to the Dhamma (the Teaching)
I go for refuge to the Saṅgha (the Taught)

For the second time, I go for refuge to the Buddha
For the second time, I go for refuge to the Dhamma
For the second time, I go for refuge to the Saṅgha

For the third time, I go for refuge to the Buddha
For the third time, I go for refuge to the Dhamma
For the third time, I go for refuge to the Saṅgha

This was the manner in which a follower gained ordination in those early days. But with the passage of time this short formula had to be expanded as various unsuitable and undesirable men sought admission into the order. As it stands now, in the Novice Ordination, the follower has to recite the ten precepts in addition to the three refuges. In the case of a Higher Ordination, *upasampadā,* the novice who is to be ordained is examined and questioned by senior monks (see the essay). It may be noted that these additions were made by the Buddha himself, and they are not later arbitrary inclusions. Hence in the conducting of a novice or bhikkhu ordination every detail has to be observed.

In the Order of the Saṅgha a novice is expected to observe the ten precepts, study the Dhamma and Vinaya (doctrine and discipline) from his elders, attend upon the senior monks, prepare himself and become eligible for the Higher Ordination. *Sāmaṇera* (*samaṇa* + *ṇera*) literally means son (*ṇera*) of the *samaṇa* or the monk, in the sense that a novice should be taught, disciplined and taken care of by a competent and understanding monk. A novice need not observe the *vassa,* the rainy season, which a bhikkhu is expected to observe. He is given the bhikkhu or Higher Ordination when he has reached the age of twenty and not before. But age alone would not do, for it is not a sufficient qualification; if he lacks in intelligence, has not studied necessary Dhamma and Vinaya for leading the bhikkhu life, he is not a fit candidate eligible for the Higher Ordination .

A bhikkhu is expected to observe the essential (*pātimokkha*) precepts which are 220[1] (227) in number. It is difficult to adequately translate the word bhikkhu. Monk may be considered as the best rendering. The words, Thera and Mahā Thera are only titles. A

1. The last 7 of the 227 are not rules, but procedures for settling legal issues in the Saṅgha. (BPS Editor)

bhikkhu who has counted ten or more years of vassa may be called a Thera (literally elder or senior), and a bhikkhu who has spent twenty or more years of vassa is eligible to be called a Mahā Thera. Still he is a bhikkhu, and as the Dhammapada (260, 261) says:

"One is not a Thera merely because his head is grey. Ripe, he is in age, and 'a man grown old in vain' is he called."

"In whom there is truth and righteousness, harmlessness, restraint and control, that wise man who has thrown off impurities is indeed called Thera."

The word "priest" cannot, however, be used as a substitute of "bhikkhu"; for Buddhist monks are not priests who perform rites or sacrifices. They do not administer sacraments and pronounce absolution. An ideal Buddhist monk cannot, and does not, stand as an intermediary between man and "supernatural" powers, for Buddhism teaches that each individual is solely responsible for his own liberation. Hence there is no need to win the favour of a mediating priest. "You yourselves should strive on: the Buddhas show the path." (Dhammapada, 276)

The purpose of "going forth" (*pabbajjā*) is to turn away from thoughts of sensuality (*kilesa-kāmā*) and objects of sense (*vatthu-kāmā*). It is, therefore, really a self-sacrifice, and the urge to do so should be a genuine one if it is to bear pleasant fruit. This is certainly not a path that all can follow; for to leave behind the world's attractive and sensuous life is no easy a task. It is not possible for all to cut themselves off from the world with all its attraction. And the Buddha does not expect all his followers to become monks or ascetics. Again the Dhammapada (verse 302) says: *"Hard it is to go forth from home to homelessness, To take delight in it is hard."*

In the Buddha's Dispensation, full liberty is granted to the disciples to leave the Order if they find it difficult to live the monk's life any more. There is no coercion or compulsion, whatsoever, and the person reverting to the lay life is not stigmatized.

Genuine renunciation, it may be borne in mind, is not escapism. Those who do not understand the real significance of renunciation, and those who judge it from bogus "recluses" who lead an indolent, worthless and parasitical life, hastily conclude that "going forth" is a sort of escapism, a selfish way of life. Nothing could be more untrue. The ideal monk, the bhikkhu, however, is an altruist of the highest type who takes least from, and gives much to society.

"As a bee without harming the flower, its colour and fragrance, takes away the honey (pollen), even so should the sage move in the village." (Dhammapada, 49).

It is true with the passage of time, many changes have taken place, yet the genuine Buddhist monk, who has given up worldly pleasures, endeavours to lead a life of voluntary poverty and complete celibacy with the high aim of serving others selflessly, within the bounds of his bhikkhu life, and attain the deliverance of mind.

There are two ways of leading the life of a bhikkhu: one entails continuous meditation (*vipassanā-dhura*) and the other part-time meditation, studying and teaching of the Dhamma (*gantha-dhura*). It is obligatory on every bhikkhu to take up one or the other of these ways according to temperament, age and environment.[2]

The robe that a novice or a bhikkhu puts on is his dress and he is expected to wear it always and not on special occasions only.

In conclusion, it must be said that the Higher Ordination or Upasampadā ordination should be conducted in a duly consecrated "chapter House" (*sīmā*) and not in any place considered convenient.

Piyadassi Thera

2. For a detailed account of the bhikkhu life the reader is referred to *The Buddha's Ancient Path,* Buddhist Publication Society, Kandy. 1979.

An Early Account of an Ordination Ceremony in Sri Lanka

by J. F. Dickson, B.A.

Reprinted from a paper published in the
Journal of the Royal Asiatic Society, 1874

In May 1872, I was invited by my learned friend and pandit Kewiṭiyāgala Unnānse, of the Malwattē Monastery in Kandy, to be present at an ordination service, held according to custom on the full-moon day of Wesak (May, June), being the anniversary of the day on which Gautama Buddha attained Nirvāna, B.C. 543. I gladly availed myself of this opportunity of witnessing the celebration of a rite of which Englishmen have but little knowledge, and which has rarely, if ever, been witnessed by any European in Ceylon.

Nothing could be more impressive than the order and solemnity of the proceedings. It was impossible not to feel that the ceremony was being conducted precisely as it was more than two thousand years ago. The chapter house (Sinhalese, *Poya-gē*) is an oblong hall, with rows of pillars forming an inner space and leaving broad aisles at the sides. At the top of this inner space sat the aged Abbot (Sinhalese, *Mahā Nāyaka*) as president of the chapter; on either side of him sat the elder priests,[3] and down the sides sat the other priests in number between thirty and forty. The chapter or assembly thus formed three sides of an oblong. The president sat on cushions and a carpet; the other priests sat on mats convered with white calico. They all sat cross-legged. On the fourth side at the foot, stood the candidates, behind the pillars on the right stood the deacons,[4] the left was given up to the visitors, and behind candidates at the bottom was a crowd of Buddhist laymen.

To form a chapter for this purpose not less than ten[5] duly ordained monks are required, and the president must be of not less

---

3. Use the word *bhikkhus* or *monks* throughout
4. Use the word *novices* throughout.
5. Not necessarily. The minimum required is five. In Middle Country, in India, it is said, that not less than ten are required.

than ten years' standing from his Upasampadā ordination. The monks attending the chapter are required to give their undivided, unremitting and devout attention throughout the service. Every priest is instructed to join heart and mind in the exhortations, responses, formulas, etc., and to correct every error, lest the oversight of a single mistake should vitiate the efficacy of the rite. Previously to the ordination the candidates are subjected to a strict and searching examination as to their knowledge of the discourses of the Buddha, the duties of a priest, etc. An examination and ordination is held on the full-moon day in Vesak,[6] and on the three succeeding Poya days, or days of quarters of the moon.

After witnessing the celebration of this rite, I read the *Upasampadā Kammavācā* or book setting forth the form and manner of ordering of priests and deacons, and I was subsequently induced to translate it. This manual was translated into Italian in 1776, by Padre Maria Percoto (missionary in Ava and Pegu), under the title of "*Kammuva, ossia trattato della ordinazio dei Talapoini del secondo ordine detti Penzi*," and a portion of it was edited in 1841, in Pali and Latin, by Professor Spiegel. Clough translated it in 1834, and Hardy has given an interesting summary of it his *Eastern Monachism*; but neither the text nor any complete translation is readily accessible, and I have therefore thought that this edition might possibly be acceptable to those who desire information respecting the practice of Buddhism in Sri Lanka, where, as is well pointed out by Mr. Childers, in his *Pāli Dictionary* (s.v. *Nibbānaṃ*, p. 272, note), "Buddhism retains almost its pristine purity."

With regard to the transliteration, I have used the system adopted (after Fausböll) by Mr. Childers in his *Dictionary*. In the translation I have placed in italics the rubrical directions in the text, and all explanations and amplifications of the text I have placed in the square brackets. I have thus endeavoured to give a translation of the text as it stands, and, at the same time, to set out the ordination service fully and completely, precisely in the form in use in Sri Lanka at the present time as I have myself witnessed it. No one who compares this form with that given in Article XV

6. It need not be a full moon day or Vesak. There is no hard and fast rule regarding the days of Ordination.

of Hodgson's *Literature and Religion of the Buddhists in Nepaul*, can fail to be struck with the purity and simplicity of the Ceylon rite as contrasted with that in use among the Northern Buddhists.

J.F. Dickson, B.A,
Kandy, 9th January, 1873.

The Ordination Service

Praise Be to the Blessed One, the Holy One, to Him who has Arrived at the Knowledge of All Truth.

The candidate, accompanied by his Tutor, in the dress of a layman, but having the yellow robes of a priest in his arms, makes the usual obeisance and offering to the President of the chapter, and standing says:

> "Grant me leave to speak. Lord,[7] graciously grant me admission to deacon's orders.[8] (Kneels down.) Lord, I pray for admission as a deacon. Again, lord, I pray for admission as a deacon. In compassion for me, lord, take these yellow robes, and let me be ordained, in order to the destruction of sorrow, and in order to the attainment of Nirvāna." (To be repeated three times.)

The President takes the bundle of robes.[9]

> "In compassion for me, lord, give me these yellow robes,[10] and let me be ordained in order to the destruction of all sorrow, and in order to the attainment of Nirvāna." (To be repeated three times.)

7. The Pali word is *bhante* which may be translated as "Venerable Sir." This is the term used by a junior monk when addressing a senior. The word "Lord" is sometimes used when referring to the Buddha.

8. Lit. "Make me go forth (*pabbājetha*)," in other words "grant me Sāmaṇera Ordination."

9. Under robe and upper robe.

10. The Pali word *kāsāva* means stained or dyed robe. It may be yellow or the colour of banyan fruit (orange colour).

And the President then gives the bundle of the robes, the yellow band of which he ties round the neck of the candidate, reciting the while the *tacapañcaka*, or formula of meditation on the perishable nature of the human body, as follows:

> "*Kesā lomā nakhā dantā taco—taco dantā nakhā kesā lomā.* Hair of the head, hair of the body, nails, teeth, skin—skin, teeth, nails, hair of the body, hair of the head."

The candidate then rises up, and retires to throw off the dress of a laymen, and to put on his yellow robes. While changing his dress he recites the following:

> "In wisdom I put on the robes, as protection against cold, as a protection against heat, as a protection against gadflies and mosquitoes, wind and sun, and touch of serpents and to cover nakedness, i.e., I wear them in all humility, for use only, and not for ornament or show."

Having put on the yellow robes, he returns to the side of his tutor, and says:

> "Grant me leave to speak. I make obeisance to my Lord. Lord, forgive me all my faults. Let the merit that I have gained be shared by my lord. It is fitting to give me to share in the merit gained by my lord. It is good, it is good. I share in it. Grant me leave to speak. Graciously give me, lord, the three refuges and the precepts."

He kneels down:

> "Lord, I pray for the refuges and the precepts."

The tutor gives the three refuges and the ten precepts as follows, the candidate still kneeling, and repeating them after him sentence by sentence:

(*I. The Three Refuges*)

I put my trust in Buddha.
I put my trust in the Law.
I put my trust in the Priesthood.
For the second time, I put my trust in Buddha.
For the second time, I put my trust in the Law.
For the second time, I put my trust in the Priesthood.
For the third time, I put my trust in Buddha.
For the third time, I put my trust in the Law.
For the third time, my trust in Priesthood.

(*II. The Ten Precepts or Laws of the Priesthood.*)

Abstinence from destroying life;
Abstinence from theft;
Abstinence from fornication and uncleanness;
Abstinence from lying;
Abstinence from fermented liquor, spirits and strong drinks which cause intoxication and heedlessness;
Abstinence from eating at forbidden times;
Abstinence from dancing, singing, and shows;
Abstinence from adorning and beautifying the person by the use of garlands, perfumes and unguents;
Abstinence from using a high or a large couch or seat;
Abstinence from receiving gold and silver;
are the ten means (of leading a moral life).

The candidate says:

> "I have received these ten precepts. Permit me.

He rises up, and makes obeisance to his tutor:

> Lord, I make obeisance. Forgive me all my faults. May the merit I have gained be shared by my lord. Give me to share in the merit of my lord. It is good, it is good. I share in it."

This completes the ordination of a deacon, and the candidate retires.

The foregoing ceremony is gone through previous to the ordination of a priest in all cases, even where the candidate has already been admitted as a deacon. If the candidate is duly qualified for the priestly office, he can proceed at once from deacon's to priest's orders; otherwise he must pass a term of instruction as a deacon. But a candidate who has received deacon's orders must solicit them again, and go through the above ceremony when presented for priest's orders.

The candidate being duly qualified, returns with his tutor, and goes up to the President of the chapter presenting an offering, and makes obeisance, saying:

> "Permit me to speak. Lord, graciously grant me your sanction and support." He kneels down, "Lord, I pray for your sanction and support; a second time. lord, I pray for your sanction and support; a third time, lord, I pray for your sanction and support. Lord, be my preceptor." (This is repeated three times.)

The President says:

"It is well"

and the candidate replies,

"I am content." (This is repeated three times.)

"From this day forth lord is my charge. I am charge to my lord." (This vow of mutual assistance is repeated three times.)

The candidate rises up, makes obeisance, and retires alone to the foot of the assembly, where his alms bowl is strapped on his back. His tutor then goes down, takes him by the hand, and brings him back, placing him in front of the President. One of the assembled priests stands up, and places himself on the other side of the candidate, who thus stands between two tutors.[11] The tutors say to the assembly:

"With your permission."

And then proceed to examine the candidate as to his fitness to be admitted to priest's orders":

> "Your name is Nāga? It is so, lord. Your preceptor is the Venerable Tissa? It is so, lord."

The two tutors together say:

> "Praise be to the Blessed One, the Holy one, to Him who has arrived at the knowledge of all Truth."

11. Tutors may be two or even three.

They then recite the following commands[12] of Buddha:

> "First it is right to appoint a preceptor. When the preceptor has been appointed, it is right to inquire whether the candidate has alms bowl and robes" (which they do as follows). "Is this your alms bowl? It is so, lord. Is this the Double Robe? It is so, lord. Is this the single robe? It is so, lord. Is this the under robe? It is so, lord. Go and stand there."

The candidate here retires, going backwards in a reverential posture, and stands at the lower corner of the assembly. The tutors remain in front of the President, and one of the them says:

> "Priests, hear me. The candidate desires ordination under the Venerable Tissa. Now is the time of the assembly of priests I will instruct the candidate."

The tutors make obeisance to the President, and go down to the foot of the assembly, and join the candidate, whom they instruct and examine as follows:

> "Listen, Nāga. This is the time for you to speak the truth, to state what has occurred. When asked concerning anything in the midst of the assembly if it be true, it is meet to say so; if it be not true, it is meet to say that it is not. Do not hesitate. Conceal nothing."

They inquire of the candidates as follows:

> "Have you any such diseases as these? Leprosy? No, lord. Boils? No, lord. Itch? No, lord. Asthma? No, lord. Epilepsy? No, lord. Are you a human being? Yes, lord. Are you a male? Yes, lord. Are you a freeman? Yes, lord. Are you free from debt? Yes, lord. Are you exempt from military service? Yes, lord. Have you come with the permission of your parents? Yes, lord. Are you of the full age of twenty years ? Yes, lord. Are your alms bowl and robes complete? Yes lord. What is your name? Lord, I am called Nāga. What is the name of your preceptor? Lord, my preceptor is called the Venerable Tissa."

12. They are not commands, but admonitions.

The two tutors here go to the top of the assembly, and make obeisance to the President, and one of them says:

> "Priests, hear me. The candidate desires ordination under the Venerable Tissa. He has been duly instructed by me. Now is the time of the assembly of priests. If the candidate is here, it is right to tell him to approach."

One of the tutors says:

> "Come hither."

The candidate comes up, and stands between the tutors, makes obeisance to the assembly, and kneels down.

> "Priests, I ask the assembly for ordination. Priests, have compassion on me, and lift me up. A third time, lords. I ask the assembly for ordination; lords, have compassion on me and lift me up." (The candidate rises up, and makes obeisance. The tutors say:)
>
> "Priests, hear me. This candidate desires ordination under the Venerable Tissa. Now is the time of the assembly of priests. I will examine the candidate respecting the disqualifications for the priestly office."
>
> "Listen, Nāga. This is the time for you to speak the truth, to state what has occurred. I will inquire of you concerning facts. If a thing is, it is right to say it is; if a thing is not, it is right to say it is not. Have you any such diseases as these? Leprosy? No, lord. Boils? No, lord. Itch? No, lord. Asthma? No, lord. Epilepsy? No, lord. Are you a human being? Yes, lord. Are you a male? Yes, lord. Are you a free man? Yes, lord. Are you free from debt? Yes, lord. Are you exempt from military service? Yes; lord. Have you come with the permission of your parents? Yes, lord. Are you of the full age of twenty years? Yes, lord. Are your alms bowl and robes complete? Yes, lord. What is your name? ...
>
> Lord, I am called Nāga. What is the name of your preceptor? My preceptor, lord, is called the Venerable Tissa."

Here ends the examination in the midst of the assembly, and one of the tutors reports the result as follows:

> "This candidate desires ordination under the Venerable Tissa. He is free from disqualifications. He has his alms bowl and robes complete. The candidate asks the assembly for ordination under his preceptor, the Venerable Tissa. The assembly gives the candidate ordination under his preceptor, the Venerable Tissa. If any of the venerable assembly approves the ordination of the candidate under his preceptor, the Venerable Tissa, let him be silent; if any objects, let him speak. A second time ... a third time I state this matter.
>
> Priests, listen! This candidate desires ordination under the Venerable Tissa. He is free from disqualifications from the priestly office. His alms bowl and robes are complete. The candidate asks the priesthood for ordination under his preceptor, the Venerable Tissa. The assembly gives the candidate ordination under his preceptor, the Venerable Tissa. If any of the venerable assembly approves the ordination of the candidate under his superior, the Venerable Tissa, let him be silent; if any objects, let him speak."

The two tutors here again make obeisance to the President, and say:

> "The candidate has received ordination from the priesthood under his preceptor, the Venerable Tissa. The assembly approves the resolution: therefore it keeps silence, so I understand your wish."

Ordination of a Bhikkhu in Kandy

By F. L. Woodward
From the Ceylon Daily News, Vesak Number, May 1940.13

At the edge of the lake at Kandy, hidden away among the trees there stands an ancient monastery, secluded and unknown to many of the visitors who throng the courts of the Temple of the Tooth on the other side. It is the Malwatte Vihāra (Flower Garden Retreat), the residence of the head of the Buddhist Order in Ceylon, the Mahānāyaka Thero, or Lord High Abbot of the Siam Sect of monks, Here is performed the ceremony of admission to the ranks of the Brethren of the Yellow Robe. An ordination may take place anywhere provided that it is conferred by a chapter of ten elders, theras, or monks of ten years standing but the seal of importance is added by the ceremony taking place at this Kandy head-vihāra, and this is usually done on Vesak Day, the great Buddhist festival, the full moon day of the month of May.

To be ordained a monk is a solemn step, and to be ordained upon his day of days, when the heart of every Buddhist is fixed upon the Birth, the Illumination, the Preaching of the Good Law, and the Parinibbāna or final passing away of the Teacher of Gods and men, and here in this place, where for centuries the ecclesiastic succession has been preserved, confers a spiritual touch and awakens associations that are in their way unique. Youths from distant villages have come up attended by their relatives and friends to receive the robes and take the vow of *pabbajjā*, renunciation of the worldly life. A boy may not do this till he is at least eight years of age. At the age of twenty he may receive full ordination (take priests orders, as Christians would say) or the *upasampadā*. Till then he is called a *sāmaṇera* or novice. All alike, whether novices or elders are termed bhikkhus, begging monks and form the Sangha or Order of the Buddhist 'Church.' On this

13. This essay was not in the original Wheel Publication, but because it complements Dickson's description, it was included this edition.

day too are present many *sāmaṇeras* attended by their tutors who have come up to Kandy from monasteries throughout the Island.

The Scene

It is the evening of Vesak Day, and all the place is lit with lamps which cast their stars upon the still surface of the lake, and white robed forms move to and fro. The hollow booming of the big tom-toms reverberates among the huge overhanging trees. A flight of stone steps leads up from the road to the ordination hall now crowded with monks and laymen. A solemnity pervades the atmosphere which is not dissipated by the subdued chatter of the numbers squatting at the lower end. As we enter he hall the first thing that strikes the eye is the great glass-enclosed Buddha before whose calmly-seated cross-legged form blink numberless little lights, amid the heaped up offerings of many-coloured flowers, in front of which, facing outwards, is seated the aged High Abbot, the president of this gathering. Next to him, on either side, in order of seniority of ordination are ranged the elder monks, and down the two sides of the hall are rows of juniors, in yellow robes of various hues, orange and ochre, russet and lemon, for the hue varies according to the process and times of dyeing. At the bottom stand the candidates, along with a gorgeously dressed figure in the Kandyan national dress, a *ratemahatma*, or chief, who is the head *dāyaka* or trustee of the temple, befrilled and padded out in white muslin and linen, his fingers decked with jewelled rings; an imposing figure of a man, in strong contrast to the meek and simply-clad close-shaven monks, an ivory-topped garden of sun-flowers. The white-clad laymen squatting on he floor form an appropriate background to this scene.

2,500 Years Ago

In thought one is carried back two thousand and five-hundred years, and pictures to oneself the first giving of the robes by the Master himself. "Come, monk! (*ehi bhikkhu*)"—this, and nothing more, marked the admission of Yasa, the eager youth, to the perpetual brotherhood of the sons of the Buddha. In aftertimes, when applicants were many, he gave permission for the robes to be conferred by a chapter of ten elders, with a view to a time when he should he no longer with them, and his ceremony has been performed unchanged age after age, until the present day. One receives the impression that these yellow-robed, shaven-headed monks, with their typical cast of features, are a rock of conservatism on which the waves of centuries of thought have beaten and been rebuffed confused and ineffectual. Our western ways, our tongue and thoughts, have passed here as the footprints of the seagull on the ocean's wave, as the gusts on a rocky promontory, tempest-buffeted, citadel-crowned.

A voice calls the gathering to order. Silence falls for a moment, soon broken by the rumble of the sonorous Pali invocation, which has resounded down the centuries.

Youth Decked in Jewels

Namo tassa bhagavato arahato sammā sambuddhassa.

Glory to Him, the Blessed Saint, the All-enlightened One.

A youth in laymen's garb comes forward. He is decked with jewels and fine clothes, lent him for the occasion by relatives and friends, the trappings of the worldly life which he has donned to enhance the effect of the sacrifice he is about to make, and which he will presently doff in exchange for the beggar's robes. He is led by a monk who has been his spiritual guide (*upajjha*) during his preparation, who has trained him in the Doctrine (Dhamma) and the Discipline (Vinaya).

Standing before the president he bows low and says:

"Give me leave, Venerable Sir, in compassion confer on me the robes. (*Kneeling*:) Venerable Sir, I beg the robes of you." (*thrice*).

He now presents to the abbot the bundle of yellow robes which he is to don, saying thrice these words:

"Venerable Sir, in compassion take these yellow robes and confer them on me for the ending of all sorrow, for the realization of Nibbāna (*sabbadukkhanissaraṇa-nibbānasacchikiriyatthāya*)."

He holds out his folded palms, on which the old monk replaces the bundle with trembling hands and fastens the band round his neck, repeating forwards and backwards:

Kesā lomā nakhā dantā taco;
Taco dantā nakhā lomā kesā.

This formula sums up the transitory nature of the human form, compounded as it is of,

> Hair of the head, hair of the body, nails, teeth and skin;
> Skin, teeth and nails, hair of the body, hair of the head.

Mendicant's Robes

Then rising, he retires with his sponsor and another monk, who disrobe him of his finery of borrowed plumes, and while the process goes on—for, he wears a series of gaily coloured suits, one over the other—prompted by them, he chants the stanzas as he assumes the mendicant's yellow robes.

> *Paṭisaṅkhā yoniso civaraṃ paṭisevāmi*
> *Yāvad eva sītassa paṭighātāya uṇhassa paṭighātāya.*
> *Daṃsamakasa-vātatapa-siriṃsapa-samphas-sānaṃ paṭighātāya,*
> *Yāvad eva hirikopīna-paṭi-cchādanatthaṃ*

> "Wisely reflecting I don the robe,
> To guard me from the heat and cold,
> From flies, and gnats, from wind and sun,
> From snakebite, and to hide my shame."

From bare necessity, not for luxury, he puts on the robes which, under the old dispensation, were made of rags picked from the dust-heap (see the sermon at the end). Bhikkhus of the present day carry umbrellas, fans, wear silken robes sometimes, and sandals; some carry purses and otherwise conform to the changing times.

Now he returns, led by his sponsor, and, again standing before the president, bows and says to his tutor:

> "Give me leave, Venerable Sir, I bow before you.
> Have patience, Venerable Sir, with my faults."

President: "I forgive what is to be forgiven."
Canditate: "May the merits I have won be welcomed by the Venerable Sir."
P: "It is well, it is well; I gladly receive."
C: "May the merit that my Venerable Sir has won be given to me."
P: "It is well, you should gladly receive."
C: "It is well. It is well, and gladly I receive them."

C: "Give me leave. Out of compassion, Venerable Sir.
Give me the Three Refuge and the Precepts Ten.
(*Kneeling*) Venerable Sir, I beg the Refuges and Precepts." (*thrice*)

Precepts

The precepts are given and repeated by the candidate in faltering tones, with occasional promptings from the tutor.

"From killing to abstain—the vow I take.
From stealing to abstain—the vow I take.
From lustful deeds to abstain—the vow I take.
From lying to abstain—the vow I take,
From drink and sloth-producing drugs to abstain—the vow I take.
From food at times unseasonable to abstain—the vow I take.
From dancing, singing, music, worldly shows,
From flowers scents and un-guents, and from wearing adornments and from beautifying this body—from all these to abstain—the vow I take.
From the use of high or wide couches or seats to abstain—the vow I take.
From taking gold and silver to abstain—the vow I take.
These ten precepts I undertake to keep. (*Rising and bowing to his sponsor*).
Give me leave. Venerable Sir, I salute you and accept with thanks." (As above).

Such is the ceremony of *pabbajjā*. If duly qualified for the full order, the candidate now retires a moment and returns to make an offering to the Abbot and says:

"Give me leave. In compassion Venerable Sir, give me aid (*nissaya*).
(*Kneeling*) Venerable Sir, I ask your aid. (*thrice*)
Be my spiritual guide." (*thrice*)
The president: "It is well."
The candidate: "It is fitting. Friend, give me leave, I accept. (*thrice*)
From henceforth the elder is my charge (*nissaya*) and I am his." (*thrice*)

He rises, bows and retires alone to the end of the assembly, where his begging bowl is fastened on his back. The tutor now goes to him and leads him up to the president. Another monk stands up and they address the saṅgha (gathering of monks).

The sponsors (*acting for the assembly*):

"Give us leave (then to the novice). Is your name (e.g.) Nāga?"

C. "Give me leave. It is so."

S. "Your preceptor is Tissa the elder?"

C. "Give me leave. It is so."

S. "*Namo Tassa Bhagavato Arahato Sammā Sambuddhassa.*"

"Glory to Him, the Blessed Saint, the all-enlightened One."

"First a spiritual guide is to be obtained. This done, we must inquire about the bowl and robes, thus:"

S. "Is this your bowl?"

C. "It is so, Venerable Sir."

S. "And this your upper robe?"

C. It is so, Venerable Sir."

S. "And this your under robe?"

C. "It is so."

S. "Go and stand yonder."

The candidate retires backwards and stands at the end of the hall. Now one of the sponsors addresses the assembly:

"Listen, reverend brotherhood. This Nāga desires ordination from the reverend Tissa. If it is seasonable to the brotherhood, I will instruct Nāga,"

Cross-Examination

They bow to the Venerable Abbot and go down to the candidate and cross-examine him thus:

S. "Hear now, Nāga. It is time to tell the truth and speak of facts. In the midst of the brotherhood of monks, when asked, 'Is it true?' It is right to make reply, 'It is true,' or as the case may be. Do not hesitate. Be not distressed in mind. I will ask you thus: Do you have diseases such as these: leprosy, or phthisis, or epilepsy?"

C. "No, Venerable Sir."

S. "Are you a human being, a male, a freeman, debtless, no soldier of the king? Do you have your parents consent? Are you of full age, and are your bowl and robes complete?"
C. "Yes, Venerable Sir."
S. "What is your name?"
C. "Venerable Sir, my name is Nāga."
S. "What is your preceptor's name?"
C. "Tissa the elder, Venerable Sir."

The examiners now return to the top end and bow to the Abbot. One of them says, addressing the Order:

"Listen, O monks. Nāga desires ordination from the Venerable Tissa. He has been admonished by me. If it be seasonable to the Venerables that he should approach, let him be told to approach." (To Nāga:) "Come hither."

The candidate comes forward, and, between the two monks, bows, and kneels saying:

"O, Venerable Sir, I ask the Brotherhood (Saṅgha) for all ordination. May the reverend Order have compassion on me and lift me up!" (*This thrice*) He rises and bows.

The Elder to the Order: "Listen to me, O reverend Order. This Nāga is desirous of ordination from the reverend Tissa." (*The same as the above examination.*)

He turns to the monks and says: "He is free from the hindrances. His bowl and robes are in order. He asks the ordination from the venerable Tissa."

Approval

He now thrice puts the motion to the chapter monks, saying:

"If anyone approves of the candidate, let him be silent. If anyone objects, let him speak."

If no objection is made, both bow to the Abbot and announces the decision:

"Nāga is ordained under the venerable Tissa. The brotherhood approves. This is their decision (*esa ñatti*). Thus I take your decision."

The ordination is now over and the formula of examination is repeated with each candidate. If there be many, as on this occasion, the proceedings are very long, the patience of the audience is exhausted and the monks find it hard to fix their attention on the words, as they had been enjoined to do. A buzz of conversation arises from the lower end. Then, when all have been duly ordained, an elder rises, and exhorts the new monks, who stand before him reverently, as follows, with the time-honoured admonitions.

The preacher: "Now should the shadow be measured. The exact time must be declared. The portion of the day must be recorded. In conjunction these things are to be told. The four supports (*nissaya*) of the monk and the four for hidden actions must be told. Food collected in a bowl is the monk's support. Thus fed must you strive, as long as life shall last.

These are the extra allowances —Food given to the Order as a whole occasional food, invitation food, ticket food, fortnightly meals, full-moon feasts, and food of the day after the full moon."

The candidates: "Even so, Venerable Sir."

P. "Robes made of rags are the monk's support. Thus clad must you strive, as long as life shall last. These are the extra allowances: robes of linen, cotton, silk, wool, hemp, or made of all these five."

C. "Even so, Venerable Sir."

P. "A seat at the foot of a tree is the monk's support. Thus seated must you strive, as long as life shall last. These are the extra allowances. A residence, a lean-to, an upstairs building, a walled house or a cave."

C. "Even so, Venerable Sir."

P. "Stale urine as medicine is a monks support. Thus remedied must you strive as long as life shall last. These are the extra allowances: butter, cream, oil, honey, and sugar.

C. "Even so, Venerable Sir."

The Four Forbidden Actions

P. "The sexual act must not he practised by a fully-ordained monk, nor any act of bestial nature. The monk that follows this pursuit is no monk, no son of the Sakya clan. Just as a man whose head is severed from the trunk can live no longer, so is a monk who follows this pursuit a monk no longer, no son of the Sakya clan. Thus restrained must you strive, as long as life shall last."

C. "Even so, Venerable Sir."

P. "Things not given to him a fully-ordained monk must not

take with thievish intent, were it even a blade of grass. The monk that takes thus thievishly a little coin, or half a coin or anything worth as much more than that, if it be not given, is no longer a monk, no longer a son of he Sakya clan. Just as a withered leaf, once severed from the stalk, hath no longer any part in greenness, even so the monk who takes dishonestly what is not given, is a monk no more, no longer a son of the Sakya clan. Thus must you refrain, as long as life shall last."

C. "Even so, Venerable Sir."

P. "No living thing, were it even but an ant must be deprived of life, with intent to slay (*sañcicca*), by a fully ordained monk. Moreover, if a monk slays a being of human form, even by slaying a foetus in the womb, he is a monk no more, no more a member of the Sakya clan. Just as a rock once split in twain can never be rejoined, so is a monk who takes life, with intent to slay, monk no more, no more a member of he Sakya clan. From this act you must refrain as long as life shall last."

C. "Even so, Venerable Sir."

P. "No superhuman powers are to be claimed, not even to the extent of saying, 'I delight to live in a lonely hut,' by a fully-ordained monk. If a monk deceitfully, for gain, falsely lays claim to superhuman qualities, be it the trance, the ecstasy, the absorption, the path or the path's fruit—he is a monk no more, no more a member of the Sakya clan. Just as a tall palmyra palm, whose top has been cut off, can never put forth shoots again, so a monk, who deceitfully, for gain, falsely lays a claim to superhuman powers, is a monk no more, no more a member of the Sakya clan. These things you must avoid as long as life shall last."

C. "Even so, Venerable Sir."

***

Our ceremony is now over and the night is far spent. The newly-robed bhikkhus go forth with eager hearts, and we, who in thought have been carried back to ages long ago, descend again to the world of rickshaws, hotels, gas-lamps and railway trains.

A Discourse to Knowers of Veda

Tevijja Sutta

A Discourse of the Buddha on the Path to the Divine

Translated by

Prof. T. W. Rhys Davids

With Introduction and Notes by

Paul Debes

WHEEL PUBLICATION NO. 57/58

Copyright © Kandy: Buddhist Publication Society (1963, 1977)

Introduction

The quest for God and the communion with him constitute among the manifold strivings of humanity its most ardent and deepest concern. At the bottom of this quest, it seems, lies an ineradicable yearning for peace, security and well-being. There seems to reside a mysterious power in the very name of God be it the Brahmā of the Hindus, Allah of the Muslims or the Heavenly Father of the Christians. Gandhi once confessed that whenever his lips uttered the name of Rāma his innermost being was shaken to its very foundations and his heart filled with unspeakable joy. Under whatsoever name God is called upon, this name has always been linked up with the idea of highest spirituality, absolute invulnerability, and final deliverance from the burden of suffering.

This spiritual potency called God is not always personified. Sometimes it is thought of as a mode of being in its loftiest possible state of immateriality without any notion of individualized existence as, for instance, the impersonal Brahmā of Hinduism or the "Godhead"—the hidden, unmanifested deity—of the great German mystic, Meister Eckhart. In Buddhism and in Jainism the concept of "God" in the Western sense is entirely unknown; although both acknowledge the existence of Divine Beings higher than Man but still imperfect and impermanent.

Nowadays, even in widely different cultural settings, wherever men believe and aspire to that communion with God, holding out for them the promise of eternal salvation, the question arises whether it will be God who takes the initiative in approaching man or, whether it is man, the creature, who must lift himself up to God. The answer to this question will depend entirely on man's image of God. If God is seen as a Father having compassion with his weak children, leading them to their heavenly home, he will be thought of as a person not unlike a human father. It is in this way that the Christian churches have depicted their God in the shape of a man, hoary with age.

If, however, God is not being conceived of as a person but as a mode of the utmost purity and spirituality of being, then the quest assumes an entirely different character. Communion, or better the Union with God, can in this case only be consummated through a steadfast and progressive purification of heart in the believer. Of this condition the Sermon of the Mount speaks: "Blessed are the pure in heart: for they shall see God."

In a similar vein Angelus Silesius, the Christian mystic of the seventeenth century, exclaims:

> "Man, do not stop at man
> The highest must thou win!
> To God, to Heaven's bliss,
> Gods only can come in."

To the enlightened mind of our day it is hardly palatable, if not to say repugnant, to conceive of an anthropomorphized Creator of the Universe who in the end destroys his own handiwork in a cataclysm of fire. And similarly the more sophisticated idea of an immaterial, i.e. spiritual, mode of being, a "World Soul" with all its accompanying connotations, religious and otherwise, can hardly find acceptance either. Utterly bewildered we ask ourselves: where shall we go from here, are there no signposts to show us the way out of this dilemma?

The answer is: go nowhere: stay where you are. From the exploration of outer Space turn your gaze inward into the depths of consciousness, from the "projection" to the projecting psyche itself. And there you will find precisely the modes of being with which you, in your former nescience, endowed a mythical creator. It is in our innermost selves wherein we discern darkness and light, creative and destructive urges, and only there, in our very inwardness, the solution to the riddle of existence.

It is exactly from these psychological, ethical, and metaphysical perspectives that the problem of "God" and the "communion" with him is viewed and understood by the Buddha. The text that follows is taken from the 13th Discourse in the Longer Collection (Dīgha Nikāya) as preserved in the Pali Canon (Tipiṭaka). First of all the following points deserve to be noted. The Brahmin priests who approach the Buddha obviously believe that communion with Brahmā equals perfect holiness and the highest state to which mortal man can aspire. Brahmā's realm means to them absolute security and eternal peace. The Buddha does not deny that Brahmā existence is indeed far above the human condition with its intermingling joys and sorrows. However, the Buddha's penetrating insight realizes that even the lofty realm of Brahmā is no more than a temporary refuge of transitory bliss and a far cry from his own teaching of final deliverance. On this deliverance the Enlightened One keeps silent and there is a reason for it. Because what he tells the priests may be for them a starting point, leading—as we may hope—to a higher development. They may in some future day surpass the Brahmā state, attain perfect holiness and complete emancipation from all fetters, human or Brahmā Divine.

On the other hand, and this is clearly shown in many of the Discourses, the Buddha's Path to final deliverance need not include the way to Brahmā or God. This goal is entirely realizable without concerning oneself with the so-called supernatural or, better to be called, the super-terrestrial.

Paul Debes

Tevijja Sutta[1]

1. Thus have I heard. When the Exalted One was once journeying through Kosala with a great company of the brethren, with about five hundred brethren, he came to the Brahman village in Kosala which is called Manasākaṭa. (1)

And there at Manasākaṭa the Exalted One stayed in the mango grove, on the bank of the river Aciravatī, to the north of Manasākaṭa.

2. Now, at that time many very distinguished and wealthy Brahmans were staying at Manasākaṭa: to wit, Caṅkī the Brahman, Tārukkha the Brahman, Pokkharasādī the Brahman, Jāṇussoṇi the Brahman, Todeyya the Brahman, and other very distinguished and wealthy Brahmans.

3. Now, a conversation sprung up between Vāseṭṭha and Bhāradvāja, when they were taking exercise (after their bath) and walking up and down, strolling up and down, in thoughtful mood, as to which was the true path, and which the false.

4. The young Brahman Vāseṭṭha spoke thus:

"This is the straight path, this the direct way which makes for salvation, and leads him, who acts according to it, into a state of union with Brahmā. I mean that which has been announced by the Brahman Pokkharasādī."

5. The young Brahman Bhāradvāja spoke thus:

"This is the straight path, this the direct way which makes for salvation, and leads him, who acts according to it, into a state of union with Brahmā. I mean that which has been announced by the Brahman Tārukkha."(2)

6. But neither was the young Brahman Vāseṭṭha able to convince the young Brahman Bhāradvāja, nor was the young

---

1. Literally, "The Sutta (spoken) to knowers of the Three Vedas." Footnotes not marked "Rh.D." (Prof. Rhys Davids) have been supplied by the editor of the *Wheel* Series.

(1), (2) etc. refer to end notes beginning at p.288.

Brahman Bhāradvāja able to convince the young Brahman Vāseṭṭha.

7. Then the young Brahman Vāseṭṭha said to the young Brahman Bhāradvāja:

"That Samana Gotama, Bhāradvāja, of the sons of the Sakyas, who went out of the Sakya clan to adopt the religious life, is now staying at Manasākaṭa, in the mango grove, on the bank of the river Aciravatī, to the north of Manasākaṭa. Now regarding that Venerable Gotama, such is the high reputation that has been noised abroad: 'That Exalted One is an Arahat, Fully Enlightened One, abounding in wisdom and goodness, happy, with knowledge of the worlds, unsurpassed as a guide to mortals willing to be led, a teacher of gods and men, an Exalted One, a Buddha.' Come, then, Bhāradvāja, let us go to the place where the Samana Gotama is; and when we have come there, let us ask the Samana Gotama touching this matter. What the Samana Gotama shall declare unto us, that let us bear in mind."(3)

"Very well, my friend!" said the young Brahman Bhāradvāja, in assent, to the young Brahman Vāseṭṭha.

8. Then the young Brahman Vāseṭṭha and the young Brahman Bhāradvāja went on to the place where the Exalted One was.

And when they had come there, they exchanged with the Exalted One the greetings and compliments of politeness and courtesy, and sat down beside him.(4)

And while they were thus seated the young Brahman Vāseṭṭha said to the Exalted One:

"As we, Gotama, were taking exercise and walking up and down there sprung up a conversation between us on which was the true path, and which the false. I said thus:

'This is the straight path, this the direct way which makes for salvation, and leads him, who acts according to it, into a state of union with Brahmā. I mean that which has been announced by the Brahman Pokkharasādī.'

Bhāradvāja said thus:

'This is the straight path, this the direct way which makes for salvation, and leads him, who acts according to it, into a state of union with Brahmā. I mean that which has been announced by the Brahman Tārukkha.'

Regarding this matter, Gotama, there is a strife, a dispute, a difference of opinion between us."

9. "So you say, Vāseṭṭha, that you said thus:

'This is the straight path, this the direct way which makes for salvation, and leads him, who acts according to it, into a state of union with Brahmā. I mean that which has been announced by the Brahman Pokkharasādī.'

"While Bhāradvāja said thus:

'This is the straight path, this the direct way which makes for salvation,, and leads him, who acts according to it, into a state of union with Brahmā. I mean that which has been announced by the Brahman Tārukkha.'

"Wherein, then, O Vāseṭṭha, is there a strife, a dispute, a difference of opinion between you?"

10. "Concerning the true path and the false, Gotama, various Brahmans, Gotama, teach various paths; The Addhariya Brahmans, the Tittiriya Brahmans,[2] the Chandoka Brahmans,[3] the Bavharijjha Brahmans.[4] Are all those saving paths? Are they all paths which will lead him, who acts according to them, into a state of union with Brahmā?

"Just, Gotama, as near a village or a town there are many and various paths, yet they all meet together in the village—just in that way are all the various paths taught by various Brahmans—the Addhariya Brahmans, the Tittiriya Brahmans, the Chandoka Brahmans, the Bavharijjha Brahmans. Are all these saving paths? Are they all paths which will lead him, who acts according to them, into a state of union with Brahmā?"

11. "Do you say that they all lead aright, Vāseṭṭha?"

"I say so, Gotama."

---

2. According to the Sub-commentary, these two are Yajurveda priests. *Addhariyā*: *addharo* (Skr.: *adhvara*) is a kind of sacrifice. Sacrificial prayers (*yajūni*) concerned with it are called *addhariya* (Skr.: *adhvaryu*), and also those who recite them. *Tittiriya* (Skr: *taittirya*) are those who recite the mantras composed by the sage Tittiri. "Tittira" is a name for the Yajurveda.

3. Chandoka (Skr.: *chandoga*). Sub-Cy.: *chando* ("verse") especially applied to the Sāma Veda.

4. Bavharijjha, Sub-Cy.: Because there are many hymns of praise in it (*bahavo iriyo thomanā ettha'ti*), the Rigveda (Pali: *irubbeda*) is called *bahvari*.

"Do you really say that they all lead aright, Vāseṭṭha?[5]"

"So I say, Gotama."(5)

12. "But yet, Vāseṭṭha, is there a single one of the Brahmans versed in the three Vedas who has ever seen Brahmā face to face?"(6)

"No, indeed, Gotama!"

"Or is there then, Vāseṭṭha, a single one of the teachers of the Brahmans versed in the three Vedas who has seen Brahmā face to face?"

"No, indeed, Gotama!"

"Or is there then, Vāseṭṭha, a single one of the Brahmans back to the seventh generation of a teacher's teacher who has seen Brahmā face to face?"

"No, indeed, Gotama!"

13. "Well then, Vāseṭṭha, those ancient Rishis of the Brahmans versed in the Three Vedas, the authors of the verses, the utterers of the verses, whose ancient form of words so chanted, uttered or composed, the Brahmans of today chant over again or repeat; intoning or reciting exactly as has been intoned or recited—to wit, Aṭṭhaka, Vāmaka, Vāmadeva, Vessāmitta, Yamataggi, Aṅgīrasa, Bhāradvāja, Vāseṭṭha, Kassapa, and Bhagu—did even they speak thus, saying: 'We know it, we have seen it, where Brahmā is, whence Brahmā is, whither Brahmā is?' " (7)

"Not so, Gotama!"

14. "Then you say, Vāseṭṭha, that none of the Brahmans, or of their teachers, or of their pupils, even back to the seventh generation of a teacher's teacher has ever seen Brahmā face to face. And that even the Rishis of old, the authors and utterers of the verses, of the ancient form of words which the Brahmans of today so carefully intone and recite precisely as they have been handed down—even they did not pretend to know or to have seen where or whence or whither Brahmā is. So that the Brahmans versed in the Three Vedas have forsooth said thus: 'What we know not,

5. Cy: The Blessed One uttered this question three times and made Vāseṭṭha confirm his reply. Why did he do that? Because sectarians, after having made an assertion, often deny having made it when refuted. Having been questioned thrice, they cannot do so.

what we have not seen, to a state of union with that we can show the way, and can say: This is the straight path, this is the direct way which makes for salvation, and leads him, who acts according to it, into a state of union with Brahmā!'

"Now, what think you, Vāseṭṭha? Does it not follow, this being so, that the talk of the Brahmans, versed though they be in the Three Vedas, turns out to be foolish talk?"(8)

"Verily, Gotama, that being so, it follows that the talk of the Brahmans versed in the Three Vedas is foolish talk."

15. "Verily, Vāseṭṭha, that Brahmans versed in the Three Vedas should be able to show the way to a state of union with that which they do not know, neither have seen—such a condition of things can in no wise be.

"Just, Vāseṭṭha, as when a string of blind men are clinging one to the other, neither can the foremost see, nor can the middle one see, nor can the hindmost see[6] just even so, it seems to me, Vāseṭṭha, is the talk of the Brahmans versed in the Three Vedas but blind talk: the first sees not, the middle one sees not, nor can the latest see. The talk then of these Brahmans versed in the Three Vedas turns out to be ridiculous, mere words, a vain and empty thing."(9)

16. "Now, what think you, Vāseṭṭha? Can the Brahmans versed in the Three Vedas—like other, ordinary folk—see the Moon and the Sun as they pray to, and praise, and worship them, turning round with clasped hands towards the place whence they rise and where they set?"

"Certainly, Gotama, they can!"

17. "Now, what think you, Vāseṭṭha? The Brahmans versed in the Three Vedas, who can very well—like other, ordinary

6. String of blind men (*andhaveni*) Cy.: The end of a stick held by a man who can see, is caught by a blind man; to him another blind man clings, to him again another. If in that way fifty to sixty blind men are joined in a line, it is called a 'string of blind men' (*andhapaveni*).

Clinging to each other (*paramparaṃ saṃsatta*) Cy.: This means: being bereft even of that seeing man who holds the stick.

In a Viennese museum there is a striking picture by the Flemish painter Pieter Breughel jr., of such a "string of blind men," led by a drunkard who takes them towards a precipice—the blindness of ignorance (*avijjā*) led on by the intoxication of craving (*taṇhā*).

folk—see the Moon and the Sun as they pray to, and praise, and worship them, turning round with clasped hands to the place whence they rise and where they set —are those Brahmans, versed in the Three Vedas, able to point out the way to a state of union with the Moon or the Sun, saying: 'This is the straight path, this the direct way which makes for salvation, and leads him, who acts according to it, to a state of union with the Moon or the Sun?'"[7]

"Certainly not, Gotama!"

18. "So you say, Vāseṭṭha, that the Brahmans are not able to point out the way to union with that which they have seen, and you further say that neither any one of them, nor of their pupils, nor of their predecessors even to the seventh generation has ever seen Brahmā. And you further say that even the Rishis of old, whose words they hold in such deep respect, did not pretend to know, or to have seen where, or whence, or whither Brahmā is. Yet these Brahmans versed in the Three Vedas say, forsooth, that they can point out the way to union with that Brahmā whom they know not, neither have seen. Now what think you, Vāseṭṭha? Does it not follow that, this being so, the talk of the Brahmans, versed though they be in the Three Vedas, turns out to be foolish talk?"

"Verily, Gotama, that being so, it follows that the talk of the Brahmans versed in the Three Vedas is foolish talk."

19. "Very good, Vāseṭṭha. Verily then, Vāseṭṭha, that Brahmans versed in the Three Vedas should be able to show the way to a state of union with that which they do not know, neither have seen—such a condition of things can in no wise be.

"Just, Vāseṭṭha, as if a man should say, 'How I long for, how I love the most beautiful woman in this land!' And people should ask him, 'Well, good friend, this most beautiful woman in the land, whom you thus love and long for, do you know whether that beautiful woman is a noble lady or a Brahman woman, or of the trader class, or a Sudra?'

"But when so asked, he should answer: 'No.'

"And when people should ask him, 'Well, good friend, this

---

7. It must be remembered that the Sun and the Moon were gods just much as Brahmā. (Rh.D.)

most beautiful woman in all the land, whom you so love and long for, do you know what the name of that most beautiful woman is, or what is her family name, whether she be tall or short or of medium height, dark or brunette or golden in colour, or in what village or town or city she dwells?'

"But when so asked, he should answer: 'No.'

"And then people should say to him, 'So then, good friend, whom you know not, neither have seen her, do you love and long for?'

"And then when so asked, he should answer: 'Yes.'

"Now what think you, Vāseṭṭha? Would it not turn out that being so, that the talk of that man was foolish talk."

"Verily, Gotama, that is so."

20. "And just even so, Vāseṭṭha, though you say that the Brahmans are not able to point out the way to union with that which they have seen, and you further say that neither any one of them, nor of their pupils, nor of their predecessors even to the seventh generation has ever seen Brahmā. And you further say that even the Rishis of old, whose words they hold in such deep respect, did not pretend to know, or to have seen where, or whence, or whither Brahmā is. Yet these Brahmans versed in the Three Vedas say, forsooth that they can point out the way to union with that which they know not, neither have seen! Now, what think you, Vāseṭṭha? Does it not follow that, this being so, the talk of the Brahmans, versed though they be in the Three Vedas, is foolish talk?"

"Verily, Gotama, that being so, it follows that the talk of the Brahmans versed in the Three Vedas is foolish talk."

"Very good, Vāseṭṭha. Verily then, Vāseṭṭha, that Brahmans versed in the Three Vedas should be able to show the way to a state of union with that which they do not know, neither have seen—such a condition of things can in no wise be."

21. "Just, Vāseṭṭha, as if a man should make a staircase in the place where four roads cross, to mount up into a mansion. And people should say to him, 'Well, good friend, this mansion, to mount up into which you are making this staircase, do you know whether it is in the east, or in the south, or in the west, or in the north, whether it is high or low or of medium size?'

"And when so asked, he should answer: 'No.'

"And people should say to him, 'But then, good friend, you are making a staircase to mount up into something—taking it for a mansion—which, all the while, you know not, neither have seen.'

"And when so asked, he should answer: 'Yes.'

"Now what think you, Vāseṭṭha? Would it not turn out, that being so, that the talk of that man was foolish talk?"

"Verily, Gotama, it would turn out, that being so, that the talk of that man was foolish talk!"(10)

22. "And just even so, though you say that the Brahmans are not able to point out the way to union with that which they have seen, and you further say that neither any one of them, nor of their pupils, nor of their predecessors even to the seventh generation has ever seen Brahmā. And you further say that even the Rishis of old; whose words they hold in such deep respect, did not pretend to know, or to have seen where or whence or whither Brahmā is. Yet these Brahmans versed in the Three Vedas say, forsooth, that they can point out the way to union with that which they know not, neither have seen! Now what think you, Vāseṭṭha? Does it not follow that, this being so, the talk of the Brahmans versed in the Three Vedas is foolish talk?"

"Verily, Gotama, that being so, it follows that the talk of the Brahmans versed in the Three Vedas is foolish talk!"

23. "Very good, Vāseṭṭha. Verily then, Vāseṭṭha, that Brahmans versed in the Three Vedas should be able to show the way to a state of union with that which they do not know, neither have seen—such a condition of things can in no wise be."

24. "Again, Vāseṭṭha, if this river Aciravatī were full of water even to the brim and overflowing. And a man with business on the other side, bound for the other side, making for the other side, should come up, and want to cross over. And he, standing on this bank, should invoke the further bank, and say. 'Come hither, O further bank! Come over to this side!'[8](11)

---

8. The Buddha, as usual, here takes the "further bank" in the meaning attached to it by the theologians he is talking to, as union with Brahmā. In his own system, of course, the "further-bank" is Arahantship. See A V 232–233, and elsewhere. (Rh.D.)

"Now what think you Vāseṭṭha? Would the further bank of the river Aciravatī, by reason of that man's invoking and praying and hoping and praising, come over to this side?"

"Certainly not, Gotama!"

25. "In just the same way, Vāseṭṭha, do the Brahmans versed in the Three Vedas—omitting the practice of those qualities which really make a man a Brahman, and adopting the practice of those qualities which really make men non-Brahmans—say thus: 'Indra we call upon, Soma we call upon, Varuna we call upon, Isāna we call upon, Pajāpati we call upon, Brahmā we call upon, Mahiddhi we call upon, Yama we call upon!' Verily, Vāseṭṭha, that those Brahmans versed in the Three Vedas, but omitting the practice of those qualities which really make a man a Brahman, and adopting the practice of those qualities which really make men non-Brahmans—that they, by reason of their invoking and praying and hoping and praising, should, after death and when the body is dissolved, become united with Brahmā—verily such a condition of things can in no wise be (12)."

26. "Just, Vāseṭṭha, as if this river Aciravatī were full, even to the brim, and overflowing. And a man with business on the other side, making for the other side, bound for the other side, should come up, and want to cross over. And he, on this bank, were to be bound tightly with his arms behind his back, by a strong chain. Now what think you, Vāseṭṭha, would that man be able to get over from this bank of the river Aciravatī to the further bank?"

"Certainly not, Gotama!" (13)

27. "In the same way, Vāseṭṭha, there are five things leading to lust,[9] which are called, in the Discipline of the Arahats, a 'chain' and a 'bond.'

"What are the five?

"Forms perceptible to the eye; desirable, agreeable, pleasant; attractive forms, that are accompanied by lust and cause delight. Sounds of the same kind perceptible to the ear. Odours of the same kind perceptible to the nose. Tastes of the same kind perceptible to the tongue. Substances of the same kind perceptible to the body by touch. These five things leading to lust are called,

9. *Kāmaguṇa*, "strands (or bonds) of sense desires," the sense objects.

in the Discipline of the Arahats, a 'chain' and a 'bond.' And these five things leading to lust, Vāseṭṭha, do the Brahmans versed in the Three Vedas cling to, they are infatuated by them, attached to them, see not the danger of them, know not how to escape from them, and so enjoy them."

28. "And verily, Vāseṭṭha, that Brahmans versed in the Three Vedas, but omitting the practice of those qualities which really make a man a Brahman, and adopting the practice of those qualities which really make men non-Brahmans—clinging to these five things leading to lust, infatuated by them, attached to them, seeing not their danger, knowing not how to escape from them, and so enjoying them—that these Brahmans should after death, on the dissolution of the body, become united to Brahmā—such a condition of things can in no wise be!" (14)

29. "Again, Vāseṭṭha, if this river Aciravatī were full of water even to the brim and overflowing. And a man with business on the other side, making for the other side, bound for the other side, should come up and want to cross the river. And if he, covering himself up, even to his head, were to lie down, on his bank; to sleep.

"Now what think you, Vāseṭṭha? Would that man be able to get over from this bank of the river Aciravatī to the further bank?"(15)

"Certainly not, Gotama!"

30. "And in the same way, Vāseṭṭha, there are these five hindrances in the Discipline of the Arahats, which are called 'veils,' and are called 'hindrances,' and are called 'obstacles,' and are called 'entanglements.'

"Which are the five?

"The hindrance of worldly lusts, the hindrance of ill-will, the hindrance of torpor and sloth of heart and mind, the hindrance of flurry and worry, the hindrance of doubt.

"These are the five hindrances, Vāseṭṭha, which, in the Discipline of the Arahats, are called veils, and are called hindrances, and are called obstacles, and are called entanglements.[10]

10. See *The Five Hindrances and their Conquest*, *The Wheel*, No. 26, Buddhist Publication Society, Kandy.

"Now with these five hindrances, Vāseṭṭha, the Brahmans versed in the Three Vedas are veiled, hindered, obstructed, and entangled.

"And verily, Vāseṭṭha, that Brahmans versed in the Three Vedas, but omitting the practice of those qualities which really make a man a Brahman, and adopting the practice of those qualities which really make men non-Brahmans—veiled, hindered, obstructed, and entangled by these five hindrances—that these Brahmans should after death, on the dissolution of the body, become united to Brahmā—such a condition of things can in no wise be!"

31. "Now what think you, Vāseṭṭha, and what have you heard from the Brahmans aged and well-stricken in years, when the learners and teachers are talking together? Is Brahmā in possession of wives and wealth, or is he not?"[11] (16)

"He is not, Gotama."

"Is his mind full of anger, or free from anger?"

"Free from anger, Gotama."

"Is his mind burdened or unburdened?"[12]

"Free from burden, Gotama."

"Is his mind tarnished, or is it pure?"

"It is pure, Gotama."

"Has he self-mastery, or has he not?"

"He has, Gotama."[13]

---

11. *Sapariggaho vā Brahmā apariggaho vā ti.* Cy.: "Owing to the absence of worldly lusts (*kāmacchanda*, 'sense desire'), he is free of possessing wives (*itthipariggahena*)" Rh.D.: ... thus restricting the "possession" to women. But the reference is, no doubt, to the first Hindrance; and the word in the text, though doubtless alluding to possession of women also, includes more. Compare, on the general idea of the passage, the English expression, "no encumbrance."

12. *Sabyāpajja-citto vā abyāpajja-citto vā'ti.* The meaning of *sabyāpajja* that applies here is, no doubt, "being oppressed", and not "malicious." Also the explanation of the Cy. in the next note points to it.

13. The Cy. identifies now the subject of the other four questions with the last four of the five hindrances: "Being without ill-will, he is free from any thought of hate. Being without sloth and torpor, he is unoppressed (unburdened) by that oppression which is also called a 'mental ailment'. Being

32. "Now what think you, Vāseṭṭha; are the Brahmans versed in the Vedas in the possession of wives and wealth or are they not?"(17)

"They are, Gotama."

"Have they anger in their hearts, or have they not?"

"They have, Gotama."

"Are their minds burdened, or are they not?"

"They are, Gotama."

"Are they pure in heart, or are they not?"

"They are not, Gotama."

"Have they self-mastery, or have they not?"

"They have not, Gotama."

33. "Then you say, Vāseṭṭha, that the Brahmans are in possession of wives and wealth and that Brahmā is not. Can there, then, be agreement and likeness between the Brahmans with their wives and property, and Brahmā who has none of these things?"(18)

"Certainly not, Gotama!"

34. "Very good, Vāseṭṭha., But, verily, that these Brahmans versed in the Vedas, who live married and wealthy, should after death, when the body is dissolved, become united with Brahmā, who has none of these things—such a condition of things can in no wise be!"

35. "Then you say, too, Vāseṭṭha that the Brahmans bear anger and burdens in their hearts, and are tarnished in heart and uncontrolled, whilst Brahmā is free from anger and burdens, pure in heart and has self-mastery. Now can there, then, be concord and likeness between the Brahmans and Brahmā?"

"Certainly not, Gotama!"(19)

36. "Very good, Vāseṭṭha! That these Brahmans versed in the Vedas and yet bearing anger and burdens in their hearts, sinful, and uncontrolled, should after death, when the body is dissolved, become united to Brahmā, who is free from anger and burdens,

---

without flurry and worry, his mind is undefiled (untarnished; *asaṅkiliṭṭha*) and pure, with regard to these and other defilements (*kilesa*). Being without doubt, he has mastery over his mind (*vasavatti*); he is not like those Brahmans who are carried away by their thoughts, are mastered by them,"

pure in heart, and has self-mastery—such a condition of things can in no wise be.

"Here then, Vāseṭṭha, the Brahmans, versed though they be in the Three Vedas, while they (confidently) settle down (in their views), are sinking down (in the mire) and so sinking they are arriving only at despair thinking that they are crossing over to dry land.[14]

"Therefore, is it that the threefold wisdom of the Brahmans, wise in their Three Vedas, is called a pathless jungle, their threefold wisdom is called a waterless desert, their threefold wisdom is called perdition!"(20)

37. When he had thus spoken, the young Brahman Vāseṭṭha said to the Blessed One:

"It has been told me, Gotama, that the Samana Gotama knows the way to the state of union with Brahmā."(21)

"What do you think, Vāseṭṭha, is not Manasākaṭa near to this spot, not distant from this spot?"

"Just so, Gotama, Manasākaṭa is near to, is not far from here."

"Now what think you, Vāseṭṭha, suppose there were a man born and brought up in Manasākaṭa, and people should ask him, who had just now left Manasākaṭa, which was the way to Manasākaṭa. Would that man born and brought up in Manasākaṭa, be in any doubt or difficulty?"

"Certainly not, Gotama! And why? If the man had been born and brought up in Manasākaṭa, every road that leads to Manasākaṭa would be perfectly familiar to him."

38. "That man, Vāseṭṭha, born and brought up at Manasākaṭa might, if he were asked the way to Manasākaṭa, fall into doubt and difficulty, but to the Tathāgata, when asked touching the path which leads to the world of Brahmā, there can be neither doubt nor difficulty. For Brahmā, I know, Vāseṭṭha, and the world of Brahmā, and the path which leads unto it. Yea, I know it even as one who has entered the Brahmā-world, and has been born within it!"(22)

---

14. *Āsiditvā saṃsidanti.* Cy: "Settling down (in their views), i e., taking the wrong path for the right one, they sink down, i e., they enter, as it were, a mire, in the belief that it is level and firm ground. Like those deceived by a mirage think that they have to cross a brimful river, they, struggling with hands and feet, press on in the belief that it is a crossing to drier land."

39. When he had thus spoken, Vāseṭṭha, the young Brahman, said to the Blessed One:

"Just so has it been told me, Gotama, even that the Samana Gotama knows the way to a state of union with Brahmā. It is well! Let the Venerable Gotama be pleased to show us the way to a state of union with Brahmā. Let the Venerable Gotama save the Brahman race."[15]

"Listen then, Vāseṭṭha, and give ear attentively, and I will speak!"(23)

"So be it, Lord!" said the young Brahman Vāseṭṭha, in assent, to the Blessed One.

40. Then the Blessed One spoke and said:

"Know, Vāseṭṭha, that (from time to time) a Tathāgata is born into the world, an Arahat, a fully awakened one, abounding in wisdom and goodness, happy, with knowledge of the worlds, unsurpassed as a guide to mortals willing to be led, a teacher of gods and men, a Blessed One, a Buddha. He, by himself, thoroughly understands and sees, as it were, face to face this universe—including the worlds above with the gods, the Māras, and the Brahmas; and the world below with its Samaṇas and Brāhmaṇas, its princes and peoples; and he then makes his knowledge known to others. The truth does he proclaim both in the letter and in the spirit, lovely in its origin, lovely in its progress, lovely in its consummation; the higher life does he make known, in all its purity and in all its perfectness.

41. "A householder (*gahapati*), or one of his children, or a man of inferior birth in any class, listens to that truth. On hearing the truth he has faith in the Tathāgata, and when he has acquired that faith he thus considers with himself:

"'Full of hindrances is household life, a path defiled by passion; free as the air is the life of him who has renounced all worldly things. How difficult it is for the man who dwells at home to live the higher life in all its fullness, in all its purity, in all its bright perfection! Let me then cut off my hair and beard, let me clothe

15. *Brāhmaṇiṃ pajaṃ*, 'the Brahmanical offspring'. Cy.: "May the venerable Gotama extricate me, the son of the Brahmans, from the road to perdition and set me on the road to the Brahmā world!"

myself in the orange-coloured robes, and let me go forth from a household life into the homeless state!'

"Then before long, forsaking his portion of wealth, be it great or be it small, forsaking his circle of relatives, be they many or be they few, he cuts off his hair and beard, he clothes himself in the orange-coloured robes, and he goes forth from the household life into the homeless state."

42. "When he has thus become a recluse he passes a life self-restrained by that restraint which should be binding on a recluse. He is possessed of right behaviour and conduct, and, seeing danger in the slightest faults, he adopts and trains himself in the precepts. He encompasses himself with goodness in word and deed. He sustains his life by means that are quite pure; good is his conduct, guarded the door of his senses; mindful and self-possessed, he is altogether happy!" (24)

43–75. "And how, Vāseṭṭha, is his conduct?

"In this, Vāseṭṭha, that the Bhikkhu putting away the killing of living things, holds aloof from the destruction of life. The cudgel and the sword he has laid aside, and ashamed of roughness, and full of mercy, he dwells compassionate and kind to all creatures that have life.

"Putting away the taking of what has not been given, he lives aloof from grasping what is not his own. He takes only what is given, and expecting that gifts will come, he lives his life in honesty and purity of heart.

"Putting away unchastely, he is chaste. He holds himself aloof, far off, from the vulgar practice, the sexual act.

"Putting away lying words, he holds himself aloof from falsehood. He speaks truth, from the truth he never swerves; faithful and trustworthy, he breaks not his word to the world.

"Putting away slander, he holds himself aloof from calumny. What he hears here he repeats not elsewhere to raise a quarrel against the people there: what he hears elsewhere he repeats not here to raise a quarrel against the people there. Thus does he live as a binder together of those who are divided, an encourager of those who are friends, a peacemaker, a lover of peace, delighted in peace, a speaker of words that make for peace.

"Putting away rudeness of speech, he holds himself aloof from harsh language. Whatsoever word is blameless, pleasant to the ear, lovely, reaching to the heart, urbane, pleasing to the people, beloved of the people—such are the words he speaks.

"Putting away frivolous talk, he holds himself away from vain conversation. In season he speaks, in accordance with the facts, words full of meaning, on the doctrine, on the discipline of the Order. He speaks, and at the right time, words worthy to be laid up in one's heart, fully illustrated, clearly divided, to the point.

"He abstains from causing injury to seeds or plants. He takes but one meal a day, not eating at night, refraining from food after hours (after midday). He refrains from being a spectator at shows, at fairs, with nautch dances, singing, and music. He abstains from wearing, adorning or ornamenting himself with garlands, scents, and unguents He abstains from the use of large and lofty beds. He abstains from accepting silver or gold. He abstains from accepting uncooked grain. He abstains from accepting raw meat. He abstains from accepting women or girls. He abstains from accepting bondsmen or bondwomen. He abstains from accepting sheep or goats. He abstains from accepting fowls or swine. He abstains from accepting elephants, cattle, horses, and mares. He abstains from accepting cultivated fields or waste. He abstains from the acting as a go-between or messenger. He abstains from buying and selling. He abstains from cheating with measures, metals, or weights. He abstains from the crooked ways of bribery, cheating, and fraud. He abstains from maiming, murder, putting in bonds, highway robbery, dacoity, and violence.

"This is part of the good conduct that he has."(25)

(Here follow another two sections on Conduct, given in detail in the Brahmajāla Sutta (DN 1) and the Sāmaññaphala Sutta (DN 2). The text continues:)

"And then, Vāseṭṭha, that Bhikkhu being thus possessed of good conduct, sees no danger from any side; that is, so far as concerns his self-restraint in conduct. Just, O Vāseṭṭha, as a sovereign duly crowned, whose enemies have been beaten down, sees no danger from any side; that is so far as enemies are concerned, so is the Bhikkhu confident. And endowed with this so noble a body of morals, he experiences within himself a sense of ease without alloy. Thus is it, Vāseṭṭha, that the Bhikkhu is possessed of good conduct."(26)

Sense-control

"And how, Vāseṭṭha, is the Bhikkhu guarded as to the door of his sense? When, Vāseṭṭha, he sees an object with his eyes he is not entranced in the general appearance or the details of it. He sets himself to restrain that which might give occasion for evil states, covetousness, and dejection, to flow in over him so long as he dwells unrestrained as to his sense of sight. He keeps watch upon his faculty of sight, and he attains to mastery over it. And so, in like manner, when he hears a sound with his ear, or smells an odour with his nose, or tastes a flavour with the tongue, or feels a touch with his body, or when he cognizes a phenomenon with his mind, he is not entranced in the general appearance or the details of it. He sets himself to restrain that which might give occasion for evil states, covetousness, and dejection, to flow in over him so long as he dwells unrestrained as to his mental faculty. He keeps watch upon his mental faculty, and he attains to mastery over it. And endowed with this so noble a self-restraint as regards the senses, he experiences, within himself, a sense of ease into which no evil state can enter. Thus is it, Vāseṭṭha, that the Bhikkhu becomes guarded as to the doors of his senses."(27)

Mindfulness and Full Awareness

"And how, Vāseṭṭha, is the Bhikkhu mindful and self-possessed? In this matter, Vāseṭṭha, the Bhikkhu in going forth or in coming back is self-possessed in his actions. And so also in looking forward or in looking round; in stretching forward his arm or in drawing it in again; in eating or drinking, in masticating or swallowing, in obeying the calls of nature, in going or standing or sitting, in falling asleep or waking, in speaking or in being still, he is self-possessed in his actions."(28)

Contentedness

"And how, Vāseṭṭha is the Bhikkhu content? In this matter, Vāseṭṭha, the Bhikkhu is satisfied with his robes to cover his body, with the alms food to provide for his stomach's needs. Whithersoever he may go, these he takes with him as he goes—just as a bird with his wings, whither so ever he may fly, carries his wings with him as he flies. Thus it is, Vāseṭṭha, that the Bhikkhu becomes content."(29)

Conquest of the Five Hindrances

"Then, being thus endowed with this so noble body of morals, endowed with this so noble sense-control, endowed with this so noble mindfulness and self-possession, endowed with this so noble contentedness, he chooses some lonely spot in the woods, at the foot of a tree, on a hillside, in a mountain glen, in a rocky cave, in a charnel place, or on a heap of straw in the open field. And returning thither after his round of alms he seats himself, when his meal is done, cross-legged, keeping his body erect, and his mindfulness alert.

"Putting away the hankering after the world, he remains with a heart that hankers not, and purifies his mind of lusts. Putting away the corruption of hate, he remains with a heart free from ill-temper, and purifies his mind of malevolence. Putting away sloth and torpor, perceiving the light, mindful, and self-possessed, he purifies his mind of sloth and torpor. Putting away flurry and worry, he remains free from fretfulness, and with heart serene within, he purifies his mind of flurry and worry. Putting away doubt, he remains as one passed beyond perplexity, and no longer in suspense as to what is good, he purifies his mind of doubt.(30)

"So long, Vāseṭṭha, as these five hindrances are not put away within him the Bhikkhu looks upon himself as in debt, diseased, in prison, in slavery, lost on a desert road. But when these five hindrances have been put away within him, he looks upon himself as freed from debt, rid of disease, out of jail, a free man and secure.

"And gladness springs up within him on his realising that, and joy arises to him thus gladdened, and so rejoicing all his frame becomes at ease, and being thus at ease he feels happy, and a happy mind finds concentration."

76. "And he lets his mind pervade one quarter of the world with thoughts of love, and so the second, and so the third, and so the fourth. And thus the whole wide world—above, below, around, and everywhere—does he continue to pervade with heart of love, far-reaching, grown great, and beyond measure."

77. "Just, Vāseṭṭha, as a mighty trumpeter makes himself heard—and that without difficulty—in all the four directions; even so, if love, the heart's liberation, has been developed, not any limited kamma (of the sense sphere)[16] will be left over there, will remain there."[17]

78. "And he lets his mind pervade one quarter of the world with thoughts of pity, ... sympathy, ... equanimity, far-reaching, grown great, and beyond measure."

79. "Just, Vāseṭṭha, as a mighty trumpeter makes himself heard—and that without difficulty—in all the four directions; even so, if pity, ... sympathy, ... equanimity, the heart's liberation, have been developed, not any limited kamma (of the sense sphere) will be left over there, will remain there.

"Verily this, Vāseṭṭha, is the way to a state of union with Brahmā."

80. "Now what think you, Vāseṭṭha, will the Bhikkhu who lives thus be in possession of women and of wealth, or will he not?"

"He will not, Gotama!"

"Will he be full of anger, or free from anger?"

"He will be free from anger, Gotama!"

"Will his mind be burdened, or unburdened?"

"Unburdened, Gotama!"

"Will his mind be tarnished, or pure?"

"It will be pure, Gotama!"

"Will he have self-mastery, or will he not?"

---

16. Sub-Cy.: "the sensuous sphere (*kāmāvacara*) is called '*kamma* with limits' (*pamāṇakataṃ kammaṃ*), because it does not suppress those defiling qualities which produce limitation" Cy.: "'Unlimited kamma' (*appamāṇakataṃ kammaṃ*) is that of the fine-material and immaterial sphere."

17. Cy.: "No kamma of the sensuous sphere is left behind in that kamma of the fine-material and immaterial sphere. What is meant by that statement? The kamma of the sensuous sphere cannot cling to or subsist within the kamma of the fine-material and immaterial sphere; it cannot establish itself there, by pervading or overpowering it, or by making room in it for itself. On the contrary, it is the kamma of the fine-material and immaterial sphere that pervades and overpowers the kamma of the sensuous sphere like a mighty flood will cover a small expanse of water; it will make room for itself and stay there; it will supersede its result, and as to itself, it will lead to union with Brahmā."

"Surely, he will, Gotama!"

81. "Then you say, Vāseṭṭha, that the Bhikkhu is free from household and worldly cares, and that Brahmā is free from household and worldly cares. Is there then agreement and likeness between the Bhikkhu and Brahmā?" (31)

"There is, Gotama!"

"Very good, Vāseṭṭha! Then verily, Vāseṭṭha, that the Bhikkhu who is free from household cares should after death, when the body is dissolved, become united with Brahmā, who is the same—such a condition of things is every way possible!

"And so you say, Vāseṭṭha, that the Bhikkhu is free from anger, and free from burdens, pure in mind, and master of himself. Then verily, Vāseṭṭha, that the Bhikkhu who is free from anger, free from burdens, pure in mind, and master of himself should after death, when the body is dissolved, become united with Brahmā, who is the same—such a condition of things is every way possible!" (32)

82. When he had thus spoken, the young Brahmans Vāseṭṭha and Bhāradvāja addressed the Blessed One and said:

"Most excellent, Lord, are the words of thy mouth, most excellent! Just as if a man were to set up that which is thrown down, or were to reveal that which is hidden away, or were to point out the right road to him who has gone astray, or were to bring a lamp into the darkness, so that those who have eyes can see external forms—just even so, Lord, has the truth been made known to us, in many a figure, by the Exalted One. And we, even we, betake ourselves, Lord, to the Blessed One as our refuge, to the Truth, and to the Brotherhood.[18] May the Blessed One accept us as disciples, as true believers, from this day forth, as long as life endures!" (33)

The Tevijja Suttanta

Translated by Prof. T. W. Rhys Davids. From *Dialogues of the Buddha,* Part 1 (Pali Text Society, London).

18. Cy.: "This was their second going for refuge. For the first time they did it after listening to the Vāseṭṭha Sutta which is included in the Middle Fifties (of the Majjhima Nikāya). Now after hearing the Tevijja Sutta they went for refuge a second time. After a few days they got first ordination, and (as reported) in the Aggañña Sutta (DN 27), they later received the full ordination and attained to holiness (*arahatta*)."

Notes

(1) Manasākaṭa is a Brahmin village. The Brahmins think of themselves as the "pure ones" (Brahmā = pure). It is the first and highest caste of the four existing at that time. To this caste belong the priests exclusively, but not all members of the caste are officiating priests. Many of them are hardly acquainted with Brahmanical lore and engaged in a variety of other occupations.

Manasākaṭa, the village of the Brahmins, therefore, must not be understood as being populated exclusively by those who performed priestly functions. The Awakened One stayed near that village on the bank of a river with a great company of brethren. The Buddha never entered a village or a town to teach, except when invited. He always dwelt outside the abode of men in the open air, in quiet groves or parks so that enquirers could come out to see him.

At that time the Awakened One was accompanied by 500 monks. These monks did not always gather round the Great Teacher. Those already initiated into the Norm and the Discipline lived in seclusion in the forest, nearly all day long given to exercises in mental concentration according to the directions given by the Buddha. The novices among them were instructed in small groups by elder and experienced brethren. In general, the monks met for talk only in the night after their period of meditation was over. At this point it might not be amiss to say a few words about the monastic life so utterly strange and foreign to the mentality of modern man. One may ask: Is it then impossible to pursue a high religious ideal as a householder, a businessman, a father of a large family? It is certainly not impossible, but very difficult; even if the ideal is restricted to the one aspired to by the Brahmin priests. Also for their ideal, the communion with God, the conditions of achieving it as mentioned by the Buddha later in this discourse, demand a degree of purity and devoted effort that is very hard to achieve for a householder. And still more so it is for one who aims at the attainment of Nibbāna, the complete eradication of greed, hatred, and delusion. Hence, from the beginning of his career the Enlightened One stresses the value of the "homeless life" of a monk. Nevertheless, many admirable virtues can be acquired by the breadwinner who cares and provides for his loved ones. The Sublimely Awakened One has only words of praise for the devout householder. Monastic life, however, a life dedicated exclusively to constant mindfulness and self-discipline, is not a calling for the many but only an ideal for the few; but many a man may make himself ripe for it. An identical point of view can be found in the Gospel where the distinction between householder and discipleship is clearly drawn. The rich young man, aspiring to the higher life, asks Jesus what he must do to be saved. To which Jesus replies: "Keep the commandments!" When the youth tells him that he had done so from childhood on, Jesus shows him the way leading from a life of disciplinary virtue to the summit of perfection: "If thou wilt be perfect, go and sell what thou hast and give to the poor, and thou shalt have a treasure in heaven; and come and follow me." Jesus himself had left his mother and sisters and did not take up married life.

(2) It was without doubt a high ideal that found expression in the young Brahmans' quest for the Path of Communion with their god. They knew well that living a righteous life, as best as humanly possible, will lead to rebirth among humans in favourable conditions, repeating itself, birth after birth, as long as they continue doing good and shunning evil.

They also knew that a still more strenuous effort along the Path will lead them to higher spheres of divine nature, realms of existence between the human and the Brahmā world, spheres of a greater happiness than human life can bestow, both in intensity and duration. Yet, both these aims—the human as well as the lower divine—left them dissatisfied. They sensed the transitoriness in them, and the dread of a possible fall into lower states of existence in human and even sub-human worlds. They knew that life in any sphere even the highest, of saṃsāric existence was subject to the Law of Kamma: as you act so you will become and having been reborn, you will through new deeds create new life, and so on ceaselessly.

Brahmā, so they were taught, was exempt from the law of causation. Effect and cause held no sway over him. In his heaven was security, eternal peace, and ecstatic bliss. Brahmā the Eternal, Brahmā the Supreme, the Absolute Ruler, Lord and Creator of the Universe, Brahmā the Father of all that is and all that is to be. The union with such a deity was their highest aspiration. The Buddha with his profound vision saw the error of their belief. Yet, with incomparable pedagogic insight he did not fulminate against the error but rather helped the erring priests along the Path of their own choosing.

(3) To behold these two young Brahmins who could not agree with each other go to the Buddha to let him be the arbiter must seem rather strange to the present-day reader. As already mentioned before, the Buddha's teaching differed fundamentally from the concepts and doctrines of Brahmanism. However, exactly here do we come to the root of that tolerance which to this very day predominates the religious climate of both India and the Far East. We find it exemplified in the Buddha's friendly attitude to Brahmans and Jains alike which won him their respect and admiration during the 45 years of his public life. In him there is not to be found a trace of that aggressive self-righteousness which is still permeating the air of religious controversy in the West. Whatever his utterances, all of them are uncontentious, factual, and convincing.

A rather curious parallel to the above can be found in the Christian Scriptures. There the Jewish priests, too, ply Jesus with questions concerning the Law of Moses, the ritual observances and the conflict of duties which might arise in serving either God or Caesar. And, similarly, they display all outward signs of respect and admiration: "We know Thou art a Master in Israel." However, they approach him not with the desire of gaining knowledge or insight but only to trap and ensnare him. Behind the mask of feigned benevolence lurks unmitigated hatred, defiance and contempt.

There is something unique and awe-inspiring in the person of the Buddha which won him fame throughout the land. Its echo is heard in a paean of praise uttered by those who have come in contact with his mighty presence. Thus we hear the two young Brahmins allude to him as:

"The Sublime Lord, the Arahat, the perfect Enlightened One, Endowed with Knowledge and Conduct, the Happy One, Knower of the Worlds, the Peerless charioteer of men to be tamed, Teacher of Gods and men, Buddha, the Lord."

This is an unusual appellation, both solemn and sublime, through which the young priest pays homage to the incomparable teacher. And here again we become aware of the wide gulf that separates Eastern and Western attitudes of religious expectation and fulfilment.

In the West an "Anointed One," a "Messiah," is expected to come down from on high. In Christianity he is identified with Jesus of Nazareth. In Judaism the "Messiah" is still expected and thought to be the Messenger of God who cares for none but the children of Israel, his chosen people. In this small and. insignificant nation the Kingdom of God shall then be established, and the Israelites miraculously transformed into light-bearers for the illumination of the benighted "heathen."

In the East and particularly in India no such national "Saviour" has ever been dreamed of, much less a divine messenger or a prophet. It is always a fully enlightened Man, a Buddha, to which the hopes and aspirations of the East have turned from time immemorial. A human being, it has to be, that makes his appearance only in the world of humans of which there have been many in aeons past and of which many more are expected in aeons to come. Not a "Saviour" who atones for the "sins" of his chosen people but a fully Awakened One who, by overcoming the Kamma of saṃsāric existence, has broken the vicious circle of birth and death; one who by his teaching and example demonstrates how deliverance can be won by all and sundry. Such a Buddha is called "The Exalted One, the Arahat, the fully Enlightened One, endowed with Wisdom and Conduct, the Happy One, Knower of the Worlds, the Peerless Charioteer of Men to be tamed, the Teacher of Gods and Men, Buddha, the Lord."

That is the meaning of "The Noble Sound of Praise" the young Brahman uttered without being aware of its full significance. For him and his companion it was Brahmā only in whom deliverance was to be found.

(4) "The Brahman priests sat down beside him." The sitting-down position, without facing each other, is worth of note. Between two people engaged in some business transaction the seating order would be different: two business men would be seated facing each other. The same would hold with two lovers. Their happiness lies in beholding the face of the beloved. The Buddha and his enquirers sit side by side because the subject-matter of their discussion calls for undivided attention, concentration and practical application. A learning situation between Master and pupil is established here which is typical for the whole East.

(5) Here the assertion is made and answered three times. The reason is obvious: Vāseṭṭha's statement is the starting point for the discussion to follow. He reiterates his conviction that the guidance of the priests towards Union with Brahmā is absolutely necessary.

(6) The Awakened One opens the discussion with a very elementary question about the source of their knowledge of the Path to Brahmā. Is there a single one among the Brahmans, he asks, who has ever seen Brahmā face to face? The biblical prophets, at least, could tell the Jews that, although they had not seen God, however, they heard his voice. The young priests are in quite a quandary here because they do not know of anybody who knew Brahmā from personal acquaintance.,

(7) Admittedly, the young priests failed to present the evidence of their ever having heard or seen Brahmā. But what about their teachers? Or the teachers of these up to the seventh generation, from Master to pupil and so on? Did not the Brahmins glorify themselves and their ancestors of being the pure offspring of Brahmā's mouth? The Buddha, pursuing this line of questioning, continues; "and what of the Rishis through whom the Vedas were given? Did they ever say they had seen Brahmā?" To all that the young priests can only answer in the negative.

(8) By pursuing this line of questioning the Buddha achieved his purpose, i.e., to arouse these tradition-bound young minds from their dogmatic slumber. In pointing out to them the unreasonableness of blind belief unsupported by any evidence, he shook their smug self-complacency, making them alert and eager to inquire further. How different we find the apostles in the New Testament narratives. When "doubting Thomas" could not believe that Christ had risen: "Except I shall see in his hands the print of the nails and put my finger into them," Jesus appeared to him saying: "Blessed are they that have not seen and yet believed." So deeply convinced was Jesus of the

rightfulness of his mission that he beseeches, as it were, his followers to pay no attention to wavering doubts but to follow him blindly and without reserve.

On the other hand, the Buddha, without being one iota less convinced of the rightfulness of his Mission, cautions his followers to beware of blind belief, hearsay, or tradition. The supreme Enlightened One knew the dangers of trusting credulity, the fallacy of hide-bound tradition, the craftiness of priests, and the exploitation of the faithful.

Thomas, the doubting Apostle, would only believe in the testimony of the senses, which is quite right as far as it goes. It would be foolish, however, to narrow the range of experience down to sense perception only. There exists an inner world in man, a world of feelings, volitions, tendencies, and mind. We cannot separate the one from the other: the two of them together constitute what is called human experience. The ideal to which we must give our allegiance is a comprehensive one which involves the total personality of body and mind. We shall later see in the Discourse how the striving for this ideal widens our outlook and deepens our insight.

(9) Here we have a paradoxical situation: the priests pretend to know the right path leading to Brahmā, yet they have never seen him nor heard his voice. They say: "We are following his footprints," without realizing that they are only deceiving themselves as did their progenitors up to the seventh generation. The Buddha compares the endless generations of priests with a string of blind men being led by a leader who is himself blind. Which brings to mind the saying of Jesus in the Gospels: "Can the blind lead the blind? Shall they not both fall into the ditch?"

(10) The parable about the most beautiful woman nobody knows, and the one that follows, about the staircase leading nowhere, illustrate two important facts. First, the absurdity of the priests attributing to Brahmā the title "highest" in complete ignorance of the criterion upon which to base such sublime an epithet. It is like an ardent lover's yearning to behold the most beautiful maiden. Only the poor youth has not the faintest idea whether such an exquisite beauty exists, let alone where to find her. Secondly, the staircase parable. The man who builds the staircase does not know where the location of the tower is he wants to climb. The priests find themselves in the same predicament. They are offering prayers, invocations, rites and sacrifices to Brahmā without knowing where he is or whether he will be able to receive their offerings and answer their supplications.

(11) In the parable of the two banks of a river, the Buddha covers the basic theme of the whole Sutta: how can the union between God and Man be brought about, or in our specific situation, the union between Brahmā and the

priests. Hither bank stands for the world of human; the bank beyond for the world of Brahmā, the abode of the gods. The twain will never meet unless man bestirs himself and, by his own efforts, crosses the river to the bank beyond.

(12) Here the Buddha applies the riverbank parable to the priests. They call themselves Brahmans, which means the "pure" ones, yet in their innermost thoughts they turned away from Brahmā leading lives that are anything but Brahmanical. So it was they that created the gulf existing between themselves and Brahmā. And for the same reason, because they are no longer "pure," a marked deterioration of character had taken place dragging them down to the level of the common herd of men.

The same sad state of affairs re-echoes through Christian teachings also. Mankind—according to them—has fallen away from its divine source, has split up into countless fragments that fight each other, has lost its original unity with its Creator. That is the meaning of the biblical myth of the "Fall" by which the progenitors of mankind were driven out of paradise; and, in the celestial realm, there was a "War in Heaven" whereby Lucifer the "Lightbearer" turned into Satan, the Prince of Darkness. He became the ruler of this manbearing globe, and with him mankind finds itself alienated from God, the Father of Light, and tainted with "original sin." It is against this sinister background that the Apostle John admonishes the early Christians:

> "Do not love the world nor what is in it. Anyone who loves the world, in him the Father's love does not dwell. For all that is in the world, the lust of the flesh, the lust of the eyes, and the pride of life, is not of the Father, but is of the world. And the world passeth away and the lust thereof: but he that doeth the will of God abideth for ever." 1 John, 15–17.

The world of men dominated by greed, hatred and lust, and the world of God, as its opposite, appear in the Sutta as the two banks of a river, separated by an unbridgeable gulf.

It is a well-known fact in the history of religions that a change of attitude manifests itself as soon as religious institutions begin to settle down comfortably in the world of men. In ages where the life of the spirit still predominates, men's thoughts turn inwardly. The great conflict between the powers of light and darkness is being fought in the heart of men. They realize that salvation is not something to be achieved by external observances, ritualistic prayers, and incantations but by treading the lonely path of purification and self-abnegation. Conversely, when men try to serve two masters at the same time, chasing after sensuous pleasures and serving their God, deterioration of both the temporal and the spiritual order will follow.

(13) The parable of the two river banks explains quite clearly the problem

of the union of man with Brahmā. However, as we shall see presently, the very act of crossing the river cannot be performed by sheer power of will; for the will finds itself obstructed, hampered and impeded by five fetters, or hindrances, as the Buddha calls them. Thus before the crossing can start at all man has to loosen and get rid of these five fetters first.

(14) The Buddha states that the five fetters binding man to the hither bank of earthly existence are his senses of seeing, hearing, smelling, tasting, and the sense of touch. We may wonder why the five senses, of all things, are denounced by the Enlightened One as if there were anything morally wrong with them. Besides, how is man to get rid of them and, if that be possible at all, survive as a human being? It stands to reason that the Buddha touches here on something far more significant than the mere *existence* of our physical sense organs. In this particular passage the Buddha does not discuss as yet the true meaning of the term "fetters"; in other words, the *ethical* side of the uses and abuses of the senses is to be elaborated later in the Sutta.

At this point it will be fitting to turn our attention once more to the world of man in which we all live and move and have our being. The mere physical aspect of it reveals a bewildering variety of drives, some constructive, some destructive, some of a neutral nature. In this teeming chaos a guiding principle is needed which the ethical teachings of all great religions set down and enunciated under the name of the "Golden Rule" which says: "Do unto others what you would want them to do unto you!" By observing the Golden Rule justice and peace can be maintained among human beings and the welfare of all guaranteed. However, the Golden Rule must not be conceived of as a panacea to bring about a miraculous change in human character with its almost unlimited potentialities for better and worse.

We have seen how this teeming mass of humanity, as soon as it organises itself into societies, cannot dispense with some principle in interpersonal relationships and how the "Golden Rule" establishes such a principle as a basic ethical standard. Although from the eagle's point of view humanity might appear as an amorphous mass, to the discriminating observer on the ground level forms are seen to be moving about. Or—to use a somewhat abstract type of reasoning—it is the existence of individual forms that makes for multiplicity. This world of innumerable things could not be apprehended were it not through individualized forms, assuming the shape of men here, the shape of beast, plant, or stone there. Form is limitation, no matter its size or shape of manifestation. Through his body man appears as form, through his sense organs he becomes aware of being localized in space and time. He hears sounds, he sees contours and colours, he smells odours, he tastes flavours, he touches bodies. He is attracted by beautiful forms and repelled by ugly and monstrous forms. Love and hatred, sympathy and antipathy are all aroused by form. Therefore, the Buddha says: "Where there is form there is hatred, rage and the shedding of blood, war and discord, quarrels and disputes, fraud and lies. In a world of no-form (*arūpa*) these cannot be found." The Buddha, now turning to the priests, points out to them the cause and cure of their predicament. Because of their being in bondage to the world of form they are fettered and chained to this world of limitation and can never reach Brahmā, unless they unshackle themselves and get rid of their fetters.

It has to be made clear, however, that sense perception by itself is ethically neutral. This cannot be said plain enough. Not the use but the abuse of sense experience leads to bondage and alienation from the Brahmā state. Bondage constitutes the inevitable effect of lustful attachment to the object of sense of which the latter is the cause. The conquest of lust, the overcoming of attachment to the world of sense experience, is, therefore, the main objective of all religious teaching, Buddhist as well as Christian. The great Christian mystic, Angelus Silesius, puts it succinctly:

"Friend, leave behind the joy,
flee what men's hearts desire
then otherwise you will
here never peace acquire.
We could have tasted lust
of the eternal bliss,
if not in carnal sphere
we ate too much of this."

For anyone who loves the world of sense objects, who craves sense satisfaction, there is no room left for the serene calm of Brahmā's world, for the bliss divine, for the union with god. Thus, we see, there exists a state of indescribable sublimity where the rules of ethics are not applicable any more, where the opposites of good and evil are transcended. In our world of greed, hatred and delusion the observation of rules regulating interpersonal relations is of paramount importance. Their disregard would cause chaos and universal anarchy. Therefore, as already mentioned, the founders of the Great Religions did lay down specific rules of conduct known either as the Ten Commandments of Moses or the Five Sīlas of the Buddha. Those who conscientiously observe these ethical rules are rightly called the just and the righteous among men. Yet there exists a more excellent way, a Path leading to heights beyond the mere disciplinary observances of the worldling, called the path of Beyondless Liberation, the Highroad to ultimate deliverance and immortality.

(15) Another parable. Again we are told of a man lying on the ground on hither side of the river. He is neither shackled nor bound but wrapped up in

his clothes to his head. He would be capable of crossing the river were it not for the restraining clothes that render any movement impossible.

(16) This dialogue is significant for the reason that the Buddha makes here a comparison between Brahmā's sublime characteristics, on the one hand, and the human foibles of the Three-Vedas-Priests, on the other. In Socratic fashion the Sublime Lord draws the answers out from the young Brahmans. A sad catalogue of human shortcomings is now being revealed while Brahmā emerges pure and undefiled.

(17) Against the radiant image of their god the Three-Vedas-Priests make a pitiful showing, indeed. Once more the priests are induced by the Buddha to admit their teachers' shortcomings. "Our teachers," they say, "bear anger and malice in their hearts. Attached to mundane possessions, surrounded by wives, children and servants, they are overbearing, harsh and contemptuous toward their inferiors." Unintentionally, however, the young priests bear witness here to their own high standard of morals by saying that a man's character is already tarnished even if he only once flares up in anger. How different from that is Brahmā's all-embracing kindness. His love, sympathy, and benevolence pervade the whole world. By his very nature he dispels even the faintest shadow of anger, malice, or ill-will. By the way: the discourse casts a rather sad reflection on our own personal weaknesses so well hidden behind the mask of polite manners but when aroused, striking like blind furies against our adversaries.

(18) Let us assume two vessels on different water levels; how can they ever meet or even hold on to the same course? Similarly, the absence of a common level separates human beings from the Brahmanic realm of absolute Oneness. And just as two vessels, sailing alongside on the same water surface, so can human beings share Brahmā's abode only by lifting themselves up to the god's level of existence.

(19) In this passage the Buddha states unequivocally that the Three-Vedas-Priests "after death and the dissolution of the body" will never achieve union with Brahmā. This may sound like a harsh saying were it not based upon the very facts of existence. Analysing these facts, we arrive at a twofold mode of human conduct, namely, the outer appearance through which man confronts his fellow beings, and the inner life through which man confronts himself. The outer appearance, that is, the bodily shape and peculiar characteristics of an individual remain fairly the same. The inner life by which we summarise feelings, tendencies, volitions and attitudes, is subject to change either for better or for worse. These forces of the inner man are moulding right now, in this present life, the exterior shape in which the life-continuum will re-emerge in its next birth. The inner life of a person may sometimes reflect itself in a beautiful

form while, on the other hand, a face of repelling ugliness may conceal a saintly character. Thus the angel of light, Lucifer, as Christian tradition has it, rebelled against God, was cast out from heaven, passed away and reappeared in hell as Satan, the Prince of Darkness. The Buddha, therefore, proclaims the Law of Moral Causation: as you act so you shall become. In other words, it is your character that builds your future abode. Consequently: let your volitions be Brahmanic and in your next existence you shall dwell with Brahmā.

(20) The daily routine of the young priests consisted primarily in learning by rote the countless Vedic Hymns and committing to memory the ritualistic directions of properly performing sacrifices. Taking the dead letter of the scriptures for their guide, they imagined themselves as the only true followers of Brahmā; although to their credit it must be said that they were not yet steeped so deeply in their self-deception as to preclude any possibility of better judgment. No wonder they become alarmed when they hear the Buddha denounce the Three-Vedas-Priests as a "waterless desert," a "pathless jungle" and a "way to perdition." Their self-confidence is shaken, and now they lift their eyes up to the Buddha seeking his guidance. But the Buddha keeps silent. It is left to the priests to ask for more light, to prove the sincerity of their interest and the seriousness of their quest for Brahmā.

(21) Again they start questioning the Buddha yet in a somewhat guarded manner. "We understand," so they say, "the ascetic Gotama knows the way to Brahmā." These words reveal the high esteem in which the Enlightened One is held even by the adherents of Brahmanism, the ruling religion of the day.

(22) The Awakened One, first of all, bypasses the question of the Path. What he does, however, is to make such a startling pronouncement that the young priests are taken by sudden surprise. The Buddha declares, namely, that he knows Brahmā face to face and, consequently, the Path leading to him; but even more: he knows how Brahmā gained dominion over his realm. The priests are baffled. If a foolish person sounded off with a statement like this, it would be downright blasphemous. Even in the mouth of a wise man it would sound reckless. But coming from no less a person than the Buddha—no exception is taken by the young priests.

(23) "Let the Venerable Gotama save the Brahman race ..."—with these words the young priests express their confidence in the Buddha and a sincere concern for the purity of their own calling. They now beg the Buddha to explain to them, step by step, the Path to Brahmā. The Buddha willingly consents.

(24) "A Tathāgata is born into the world, an Arahat, a fully Awakened One, abounding in Wisdom and Conduct ..." With these solemn words the Great Way of a World-Illuminator, a Buddha, is declared open; we find these words spoken in many Suttas, particularly in the Dīgha Nikāya. The Path is declared

open, the landmarks of the Dhamma are being laid out, the steep ascent to the summit of final Liberation is now made possible. Householders or their sons hear the call, abandon worldly life, free themselves from sensual attachments and, under the guidance of the Buddha, attain to Sainthood or Arahatship.

Only a Buddha possesses all the qualifications that are spoken of in the above solemn annunciation. He has not only realized the Path by going it: he has become the Path itself. What is this Noble Path and what are its stages?

The first stage of the Noble Eightfold Path is designated by the Buddha as Right and wholesome View, the first prerequisite to be acquired by the pilgrim. "Right" and "wholesome" have here quite specific connotations. Right refers to the Buddha's Norm and wholesome to the Buddha's discipline which, when adhered to, results in wholesome consequences.

In aeons past all the Buddhas have taught the same Doctrine of universal suffering and the way out of it. Because the human situation has not changed—and history bears witness thereto—the Buddhas promulgated in essence the same truth of humanity's fatal clinging to evanescent possessions in its endless turning on the wheel of birth and death. The Noble Path of the Buddhas includes the one leading to Brahmā. However, the Pali Texts firmly put Brahmā in his proper place; he is neither omniscient nor omnipotent, and his present position, like that of other beings, is the result of past actions—Kamma. He occupies a lofty, but still mundane plane of existence.

"Full of hindrances is the household life, a path defiled by passion ... how difficult it is for a householder to live the higher life in all its fullness, in all its purity, in all its bright perfection." Out of these considerations householders or their sons leave their families and devote themselves to wholesome pursuits that lead to the state of holiness or Arahatship.

Family life is part and parcel of life's manifold expressions; it is the sphere of social intercourse which can be either one of hostile encounter or one of gentle approach. In this mingling of groups with their conflicting interests, the family stands out as an island of peace and order, the maintenance of which works for warmth and security. Through unity and concord within the family, all its members are sheltered from disaster caused by unbridled greed with all its dire consequences of rivalry, hate, quarrel, and destruction. In family life the art of the gentle approach is cultivated; therefore, it is justly spoken of as good and valuable, while those tendencies that cause the family to split asunder are spoken of as dangerous and disruptive.

However, on a higher level, beyond mankind's manifold strivings, there exists a world of Oneness which in all religions is designated as the sphere of the Divine. There the longings for the affections of family life are transcended and transformed. Because "from affection," declares the Buddha in the Dhammapada, "is born grief; from affection fear is begotten" (213).

Only *mettā*, the all-inclusive love, leads to the state of union with Brahmā. As the Christian Gospels say: "The children of this world marry and are given in marriage. But they which shall be accounted worthy to inherit that other world and the resurrection of the dead neither marry, nor are given in marriage" (Luke, 20, 34). Consequently, in the Brahmanic sphere of oneness neither separation of the sexes nor their mating takes place any more. Family life, celibacy, chastity or its counterpart, have entirely lost their meaning.

The resolve of a householder to leave family and possessions, to go forth into homelessness can be included into the second stage of the Noble Eightfold Path, namely: Right Aspiration or Right Resolve.

(25) Here the Path of Purification begins, leading from the state of the worldling to the state of Brahmā. In this passage the pilgrim's first steps on the Path are outlined in detail, not unlike a compendium of Buddhist ethics—however, with one fundamental difference: in the Ten Commandments a personal God is the Law-giver meting out rewards or punishments, according to obedience or disobedience of the doer. In Buddhist ethics no external Law-giver determines the motive of man's actions. Buddhists do not rely on such external sanctions as God, Church or State. In the Buddha's Code of Ethics we, too, are enjoined not to take life nor to lie or to bear false testimony, etc. However, the Buddha counsels, he never threatens. Instead of saying: "Thou shalt not...!" he says: "He (the disciple) avoids the killing of living beings and abstains from it." And likewise: "he avoids taking what is not given to him and abstains from it." Here the Buddha emphasizes not so much the outer deed but rather the inner or mental attitude of the doer. Not by a cold command is the latter motivated from taking life, nor does he feel that formal compliance with a disciplinary code renders his deeds ethically meaningful—it is compassion and kindness that move him and not fear of punishment. The same inner attitude obtains in the case of theft, unchastity, lying, calumny, and rudeness of speech. By keeping the Buddha's counsels in mind and applying them to his daily actions, the disciple will soon discover a new and purified atmosphere around him in which virtue comes with joy and voice loses the lure of its seductive power.

The third precept enjoins complete abstention from sexual intercourse upon those who tread the Path of Brahmā and upon others on the Path to even higher perfection. From those who cannot leave their families the Buddha demands self-control as against licentiousness and self-indulgence. He warns against seduction of virgins still under parental guardianship and against unlawful sex practices with persons under the bond of matrimony. The second counsel concerning speech requires abstinence from frivolous and senseless talk. Not only calumny is frowned upon but also reporting with malicious intent what is meant to be secret.

The first three commands deal with the acts of men, the others with his speech. The four demands of speech belong to the third and the three commands of acting belong to the fourth stage of the Noble Eightfold Path. All the other commands beginning with ... "he holds himself aloof from causing injury to seeds or plants ....," till the end of this passage, belong to the fifth stage of the Noble Eightfold Path and are principally, but not exclusively, for the monk who wants to detach himself from the turmoil of the world. The last lines, however, are directed to all and sundry, because their observance tends to make human life smooth and tolerable.

(26) The two fruits of virtuous conduct named here can be reaped already in this life. If the doer, by steadfast practice, acquires the habit of clean living, he will—in spite of occasional relapses—gain in strength of character and eventually overcome the promptings of his lower nature. On the other hand, an immoral conduct, marked by a brazen defiance of every rule of decency, leads only to harsh encounter and violence; whereas a kindly person full of consideration to his fellow human beings calls forth the same qualities in others. Not infrequently, alas, even the kindest of men meets with adversity of fate, painful encounters, and tragedies which must be attributed to moral failures in former lives. However, if he clings to right conduct and fair play in all his dealings he can be assured of his well-being in this life and the life to come. And this may justly be called the first fruit of virtue.

The second fruit consists in an inwardly felt sense of unalloyed happiness which cannot be diminished nor taken away from him. Just as the body of a sick person is being restored to its former physical health and well-being, so does moral health strengthen the inner man, moulding him to a well-integrated personality.

(27) Restraint of the senses or, better, *guarding* the doors of the senses, constitutes the first step on the Path to sainthood; it leads to a higher mode of living than the mere virtuous conduct of which we spoke before and is harder to achieve. A virtuous person is not entirely free from tensions and inner conflicts. Objects of desire present themselves, attractions are felt, and yet he will not yield. Situations arise that are charged with emotions, yet he will exercise moderation. Feelings of extreme dislike will suddenly well up, yet he will bring them under conscious control. All these attitudes—praiseworthy in themselves—are not at par with "guarding of the sense-doors," for the virtuous person is still of the world entangled in its multitudinous cares, whereas the guardian of his sense-doors aims at nothing less than the *overcoming* of the world.

At this point we have to make a clear distinction: when we speak of restraining the senses we do not mean to put a stop to their normal functioning. It stands to reason that to do so would make a person totally unfit to live in this world. Besides, it is not in the sense organs as such where we must look for the seat of covetousness and the wellsprings of craving; the roots lie deeper. The guardian of his senses perceives everything just like anybody else, however, with one fundamental difference: he does not clutch the object of desire to his heart, he is not losing himself in it. He will never say to the passing moment, "Oh linger on, how fair thou art..." As we said before, by suppressing the instruments of perception no virtue is won. Behind them lurks the dragon-head of covetousness, and not until this dragon is slain will victory be won.

Earlier in the text we have noted that the Buddha compares the five senses to fetters by which a man is chained to this river bank of worldly desire. We have seen that not the sense organs but the insatiable craving behind them is the real culprit. This culprit has been forging the chains that bind every one of us to the object of sense gratification. The guarding of the sense-doors is then, indeed, the first stage in the removal of the chains which in the end leads to untrammelled freedom.

Alas, our present state of mind is still a far cry from the goal so ardently desired. To mention an example: there goes a charming figure—and longing arises. Lo! An enchanting voice sends its seductive tunes over the air-and we are all ears. Forgotten are the most pressing duties of the hour. We are as if hypnotically entranced, irresistibly drawn to the source of our spellbound condition. And then again, when eager desire meets with resistance frustration sets in, ill-humour, and irritation. A whole hornet nest of bitter feelings is stirred up; we plot vengeance and want to get even with the world. If we only realised that the fault lies entirely with us, and the world at which we now look with jaundiced eyes is nothing but a miscreation of our own deluded minds! How are we going to disentangle us from this our self-made dilemma. It is no easy task. First, we must realise that frustration is the twin-sister of desire. Second, we must try to keep our emotions on an "even keel." From past experience we ought to know by now that, arousing them, there is trouble brewing. Sense impressions, awakening desires, come and go ceaselessly; we cannot and must not withdraw from them. However, we must pay attention to the road we are travelling. We have to keep our eyes open for the stop-signs and the dangerous crossings. We must learn to think objectively and watch our feelings; they may lie in ambush eagerly waiting for the weak moment to attack, conquer, and subdue us. By trying to work out the foregoing suggestions we shall eventually develop an attitude of detachment in the face of tempting objects. And as a result the turgid waters of our stormy cravings will subside; peace and serenity will enter again into our troubled hearts.

A word of caution must be added here: what was said before was not meant to be a shortcut to the summit of perfection. There are no child prodigies in the arena of spiritual combat; first things will have to come first. This is said explicitly in the 125th Sutta of the Majjhima Nikāya:

"And when the noble disciple has become steadfast in morals, in noble virtue firmly established, pure and undefiled in all his dealings, watchful for the slightest error in conduct, an intrepid warrior never relenting, then the Exalted Lord admonishes him further, saying: "Come you, monk, be watchful at the doors of your senses."

From this solemn utterance of the Buddha it becomes imperative that the code of morals, obligatory for all of us, has to be adhered to first. This is the irremissible prerequisite upon which to build the guardianship of the senses. It would be futile—if not downright dangerous—for a person who is still given to lying to begin practising restraint of the senses. As indicated already, not a "perfect" observance of the ethical code makes one eligible to enter the Path. What matters above all is steadfastness of character, persistence in practice and watchfulness over one's conscience. It goes without saying that relapses will occur, temper may rise, "white" lies be said to escape from embarrassing situations. What matters most, however, has been emphasized and need not repeating.

(28) From the first step on the Path to Deliverance, the guardianship of the senses, we arrive now at the second step called mindfulness. The guardianship or restraint of the senses belongs to the sixth stage of the Noble Eightfold Path of which mindfulness is the seventh. Stages six and seven complement each other. They cannot be separated as they always go together. Likewise must it not be understood that the single factors of that Path have to be taken up consecutively, one after the other, in fact, all Paths and their respective stages interpenetrate each other.

In actual practice the following results will emerge: in spite of the same intensity of external stimuli their impressibility and suggestibility will be felt less and less. What before seemed exciting is now perceived as a hindrance, if not an annoyance, on the way to that inner calm which is the precious fruit of sense-control. The disciple is now disengaged; his attention can be focussed on the next task on hand: to keep the mind's eye steadily on specific body movements and functions. This exercise goes against the grain of most average, i.e., habit-ridden people. With them the trouble lies in their being "enfleshed" so hopelessly in their bodies as to be hardly aware of anything else. With those people the body is the EGO writ large; the only true centre of their being. The aim of the practice of mindfulness is just the reverse: to make the body the object of observation.

Let us consider for a moment how this can be done. First, we try to focus our attention on a single body movement, say, breathing. Mindful we breathe in, mindful we breathe out. This may sound very simple, but it is not. For ours is a wandering mind that, like a grasshopper, hops from one spot to the other. To discipline the mind we shall have to put a stop to the flow of distracting thoughts. It will be sufficient, if we catch only one moment of fixed attention, to recognize that this body of ours is something distinct from the observing "I," just as the writing pen is distinct from the hand that guides it. By the same token the body is seen as a mere instrument through which we satisfy our feelings, desires, volitions, drives, urges, and so on. Now let's go one step further. This body of ours which has become an object of our fixed attention reveals itself as an intricate network of bones, muscles, sinews, interior organs, water, lymph, slime, etc; thus we have detached the body from the subject. We have made it an object for the onlooker; we are not identifying any more our personality with its instrument, the body.

If we succeed with the practice of mindfulness, which, of course, cannot be done in one day, we shall find ourselves on the threshold of a new consciousness. We begin to see ourselves, the things around us, the whole exterior world in an entirely new light.

(29) The meaning of Contentment along the Path will be easily understood. It is not that the disciple in training is at every moment contented. Contentment has to be won; it is just as much a matter of exercise and constant practice as is the perfection of mindfulness which has been spoken of before. Of course, in those rare moments when the practising disciple experiences the indescribable raptures of heavenly bliss, both contentment and discontent have lost their meaning for him. Yet, the award is not for the beginner in the race but only for the swift runner who, in spite of obstacles, undaunted, keeps his eyes uplifted toward the shining goal.

Contentment still remains a boon which cannot be dismissed lightly. Without it even the noblest endeavours are bound to weaken. Take an apprentice, for instance, in whatsoever trade he may exert himself; unless he has the aim of mastery constantly before his mind the pains, the failures, the frustrations inherent in the process of learning, do not count. From this attitude only contentment is begotten and with it the firm assurance of ultimate success.

(30) We come now to the discussion of the five mental hindrances, so called because they hinder, obstruct and impede the Mind from progressing in the practice of the Buddha's Teaching in general and meditative training in particular. Among the many obstacles that block the road to spiritual progress, five are named specifically in the Suttas:

1. Sense desire
2. Ill-will
3. Sloth and torpor
4. Restlessness and worry
5. Sceptical doubt.

Here we have the five root-causes of that obfuscation of mind from which we all suffer, carrying in its wake all those debilities which obstruct our best mental efforts. We have already spoken of them when we compared the Brahmanic frame of mind with its human counterpart. The Buddha elucidates the difference in two parables.

He likens the person driven by sense-desire to a business man who has gotten into heavy debts of which the burden becomes intolerable. The business activities of this man are compared with the innumerable sense objects that crowd around him and call for attention. The burden of the man's debts the Buddha likens to the futile chase after gratification through sense-desires which will not bring satiety, just as the drinking of salt water never quenches the mariner's thirst.

The second hindrance, ill-will, the Awakened One compares with a sick person who is unable to digest food and wastes away. In the same way ill-will spoils all goodness, destroys harmony and kills joy.

The third, sloth and torpor, he compares with a prison. Just as a prisoner is prevented from escaping his cell by walls and iron bars, so do sloth and torpor bind a person to the prison of his own obtuse mind.

Restlessness and worry are compared with slavery. As a slave follows his master's bidding, often against his own will, so the restless mind of a man compels him to think confused thoughts. It shuts out that stillness and lucidity of mind which leads to single-pointedness and insight.

Sceptical doubt the Buddha compares to an endless road leading nowhere and beset with dangers. But the one who overcomes sceptical doubt is likened to a person who has set foot on firm ground, who has found the way home. These are the five hindrances which impede the mental life of most of us. To such an extent are they part and parcel of our natures that—for lack of comparison with their opposites—we simply take them for granted.

In the second parable the Buddha compares the mind free of the five hindrances with a crystal-clear lake where the pebbles on the bottom can be seen and the fishes gliding swiftly to and fro. Conversely, trying to meditate while the mind is disturbed by the hindrances is like expecting to see the reflection of one's face in water wherein various colours have been mixed, or in boiling water, or in water covered by aquatic plants, or in water whipped up into waves by the wind, or in water that is turbid and muddy. How the nature of mental dispositions and propensities depends on the prevalence of the five hindrances has been clearly shown in the foregoing parables. However, the Tevijja Sutta, which is the main subject of our present discussion, seems to contradict the above statements. Yet, on closer scrutiny, we shall see that this is not the case.

We remember how the Buddha compared the five objects of craving with a man, bound with chains to the hither bank of a river, whereas the five mental hindrances are likened to a man lying there without chains. In the same context the Buddha emphasizes "restraint of the senses" combined with "body-mindfulness," first, and only after that, he mentions the suppression of the five mental hindrances as a special exercise. This seeming paradox can easily be dissolved: for the five objects of craving are identical with the first hindrance, i.e., sense desire. The overcoming of the five objects of craving means, therefore, the suppression of mental hindrance number one. Furthermore, sense desire cannot be overcome in the presence of sloth and torpor, which constitutes mental hindrance number three. Again, we recall "sense restraint" and "body-mindfulness" recommended as a practice continually to be performed which cannot be done under the strain of "restlessness and worry," much less in the face of "sloth, torpor, and sceptical doubt" (hindrances Nos. 4, 3, 5). "Ill-will" which is hindrance number two, is always closely coupled with "sense desire." The latter is by nature ambivalent; i. e., manifesting always in pairs of opposites: love-hate, attraction-repulsion, sympathy-antipathy. Thus the conquest of "sense desire" results in the ultimate elimination of "ill-will."

The river-bank parable will confirm this even more. Common sense contends that the man in chains is in no condition whatsoever to reach the farther shore, as compared with the man who, of his own free-will, lay down, unfettered and unimpeded. In reality, however, this is not quite so. The man in chains suffers and, through marshalling his wits and will-power, will eventually free himself, cross the river and make the other shore. The other fellow has by his own volition incapacitated himself; he will lie there forever, until he bestirs himself and changes his mind.

By the same token willpower is called for when treading the path of purification. The aim is the uprooting of the five mental hindrances. This is the ever recurring theme of the Suttas. Purification of the inner man cannot be achieved in one fell swoop; it has to be done gradually one step after another. To use a simile: first the coarse layers of filth must go; then comes the removal of the remaining impurities, hidden, as it were, in crevices and crannies.

The general cleansing consists in breaking the chains of covetousness which is the prime cause of all the hindrances that open the gulf between Brahmā and the priests, between God and man. This purpose is served by the above-mentioned four exercises: virtue, sense-restraint, mindfulness, contentment. This done, the removal of the hidden impurities can begin, thereby coming to grips with the five mental hindrances.

We must now direct our attention to the removal of the finer impurities in order to begin with the above-mentioned important task. It is said in the Scriptures: "Putting away the hankering after the world, he (the disciple) remains with a heart that hankers not, and purifies his mind of lusts." This quotation contains three essential criteria. First, he repudiates worldly lust according to the insight gained by practising the first and second stages of the Noble Eightfold Path. The second criterion: he remains with a heart that hankers not. And the third specifies: "he purifies his mind of lusts." That means: a monk who, for a long time, has successfully loosened the fetters of the five hindrances, well-nigh gotten rid of them, chooses a lonely spot and seats himself cross-legged. In this posture he remains, unruffled, without the faintest stirring of worldly lust, "remains with a heart that hankers not." All the same, he is well aware that, at any other time and in different surroundings, sense desire may rise again. For this reason he holds fast to the "blessed mood," lets its bliss suffuse his whole being, taking umbrage in its calming and purifying light. He is now unshackled and free, flooded with an overwhelming joy of untrammelled freedom that cannot be described: it defies verbal communication. Neither is this joy connected with sensual pleasure nor with the feeling of triumphant victory. It passes on to tranquil felicity, fills the body to its brim until, overflowing, the awareness of the body itself is left behind and fades away. With the body-consciousness gone, nothing is left but a radiant centre of timeless bliss.

We cannot do better than letting the Exalted Lord himself indicate the unique flavour of the four sublime contemplations (*jhāna*) by quoting his utterances of breath-taking beauty and power:

"Free from sensual desires, free from evil thoughts he attains and abides in the first jhāna of joy and pleasure, which is accompanied with reasoning and investigation and arises from seclusion. He suffuses, pervades, fills, and permeates his body with the pleasure and joy arising from seclusion, and there is nothing in all his body untouched by the pleasure and joy arising from seclusion.

"Again the monk with the ceasing of reasoning and investigation, in a state of internal serenity, with his mind fixed on one point, attains and abides in the second jhāna of joy and pleasure arising from concentration, and free from reasoning and investigation. He suffuses, pervades, fills, and permeates his body with the pleasure and joy arising from concentration, and there is nothing in all his body untouched by the pleasure and joy arising from concentration.

"Again the monk with indifference towards joy, abides with equanimity, mindful and self-possessed, and with his body experiences what the noble ones call, 'dwelling with equanimity, mindful, and happy,' and attains and abides in the third jhāna. He suffuses, pervades, fills, and permeates his body with pleasure without joy, and there is nothing in all his body untouched by his pleasure without joy.

"Again the monk, with the dispelling of pleasure and pain, and the disappearance of elation and depression achieved before attains and abides in the fourth jhāna which is without pain and pleasure and with the purity of equanimity and mindfulness. He sits permeating his body with mind purified and cleansed, and there is nothing at all in his body untouched by his mind purified and cleansed."

These supramundane (not: supernatural) meditative absorptions, or jhānas, do not in themselves vouchsafe that Unshakable Deliverance of the Mind which is the goal of even profounder meditations. And yet they are able to lift the practitioner immeasurably above the mundane sphere of common sense pleasures, in spite of their being only temporary and evanescent. However they give a foretaste of Brahmanic bliss and are a mightily strengthening influence for the pilgrim on his Path to the union with Brahmā.

In the foregoing discussions much space was given to the elucidation of those exercises which lead to the overcoming of the five sense objects of craving and elimination of the five hindrances. If this meant a complete emptying of the mind of all worldly objects, so does the exercise of *mettā*, of which more presently, manifest the positive nature of the disciple's self-sacrifice. *Mettā*, unbounded benevolence and loving-kindness, of which the Buddha says: "This is the Path to the state of union with Brahmā." The exercise of *mettā*, which, psychologically speaking, is a moral attitude, tends to the cultivation of goodwill rather than meditation itself. *Mettā* does not consist in thinking of oneself as expanding the feeling of loving-kindness until it becomes all-embracing but in expanding the actual feeling of loving-kindness itself—a subtle but supremely important distinction. Of the four methods of practising *mettā* that appear in the Doctrinal Discourses, the one in the Tevijja Sutta deals principally with the method of "suffusing." This consists in suffusing the whole world with the thought of *mettā*, expanded in all directions, and is associated with the "jhānas" or meditative absorptions. The method of *mettā* as depicted above marks a high level of achievement which is beyond the attainment of the ordinary mortal. For him the exercise should start from a lower level. Let him think of any beloved or less beloved or even disliked person with benevolent thoughts. Feelings of anger and malice will arise in him who thinks of an enemy. Feelings of lust may arise in him who develops *mettā* towards his wife or any person of the opposite sex.

When this happens the beginner must enter upon a series of meditations, to dispel either lust or hatred by persistently dwelling upon love, directed towards this person and so continue until his mind is rendered tender and calm. Once this tenderness is cultivated and the five hindrances overcome he pervades the whole universe with his power of loving-kindness. And like unto a mighty trumpeter who makes himself heard in all four directions without difficulty, so does he radiate loving-kindness from one direction to the second, the third, the fourth; from above and below until, like the sun, he becomes a radiant centre of light, the embodiment of the very spirit of loving-kindness. Many are the blessings of *mettā* enumerated in the Scriptures: happy he sleeps, happy he awakes; he is dear to men; dear to non-human beings; the gods guard him and, if he realizes no further attainment, he goes to the world of Brahmā.

(31) Such a monk is free of wife and wealth, free from the world's cares; he is untrammelled like Brahmā. Anger, malice, impure thoughts no longer arise in him. He has attained to purity of mind, has his emotions under control, has achieved self-mastery like Brahmā. He reflects now Brahmanic qualities on earth as Brahmā does in his heaven, and "after death when the body is dissolved he can be united with Brahmā."

(32) The same thought is being repeated. More characteristics are enumerated which make for Brahmanic qualities in a true follower of Brahmā. And so the Buddha's teaching of the Path leading to the state of union with Brahmā is completed.

(33) The two young priests have fully understood. They beg to be the followers of the All-Enlightened One. Their request is granted and they become members of the Noble Brotherhood.

Stories of Old

Gathered from the Pali Commentaries

WHEEL PUBLICATION NO. 59

Copyright © Kandy: Buddhist Publication Society (1963, 1980)

Sources and Translators

These stories have been collected from the ancient commentaries to the Pali Canon that were compiled and translated in Sri Lanka by Venerable Buddhaghosa in the 5th century CE.

1 *The Arahat Milakkha Tissa* is a free rendition by Ñāṇamoli Thera from the *Manorathapurāṇī* (the Commentary to the *Anguttara Nikāya*).
2 *The Elder Tissa of Cittalapabbata* is a free rendition by Ñāṇamoli Thera from the *Manorathapurāṇī.*
3 *The Elder Dhammadinna's Ministry* was translated by Ñāṇamoli Thera from the *Manorathapurāṇī.*
4 *The Elder Mahā-Siva* was translated by Ñāṇamoli Thera from the *Manorathapurāṇī.*
5 *The Elder Tissabhūti* was translated by Ñāṇamoli Thera from the *Manorathapurāṇī.*
6 *Sabhiya* was translated by Nyanaponika Thera from the Commentary to Suttanipāta.
7 *The Red Lotus* was translated by Nyanaponika Thera from the Commentary to Suttanipāta.
8 *The Unattractive Tree* was translated by Nyanaponika Thera from the Commentary to Suttanipāta.
9 *The Thorn in the Flesh & the Thorn in the Heart* was translated by Nyanaponika Thera from the Commentary to the Samyutta Nikāya.
10 *How to Recognize Saints* was translated by Nyanaponika Thera from the Commentary to the Samyutta Nikāya.
11 *Slow to Fade Away* was translated by Ñāṇamoli Thera from the *Manorathapurāṇī.*
12 *The Story of King Halfpenny* was adapted from the Pali by Soma Thera.

The first five stories are sited in ancient Sri Lanka.

Rohana (Sinhalese 'Ruhunu'), mentioned in the first story, is an old regional division of Sri Lanka in its south.

Mahāgāma, now called Māgama, was the capital of Rohana.

Tissamahārāma (in the second story) is also in the south of Sri Lanka, and still exists under the same name as a place of pilgrimage. Tissamahāvihāra is identical with it.

Cittalapabbata (also in the second story), was a monastery 20 kms east of Tissamahārāma. It is frequently mentioned in the *Visuddhimagga* as an abode of arahats, and is the present-day historical site called Situlpava in the Yala National Park, 20 kms. East of Tissamahārāma.

Talāṅgara (or Talaṅgara) (in the third story) may be identical with the town of Tangalla, in Sri Lanka's South, 40 kms. West of Tissamahārāma.

1. The Arahat Milakkha Tissa

About two thousand years ago there was a young man living in Rohana not far from the southern capital of Mahāgāma. He came from a family of hunters, and they lived near the great monastery of Gāmendavāla.

When he grew up, he decided to take a wife and raise a family. So he worked hard, trapping creatures in the jungle, selling the meat and making a profit. He was in fact very diligent in this for some years, and he was able to lay up for himself quite a little money and quite a lot of future suffering.

One day he went into the woods as usual, and as he felt hungry, he killed a deer caught in one of his traps, grilled the meat over a fire and ate it. Then he was thirsty but there was no water, so he had to walk a long way to the great monastery of Gāmendavāla. When he got there, he went to where the drinking water was kept; but though ten pitchers were there as usual, he found them all empty. He was parched by then, and losing his temper a little, he exclaimed:

"Well really! All these bhikkhus living here and not a drop of water for visitors!"

The Elder Cula Pindapātika Tissa overheard him, and went to him; but glancing at the water pitchers, he saw that they were all full. He thought, 'This man is about to turn into a living ghost.' He said:

"Lay follower, if you are thirsty, here is water, drink it."

Taking one of the pitchers, he poured some water into the man's hands. As he drank, it seemed to vanish away as if put in a red-hot pan. Though he drank till all the pots were really empty, his thirst was still not quenched.

The Elder, who knew him well, said:

"Lay follower, you are half a ghost already. It is because of all the cruel things you do. What is going to become of you?"

The young man said nothing, but after he had saluted the Elder and departed, the words worked like jungle thorns deep into his mind as he walked along. Suddenly his indecision left him. He went the round of all his traps and broke them. He returned home, where he told his wife that he must leave her and the children and he made arrangements for their welfare. Then he loosed the deer and birds he had caught and caged, broke his spear and turned his back upon his home.

He went straight to the monastery and asked to be admitted as a novice. The same Elder told him:

"Friend, life gone forth into homelessness is hard. Will you be able to live it?"

He assured the Elder that his experience, as he saw it, allowed him no alternative. So the Elder admitted him and gave him the monk's name of Milakkha Tissa. He duly instructed him in the general meditation on the parts of the body. He lived quietly for a while, studying the Buddha's word, meditating and doing the various duties.

Reading the discourses one day with his teacher, they came to the passage in the Devadutta Sutta, which, says: 'Then the warders of hell throw him back into the great hell again.'

He asked: "Do they really take a being who has just escaped from such immense suffering and throw him back again into the great hell, venerable sir?"

"They do, friend. All that is made by beings' evil deeds alone."

"Can it be seen, venerable sir?"

"No. But I will show you something like it."

The Elder called the novices and had them pile wet wood on the top of a flat rock. Then they saw him so act as to draw from hell by supernormal power a tongue of fire no bigger than a firefly, which he guided towards the wood. As soon as it reached it there was a flash, and the wet wood was turned to ashes. The other looked at the Elder and asked:

"Venerable sir, how many vocations are there in this dispensation?"

"There are two, friend. The *vasadhura,* or vocation of practice; and the *ganthadhura,* or vocation of books."

"Venerable sir, books are for clever people. But I have faith, and that is based on suffering, which I can see for myself. Let me follow the vocation of practice. Give me a special meditation subject, venerable sir."

The Elder told him all that he must do, and he expounded a special meditation subject to him, explaining to him how to develop both concentration and insight into the true nature of experience.

From then on he lived very strictly, doing the regular duties now at the monastery of Cittalapabbata, now at Gāmendavāla and now at Kājaragāma. He was so anxious not to neglect his task that whenever he felt drowsy he would put a plait of wet straw on his head and sit with his feet in water.

Once at Cittalapabbata after meditating through two watches of the night, he put the wet straw on his forehead to keep off the sleepiness that weighed down on him towards dawn. Then he heard the voice of a novice chanting on the slope of the Eastern Rock this verse from the Arunavatiya Sutta:

"Arise, arise, bestir your hearts
And strive to know the Buddha's word
As tuskers crush a shed of rushes
Deal Māra's hordes the final blow
Since he that will in diligence
Live out this Law and discipline
Shall leave the roundabout of rebirths
And make an end of suffering"

The words seemed as if addressed directly to him. The flooding happiness they brought him heralded the onset of concentration. Then the new transparent clearness in his mind enabled him to see for himself without depending on others the true conditioned nature of all existence, and he reached the fruit of the path of non-return. Soon afterwards, with a supreme effort he attained arahatship, whereon he uttered this exclamation:

"With wetted straw upon my head
I walked the night until I knew
The path's fruit that is last but one
But now I have no doubts at all."

2. The Elder Tissa of Cittalapabbata

Many centuries ago there was a novice called Tissa who lived with his preceptor at Tissamahārāma. Gradually he found himself growing discontented with the bhikkhu life though he could not explain to himself for what reason; and in spite of himself a wish to return to lay life kept troubling his mind. For some time he did his best to get rid of this thought by busying himself with the dyeing and washing of robes, the baking of his bowl with oil, the mending of old robes, and by as many other devices as he could think of, but with no success. So at length he went to his preceptor and told him about it.

Now the old teacher knew his pupil well, and he had seen in him the latent possibility of great spiritual advancement; now too he saw that with the help of favourable circumstances the novice's discontent might disappear. However, he knew that it would be useless and even harmful to try and persuade him by direct argument; his pupil would have to be helped to discover for himself his own talents. So the Elder said to him:

"Tissa, we are getting old. And here at Tissamāharāma all the bhikkhus' lodgings belong to the community. We have nowhere a place of our own where we can grow old and die in peace. Will you go to Cittalapabbata and make a dwelling place there for us according to the vinaya rules that shall be our own personal property?"

The novice did not have to be asked again before he agreed, and at once he was eager to set off in order to start the work. His preceptor told him:

"Tissa, while you are doing the building work there, do not forget the way you have been taught; keep your meditation subject always in mind and practice the development of it at regular intervals."

The novice promised to follow this advice. Then he took leave of his preceptor and set out for Cittalapabbata eighteen miles away through the jungle. When he got there, he first put up at the monastery in the forest; and then began looking for a suitable place nearby to make into a dwelling for his preceptor. Eventually he found a suitable overhanging rock.

After getting the consent of the resident bhikkhus, and after making sure that no creatures' nests or even anthills would be destroyed, he set about thoroughly clearing the site and levelling the ground under the rock. Then he built a wall which had the rock's overhang for its roof, and in that wall he fitted a door and a window. Then he prepared a floor in the new room and made a step in front of the door. And outside he constructed a long walk for walking up and down on. As furniture for the room, he made a bed and chair. All this took him a long time with much hard work. All the days that he was engaged on it he kept up his study of the Samyutta Nikāya; and he never let a day pass without a period spent on practicing his meditation subject. At last it so happened that one day, simultaneously, he finished the building work and got the room ready for occupation; completed his study of the Samyutta Nikāya; and succeeded in attaining a measure of concentration by means of his meditation subject. Since all these three things came to fruition at the same time, it was with no little satisfaction that he went on the following day to Tissamahārāma. And he told his preceptor:

"Venerable sir, the work on the cave is finished. Now it is ready for you to live in."

The Elder paused in thought. Then without looking up he said quietly:

"Tissa, all this has been very difficult for you, and you have worked hard. Now go back there today and live alone in that cave by yourself for this one night."

The novice was surprised, but he agreed; and that same day he made the long journey back to Cittalapabbata. He was tired when he arrived. However, he washed his feet and entered the cave and sat down. The sun had already set, and the stillness of the night was all around him. In that transparent quiet he considered step by step the work he had just completed and the thought came to him:

"A work of pure love has been done by me for my preceptor."

For a long time this thought sustained him until suddenly rapture arose and came flooding over him like the breaking of an ocean wave. In that propitious moment all conditions favoured him, and for that reason he was able to master the rapture and to establish insight upon it. He saw this experience of his as due to conditions; and this insight he was able to extend to the whole of the three planes of existence. In all kinds of existence he saw that there could be nothing not subject to impermanence, to suffering, and to the law of no-self; that whatever is inseparable from the idea of arising is inseparable from the idea of cessation. During the course of the night he was able to carry this insight so far in strength that all craving in him ceased, and with the exhaustion of all taints he reached arahatship.

After many years, when the novice Tissa had become the Elder Tissa, long after his preceptor had passed away, he completed his lifespan in that same cave, and he attained final Nibbāna there, by the element of extinction without result of past clinging left. He had long been known as the Elder Tissa of Cittalapabbata. They took his relics and built a shrine over them, and they called it Tissa's Shrine.

3. The Elder Dhammadinna's Ministry

A. The Elder Mahā-Nagā's Cure

The Elder Dhammadinna, who lived at Talāṅgara, was the instructor of a large community of bhikkhus. He was one of the great ones with cankers destroyed who possessed the four kinds of analytical knowledge. One day, as he was sitting in his own day-time quarters, he wondered:

"Has our teacher, the Elder Mahā-Nagā who lives at Uccavālika, brought his work of recluseship to its conclusion or not?"

He saw that the Elder Mahā-Nagā was still an ordinary man, and he knew that if he did not go to him, he would die an ordinary man. He rose up into the air with supernormal power and alighted near the Elder who was sitting in his day-time quarters. He paid homage to him, doing his duty, and sat down at one side. To the question:

"Why have you come unexpectedly, friend Dhammadinna?" he replied:

"I have come to ask a question, venerable sir."

"Ask, friend. If we know, we shall say."

He asked a thousand questions.

The Elder Mahā-Nagā replied without hesitation to each question. To the remark:

"Your knowledge is very keen, venerable sir; when was this state attained by you?"

He replied:

"Sixty years ago, friend."

"Do you practice concentration, venerable sir?"

"That is not difficult, friend."

"Then make an elephant, venerable sir."

The Elder Mahā-Nagā made an elephant, all white.

"Now, venerable sir, make that elephant come straight at you with his ears outstretched, his tail extended, putting his trunk in his mouth and making a horrible trumpeting."

The Elder did so. Seeing the frightful aspect of the rapidly approaching elephant, he sprang up and started to run away. Then the Elder with cankers destroyed put out his hand, and catching him by the hem of his robe, he said:

"Venerable sir, is there any timidity in one whose cankers are destroyed?"

Then he recognized that he was still an ordinary man. He knelt at Dhammadinna's feet and said:

"Help me, friend Dhammadinna."

"Venerable sir, I will help you; that is why I came. Do not worry."

Then he expounded a meditation subject to him. The Elder took the meditation subject and went up on to the walk, and with the third footstep, he reached arahatship.

3. The Elder Dhammadinna's Ministry

B. The Elder Mahā-Tissa's Cure

There was an Elder, Mahā-Tissa by name, who had obtained the eight meditative attainments when he was still a novice. The defilements of mind, being suppressed by his attainments, did not make an appearance, and his instruction showed him to be close to the noble path. So for sixty years he was unaware of his still being an ordinary man, and not an arahat.

Then one day, the order of bhikkhus sent a message from Tissamahāvihāra at Mahāgāma to the Elder Dhammadinna, who was dwelling in Talāṅgara, to come and preach a sermon on the norm. After the elder consented, he thought:

"There is no bhikkhu who is more senior with me. Having made the Elder Mahā-Tissa, my meditation teacher, the senior of the order (*sangha-thera*), I will go..."

Surrounded by the order of bhikkhus, he went to the Elder's dwelling, and offering his duty to the Elder he sat down at one side.

The Elder said: "Well, Dhammadinna, it is long since you came."

"Yes, venerable sir. The order of bhikkhus sent me a message from Tissa-Mahāvihāra. I will not go alone but would like to go with you. That is why I came."

After a long and friendly talk, he asked "When, venerable sir, did you attain this state?"

"As many as sixty years ago, Dhammadinna."

"But, venerable sir, do you practice the attainments?"

"Yes, friend."

"Can you construct a lotus pool, venerable sir?"

"That is not difficult, friend."

He constructed a lotus pond in a place opposite to them.

"Make a lotus plant there, venerable sir,"

and the Elder did so.

"Now show a big flower there,"

and it was done.

"Show the form of a sixteen-year-old maiden in it," and the Elder did as was said.

Thereupon Dhammadinna said: "Venerable sir, reflect upon her as beautiful again and again."

As the Elder looked upon the form of the maiden created by him, lust arose in him. Knowing thus that he was still an ordinary man, he knelt down by his pupil saying:

"Good man, be my support!"

"It is for that reason I came, venerable sir."

He calmed the Elder by means of the contemplation of the foul; expounded a meditation subject to him; and went outside in order to give the Elder an opportunity. Having dissolved the formation (created by his supernormal power and his lustful thought-formation as well), when he came out of his day-quarters, he had already reached arahatship, together with the four kinds of analytical knowledge.

Then, after making him senior of the order,[1] the Elder Dhammadinna went to Tissamahāvihāra and preached a sermon on the norm.

4. The Elder Mahā-Siva

In the Tissamahāvihāra at Mahāgāma lived the Elder Mahā-Siva who was the teacher of a large community of disciples, expounding to them the Tipiṭaka by way of text and meaning. Guided by his instruction, a very great number of bhikkhus had attained to sainthood.

In one of these bhikkhus, joy had arisen due to his full penetration of truth, and he thought: "Is there this bliss in our teacher?"

On directing his attention to it, he knew that the Elder Mahā-Siva was still a commoner. He thought: "There is a way by which I shall arouse the Elder's sense of urgency!"—and he went out from his own dwelling place to visit the Elder. He paid homage to him and after offering the duty he sat down.

---

1. It seems that he goes alone. The story is not so clear on the reasons for making the Elder Mahātissa the senior monk of the community. One would expect this to be for the reason that Mahātissa would take care of the monastery in his absence because Dhammadinna says that there is no more elder monk staying near him (*mama santike*). However, when Dhammadinna goes to Mahātissa he says that he would like him to come along. (BPS editor)

Then the Elder said to him: "Why have you come, friend the alms-food eater (*pindapātika*)?"

"If you will grant me an opportunity, I have come to learn a portion of the Dhamma, venerable sir."

"Many, friend, are learning. I cannot tell you a time."

When that monk did not get an opportunity in the whole day and night, he said to the Elder: "Since there is thus no time, how will you find time for death?"

Then the Elder thought: "This one has not come for learning; but he has come for arousing a sense of urgency in me."

The other then said: "Venerable sir, an Elder bhikkhu should be as I am"—and he paid homage to the teacher and then rose up into the sapphire-coloured sky and departed.

From the time of the other's departure, the Elder was filled with a sense of urgency. He delivered his day lesson and evening lesson, and placing his bowl and outer robe within his hands' reach, he took the lesson in the early morning. Then taking his bowl and outer robe he went out of the monastery with another bhikkhu who was leaving; and resolved on the thirteen strict ascetic virtues (*dhutanga*). He took as his resting place an overhanging rock outside the village. Preparing the cave, he put aside bed and chair, and made the mental resolution: "Without reaching sainthood, I will not spread my bedding on the couch," and he betook, himself to the ambulatory.

While he was applying himself, saying: "Today I shall obtain sainthood! Today I shall obtain sainthood!" the *pavāraṇā*[2] ceremony came round. When the *pavāraṇā* ceremony drew near, thinking: "I shall abandon the commoner's state. I shall celebrate the *pavāraṇā* in purity," he fatigued himself exceedingly in striving. Being unable for that *pavāraṇā* to arouse either Path or Fruition, he said: "Even for one like me who has initiated insight it is unobtainable. Ah, difficult it is to obtain arahatship!"

Continuing the practice, with chiefly standing and walking, he did the duties of a recluse for thirty years. Now one day, while the great *pavāraṇā* ceremony was going on, he saw the full moon.

---

2. *pavāranā* (lit. "invitation") is the ceremony at the end of the monastic rainy season when the monks invite each other to point out any faults, before they declare their purity from unconfessed offences

Thinking: "Which is the purer, the moon's disc or my virtue?"—he observed: "On the moon's disc, there is the mark of the hare to be seen, but since my higher ordination up to this very day there has been no spot or stain,"—and he became filled with rapture and joy. Because his knowledge was mature, he suppressed the rapture and reached arahatship together with the four kinds of analytical knowledge.

5. The Elder Tissabhūti

An Elder, Tissabhūti by name, came to stay in the great Maṇḍalārāma monastery at Kallagāma. While he was in the village on his alms-round, he noticed a person of the opposite sex. Lust arose in him. Without moving from where he stood, he poured the rice gruel into his young attendant's bowl. He suppressed the improper thought by means of insight, and returned to the monastery. But it reappeared to him in a dream. He considered: "If this thought grows, it will drag me to the four states of woe."

He went to his teacher. After paying homage to him, he stood at one side and said: "I have caught a sickness. If I can cure it, I shall come back. Do not expect me for the day recitation or the evening recitation, but expect me for the morning one."

Then he went to the Elder Mahā-Saṅgharakkhita. The Elder was repairing his leaf hut. Without looking up he said: "Put down your bowl and outer robe, friend."

"Venerable sir, I have caught a sickness. I shall put them down, if you can cure it."

"Friend, you have come to one who can cure your sickness. Put them down."

He thought: "The bhikkhu, our teacher, speaks kindly. He would not speak like this unless he knew." And he put down the bowl and the outer robe. Then after he had undertaken the duties to the Elder, he sat down at one side.

The Elder knew that he was of lustful temperament, and so, as a meditation subject, he expounded the contemplation of the impurity of the body to him; that is, the progressive stages of a decaying corpse. Then the Elder Tissabhūti got up. After he had slung his bowl and outer robe over his shoulder, he paid repeated homage to the Elder.

"Why do you show such gratitude, Tissabhūti?"

"Venerable sir, if I succeed in doing what I have to do, it will be well. If not, then this is the last time you will see me."

"Go, friend Tissabhūti. For one, who is as devoted to his practice as you are, it will not be hard to gain jhāna or insight or path or fruition."

When he had made a suitable reply to the Elder's words and had shown his gratitude, he went to the shade at the root of a bush that he had noticed as he came. He spread his refuse-rag robe, and seating himself on it cross-legged, he made the contemplation of the impurity of the body as his meditation subject clear before him. He established insight and severed his greed for the five strands of sense desire by means of the path of non-return. Then he arose and paid homage to his teacher. Next day he arrived back for the morning recital.

6. Sabhiya

In the Sabhiya Sutta of the Sutta-nipāta we read about a wandering ascetic called Sabhiya. A deity, who in a former life had been a kinsman of his, appeared to him and taught him certain questions which he should put to ascetics and brahmins whom he might meet on his wandering. "Under him who can give an answer to these questions, thou shouldst live the holy life" said the deity.

That deity however, say the teachers of old, was not exactly a blood relation of Sabhiya, but a fellow monk of his in a previous existence, who dearly wished his welfare and progress as parents do for their own child. Here is the story of their past.

Under the dispensation of Kassapa Buddha[3] when that Awakened One had already passed away, three sons of noble families went forth into the homeless life as monks. They lived in the forests and only now and then they visited the nearest city to worship there at the golden cetiya[4] and to listen to an exposition of the Dhamma. But sometimes even that short absence from the forest was unwelcome to them and they preferred to remain in their sylvan solitude striving earnestly for mind's deliverance.

3. A Buddha of the past

4. *Pagoda, dagoba*

But, in spite of their strenuous life, they could not gain even the smallest attainment. Finally they spoke among themselves: "By going out for alms food, we still pay too much regard to our life. But he, who is so anxiously concerned to preserve his life, surely cannot win to any supramundane state. And to die as an ordinary man unfreed of the fetters is most grievous and shameful. Let us then tie a ladder, climb on a steep rock and, discarding the ladder without regard for life and body, let us do the recluse's work!" So they did.

The oldest among the three, endowed with favouring qualities of mind, attained on that very day to sainthood, together with the six supernormal powers (*abhiññā*). By his magic power he rose up into the air and went to the Himalayas. The almsfood obtained there, he brought to his fellow monks on the lonely rock.

But the others said: "Your own work, venerable sir, has been done. Your task is accomplished. But for us who are still unfreed, it will be a waste of time even to talk to you. Please do not come here again!"

When the Elder saw that in no way could he persuade his friends, he left.

After two or three days, one of the other two became a non-returner,[5] endowed with five of the supernormal powers. And when he had done like the first Elder and failed to persuade the third to accept almsfood, he also left. But the third monk, in spite of strenuous effort, could not attain to any higher achievement.

On the seventh day after their ascent of the rock, he died and was reborn in a heavenly world of the sense sphere. On that very day the other two also passed away; the canker-free saint into parinibbāna, and the non-returner appeared in the sublime heaven of the pure abodes where non-returners spend their last existence.

The third of the friends, reborn as a deity, traversed to and fro, through many existences, the six heavenly realms of the sense sphere, enjoying whatever happiness they can give. After exhaustion of that kamma he departed from these worlds and,

5. A non-returner has reached the third of four stages of emancipation culminating in sainthood (arahatship); he does not come back to this world but, during the one existence before him, in the pure abodes, he reaches perfect deliverance.

during the time of our Buddha Gotama, he was reborn on earth, in the womb of a female ascetic. He received the name Sabhiya and, having come to age, he became a wandering ascetic. He was an accomplished disputant and was widely feared and never conquered in religious controversies.

Now that brahma of the pure abodes, his former companion in the holy life, remembered him, and he saw that Sabhiya had no knowledge that there was a Buddha on earth. In order to set Sabhiya on the road where he could meet the Buddha he taught him those several questions which are recorded in the discourse, and said: "Under him who can answer them, lead thou the holy life!"

He did not tell Sabhiya of the Buddha because he knew that if he was an earnest seeker after the goal, and saw the shallowness of the other ascetics and priests, he would not fail to recognize the Buddha. Therefore, he only told him how to question well and wisely.

As we read in the discourse, Sabhiya met the Buddha and had all his questions answered. He became a bhikkhu and soon attained to sainthood.

7. The Red Lotus

Once the Blessed One lived near Sāvatthī at the Jeta Grove in Anāthapiṇḍika's monastery. At that time the venerable Sāriputta had as his personal attendant a young monk who had been ordained under him and was a goldsmith's son. The venerable Sāriputta thought: "For young people, the contemplation of the body's impurity is a suitable subject of meditation," and for conquering lust, he instructed him in that meditation.

But the young monk's mind could not get even to the stage of becoming familiar with the subject, and he said so to the venerable Sāriputta: "This is of no help to me."

But the thera[6] thought: "For young people this is surely suitable," and he gave him again the very same subject of meditation. But even after four months of effort the monk did not obtain even the smallest result. Thereupon the thera took him to the Blessed One, and the Master said:

6. The elder Sāriputta.

"To know what is suitable for him, is not within the range of your capacities, Sāriputta. He is one who has to be guided by a Buddha."

The monk had been born in a goldsmith's family throughout five hundred lives. Hence the Blessed One knew: "A red object will be suitable to him."

And the Blessed One, by his supernormal power, created a red lotus of radiant colour, and placed it into the hands of the monk, saying: "Well, O monk, plant this lotus in sandy soil at a shady spot of the monastery. Then, facing it, sit down with legs crossed, and think, "Red, red."

The monk did as he was told, and almost immediately he attained, in succession, to all four jhānas, those sublime states of full meditative absorption, and he even was able to enter into them in their reverse as well as their normal order.

Now the Master resolved in his mind: "May the lotus whither!"

When the monk emerged from his meditation, he saw the red lotus withered and discoloured, and he thought: "This radiant form has now been crushed by decay!" Obtaining from that a vivid perception of impermanence, he then applied it to himself, and, continuing his contemplation, he understood: "What is impermanent is suffering. What is suffering is not self," and he saw the three planes of existence as if enveloped in flames.

Not far from him there was a lotus pond. Boys had gone into it gathering lotus flowers and had put them on a heap at the shore. When the monk looked at the scene, the red lotus blossoms which were still in the water, appeared to him like tongues of flames in a burning reed thicket; and the falling petals seemed to plunge into a chasm. And among the flowers that were lying on the land, those on top that were withered appeared to him as if seared by fire.

Stirred by that sight he contemplated on life's processes, and still more the three planes of existence appeared to him like a house enveloped in flames that does not give any refuge and safety.

Then the Blessed One, sitting in his room, emitted his bodily aura that rose above the monk and spread over his face. The monk looked up and thought: "What is that?"

Then it appeared to him as if the Blessed One had come and stood close by. Seeing this, the monk rose from his seat and paid homage with clasped hands. Then the Master, knowing his fitness, taught Dhamma by speaking this illuminating verse:

"Who severs lust entire,
Like into the pond descending
One uproots lotus plants,
Such a monk discards 'here' and 'beyond'
As snakes slough outworn skin"

8. The Unattractive Tree

Once there lived a king of Benares called Brahmadatta. Every four months he used to ride to his royal park to amuse himself in sports and frolics. One day in the middle of the summer, when he had gone again to the park, he saw at the entrance of it an ebony tree in full bloom and with dense foliage. Plucking one of the flowers, he entered the park.

The courtier who rode behind him thought, "This must be a very distinguished flower that the king has taken!" and sitting on his elephant's back, he too plucked a flower. So too did the entire large entourage. And when, finally, there were no blossoms left, they took the leaves. Void of blossoms and leaves, the tree was left with its bare trunk.

And so the king saw it when he returned from the park in the evening.

"What has happened to the tree?" he thought. "When I went to the park, coral-like blossoms adorned it, shining through the emerald green of its leaves. And now it is quite bare, and neither blossoms nor leaves are to be seen!"

While he so mused, he saw close-by another tree, without any blossoms but amply covered with foliage. And the king thought: "That other tree, with its branches heavy with beautiful flowers, was attractive to the crowd, and within a short time distress befell it. But this tree here, because it has nothing attractive to show, still stands inviolate and unharmed. So also my kingdom is attractive and desirable to many, like that blossoming tree.

"But monkhood is unattractive like this tree without blossoms. Hence, as long as this kingdom of mine has not yet been plundered and ransacked like that blossoming tree, it is fit to go forth into the homeless life clad in the monk's dull-coloured and inconspicuous robes, like that other tree with its unattractive foliage."

Thinking thus, he gave up his kingdom and became a monk. Developing insight, he realized a Silent Buddha's Awakening (*pacceka-bodhi*).

Hence it was said:

> "Discarding laymen's garb and ways
> Like coral tree its foliage sheds,
> Clad in the ochre robe go forth
> And fare alone like the rhinoceros!"

(Sutta Nipāta v. 64)

9. The Thorn in the Flesh and the Thorn in the Heart

Once there lived twelve monks in a forest, devoted to meditative effort. One day when at sunset the gong had been sounded, one of the monks, an Elder, had left the ambulatory and, for shortening the way, he went across a grassy patch. A thorn hidden in the grass pierced the sole of his foot. The thorn was very long and sharply pointed, and caused severe pain as if a heated iron rod had pierced the foot.

The Elder thought to himself: "Now, shall I pull out this thorn or that other thorn that constantly pierces our heart?"

And he thought further: "When pierced by an external thorn, there is no fear of falling into the states of woe; but there is such danger from that other thorn that always hurts us inwardly."

So he ignored the pain and, walking the whole night up and down on the ambulatory, he did his meditation.

At daybreak he gave a sign to a monk who passed. When that monk came near and asked him what he wanted, he said: "A thorn has hurt me, friend."

"When did it happen, venerable sir?"

"Last evening, friend."

"But why did you not call, venerable sir? We would have come and extracted the thorn and treated the wound with oil."

"I have striven, friend, to pull out that other thorn that constantly hurts us deep within."

"And did you succeed, venerable sir?"
"Partly, friend."

10. How to Recognize Saints

At the monastery on the Cittala Hill, there lived an Elder who was a canker-freed saint. As his personal attendant he had a novice who was ordained in old age. One day the old novice went on almsround together with the Elder, and carrying the Elder's alms bowl and outer robe, he walked behind him. While they so went, the old novice asked the Elder: "Those who are saints, how do they look? How can we recognize them?"

The Elder said: "There is an old person who carries a saint's bowl and robe, fulfils all duties towards him, and even goes along with him—yet he cannot recognize saints. So hard to know, friend, are the saints!"

And not even then did the old novice understand.

11. Slow To Fade Away

"Lust" said the Enlightened One, "is slow to fade away." It is, add the teachers of old, like lampblack that sticks for a long time. Lust does not go away even for two or three successive existences. To illustrate this, there is a story.

A man, it seems, had an illicit relation with his brother's wife. He was dearer to that woman than her own husband. She said to him: "If this affair becomes known there will be a great scandal. Kill your brother."

He was shocked and said: "Stop it, hag. Do not say that again."

She was silent. After a few days had passed, she spoke of it again. His mind wavered. After that, when she had mentioned it for the third time, he said: "What shall I do to find an opportunity?"

Then she explained the means to him: "Do as I tell you. In a certain place near a big hollow tree there is a washing place. Wait there with a sharp hatchet." He did so. When the elder brother came home after working in the forest, she pretended to be nice to him and said: "Come, husband, I will look at your head." After she had looked, she said: "Your head is dirty." Then she gave him a ball of crushed myrobalan paste, and sent him off, saying: "Go and wash your head at such and such a place, and come back."

He went to the washing place she had told him. He smeared his head with myrobalan paste, bent forward to pour the water on his head and began to wash. Then the other came out from inside the hollow tree and struck him on the spine, killing him, and then went home.

The other was unable to throw off his affection for his wife and was reborn in that same house as a rat snake. He would go near to her over where she was standing or sitting and fall on her body from the roof. Then, thinking: "This must be him again!"—she had him killed.

On account of his affection for her, he was again reborn in that same house as a dog. As soon as she set out anywhere on foot he went after her. When she went to the forest, he followed her. When people saw this, they mocked her, saying: "The hunter has gone out with the dog! What place are they going to?" So she had him killed again.

Again he was reborn at the same household as a calf, and likewise he followed her everywhere. Then when people saw her they mocked her, saying: "The cow herd has gone out. Where will the cows wander?" She had him killed on the spot.

Since he was still unable to break off his affection for her, he was reborn for the fourth time, this time in her womb with the recollection of former lives. Eventually, he saw that he had been killed by her in his last four existences; he thought: "I have been reborn in the womb of such an enemy!" From then on he would not let her touch him with her hand. If she touched him he shrieked and cried. Only his grandmother could look after him.

Later on, when he was grown, his grandfather said: "My dear, why would you not let your mother touch you with her hand, and why, when she touched you, did you cry out aloud and shriek?"

When he was asked this by his grandfather, he said: "She is not my mother, she is my enemy." He then told him all that had occurred. The grandfather embraced him and wept saying: "Come, my dear, what business have we living in such a place."

The grandfather then went with him to a certain monastery. They both went forth into the monk life and living there they both attained arahatship.

12. The Story of King Halfpenny

For long, men have:

craved for the unlovely, believing it to be lovely;
craved for unhappiness, believing it to be happiness;
craved for the impermanent, believing it to be permanent; and
craved for what is not self, believing it to be self.

In those who have such a perverted view of the facts of life, craving grows. "Like a creeper grows the craving of the negligent man"—that is, of a man who has not taken pains to understand the true nature of life. "He leaps hither and thither desiring fruits, like an ape in the woods."

Most complex is this craving in the common man who has not been instructed in the Buddha's teaching. It often seems as if it would be futile to expect any movement on his part towards right understanding which leads to the cessation of craving. Still, even such an uninstructed man's conscience may prick him, owing to some good training in past lives, and make him change his character, as the following story shows.

Long ago, a labourer, who lived at the north gate of Benares, had earned a halfpenny (*addhamāsaka*) by carrying water, and hid it under a tile of the boundary wall near the gate. While earning his livelihood as a water-carrier he lived, from time to time, with a poor woman at the south gate of the town.

One day she told him:

"Today there is a festival in the town. Let us amuse ourselves, if you have money."

"I have," said the man.

"How much?"

"A halfpenny."

"Where is it?"

"Under a tile of the north boundary wall, twelve yojanas from here, is my treasure. Have you any money on you?"

"I have," said the woman.

"How much?"

"A halfpenny."

"Then with your halfpenny and my halfpenny, we have a penny. And with the penny we can buy garlands, perfumes and drink and find pleasure."

"Fetch your halfpenny," said the woman.

"My dear, don't worry. I shall fetch it," said the man, and went to bring his treasure, pleased and excited, because he had got the idea of enjoyment from the woman.

The labourer, who was strong as an elephant, covered six yojanas. He was excited with greed, and at midday was going along the road near the king's palace, treading on hot sand which was like flameless glowing coal spread out. The man had rolled palm leaves stuck in his ears for ornament, was dressed in dirty rags, and was singing a wanton song.

The king of Benares at that time was the bodhisatta; his name was Udaya. King Udaya, who was standing at the open window, saw the labourer and was curious to know about the man's errand. He had the labourer brought to the palace. To the labourer the king said:

"The earth has turned to live coals; the ground is like burning cinders; but you sing a wanton song. Does not the heat burn you? The sun glows above and the sand scorches below. But you sing a wanton song. Does not the heat burn you?"

"No, sire, the heat does not burn me; desires burn me. The many things that I have to do because of passion, these do burn me; the heat does not."

Then he made known his errand to the king, and added:

"Her words, when she sent me off on this journey, 'Fetch the halfpenny, then both of us will amuse ourselves,' do not leave my heart, and as I ponder on them the fire of passion burns me."

"But in this hot weather what is the comforting thought owing to which you go singing a wanton song?"

"Sire, the thought, 'Having got the money, I shall amuse myself with her' makes me content, and sing."

"Does the treasure you have hidden at the north gate amount to a hundred thousand?"

"No, sire."

"Does it amount to half a hundred thousand?"

"No, sire."

Then questioning him further, the king found out that the treasure was a halfpenny, and said this:

"Good man, don't go at this hot time. I shall give you a halfpenny."

But the man wished to have both the king's halfpenny and the halfpenny under the tile of the boundary wall. Although the king increased his offer to a crore and more, the man would not stop the journey to get his halfpenny. Then the king offered the man half of Benares, and only then did the labourer agree to cancel his journey to the north gate. But it is said that he chose that half of Benares where his halfpenny was hidden! Later the labourer was known as King Halfpenny (Addhamāsaka Rāja).

One day the two kings went to a park. There, after amusing himself, King Udaya rested with his head on King Halfpenny's lap and fell asleep. And when Udaya was sleeping, Halfpenny thought:

"Why should I not kill King Udaya and become king of the whole of Benares?"

But quickly remorse overtook Halfpenny, and he awoke King Udaya, and confessed to him the treacherous thought that had crossed his mind. King Udaya offered to Halfpenny the whole of Benares and agreed to be Halfpenny's viceroy. But Halfpenny said:

"I have no use for the kingdom, sire. Take back your kingdom. I shall go forth. I have seen the root of sensuality. Sensuality grows with the thought of it. I shall never more think sensually."

And then he said this:

"Desire, I saw your root.
From thought do you spring.
I shall not think of you, and you shall not be in me.
Little desire is not enough,
and much desire does not bring satisfaction.
Truly he who is awake should penetrate foolish prattling desires."

Then the labourer who became King Halfpenny renounced the world and became a Paccekabuddha.[7]

7. A Silent Buddha.

The Satipaṭṭhāna Sutta and Its Application to Modern Life

by

V. F. Gunaratna

WHEEL PUBLICATION NO. 60

Copyright © Kandy: Buddhist Publication Society (1981)

The Satipaṭṭhāna Sutta and Its Application to Modern Life

The *Satipaṭṭhāna Sutta* and its application to modern life—this is the theme of my talk this evening, and it will be my endeavour, first, to give you some idea of what *satipaṭṭhāna* really is, and thereafter to show you that the special and peculiar conditions of the modern age are such that the doctrine of *satipaṭṭhāna* was never more urgently needed than it is today.

The *Satipaṭṭhāna Sutta*,[1] as you know, deals with the fourfold development of a very great quality of the mind, viz. *sati* or "mindfulness." *Satipaṭṭhāna* means the establishment of mindfulness or the practice of mindfulness. The four types of mindfulness dealt with in the Sutta are:

(1) Mindfulness of the body (including mindfulness of the breath): *kāyānupassanā*,
(2) Mindfulness of sensations: *vedanānupassanā*,
(3) Mindfulness of thoughts: *cittānupassanā*, and
(4) Mindfulness of mind-objects: *dhammānupassanā*.

Mindfulness is one of the eight factors of the Noble Eightfold Path. It is one of the five *indriyas* or faculties and it is also the first of the seven *bojjhaṅgas* or factors of enlightenment.

You will thus see what an important place is assigned to mindfulness (*sati*) in Buddhism. Indeed, it has been called by the Buddha the one and only way (*ekāyano maggo*) for the purification of beings (*sattānaṃ visuddhiyā*), for the overcoming of sorrow and lamentation (*sokapariddavānaṃ samatikkamāya*), for destruction of suffering and grief (*dukkha domanassānaṃ atthaṅgamāya*), for entry into the Noble Path (*ñāyassa adhigamāya*), and for the realization of Nibbāna (*nibbānassa sacchikiriyāya*).

From the average man's point of view also, mindfulness is a very desirable quality. Common sense will tell us that the

---

1. A translation of the *Satipaṭṭhāna Sutta*, with Introduction and Notes, by Nyanasatta Thera, has appeared as No. 19 of *The Wheel* series, under the title *The Foundations of Mindfulness*.

practice of mindfulness makes us more precise and more alert, and minimizes the possibilities of errors, mistakes, lapses, and accidents. Common sense will also tell us that the habit of mindfulness will also induce a healthy balance, a sense of proportion, and a sense of mental alertness, keeping us constantly on our guard. But please remember that the Buddha tells us much more. He tells us in no uncertain terms (which I have just quoted) that mindfulness has the effect of purifying beings, overcoming sorrow, causing entry into the Noble Eightfold Path, and ultimately of realizing Nibbāna itself. Now how is it possible to obtain these greater and grander results?

These results are attainable if the mindfulness practised is not merely mundane (*lokiya*) or worldly mindfulness, but mindfulness of a very special spiritual or supramundane (*lokuttara*) nature. There is a very special and particular technique to be adopted in order to achieve this. The *Satipaṭṭhāna Sutta* mentions these special types of mindfulness and also the special procedure necessary. So when the special type of mindfulness is practised in the special way prescribed, all the promised results can be realized.

Mindfulness proper has this special feature about it, namely, that it involves a method of looking at things objectively and not subjectively. Not until mindfulness brings in this all-important element of looking at things objectively will it became mindfulness in the Buddhist sense, the real *sati.* It is necessary to grasp this distinction between objective and subjective looking. When Pythagoras was asked to define who a philosopher is, he said something to this effect: When all are invited to the feast of life, some go there to enjoy, some go there to win name and fame, and there are yet others who go there just to look on. These others are the philosophers. What is meant thereby is that the philosopher does not identify himself with life. He looks at life standing as it were outside life. That is how the trainee in *sati* should look at things.

When you look at a thing subjectively, there is a mental affinity between yourself and the thing you are looking at. You bring yourself mentally very close to what you are looking at. You connect yourself with the object and if there is any relationship between yourself and the object, you make no effort to ignore that relationship. On the contrary, that relationship influences you a great deal and colours your observation. In short, you are an interested observer. On the other hand, if you look at a thing objectively, you keep yourself mentally far removed from the object, you disconnect yourself from the object and if there is any relationship between yourself and the object, you will not allow that relationship to influence your observation. In short, you are a *bare observer* as distinguished from an *interested observer.* A bare observer uninfluenced by extraneous considerations must necessarily see more clearly and better than an interested observer, since the interested observer's vision can be affected by the particular nature of his interest. A spectator sees more of the game than a player or a partisan. In the practice of mindfulness, one must therefore free oneself from all notions of self and self-interest and must try to fix the mind solely on the object without any assumptions and presumptions, bias and prejudice, and all other preconceived considerations. In short, one must strive to have the true picture of the object and that only. It is this special quality of mindfulness that one has to cultivate.

I have said that there are four objects of mindfulness: body, sensations, thoughts, and thought-objects. In regard to every one of these four, mindfulness must be practised in the objective way. Whatever the object of mindfulness, you have to see that object and that object only. This is the secret of successful *satipaṭṭhāna* and this secret the Buddha had clearly explained on many occasions. You can imagine how important this is when I tell you that, on one occasion, the Buddha while on his begging rounds, halted to explain this to a certain individual. The Buddha had a set timetable and worked according to a set routine, and never had he been known to have halted, while on his begging rounds, to do anything else. But here, in this particular instance, he halted to discourse to Bāhiya, a leader of a religious sect.

This Bāhiya had led a good life and had flattered himself with the belief that he may have reached the stage of an Arahant (a Saint), but a deity told him:

"You are neither an Arahant nor have you reached the Arahant's path. You do not know the technique [*paṭipadā*] whereby you can become an Arahant. Go and enquire from the Buddha. He is an Arahant and teaches *dhamma* for reaching Arahantship. He lives in the far off town of Sāvatthī."

Then Bāhiya, greatly stirred by the words of the deity, lost no time in proceeding to Sāvatthī.

He was so keen to learn the technique of becoming an Arahant that, it is said, he stopped only one night throughout the long journey. When he came to the Jetavana in Sāvatthī, he heard that the Buddha had gone on his begging rounds. Greatly agitated, he followed the direction in which the Buddha went, met him, fell with his head at his feet and implored the Buddha to teach him this technique. Twice the request was made and twice the Buddha refused him, saying, "You come unseasonably, Bāhiya. We have entered in request of alms." When for a third time the request was made, the Buddha, perhaps seeing that Bāhiya was destined to die that day, explained the technique in a few words, but they were sufficient for Bāhiya to understand.

> "Bāhiya," said the Buddha, "this way you should train yourself: In the seen there will be to you just the seen. In the heard there will be to you just the heard. In the thought there will be to you just the thought. In the cognizing there will be to you just the cognizing."

> *"Diṭṭhe diṭṭha-mattaṃ bhavissati, sute suta-mattaṃ bhavissati, mute muta-mattaṃ bhavissati, viññāte viññāta-mattā bhavissati."*

These are pregnant words with deep meaning, but from what I have told you before, you will, I am sure, not find it difficult to grasp their deep import. If you have to practice mindfulness of sight on any object, it should be the sight of it and nothing more. The thoughts and emotions that flow from the observation of the object in question, aroused by the particular interest you have in the object, should not mar your vision. When the object of mindfulness is any sound or hearing, it should be just that sound or hearing without the thoughts and emotions aroused by the particular interest in that sound or hearing. Similarly, this ideal should be kept in mind in regard to the other types of mindfulness.

Returning with his disciples from the collection of alms, the Buddha saw Bāhiya dead by the roadside attacked by a young calf. The Buddha asked his disciples to take the dead body and cremate it.

The Buddha then said, "Bāhiya has followed the instructions given by me. Bāhiya has attained to Arahantship."

We can now see the importance of looking objectively at what comes our way. When anything comes our way, we must not readily succumb to its influence. We must watch it objectively. What comes our way may be a sight, a sound, a taste, a smell, a touch, or even a thought. There is no suitable English word to express the idea of "what comes our way." The Pali word is *ārammaṇa*, usually rendered by "object". These are the things that come our way in life, and if we instead of being dominated by them, look at them objectively, we are going through life in the correct attitude. Today, the world is suffering from an imperfect observation of these "encounters". To that observation are added the memory of our previous reactions to them and our present tendencies in regard to them. Then we rush into action. This is folly.

Let the picture impress itself fully on our mind. Today, we do not wait to catch the full import of such an encounter. Influenced by its superficial features we just rush to action.

Look, for instance, at anything which is considered evil. Look at it objectively instead of permitting the habitual reactions of thought that are likely to arise hereby. Try to get the full import of the sight. Look at it fairly and calmly. Look at it long, undisturbed by the desires, emotions and considerations which such a sight may arouse in you. Do not draw conclusions and deductions.

Just keep on looking, looking objectively, and the superficial gloss surrounding that evil will shed itself and you will not be deluded by that sight. The external comely appearance which characterizes and allures many an unsuspecting weak mind will fade away before the steadfast gaze of the bare observer and he will see things in their true light. He will see things as they are (*yathābhūtañāṇadassana*). When you see things as they truly are, you are no more a victim of delusion. This is the great message of *satipaṭṭhāna*. I have just spoken about the special meaning attached to mindfulness.

Now, let us proceed to the special procedure attached to the practice of mindfulness. At the outset it must be stated that this special procedure refers to the practice of the first object of mindfulness, namely, mindfulness of the body, and more especially to that special type of mindfulness of the body known as *ānāpānasati* or mindfulness of in-breathing and out-breathing. This type of mindfulness needs a special time and a special posture. The other types of mindfulness can be practised anywhere, at any time, as the occasion arises.

Now, what is the type of place that has been recommended for the practice of *ānāpānasati* or mindfulness of breath? The Sutta says, *araññagato va rukkhamūlagato va suññāgāragato va*: "In a forest, at the foot of a tree or in an empty house." The three types of places given connote a place of quiet, a place to which one can retire secure from the din, turmoil and bustle of a busy life. This is something that the modern world badly needs. As for forests, they are fast decreasing in number. In towns you find very few gardens with large shady trees. In the village you do find gardens and trees, but villages are fast being converted into towns and they are no more the isolated places of silence and quiet they once were. Those living in busy towns and busy villages are therefore left with only the third type of place: *suññagāra*, an empty house. Even this is not easy to find and one must therefore look for an empty room. Modern housing problems are such that even an empty room is not available to many. Overcrowding in houses and the system of living in flats make it still more difficult to secure an empty room. The next best thing is to select a quiet corner in a room, or better still, this practice of mindfulness can be done on your bed at night or in the early hours of the morning when silence reigns supreme.

Having found a place, you must stick to it. You lose much if you keep on shifting the place of practice. You must also have a special time and rigidly adhere to it. Remember the practice of *ānāpānasati* is a meditation. It must be regular, and you must, realising its importance, not allow anything to interfere with its regular practice. It must be the same place every day and it must be the same time every day. These are important psychological factors that make for the efficacy and success of the meditation. The make-up of the human system is such that it easily responds to the rhythm of regularity. If you are accustomed to have a particular place and a particular time for your meditation, and if you are regular and sincere, when the meditating time approaches, you will not feel like doing anything else at that time, and you will be very greatly disappointed if something unavoidable prevents your meditation. Furthermore, as the time for meditation approaches, you will be pleased to see yourself getting into the meditative frame of mind. You will be surprised to see how bad thoughts will cease to enter your mind at that sacred hour, and even as you approach that habitual place of meditation, that place which should be sacred to you, you will again be surprised to see how easily the mind will respond to the discipline to which you have subjected it and how bad thoughts will cease to enter your mind. Even if they do, they will give way to good thoughts with great ease. So you must have a particular time and a particular place for this meditation.

I must also remind you that it is necessary, at available moments during the day, to hearken back to this meditation that you have practised at night or early morning. At odd moments during the day you should be able to retire to the silence of your mind, be restful amid the restless, and practise this meditation (even if only for a few minutes). At such moments the requirements of special time, special place and special posture must necessarily be dispensed with. You may feel prompted to ask me "When can I, in this busy world, find the time during the day to practise any meditation at all?" My answer is, "You certainly have the time."

This is no doubt a busy age, an age of speed and tension. A quick moving vehicle brings you to a place. Maybe you have to wait a little before you get into the next vehicle, which takes you to your destination. It is an impatient waiting for you. It is all tension. Here is one place where you can practise a little mindfulness of breathing (*ānāpānasati*). You come to a railway station to buy a ticket. It is a long queue. You wait impatiently for your turn. Here is another place where you can practice *ānāpānasati*. You board a train and detrain at a railway junction, where you are impatiently walking up and down the platform waiting for the connecting train. It is tension for you.

Here is yet another place where you can practise *ānāpānasati*. You come tearing down in your car and as you approach a junction, the green colour of the traffic lights has just given place to amber. You curse, and come to a halt. It is all tension for you as you impatiently wait a seeming eternity until the red colour gives way to amber, and another seeming eternity until amber gives way to green. In those two seeming eternities you can practise a little *ānāpānasati*. Your tension will go, you will be all the calmer and better equipped to face whatever problems are awaiting your attention. In the waiting room of a railway station, in the waiting room of a professional consultant, in train, in car or bus, you can practice a little *ānāpānasati*. You will see that in the daily life of the busy, modern world there are opportunities to retire into the silence of your mind and practise mindfulness for a few moments.

We shall now proceed from consideration of place and time to considerations of the posture necessary for the practice of *ānāpānasati*. The Sutta says, *nisīdati pallaṅkaṃ ābhujitvā ujuṃ kāyaṃ panidhāya:* "He sits down cross-legged, keeping his body erect." This is a posture in which we should be able to remain motionless for quite a long time. Some people find it very difficult to remain still even in a comfortable chair for at least half an hour without shifting the position of the hands or legs. It is necessary however to learn to adopt the cross-legged position and to remain motionless. This is especially necessary for the modern age which is essentially an age of motion.

Look around you and it is all motion, motion, motion; and motion leads to commotion. All sense of calm is completely destroyed, and with disappearance of calm, the mind loses its healthy balance. Calm is the first step towards mental purity and mental strength, and this calm is distinctly lacking in the modern man. Once in a while, break away from this motion and commotion. Go to some quiet spot and remain motionless. This can have a remarkably soothing effect on the agitated mind of the modern man. The very act of remaining still will not only make you calm, but give you mental strength. It has a tonic effect on the mind, and even for that one moment of quiet and restfulness you will have a vague feeling that you are awakening to a sense of security and strength. By reason of the multiplicity of motions we have to perform in the modern world, by reason of the multiplicity of hurried actions, tense moments and anxious situations, there is great waste of mental energy. Therefore, once in a while, if you can, just sit still for some time. You are conserving mental energy. The cross-legged position, the *padmāsana* posture, is best able to help you maintain sustained motionlessness.

By the fact that your legs are interlocked and your hands are brought together, there will not be any escape of the mental energies that are conserved by your meditative processes. It is also a physically well balanced position, the body weight being equally distributed, and so you will find it easy to remain motionless in this position longer than in any other. By reason of keeping the upper part of body erect, there is perfect control of your breath. You can breathe more freely. Besides, there is an intimate connection between the spinal cord and the emotions. When you are in that position you can have easier control of your emotions. Those who find this posture difficult may sit on a straight-backed chair, keeping the body erect. The legs should rest on the ground without strain.

Now we shall proceed to explain the method of practising mindfulness of breathing (*ānāpānasati*). Having chosen a special place, and time, and having adopted the special posture prescribed, you must now commence the practice of conscious breathing. Breathe calmly and while breathing, be fully aware of your breath, but avoid strain. Do not breathe forcefully. Breathe naturally and calmly, observing your breath all the while. *Dīghaṃ va assasanto dīghaṃ assasāmīti pajānāti; dīghaṃ va passasanto dīghaṃ passasāmīti pajānāti*: "Breathing deeply in, he knows he is breathing deeply in. Breathing deeply out, he knows he is breathing deeply out. Similarly, taking a short breath in, he knows he is taking a short breath in, and taking a short breath out, he knows he is taking a short breath out."

The disciple must not identify himself with his breathing. He must view the breathing objectively and not subjectively. He must not dwell on the fact that it is he who is breathing. He must contemplate this bare act of breathing and nothing else. He must maintain awareness of this breath at all costs. All that is needed is this quiet awareness of the inflow and outflow of the breath. Remember this is not a breathing exercise. This is an exercise in mindfulness of breath. No retention of the breath is needed, as is required by the Yoga Sūtra of Patañjalī and other Hindu books. Perseverance in this mode of observation of breath will result in a deepening of the breath rhythm, and the first noticeable effect will be a growing sense of calm and tranquillity. There will also be better aeration of the lungs and a sense of physical well-being, but this is a by-product. Continued practice of *ānāpānasati* leads one on to the higher levels of tranquillity-meditation (*samatha-bhāvanā*), bringing in their wake those exalted ecstasies known as the *jhānas.* The disciple can, however, instead of pursuing the *jhānas,* elect to pursue the path of *vipassanā-bhāvanā* (meditation on higher insight) and obtain *vipassanā* (higher insight).

That the observation of the rise and fall of the breath can lead to all these great results is difficult for the modern man to appreciate. The Venerable Nyanaponika Thera in his book, *The Heart of Buddhist Meditation,*[2] says that "breath stands on the threshold between the voluntary and the involuntary bodily functions, and thus offers a good opening to extend the scope of conscious control over the body". We can therefore understand the great possibilities underlying systematic mindfulness of breath. He goes on to say that by reason of the continued observation of the rise and fall of the breath, "the heaving of the Ocean of Impermanence, its continuous rise and fall can be observed well." The rise and fall of all beings and all things will be clearly perceptible to the disciple. This is not an intellectual understanding but a deep spiritual experience of a higher plane which comes with the realization of the rise and fall of the breath. Henceforth the disciple ceases to act unwisely with regard to the body. He ceases to be the body's slave. Rising beyond the physical plane, he finds that there is no basis within the body which could logically support any notion of "I" or "mine." It is no more a case of "I am breathing." The disciple will thus find that there is no permanent principle within this body to which it is desirable or profitable to cling. *Anissito ca viharati na ca kiñci loke upādiyati*: "He depends on nothing and clings to nothing in this world." Realizing the impermanence of the body, he realizes the impermanence of all things. He comes to understand things as they are. He touches a higher plane. That way lies Nibbāna.

There are yet other types of mindfulness of the body. There is mindfulness of the various parts of the body. The Sutta enumerates a list of 31 parts which are often heard repeated by pious devotees when they are observing the eight precepts. *Atthi imasmiṃ kāye kesa-loma-nakha-danta-taco maṃsaṃ nahāru aṭṭhi,* etc. "There are

2. Buddhist Publication Society, Kandy, Sri Lanka.

in this body: hair of the head, hair of the body, nails, teeth, skin, flesh, sinews, bones, etc." The Sutta continues thus:

"Just as if, O monks, there were a basket with two openings, full of various kinds of grain, namely hill paddy, paddy, green gram, cow-pea, sesame, rice; and a man with sound eyes, having opened it, should reflect thus: 'This is hill-paddy, this is paddy, this is green gram, etc.' In the same way a monk reflects on this body enveloped by the skin and full of manifold impurities, from the soles up and from the top of the hair down, thinking thus: 'There are in this body hair of head, hair of body, nails, teeth, skin, flesh, etc.'"

Another method of meditation on the body is to take each part separately, think of its location, its colour and shape, and consider how loathsome and repulsive each part is. This minute dissection of the body into its various component parts will help to remove the illusion of "the body beautiful" and reveal its inherent impurity. The Commentary states:

"No one who searches earnestly throughout the whole of this fathom-long carcass, starting from the soles of the feet upwards, starting from the top of the hair downwards, and starting from the skin all round, ever sees even the minutest atom of pureness; on the contrary, he sees nothing but various very malodorous, offensive, drab-looking sorts of impurity consisting of the head-hairs, body-hairs, and the rest."

This meditation is necessary to the modern world, which places an exaggerated importance on the body. Man is so attached to his body, regarding it as his own precious possession, that nothing short of a drastic dissection (as contained in this meditation) will arouse the sense of repulsion necessary to establish that elevating and lofty detachment with regard to one's body which ultimately leads to a realization of the rise and fall of all things. He comes to see things as they are. He touches a higher plane.

There are two other types of mindfulness of the body, namely, mindfulness of the four elements and mindfulness of the decomposition of the body. In the former, there is a different kind of dissection of the body. The body is reduced to the four fundamental manifestations of matter, namely, the element of earth, the element of water, the element of fire, and the element of wind. These elements the human body possesses in common with all forms of inanimate matter. These fundamental qualities of matter are sometimes referred to as solidity, adhesion, caloricity, and motion. This mode of dissection (bringing out the thought that the body is not different from inanimate matter) helps to establish in the mind the impersonal and impermanent nature of the body which is forgotten and obscured by reason of the great emphasis on the body placed by the modern age, and ultimately leads to a realization of the rise and fall of all things. Seeing things as they are, he touches a higher plane.

The mindfulness of the decomposition of the body is just as beneficial in its effect as any mindfulness based on the dissection of the body. When one contemplates the various stages of decomposition of the dead human body; how it becomes bloated; how it turns blue; how matter oozes out of the eyes, nose, mouth and other openings of the body; how it becomes a prey to a myriad of worms; how the flesh comes off the bones; one cannot avoid considering that the same fate can befall one's own body which one views so tenderly. These drastic contemplations (especially recommended for those obsessed with thoughts of lust, which the tendencies of the modern age seem to engender rather than reduce), will also arouse the sense of repulsion necessary to establish that elevating and lofty detachment with regard to one's body which ultimately leads to a realization of the rise and fall of all things. Seeing things as they are, he touches a higher plane.

We have concluded a detailed (though still incomplete) consideration of the first type of mindfulness, namely mindfulness of the body (*kāyānupassanā*). Now we proceed to the second type, namely, mindfulness of sensations (*vedanānupassanā*). Here too, the disciple must view the matter objectively. He must not identify himself with any sensation that he experiences. Sensations are pleasant, unpleasant and indifferent, and in regard to each of these sensations one must view the sensation and the sensation only. A man suffering from pain normally tends to identify himself so closely with the pain-feeling that he is unable to take a detached view of it. The pain is all-important. He is overpowered by it. Similarly, with regard to a pleasure sensation. Mindfulness of sensation helps one to stand out of one's body, as it were, and view these sensations with the detachment of a spectator.

The commentary to the *Satipaṭṭhāna Sutta* mentions the case of a Thera whose objective contemplation of a severe pain was so intense that when he was asked where the pain was, he was simply unable to locate the seat of pain. To the disciple who thus trains himself to look with dispassionate calm upon the sensations without identifying himself with them, they sooner or later cease to assume the all-important, all-compelling nature they once did. Sensations too will be regarded as part of the ever changing phenomena which constitute the life process. He knows that these sensations are not permanent. They too arise and pass away. Just as in respect of the body, so in respect of the sensors, he will find that there is no basis which can logically support any notion of "I" or "mine." It is not a case of "I feel" but "there is a feeling." In none of these fleeting sensations is there to be found any permanent principle to which it is profitable or desirable to cling. When the nature of sensations (their rise and fall) is thoroughly comprehended, the disciple is no longer moved by them. By observing the rise and fall of sensations, he observes the rise and fall of all things. He sees things as they are. He touches a higher plane.

The third type of mindfulness is mindfulness of thoughts (*cittānupassanā*). Just as the disciple is expected to watch objectively the play of sensations in him, so he is expected to watch objectively the play of thoughts upon him. It is highly beneficial to mind the mind this way. Do we ever deal with thousands of visitors every day? Yes we do. Every day thousands of thoughts enter our minds. We are so accustomed to this that we take these visitors for granted. Every thought we think influences us for good or bad. A subsequent thought however can modify the influence of the previous thought. A thought of anger, for example, has injurious effects on one's mind, and even on one's body; but if the immediately subsequent thought is one of an opposite nature, or one of repentance and a realization that what was done was wrong, the injurious effects of the angry thought may be modified. If we develop the habit of looking at any bad thought objectively, we can easily arrest the progress of that bad thought. Practising mindfulness of thought is the cultivation of the habit of looking objectively at a thought, and not subjectively, and of being deeply aware of its presence.

No thought should be able to enter the portals of our mind without our being fully aware of it. Then only are we free from being blindly led by the force of thoughts. When a thought of anger arises, one must be fully aware of this and tell oneself, "Now look, a thought of anger has entered my mind." By this introspection a subtle effect is produced. The angry thought loses its compelling nature. It has spent its force and cannot express itself as an angry deed. This objective way of looking at any evil thought thus protects the disciple from its pernicious influence.

Whenever any evil thought enters the mind, the watchdog of *sati* barks at the unwelcome visitor and cautions the disciple who can then induce a thought of an opposite nature to counteract the evil thought. The commentary to the *Satipaṭṭhāna Sutta* mentions the case of Phussadeva Mahāthera, who would stop walking if in the midst of a walk an evil thought were to enter his mind. He would not resume his walk until he had banished the evil thought.

The people of the place who had noticed this used to wonder whether he lost his way or had forgotten something. But when at the age of twenty he became an Arahant, only a few would have known how he achieved this. When an evil thought enters your mind, you must look at it fairly and squarely. Think of that thought and that thought only, and not of the circumstances that gave rise to that thought or the mode of action suggested by that thought.

Do not dwell on any such related questions. Look straight into that thought and dwell on it only. You will then be surprised to find how gradually that evil thought will lose its inviting nature. Persist in looking on. Like the philosopher defined by Pythagoras, just look on. That is all. The evil thought will no more incite you to action. It may even disappear.

It is not always easy to look into one's own mind. Man generally fights shy of looking too closely into his own mind since the awareness of his own silent evil thinking upsets his good opinion of himself. Continued practice of mindfulness of thoughts will help the disciple to understand that his thoughts are not himself. He will not identify himself with his thoughts. He will grow into the realization that, like the body, the mind also is not an entity but a temporary combination of passing things. This temporary assemblage gives the illusion of a permanent entity. As the constituent parts are impermanent and subject to change, so is the constituted combination. Just as the body is nothing more than a combination of hair, flesh, nails, teeth, all of which must perish, so is the mind nothing more than a combination (or rather a succession) of thoughts, all of which arise only to pass away. The mind is compared to the flow of a river. *Nadi-soto viya*: "The flow of thoughts makes the seeming entity of the mind." Just as drops of water, one following the other in rapid succession, give the impression of a line of water, similarly one thought follows another with such rapidity of succession that one is deluded into the belief that there is an entity called mind. Only the practice of *cittānupassanā*, mindfulness of thoughts, will reveal that thoughts are impersonal in their nature, and that they are distinctly fleeting phenomena. They come and go; they arise and pass.

The disciple thus realizes the rise and fall of thoughts. So, in respect of thoughts also he will find that there is no basis which can logically support any notion of "I" or "mine." It is not a case of "I think" but "there is thinking." In none of these fleeting processes can there be found any permanent principle to which it is profitable or desirable to cling. He depends on nothing. He clings to nothing in this world. He sees the rise and fall of all things. He touches a higher plane, and that way lies Nibbāna.

We now come to the last and a very different type of mindfulness, mindfulness of mental objects (*dhammānupassanā*). The word *dhamma* has here a very special meaning. It means "contents of thought" or "mental objects," and specially refers to the five mental hindrances (*pañca nīvaraṇā*),[3] the five aggregates of clinging (*pañca upādānakkhandhā*), the six bases (*saḷāyatana*), seven factors of enlightenment (*satta bojjhaṅga*),[4] and the four noble truths (*cattāri ariyasaccāni*).

These are the *dhammas* referred to in the *Satipaṭṭhāna Sutta*. Through the disciple's daily experiences he must be able to observe these *dhammas* or special mental objects. He must be alive to these conditions if they arise in him, and if they have not arisen in him, he must be aware that they have not arisen in him. It is not a theoretical knowledge of these *dhammas* that matters. One must actually experience them and know them as such when

---

3. They are sense desire, ill-will, sloth and torpidity, restlessness and worry, and sceptical doubt. See *The Wheel* No. 26: *The Five Mental Hindrances*.

4. See *The Wheel* No. 1: *The Seven Factors of Enlightenment*, by Piyadassi Thera.

they arise. For instance, the five hindrances are not merely to be known theoretically as obstructions to spiritual progress, but one must be on the lookout to recognise them as soon as they arise in the mind. Similarly, whenever there is a dawning of the Truth, for instance the First Noble Truth, he should be able to recognise it as such.

This meditation is both an antidote to evil thoughts and a preparation for the reception of the Truths of the *Dhamma*. In this manner all the daily experiences of the disciple can be brought into conformity with the contents of the *Dhamma* at some point or other. Contemplating thus the mental objects as they arise, the disciple again finds that there is no permanent principle to which it is profitable or desirable to cling. He depends on nothing. He clings to nothing. Again he touches a higher plane, and that way lies Nibbāna.

Enough has been said with regard to the theory and practice of *satipaṭṭhāna*. Now we shall proceed to examine its applicability to modern life. First let us see how modern world-conditions have evolved.

The 17th and 18th centuries saw a fairly contented world with a childlike faith in the comforts and hopes that religion affords. Then the next century saw the dethronement of Religion by Science. Science reigned supreme and the modern world was busy constructing all kinds of powerful instruments and mighty machines for the convenience of man. Later, desire for world power made its appearance, threatening to take the place of Science. This led to a coalition between these two and, from that moment onwards, Science was prostituted for the sake of making instruments and machines, not for the convenience of man, but for his destruction. The First World War, followed by the Second World War, brought about tremendous changes in the world, changes in the social structure, economic upheavals and political revolutions. Man began to lose faith in the ancient ways of thinking. Man began to decry religion. Future rewards for moral goodness ceased to interest him and his one desire was the full enjoyment of the present. Collectively as a nation the desire was for full enjoyment of power, world power.

Consequently there was a falling off of moral standards; the two World Wars have proved this. The so-called civilization of the modern world is but a thin coating of conventional politeness. The two world wars scratched that coating and laid bare the beast in modern man. The mass destruction of human life, the agonies in concentration camps, the unspeakable horrors of Hiroshima and Nagasaki, all bear witness to the unfortunate fact that the modern world is heading towards destruction. Unless we cry halt we will be swept off by our own iniquities.

The scientist of the modern world seems to think that he has done a service to humanity. What, I ask you, is the test of service? The modern scientific age has alleviated pain. Yes, it has cured diseases, discovered drugs and lengthened life. The modern Scientific Age has built great cities, great bridges and great factories. It has constructed marvellously efficient vehicles to travel on earth, on sea and through space. It has shattered distance, economised labour and captured time. But I ask you: has the modern scientific age invented one single instrument to make man more noble? Has the modern scientific age invented one single instrument to help man to eliminate his lust, his hate or his delusion? Science has probed the external world and wrested from nature her secrets, yet it does not deliver salvation to man. There is another world, a more fruitful world for exploration, and that is the world of the mind. By dint of meditation, explore that world and you will be rewarded with the intuition which will solve the problem of life. You will then secure that *paññā* or higher wisdom which will make you see things as they really are. Every little step you take in that direction is a step towards emancipation, a step towards Nibbāna. The great drift, the dangerous drift today, is away from true progress, and therefore the necessity for a counterdrift is as great. This is where the practise of *satipaṭṭhāna* is important and relevant. By giving the modern man the necessary wisdom to understand evil tendencies as such, *satipaṭṭhāna* helps to give a powerful pull in the right direction. Whenever the tendencies of the modern age drag you away from the path of righteousness, almost without your knowing it, the faithful watchdog of *sati* can be depended upon to pull you back. Such is the strength of *satipaṭṭhāna*.

The modern age is essentially an age of rush and speed. Man really has no time to do any serious thinking. If he has any time to think, it is only to think as much as is necessary to run the giddy round of life from day to day. The consequence of not accustoming oneself to serious deep thinking is the liability to lose that power. If you do not use your hand for six months, it is liable to be atrophied. Similarly, if you do not engage in deep thinking, that faculty too is liable to be atrophied. The danger is that you will then blindly adopt the patterns of thought set before you by the few who can dominate you. This is what is happening today. In the field of business, in the field of agriculture, in the field of education, in the field of politics, in the field of human activity, a few dominate the minds of the many. The majority just follow the thought patterns of the thinking few.

Consider the amount of thought created for you today. You do not always consciously and deliberately decide on the type of requirements you need, do you? The profound effect of large-scale advertisement in the modern world is such that some of your requirements are selected for you. Often without your knowing it, your clothes are selected for you, the books you read are selected for you and the medicines you take are selected for you. Such is the subtle psychology of advertisement. Newspapers also are responsible for creating such impressive thought patterns. The majority of men are content to accept these views without question. There is very little original independent thinking today. This can only mean that the powers of concentration of the majority are very weak. The resultant danger is that modern man is handicapped in his spiritual progress, for no one can progress spiritually unless he can concentrate and meditate.

However good a life you may lead, unless you practise meditation there is no guarantee of permanent moral rectitude. You may at any moment fall away from goodness. The easiest way to develop the power of concentration is to practise a little *ānāpānasati* each day. No other type of meditation can modern man use so easily. It is the only meditation that can ensure immunity from external influences.

Another feature of modern life is the stress that is laid on sex. Most things are managed and conducted today in such a way as to stimulate lust (*rāga*) in you. Look around and see for yourself whether this is not true. Look at the number of trashy novels and obscene publications which in the name of literature find a place in any wayside bookshop, and you will realize the dismal depths to which human depravity has sunk. Look at the cinemas and dances of the modern world. What good, I ask you, have these cinema and dance halls, these beauty parades and these night clubs, done to the modern man except to stimulate his lust? Unless from time to time the modern world is reminded of the correct view regarding the human body, the emphasis on sex and the body will continue to becloud the mind of modern man to such an extent that all sense of proportion will be destroyed and the unreal will be mistaken for the real. The result will be confusion, disharmony and degradation.

Another feature of the modern world is the morbid craving for variety. The inability, due to the absence of *sati*, to see things as they really are, and to distinguish the essential from the non-essential, has resulted in a state of mental indecision and chronic dissatisfaction. The even tenor of life is too dull for the modern man. He craves sensations; he is fed on sensations. He will continually yearn for something fresh, something new. He cannot content himself with existing methods, situations and conditions. He will always look forward to new methods, new machines, new drugs, a new way of life, a new ideology. He is soon tired of existing things. Life is disappointing if there are no sensations. The morning paper is disappointing if there are no banner headlines. This attitude is symptomatic of a disease: mental unrest. The advertiser and the business man are quick to exploit this weakness of the modern man. Before one model of any article goes out of use, another model is brought to the market. See the changing fashions of dress.

See the changing types of furniture and other equipment. All these changes pander to this dangerous craving for variety. The only remedy for this ailment is to learn the art of looking at things as they really are. Once a customer is initiated into the art of looking at a thing objectively, he will not be easily influenced by advertisements. Objective observation will also help him to discover plenty of old wine in new bottles. The delusion of the importance of novelty is destroyed. Fully perceiving what is really essential in life, and fully distinguishing the essential from the non-essential by the aid of *sati*, he is no more a victim of this craze for sensations.

Now that I have shown to you the application of the *Satipaṭṭhāna Sutta* to modern life, there is one more aspect of the subject which needs attention. You may perhaps think that the way of *satipaṭṭhāna* is long and weary and that within the space of one life the much-spoken of results of the practice of *satipaṭṭhāna* cannot be achieved. Has the Buddha ever said so? Has the Buddha ever said that Nibbāna cannot be attained in this life itself? In a powerful oration in the *Satipaṭṭhāna Sutta*, the Buddha has emphatically declared that if any one practises these four types of mindfulness for seven years, then one or another of these two results may be expected by him: Arahantship here and now (*diṭṭhe dhamme*) or at least the state of *Anāgāmi* (Non-returner). In the next sentence the Buddha says, "Let alone the question of seven years, O monks, six years is sufficient." In the next sentence he says in similar style that five years is sufficient.

Thus in successive sentences He brings it down from six years to five, four, three, two, and one year; and thereafter to seven months, six months, five, four, three, and two months; then to one month, half a month and finally to seven days.

Thi shows that the ability to attain to Nibbāna is not so much a question of time as a question of the intensity and eagerness of the mind of the disciple. Just consider seven days to attain to Nibbāna. Quick results, are they not? The impatient modern man always yearns for quick results. Here is a guarantee of quick results.

Why does not modern man accept this offer? Perhaps he feels that the promise is too good to be true. What is important is not views but action. The proof of the pudding is in the eating of it, and not in any learned chemical analysis of its component parts. Therefore, I would finally make this appeal to you all, namely, stop all academic discussion about *satipaṭṭhāna*. Practise it quietly and observe the results for yourselves. "*Ehipassiko*," said the Buddha, "Come and see for yourself."

ABOUT PARIYATTI

Pariyatti is dedicated to providing affordable access to authentic teachings of the Buddha about the Dhamma theory (*pariyatti*) and practice (*paṭipatti*) of Vipassana meditation. A 501(c)(3) nonprofit charitable organization since 2002, Pariyatti is sustained by contributions from individuals who appreciate and want to share the incalculable value of the Dhamma teachings. We invite you to visit www.pariyatti.org to learn about our programs, services, and ways to support publishing and other undertakings.

Pariyatti Publishing Imprints

Vipassana Research Publications (focus on Vipassana as taught by S.N. Goenka in the tradition of Sayagyi U Ba Khin)

BPS Pariyatti Editions (selected titles from the Buddhist Publication Society, copublished by Pariyatti)

MPA Pariyatti Editions (selected titles from the Myanmar Pitaka Association, copublished by Pariyatti)

Pariyatti Digital Editions (audio and video titles, including discourses)

Pariyatti Press (classic titles returned to print and inspirational writing by contemporary authors)

Pariyatti enriches the world by

- disseminating the words of the Buddha,
- providing sustenance for the seeker's journey,
- illuminating the meditator's path.

www.ingramcontent.com/pod-product-compliance
Lightning Source LLC
Chambersburg PA
CBHW020348170426
43200CB00005B/91
9781681721361